Dhaka's Changing Landscape

Dhaka's Changing Landscape

Prospects for Economic Development, Social Change, and Shared Prosperity

RITA AFSAR
MAHABUB HOSSAIN

UNIVERSITY PRESS

OXFORD
UNIVERSITY PRESS

Oxford University Press is a department of the University of Oxford. It furthers the University's objective of excellence in research, scholarship, and education by publishing worldwide. Oxford is a registered trademark of Oxford University Press in the UK and in certain other countries.

Published in India by
Oxford University Press
22 Workspace, 2nd Floor, 1/22 Asaf Ali Road, New Delhi 110 002

First Edition published in 2020

ISBN-13 (print edition): 978-0-19-012111-2
ISBN-10 (print edition): 0-19-012111-4

ISBN-13 (eBook): 978-0-19-099124-1
ISBN-10 (eBook): 0-19-099124-0

Typeset in Arno Pro 11/13
by The Graphics Solution, New Delhi 110 092
Printed in India by Replika Press Pvt. Ltd

This book is dedicated to the everlasting
memory of the co-author
Dr Mahabub Hossain

Contents

Figures

Tables

Boxes

Foreword

One of the great transitions of recent times has been the increasing proportion of the world's population living in towns and cities. United Nations' figures suggest that less than 30 per cent of the world's population lived in urban areas in 1950, a proportion that had increased to almost 56 per cent in 2019, which represented some 4.3 billion people. We are already living in an urban world in which the management of cities, and particularly that of large cities, known as 'mega-urban areas', has emerged as one of the critical challenges for the twenty-first century. That transition from rural to urban has been much more dramatic in the developing world and no better example can be found than the case studied by Dr Rita Afsar and Dr Mahabub Hossain in Bangladesh. Essentially a primarily rural 'rice basket' at the time of Partition, with less than 1 per cent of its population living in towns and cities, Bangladesh today has around 12 per cent of its population classified as urban. These bold figures, however, give little indication of the real impact of cities because the country remains one of the most densely populated rural areas in the world, and the real size and growth of the cities have been astonishing.

From a relatively small regional centre of the Moghul Empire in eastern Bengal, the population of Dhaka grew to between 200,000 and 300,00 at the time of Partition, when it represented but a tiny proportion of the population of what was then East Pakistan. By the time of independence in 1971, the city's population was around 1.5 million, a figure that had doubled by 1980 and then more than tripled to reach 16.3 million in 2000. Today, including the entire metropolitan area, its population is estimated to be in excess of 20 million people, representing a truly remarkable growth to global megacity status in some 50 years.

Equally remarkable has been the economic and social transformation of the country. From Henry Kissinger's perhaps unkind classification of Bangladesh at the time of independence as the 'world's basket case', the World Bank has estimated that the poverty rate fell from 82 per cent in 1972 through 18.5 per cent in 2000 to 13.8 per cent today. Fertility fell from 6.9 children per woman around the time of independence to 2.9 in the period 2000–5, to around the replacement level of 2.1 today. Afsar sets out to unpick the complex interplay of factors in this rapid growth of Dhaka in the context of recent (1991–2010) economic and social development. Following on from Afsar's earlier work *Rural-Urban Migration in Bangladesh* (2000), Afsar focuses in on the national capital to examine the role of migration in its growth. Using longitudinal data, she draws out differences between migrants and non-migrants, slum dwellers and non-slum dwellers, and a number of basic socio-economic variables to see who benefit or who remain disadvantaged within the urban environment. In a country where the fertility decline has been so marked, her gender perspective on access to basic services is instructive.

More broadly, Afsar's and Hossain study of the megacity of Dhaka will serve as an example of how to approach the analysis of urban growth, migration, social change, and poverty in other parts of the world, perhaps most specifically in the cities of sub-Saharan Africa, which are experiencing similar change through the emergence of large cities. This book does not shy away from an examination of policy and it is to be hoped that academics and practitioners in these other parts of the world will engage with the debates herein to see the extent to which a 'Bangladesh model' might be relevant to their contexts. This is certainly not to say that the model is perfect or that Bangladesh has solved all its urban problems, but this book does represent the analysis of an important case of urbanization and development from which many can and should learn. It is a step along the way towards any strategy to 'manage' large cities in poor economies.

Ronald Skeldon
Emeritus Professor, University of Sussex, Falmer, UK
Professor of Human Geography, Maastricht University,
The Netherlands

Preface

This book is the outcome of my long and arduous journey that started exactly eight years and ten months ago. The journey surpassed most of my life challenges so far, be it obtaining my PhD, which took two-and-a-half years, or giving birth to my two precious children. The most tragic casualty during this period—and one that was a massive blow—was the sudden demise in 2016 of Dr Mahabub Hossain, the co-author of, and the main architect behind, this longitudinal study. He was the key person who managed funding for this research. More importantly, he was the main driving force and without his support it would not have been possible to complete the three repeat surveys that formed the basis of this book or use the cleaned and congruent dataset. It took me some time to overturn my grief into a promise, which is embodied in the publication of this book. During this period, I was also greatly saddened by the loss of my two lovely sisters, Neeta Banerjee and Gita Mukherjee. I commuted between Perth and Dhaka several times to work on the manuscript, grasping every possible moment in pursuit of completing the manuscript, which was my personal promise and endeavour, while I worked full-time for the Western Australian government. At the same time, I was blessed with the birth of my five grandchildren who showed light through the dark tunnel of my journey, making both the work and life more meaningful and enjoyable.

The book is about residents of Dhaka: migrant and non-migrant, poor and non-poor, men and women, young and old. It is about how they have experienced the city's rapid transition for the two decades between 1991 and 2010 in terms of quality of life and livelihoods, and their prospects for a shared future. It is not so common to come across urban studies based on longitudinal data largely due to the high mobility of urban households. Their experiences in the early 1990s have been covered in my earlier book *Rural–Urban Migration in Bangladesh: Causes, Consequences and Challenges,* based on the first round of the survey conducted in 1991, which was the abridged and updated version of my PhD thesis. Actually, my long experience of working with the poor and underprivileged in Dhaka provided impetus for this journey in order to establish the urban poor's share in the city's prosperity through systematic research.

However, over the 20-year period, the city's population more than doubled and reached double digit figures at 15 million. At the same time, its contribution to the national economy almost trebled from 13 per cent to 36 per cent. An unmistakable trend of economic growth is evidenced along with the rapid decline of urban poverty and a downward trend in inequality in the country during the same reference period. At the other end of the spectrum are the environmental challenges in the context of high density and Dhaka's worst liveability ranking. The book answers some of the doubts generated by these contradictory signals of rapid urbanization: is the poorer segment of urban population that migrates with dreams for better lives and livelihoods benefitting from positive economic trends? Are these benefits sustainable in the long run? Have these benefits brought qualitative changes creating scope for this group to have a stake in the city's growing prosperity like their non-poor counterparts?

Addressing these compelling questions is necessary to create a right vision to make the city prosperous, inclusive, and sustainable, prerequisites for the New Urban Agenda and Sustainable Development Goals (SDGs). The book revisits the debates on rapid urban growth and congestion versus benefits of agglomeration, and analyses population and other features of urbanization by comparing Dhaka with other megacities. Also, it provides a systematic review of urban poverty, analyses progress made in employment options and occupational mobility for cross-sections, and identifies the determinants of income, factors contributing to income inequality, and those having an equalizing effect. The book presents access, quality, and equity issues in achieving quality of life for all, with a major focus on the poor and women in regard to basic amenities such as housing, water, sanitation, and air quality as well as health and education outcomes.

Implications of these findings are critically analysed from a policy perspective together with better practice analysis, drawing lessons across the globe from which strategic policy measures are recommended in this book. In the context of changing policy discourse that recognizes the role of urbanization in promoting economic development in place of traditional hostility, the book provides policy options on how cities can be transformed to better drive economic growth and poverty reduction, as well as to become better places in which to live. By defining the way in which cities should be planned and managed to best promote sustainable and equitable urbanization and integrating this with the national development agenda, this book has provided a road map that would create the scope for sharing prosperity equitably for all citizens, not only for Bangladesh but also for other rapidly urbanizing countries.

Going beyond the push–pull debate, the book recasts migration theories by considering migrants' intrinsic qualities—their self-confidence, hopes, aspirations, and resilience, and blending broader structural and institutional forces with migrants' agency and aspiration. It unbundles the contexts and conditions that influenced migration motivations by estimating district level poverty and the level of physical and social infrastructure development at migrants' birthplaces to generate a better understanding of migration, space, and poverty as well as development nexus.

Another distinct feature of this book lies in the fact that it provides a rich analysis of the connection between migration and modernization, thereby contributing to the sociological theories. It examines some pertinent theories of social change by analysing attitudinal changes associated with urban living such as the attitudes of migrants towards gender division of labour, women's higher education and their participation in the labour market. It also assesses whether, how, and to what extent gender and generational relations are redefined and impacted in relation to migration, and identifies the factors that are conducive towards progressive attitudes and practices, and those which impede progress.

Rita Afsar
20 September 2019
Perth, Australia

Acknowledgements

During my work on this book for almost a decade, a great many people helped, supported, and inspired me. First of all, I would like to pay my tribute to the late Dr Mahabub Hossain, who was instrumental in the fruition of this longitudinal study since its inception in 1991. I am thankful to the two former directors Dr Syed Masud Ahmed and Professor Abdul Bayes of the erstwhile Research and Evaluation Division (RED) of the Bangladesh Rural Advancement Committee (BRAC) for sponsoring the study and providing necessary logistic and other support for the fieldwork and at the time of preparation of the manuscript. I express my deepest gratitude to A.S.M. Mahfuzur Rahman for programming, data management, processing, and analysis as well as supervising the field staff. His contributions in terms of data support is crucial for the preparation of the book. I must also acknowledge the tireless efforts made by Swapan Deb Roy of BRAC in providing necessary data support to me even during holidays and weekends, while I was writing the manuscript.

The research team composed of Shameem Hossain and Arifeen Akter, as coordinators, and five internees who were masters' students from the Institute of Social Welfare and Research (ISWR), Dhaka—Md. Tawhidul Huque, Afroza Parvin, Md. Syful Islam, Shahidul Haque, and Md. Khalid Hasan—deserves great appreciation for their hard work. In the context of high mobility of urban households, they made painstaking efforts to complete the household survey and collect the qualitative information. Assistance provided by my former research team members Anjan Kumar Roy and Iam Hossain of the Bangladesh Institute of Development Studies (BIDS) during the reconnaissance visit to help in locating the study areas is thankfully acknowledged.

I am most grateful to Professor Ronald Skeldon, professorial fellow in the Department of Geography at the School of Global Studies at the University of Sussex, and professor of human geography in the Graduate School of Governance, Maastricht University in the the Netherland, who wrote the foreword for this book in such a short time. I must acknowledge that the useful comments made by the anonymous reviewers helped in enriching the book. I express my deepest gratitude to my friend and colleague Annie Kewe, senior editor in the western Australian government, who provided unconditional editorial support for some of the essential parts and chapters of this book. Comments and support that I received from my friends Susanna Price, lecturer (Hon), Australian National University (ANU) College of Asia and the Pacific; and Professor Samina Yasmeen, School of Social Sciences, University of Western Australia (UWA), and the director and founder of the University's Centre of Muslim States and Societies, are gratefully acknowledged.

I would like to thank the team at Oxford University Press (OUP) for its support and cooperation. Vijay Tandon, my friend, deserves special thanks for his encouragement. I must acknowledge the commitment shown by Professor Amitabh Kundu, a distinguished fellow at the Research and Information System for Developing Countries, Dr Rushidan Islam Rahman, former research director, and Dr Anwara Begum, senior research fellow at the Bangladesh Institute of Development Studies, for their willingness to be available to comment on the book.

My acknowledgements would remain incomplete if I do not thank my family members, especially my grandchildren Elora, Irfan, Mikayl, Ishaan, and Aarya; my daughter Swarna Afsar; daughter-in-law Maryum Afsar; son Swarup Afsar; my husband Q.M.D. Afsar Hossain Saqui; and my friend Dr Zahurul Islam, who assisted me in various capacities in this long journey. Contributions made by my son-in-law, Tasneemul Galib, particularly in terms of providing graphic design ideas for the front cover page of the book is highly appreciated. Over and above, I am indebted to all those residents of Dhaka city who shared with us their experiences and told their stories, which formed the basis of the book. None of them is responsible for the remaining errors and inadequacies in the book: for those I take the sole responsibility.

Abbreviations

ADB	Asian Development Bank
ADP	Annual Development Programme
ANU	Australian National University
ARI	acute respiratory infection
BBS	Bangladesh Bureau of Statistics
BCCI	Bangladesh Chamber of Commerce and Industry
BDHS	Bangladesh Demographic and Health Survey
BIDS	Bangladesh Institute of Development Studies
BRAC	Bangladesh Rural Advancement Committee
BRT	bus rapid transit
BUHS	Bangladesh Urban Health Survey
CI	corrugated iron
CPD	Centre for Policy Dialogue
CPI	City Prosperity Index
CWR	child–woman ratio
DCC	Dhaka City Corporation
DESA	Dhaka Electricity Supply Authority
DHS	Demographic and Health Survey
DMC	Dhaka Megacity
DMDP	Dhaka Metropolitan Development Plan
DWASA	Dhaka Water Supply and Sewerage Authority
EIU	Economic Intelligence Unit
EPI	expanded programme on immunization
FAO	Food and Agriculture Organization

FGD	focus group discussions
FSS	female stipend scheme
GDP	gross domestic product
GLS	generalized least square
GNI	gross national income
GSS	Ghana Statistical Services
HCR	head count ratio
HDI	human development index
HIES	Household Income and Expenditure Survey
HSC	higher secondary school certificate
ICDDRB	International Centre of Diarrhoeal Disease, Bangladesh
ICT	information and communication technology
ID	index of dissimilarity
IFI	international financial institution
ILO	International Labour Organization
ISO	International Organization for Standardization
ISWR	Institute of Social Welfare and Research
JMP	Joint Monitoring Programme
LDC	least developed countries
LFS	Labour Force Survey
MBBS	Bachelor of Medicine, Bachelor of Surgery
MDGs	Millennium Development Goals
MFI	micro-finance institution
MGI	McKinsey Global Institute
MHHDC	Mahbub ul Haq Human Development Centre
NCD	non-communicable disease
NEG	new economic geography
NGO	non-governmental organization
NHA	National Housing Authority
NIPORT	National Institute of Population Research and Training
PM	particulate matter
PPP	purchasing power parity
PRSP	Poverty Reduction Strategy Paper
R&D	research and development
RAJUK	Rajdhani Unnayan Kartripakkha
RED	Research and Evaluation Division

REHAB	Real Estate and Housing Association of Bangladesh
RHD	Roads and Highways Department
RMG	ready-made garment
RTA	Road Transport Authority
SAP	structural adjustment policies
SDG	Sustainable Development Goal
SRNDP	Southwest Road Network Development Project
SSC	secondary school certificate
SSNP	Social Safety Net Program
TFR	total fertility rate
TVET	technical and vocational educational training
UBT	urban bias theory
UDD	Urban Development Directorate
UN	United Nations
UNCSD	United Nations Conference on Sustainable Development
UNDP	United Nations Development Programme
UNESCAP	United Nations Economic and Social Commission for Asia and the Pacific
UNESCO	United Nations Organization for Education and Culture
UNFPA	United Nations Family Planning Agency
UN-Habitat	United Nations Human Settlement Programme
UNICEF	United Nations Children's Fund
USAID	United States Agency for International Development
UWA	University of Western Australia
WHO	World Health Organization

1 Dhaka's Changing Landscape and Fortune

The Three Compelling Questions

The world is increasingly becoming urban with an estimated 4.3 billion people, or more than half (55 per cent) of the world's population, now residing in urban areas—a rapid growth since 1960 when, for the first time, the world's urban population crossed the 1 billion mark (UN 2018). Urban growth is spectacular in Asia, which has a similar proportion of urban populations (54 per cent) and 18 out of the 33 megacities globally with populations of 10 million or more (UN 2018). In Bangladesh, the level of urbanization has quadrupled from 7.6 per cent to 30.5 per cent of the total population in the 40 years between 1970 and 2010. It is estimated to have reached 34.3 per cent in 2015 and will increase further to 38.2 per cent in 2020 (UN 2018). Bangladesh, together with India, Pakistan, Indonesia, and China, is projected to contribute nearly two-fifths (37.4 per cent) of the world's 2.7 billion incremental urban population between 2015 and 2050 (UN 2018).

RAPID URBANIZATION AND ECONOMIC GROWTH

With an estimated population of 18 million, Dhaka, the capital and the primate city of Bangladesh, alone contained around one-third of the country's urban population (32.5 per cent) in 2015 (UN 2018). Based on these trends, by 2030 Dhaka will become the fourth largest city in the world, containing a population of 28 million people or almost the same proportion (33 per cent) of the country's urban population. This high concentration of urban population in a single megacity contradicts patterns and trends of urbanization in most developing countries where cities with populations of 1 million or more will continue to grow, containing almost one-fifth of the world urban populations by 2030 (UN 2018). Despite renewed attention to the positive benefits of agglomeration, the persistence of Dhaka's primacy over time raises questions regarding its sustainability, liveability, and the scope for poverty reduction, income growth, and equitable distribution and prosperity (McKinsey Global Institute 2011; Glaeser and Joshi-Ghani 2013; UN-Habitat 2013).[1]

Cities are central to national economies and urbanization has played a vital role in economic development across the world. Research shows that globally there is a clear association between national income and the level of urbanization (Annez and Buckley 2009; Henderson 2010; Duranton 2014). For example, the economies of Asia's largest and most globalized cities are greater than those of many of the region's countries. In 2010, Tokyo generated almost US$ 1.9 trillion of Japan's gross domestic product (GDP). Similarly, cities of China contributed 74 per cent of the national GDP but represent less than 50 per cent of the population (McKinsey Global Institute 2011).

Arguably, however, association between national income and rate of urbanization is still debated. For example, of the 38 countries with annual urbanization rates over 1.5 per cent between 1990 and 2014, less than one-quarter (23.7 per cent) were upper-middle income countries, while the larger proportions fall in middle income (34.2 per cent) or low-income (36.8 per cent) categories (UN 2015c). However, based on such association, it would be unwise to conclude that urbanization cannot stimulate economic growth, or vice-versa. Rather following Turok (2018: 103), we can emphasize:

> Urbanisation is neither simply a cause of growth, nor merely a symptom. By increasing density and proximity between human activities, it both enables growth and is an outcome of growth. These interactions also transform how economic growth itself evolves, so it is more accurately referred to as development. Urbanisation involves the

> spatial concentration of capital as well as labour. It is an integral part of economic development, and fuels continuing prosperity. The strength of the connection depends on the context—the relationship does not occur in a vacuum. Much depends on the form of urbanisation and the composition of the economy.

However, there is ample evidence that agglomeration provides some tangible benefits such as more opportunities for informal knowledge sharing and networking (Storper and Venables 2004). These benefits, such as accumulated knowledge, comprise 'common-pool resources or positive externalities' (Turok 2018: 94) that raise the efficiency and flexibility of firms, encourage investment, and increase productivity, which in turn spur growth in output and income (Henderson 2003; Glaeser 2011; Storper 2013; Turok 2016). More than simply being major manufacturing centres, cities across the world are increasingly leading in education and science, technology and innovation.

POVERTY, INEQUALITY, AND THE SCOPE FOR SHARED PROSPERITY

It should be noted that urban poverty and inequality have received renewed attention from researchers and policymakers ever since the publication of the World Bank's seminal report *Reshaping Economic Geography* (2009). The concern regarding distribution of economic benefits and well-being for all emerged from the increasing level of urbanization, given that an estimated three-fifths (60.4 per cent) of the world's population will be living in urban areas by the year 2030 (UN 2018). More than that, the share of urban poor in developing countries will also rise and is estimated to reach 50 per cent around 2030 (Ravallion, Chen, and Sangruala 2007). It is also widely recognized that while economic growth is good for poverty reduction, the poor do not necessarily benefit automatically from such growth.

There are stories of the economic successes and transformations of cities, most prominently in East Asia, that lifted millions of people out of poverty (UN-Habitat 2016). Research shows that the estimated number of the middle class in the Asia Pacific region will reach 3.2 billion by 2030, representing 80 per cent of the world's total middle-class population (Kharas and Gertz 2010). However, the rise of the middle classes has not necessarily been an inclusive process as evident from poor people and migrants who often are greatly disadvantaged with respect to their rights and increasing inequality, as shown by the Gini coefficient for many cities in the region (UN-Habitat 2010).

Bangladesh has made notable reductions in poverty and impressive progress in social indicators such as reduction in infant and child mortality, increased enrolment rates and gender parity at primary and secondary levels, and sustained fertility control. Both official estimates and those from micro-level surveys indicate that incidence of income poverty is lower in urban than in rural areas in Bangladesh, as is the case in many other developing countries. Household Income and Expenditure Survey (HIES) data generated by the Bangladesh Bureau of Statistics (BBS) shows that the headcount index (upper poverty line) for urban poverty halved (from 44.9 per cent to 21.5 per cent) between 1991–92 and 2010 (BBS 2011a; World Bank 2015). During the same period, the magnitude of rural poor declined from three-fifths (61.2 per cent) to little over one-third (35.2 per cent). One obvious reason for greater income gains for urban dwellers including the urban poor is their easy entry and access to gainful employment, and better income earning opportunity, as revealed from the empirical studies (Hossain, Afsar, and Bose 1999; Afsar 2004; World Bank 2015).

However, with more people migrating from rural areas, the share of urban poor in the country's poor population is increasing over time. In 1991, the urban poor comprised 10 per cent of the national poor population, which increased to 14.4 per cent and 17.7 per cent, respectively, in 2000 and 2010 (Table 1.1). In absolute terms, their numbers increased by 2.1 million between 1991–92 and 2010, while the total number of rural poor declined by 17 million over the same period (BBS 2011a; World Bank 2015).

It is argued that the pace of poverty reduction depends on the rate of average income growth and the degree of inequality over time. Research shows that poverty reduction is fastest in countries where income growth is combined with falling inequality (UN-Habitat 2010). However, the values of the Gini income index obtained from the HIES data are consistently higher for urban areas in Bangladesh, indicating greater income inequality compared with rural areas (Table 1.1). A similar rural–urban differential, with a lower degree of inequality, can be observed from the estimates of the Gini index based on the real per

Table 1.1 Number of Poor People in Bangladesh, Incidence of Poverty, and Income Inequality at the National, Rural, and Urban Levels

	1991–92			2000			2010		
	National	**Rural**	**Urban**	**National**	**Rural**	**Urban**	**National**	**Rural**	**Urban**
Poor people (million)	61.7	55.5	6.2	61.7	58.7	8.9	46.8	38.5	8.3
% of total population	56.8	51.1	5.7	48.9	41.8	7.1	31.5	25.9	5.6
% of national poor	100	90.0	10.0	100	85.4	14.4	100	82.3	17.7
Poverty head-count rate (%)									
Upper poverty line	58.8	61.2	44.2	48.9	52.3	35.2	31.5	35.2	21.5
Lower poverty line	42.7	46.6	23.3	34.3	37.9	19.9	25.1	21.1	7.7
Inequality									
Gini income index	0.39	0.36	0.40	0.45	0.39	0.50	0.46	0.43	0.45
Gini consumption index	0.26	0.24	0.31	0.31	0.27	0.37	0.32	0.27	0.34

Source: Computed from HIES data from BBS (various years), and 2002, 2008 and 2013 Poverty Assessments, World Bank.

capita consumption (World Bank 2015). Although there are increases in the values of the Gini index mostly since the 1990s for both rural and urban areas, we can observe downward trends for urban areas in the post-2000s. However, for rural areas it has increased or remained unchanged. Note that there are debates on income measures that contest the declining trend in urban inequality, mainly on the grounds of what should and should not be included to measure household income.[2]

URBANIZATION AND SUSTAINABLE DEVELOPMENT

Leaving aside the income inequality debate, there are also concerns that economic gains experienced by rural migrants in urban areas can be short-lived if not well protected against the vulnerability that could arise from ill health, natural calamity, violence and other socio-political threats, death of the income-earning members of family, and weakening of social capital (Rahman, Hossain, and Sen 1996; Hossain, Afsar, and Bose 1999; Kothari 2002). According to the United Nations (2015a), urbanization is integral to sustainable development, which consists of economic and social development, and environmental protection. The outcome of the Rio+20 United Nations Conference on Sustainable Development (UNCSD), recognized both the plight of the urban poor and the need for sustainable cities as matters of great urgency for its development agenda to promote equity, welfare, and shared prosperity in an increasingly urbanizing world.[3] The newly adopted 2030 Agenda for Sustainable Development presents 17 Sustainable Development Goals (SDGs) that replace the previous Millennium Development Goals (MDGs) with broader scope and coverage—all having an urban dimension addressing a wide variety of facets of inequality (Winkel 2015; UNESCAP 2017).[4] While cities were not specifically represented in the MDGs, Goal 11 of the new Sustainable Development Agenda seeks to 'make cities and human settlements inclusive, safe, resilient and sustainable' (UNDP 2015c: 24). The United Nations' report *Transforming Our World: the 2030 Agenda for Sustainable Development* that provides the basis for the SDGs places great emphasis on equality of opportunity and shared prosperity as it states:

> Sustained, inclusive and sustainable economic growth is essential for prosperity. This will only be possible if wealth is shared and income inequality is addressed. (UN 2015c: 7)

THE NEED FOR A COMPREHENSIVE ANALYSIS OF URBAN DYNAMICS, REALITIES, AND POLICY IMPERATIVES

Existing studies on urban poverty in Bangladesh have largely been patchy, fragmented, and often lack rigorous analytical approach (Islam 1996; 2005; CUS 2006). Most of these studies are limited to a collection of chapters based largely on non-representative samples or focus on microscopic analysis of slums alone without comparison with diverse groups of poor or between poor and non-poor populations (CUS 1996; Islam et al. 1997; World Bank 2007). K. Siddiqui et al. (2010) provided multiple perspectives regarding poverty and progress made over time by narrating experiences and perceptions of different classes in Dhaka city. However, the sampling frame of the study—a municipal holding number from which 100 households were drawn—excludes poor households. Although they conducted a large number of interviews and focus group discussions (FGD) with different occupation groups, this does not provide a random basis that is necessary for a systematic, valid, and reliable analysis of poverty over time.

It should be noted that lack of comprehensive and reliable data constrains research on the nature, magnitude, and the trend of urban poverty in Bangladesh that is needed to understand how it is changing over time, and to identify determining factors and impacts on different cross-sections. Whatever data exist on incomes and levels of living of urban population, they are gathered mostly from one-shot surveys, and there are glaring discrepancies in the findings from different studies. Differences in sampling methodologies and analytical approaches make it difficult to carry out intertemporal comparisons of the changes in levels of living. Besides, there has been a clear dearth of intertemporal studies through repeat surveys of the same areas and households required for a systematic review of the trends in urban poverty.

Without proper conceptualization and monitoring of economic activities and social progress, it is difficult to capture the process of income generation and the accumulation of physical and human capital that shape the dynamic process of economic and social development and alleviation of poverty. This requires far better understanding of long-term implications of poverty, poverty dynamics, and social and economic mobility. Longitudinal studies are considered best suited for this purpose. It is argued that longitudinal data allows the analysis of duration and permits measurement of differences or change in a variable from one period to another. It can be used to identify the causes of social phenomena (Menard 1991: 5) and connections between factors and events that are widely separated in time (Hakim 1987). Accurate and consistent data on trends in urbanization and the city's demographic, economic, and social landscape, along with concomitant changes in the lives of the people, are critical for 'current and future needs with respect to urban growth and for setting policy priorities to promote inclusive and equitable rural and urban development' (UN 2014: 4).

A longitudinal study by the BIDS on the 'Analysis of Poverty Trends' has demonstrated the usefulness of repeat surveys to generate panel data needed for better understanding of the dynamics of poverty alleviation. Using household-level data at different points in time, it has highlighted the role of technological progress, infrastructure development, and human capital formation in reducing poverty. However, the study confines its investigation to rural households only. A similar study for urban areas is urgently needed. The book fills gaps in the existing literature by extensive use of the longitudinal data and building a bridge between quantitative and qualitative research traditions by analysing patterns, scale, complexity, and trends in urban poverty and post-migration developments in socio-economic conditions of slum and non-slum residents of Dhaka city.

THE THREE COMPELLING QUESTIONS OF THIS BOOK

The book is about residents of Dhaka: migrant and non-migrant, poor and non-poor, men and women, young and old. It is about how they have experienced the city's rapid transition for the two decades between 1991 and 2010 in terms of quality of life and livelihoods, and their prospects for a shared future. Their experiences in the early 1990s have been covered in a book by Afsar (2000), *Rural–Urban Migration in Bangladesh: Causes, Consequences and Challenges*, based on the first round of the survey conducted in 1991, which was the abridged and updated version of her PhD thesis.

However, over the 20-year period, the city's population more than doubled and reached double digit figures at 15 million. At the same time, its contribution to the national economy almost trebled from 13 per cent to 36 per cent (Afsar 1995; Muzzini and Aparicio 2013). An unmistakable trend of economic growth is evidenced along with the rapid decline of urban poverty and a downward trend in inequality in the country during the same reference period. At the other end of the spectrum are the environmental challenges in the context of high density and Dhaka's worst liveability ranking. The book answers some of the doubts generated by these contradictory signals of rapid urbanization by addressing three compelling questions: first, is the poorer segment of urban population that migrates with dreams for better lives and livelihoods benefitting from positive economic trends? Second, are these benefits sustainable in the long run? Third, have these benefits brought qualitative changes creating scope for this group to have a stake in the country's growing prosperity like their non-poor counterparts?

Addressing these compelling questions is necessary to create a right vision to make the city prosperous, inclusive, and sustainable, prerequisites for the New Urban Agenda and SDGs. The book draws on longitudinal data generated from three rounds of repeat surveys conducted in 1991, 1998, and 2010 of the same cross-section of 600 slum and non-slum households randomly selected from four wards of Dhaka city. This gives it rigour, depth, and validity, which is generally missing in other books on similar topics. To address the first question, the book estimates poverty and income and examines livelihoods and labour market outcomes for cross-section of Dhaka's residents and the changes over time. Also, it encapsulates the changes in the causes and context of rural–urban migration and analyses progress made in employment options and occupational mobility. To address the second and third questions, it examines the scope for income growth and equitable distribution, social and human capital development, and quality of life, together with changes in attitudes, aspirations, and gender and generational values and relations since the 1990s. Each of these aspects are covered by the themes. For example, question one is addressed with the help of three themes: urban poverty, income growth, and inequality; migration, poverty, and space—interlinkages and transformative potential; and migration, livelihoods, and inclusive development. Questions two and three are answered by three themes: quality of life (sustainability matters); urbanization and the demographic dividend; and migration and modernization. Each of these themes are discussed below to generate an understanding of the reason these themes were chosen and their suitability to address the three compelling questions.

Urban Poverty, Income Growth, and Inequality

Based on the electoral rolls as the sampling frame, which allowed us to draw both poor and non-poor households, the book generates a better understanding on the changes in the incidence, intensity and severity, trends and determinants of urban poverty, and income growth and income inequality. Together with the analysis of the trends and changes in human capital, livelihoods, and asset base of different cross-sections, it examines the level and composition of income and employment as well as real earnings for different occupational groups. Also, it highlights factors including policies and strategies as well as pathways that can potentially lift people out of the poverty trap and help minimize inequality in income distribution. Therefore, by providing a systematic review of poverty, income, and inequality, it contributes to a better understanding of the needs related to urban infrastructure and services as well as employment and mobility trends. This understanding is critical to develop and adopt innovative solutions to emerging challenges common to many developing countries, which ultimately would help both local and national governments maximize impacts of SDGs.

It especially emphasizes consequences arising from migration in a rapidly urbanizing megacity and examines implications for poverty alleviation, sustainable development, and the scope for its residents in sharing its growing prosperity. This knowledge is necessary for developing compact, sustainable, and equitable national urban policy.[5] It analyses progress made in employment options and occupational mobility, examining the scope for income growth and equitable distribution. To examine prospects for shared prosperity for the poor and disadvantaged, the sample for this study included diverse categories of both poor and non-poor populations. Each of these categories is disaggregated further by slum and non-slum residence, migration status, age, gender, length of stay in Dhaka, level of education, occupation and income to identify who benefitted most or remained most disadvantaged, and factors contributing to their benefits or disadvantages. In this way, it is poised to contribute to the body of knowledge and better-informed policies, programmes, and development of appropriate services by the government—both national and local—non-government organizations (NGOs), private sector, and development partners.

The importance of this book can hardly be overemphasized in the context that it examines the process and consequences of urbanization from a multidimensional perspective for a country like Bangladesh that has often drawn international attention for all the wrong reasons. From the American Secretary of State Henry Kissinger, who ridiculed the country as a 'bottomless basket', to numerous reports and media coverage focusing on its environmental disasters, positive stories, particularly about Bangladesh's achievements in the areas of social development since the 1990s have been ignored. For example, between 1990 and 2017, the value of the Human Development Index (HDI) for Bangladesh improved from 0.387 to 0.608 showing a 57.1 per cent increase, which raised its ranking to 136 and placed the country in the medium development category (UNDP 2018). Similarly, the per capita gross national income (GNI) almost trebled from US$1,320 to US$3,677 showing a growth rate at 3.8 per cent per year during this period. Life expectancy at birth increased by 14.4 years (from 58.4 to 72.8 years), mean years of schooling increased by 3.0 years (from 2.8 to 5.8), and expected years of schooling doubled by 5.8 years (from 5.6 to 11.4 years) (UNDP 2018).

Migration, Poverty, and Space: Interlinkages and Transformative Potential

Urbanization is always associated with development and innovation but is increasingly acclaimed for its potential to transform the developing world with greater understanding, vision, and right policy. However, there are debates about whether this development has been at the expense of the countryside.[6] While location matters, it should also be noted that capital, goods, and peoples' livelihoods transcend boundaries, and the questions of productivity, economies of scale, and migration/mobility are of equal importance (Jones and Corbridge 2010). For Bangladesh, experiencing rapid urbanization, high income growth, and persistent income inequality, planners, interventionists, and policymakers require greater understanding on the consequences of urbanization, including the impact of rural–urban migration on urban poverty, welfare, and the scope for shared prosperity for different cross-sections in the city. This becomes even more important in the context of the country's Seventh Five-Year Plan (2016–20) that includes an urbanization strategy to achieve 'compact, networked resilient, inclusive and smart urban development' (GOB 2015c: 480). Similarly, in South Asia there is growing recognition of the importance of urban policy to optimize gains from urbanization with gradual weakening of the traditional hostility of policymakers (Ellis and Roberts 2015). The understanding generated by the book would be helpful to guide the informed policy with inclusiveness, prosperity, and sustainable development at its core, particularly in the context of changing policy discourse.

Dhaka presents a fertile ground to examine whether causes, context, and consequences of migration are changing over time due to persistent mobility of people, capital, information, and knowledge. The city also exhibits a high growth of per capita income and yet growing inequality. Therefore, another important theme that the book focuses on is the intersection between migration, poverty, and social change: whether and to what extent the gains from migration are reflective of people who live in urban areas. In particular, the focus is on the urban poor who are often blamed for transferring rural poverty to urban areas in a country where urbanization is often equated with 'slumization' (Siddiqui et al. 1993; Islam 1996; Hossain 2008).[7] Such views are not conducive to understanding the changing landscape—the blurring of the divide between rural and urban spaces—or the increasing interactions and interdependencies between rural and urban areas in terms of capital, goods, information, people, environmental services, and more, including diversity of migrants and their reasons for migration, all of which are important for a balanced, sustainable, and inclusive development policy.

The book unbundles the contexts and conditions that influence migration motivations and link these to broader structural and institutional aspects together with agency and micro-level factors that impact the implementation process of the migration decision. In this process, it presents a nuanced debate regarding the nexus between migration and development as reflected in pertinent theories such as the East–West divide, rural development and migration, new economic geography, social network and migrants' agencies, women's empowerment, and the frontiers of push–pull migration and their applicability in the context of Bangladesh. Going beyond the push–pull debate, the book recasts migration theories by considering migrants' intrinsic qualities—their self-confidence, hopes, aspirations, and resilience—and blending broader structural and institutional forces with migrants' agency and aspiration. It analyses the whole gamut of population dynamics and migration, including regional connectivity and rural–urban links, and constructs relevant theoretical approaches to capture emerging trends and nuances of migration motivation.

Also, the book emphasizes the transformative potential of urbanization, particularly rural–urban linkages in eradicating rural poverty. Empirical evidence shows that migration is a cornerstone for enhancing upward economic mobility, with labour migration playing a key role in building diversification and resilience of rural households (USAID 2015). Similarly, urban–rural linkages contributed a reduction of 13–25 per cent in rural poverty in India between 1983 and 1999 (Cali 2013). Therefore, the book focuses on changes in rural poverty, the role of physical and infrastructure development, and intra and inter-personal factors in examining migration motivation, and whether and how it is changing over time. Also, it examines the links between migration motivation and migration outcomes to connect two dominant traditions in migration literature and to analyse migration, space, and poverty as well as development nexus.

Migration, Livelihoods, and Inclusive Development

Employment-related reasons, whether it is the search for a job and/or a better job or income, looms large in the literature related to migration motivation, including the results of our three rounds of surveys. Obviously, questions that arise are what happens to migrants after migration? Do they achieve their goals and realize their aspirations for better employment and/or livelihoods or income? It is important to understand how structural changes in the Bangladesh economy from predominantly agricultural to a more modern economy, particularly with an expanding service sector, are affecting productivity and changing livelihood options for migrants and their family members.

The book addresses all these questions and, by going beyond the formal and informal sector debate, it highlights the scope for inter-sectoral movement and upward mobility—either within the same sector or across different sectors of the economy—for migrants, particularly the poorer ones, to understand the dynamics of the urban labour market. It also assesses their level of job satisfaction and plans for future change to narrate the supply side of the story.

Quantitative data is supplemented and complemented by qualitative data derived from in-depth interviews and FGDs of men and women engaged in different occupations such as construction labourers, ready-made garment (RMG) factory workers, hawkers, rickshaw pullers, and auto-rickshaw drivers. Qualitative data helped with generating insights into nuances and specificities of contexts and conditions regarding migration decision making and the implementation process, the role of social networks in migration and the settlement process, occupational hazards and training needs necessary for narrowing the gap between top-down urban policies, and needs-based policy for poor people in urban areas.

Existing literature also highlights that urban policies that aimed to reduce rural–urban migration succeeded neither in reducing migration nor in alleviating rural poverty and disadvantages, which often exacerbate rural–urban migration. M. Awumbila, G. Owusu, and J.K. Teye (2014) cited examples of forced evictions of migrants in Harare and Dhaka in 2007 as responses to the failures of city authorities, similar to their research findings in Ghana, where migrants were also repeatedly harassed by the city authorities. However, it is encouraging that policy environment is changing even in many developing countries. In South Asia, for example, the policy discourse is changing in favour of leveraging benefits of urbanization for growth and prosperity (Ellis and Roberts 2015). Similarly, in Bangladesh the Seventh Five-Year Plan commits to formulate an urbanization strategy to achieve 'compact, networked, inclusive and smart urban development' (GOB 2015c: 480).

Quality of Life: Sustainability Matters

While changes in employment, occupational mobility, and income gains are important for survival and sustenance of life, a major part of sustenance also depends on access to basic services such as safe water and sanitation, electricity and piped gas connections, and the quality of human capital. For a rapidly urbanizing city like Dhaka that has accorded a low city prosperity index (CPI) and the second-worst ranking in the city liveability index (Economist Intelligence Unit 2015), meeting Goal 11 that calls to 'make cities and human settlements inclusive, safe, resilient and sustainable' (UN-Habitat 2013; 2016), issues related to access, quality, and equity in basic services including health and education become even more important.

Therefore, this book analyses whether material gains of migrants can be sustained in the long run by examining whether access to and quality of basic amenities such as housing, water and sanitation, and gas and electricity improved over time for respondents, especially the poor and women, in the first place. This is supplemented by assessing progress in relation to health and education for different cross-sections, inter-generational indicators of equality, necessary for measuring the scope for shared prosperity. The book identifies factors contributing to these changes. Also, it presents trends in adult literacy and educational attainment to examine whether quality of human capital has improved, and examines particularly whether poor migrants have enough incentives to spend on their children's health and education and outcomes.

Urbanization and the Demographic Dividends[8]

Urbanization is associated with fertility decline. Based on the last two rounds of our survey results, we found that family size is becoming smaller for both slum and non-slum households, although there was a considerable gap in the fertility rate between eligible women from slum and non-slum households. Therefore, the book assesses whether a smaller family size is associated with the demographic transformation yielding the demographic dividends, particularly for slum dwellers. It examines best practices and the types of policies and governance framework necessary to turn the gift of Dhaka's demographic transition to sustained economic growth. The book revisits the debates on rapid urban growth and congestion versus benefits of agglomeration and analyses population and other features of urbanization by comparing Dhaka with other megacities. It also examines the prospects for shared prosperity in the light of SDG and some of the CPI measures prepared by the United Nations Human Settlements Program (UN-Habitat 2013) such as poverty and prosperity, quality of life and human capital, infrastructure development and environmental sustainability to attain the main outcomes: equity and social inclusion.

Migration and Modernization

Urbanization is often associated with innovation, and demographic, social, and economic transformation. Cities are recognized as the engines for growth and change (Dwyer 1972). It is believed that urban living is conducive to changes of attitudes, aspirations, behaviours, and personal relationships no matter how briefly migrants may have experienced it. However, in the context of the dearth of studies in Bangladesh related to migration and its impact on modernization and social change, the book examines whether the attitudes and aspirations of the respondents have changed over time, particularly to measure how and to what extent gender and generational relations within families are redefined and impacted in relation to migration in the urban milieu.

A 20-YEAR REPORT CARD AND A ROAD MAP TO SUSTAINABLE AND EQUITABLE DEVELOPMENT

Finally, the book presents a report card on the changes that Dhaka's residents experienced over time, the impacts of these changes on their lives, livelihoods, well-being, and future prosperity along with issues that need attention based on the major findings. Implications of these findings are critically analysed from a policy perspective together with better practice analysis, drawing lessons from across the globe from which strategic policy measures are recommended in this book. In the context of changing policy discourse that recognizes the role of urbanization in promoting economic development in place of traditional hostility, the book provides policy options on how cities can be transformed to better drive economic growth and poverty reduction, as well as to become better places in which to live. By defining the way in which cities should be planned and managed to best promote sustainable and equitable urbanization and integrating this with the national development agenda, this book has provided a road map that would create the scope for sharing prosperity equitably for all citizens, not only for Bangladesh but also for other rapidly urbanizing countries.

NOTES ON THE DATA SOURCES AND METHODOLOGICAL APPROACHES

As mentioned before, the book is based on longitudinal data generated from three repeat surveys—conducted in 1991, 1998, and 2010—on a randomly selected cross-section of slum and non-slum households from four wards of Dhaka city: Lalbagh, Purana Paltan, Jurain, and Mirpur. These wards were also randomly selected as representative wards of Dhaka city and the first and second rounds of surveys were conducted on all the four wards to which Motijheel was added in 2010 for the sake of consistency, as discussed in Table A.1 in the Appendices.

In the first two rounds, we drew 600 slum and non-slum households by using stratified random sampling procedure to ensure adequate representation of poor and non-poor populations. We used the 1989–90 and 1996 electoral rolls as the sampling frame for these two rounds of surveys, respectively, in the absence of census data at the time of the survey. By stratifying sample households proportionately to population based on occupation of the electorates, we drew 100 non-slum households from each ward.

Representativeness, Precision, and Consistency

As the electoral rolls of 1989–90 suffered from under-enumeration of households in slum and squatter settlements, we conducted a supplementary census in all slums in the selected wards to ensure representativeness of the sample households. From the census, we listed households based on major sources of income. We then stratified these households by three major sources of income—transport operation, construction, and other—as these are the dominant occupations of slum dwellers (CUS 1996; Hossain, Afsar, and Bose 1999; Afsar 2000). Accordingly, we selected 50 households randomly from each of the wards to represent poor population. In this process, we selected 150 households from each ward for the survey, of which one-third were slum dwellers, which was consistent with the proportional strength of slum population in Dhaka city as estimated by the BBS in 1989 (BBS 1992). Quoting from BBS (2015), G. Jones, A.Q.M. Mahbub, and I. Haq (2016) reported that Dhaka Megacity (DMC) accounts for 39 per cent of all slum dwellers of Bangladesh, which lends support to the proportional strength that we used given that the survey was conducted in 2010 and in Dhaka City Corporation (DCC).

For the second-round survey in 1998, we followed the same process. However, given that the 1996 electoral rolls (the sampling frame for the 1998 survey) had comprehensive coverage of slum and squatter settlements, we did not have to conduct a supplementary census. Following the same process of random stratification used in the first round, we drew 150 households—100 from non-slum and 50 from slum and squatter settlements based on the major sources of income.

It would have been ideal had we re-surveyed the same households to help generate panel data from the second and third-round surveys. However, panel data does not constitute a viable option given the difficulty of tracing many households living in rented accommodation due to greater mobility in the cities, particularly in a megacity like Dhaka, compared with rural areas.[9] In view of the above problems, we conducted the third-round survey in 2010 in the same wards using the same random sampling method. We used the 2008 electoral rolls as the sampling frame to draw 600 households from the same cross-section of slum and non-slum households to ensure the representativeness and precision required to establish trends in this survey.

To keep consistency with the last two rounds of data, we included a part of Motijheel *thana* (Ward No. 33) in order to have representation from slum households because, with the demolition of the Drainpar *bostee,* Purana Paltan no longer had any slum or squatter settlements. For similar reasons, Shahid Nagar (Ward No. 60) was added to the sample in the case of Lalbagh (Ward No. 62). Further, due to changes in administrative set-up, Jurain was brought under a new Thana—Shyampur and, subsequently, we could not find some of the old mahallas surveyed in the first two rounds in Ward No. 90 (Table 1.2). It should be noted that at the time of our third-round survey Dhaka district was divided into 96 thanas, 92 wards, and 855 mahallas, while in 2001, there were 90 Wards and 731 mahallas (BBS, 2012a).

However, unlike in 1996, the 2008 electoral rolls did not specify slum areas separately. Thus, during reconnaissance visits we had to ensure representation of urban population from slum households based on two indicators—population density in the house enlisted, and the shared mode of basic services such as the source of water, gas burners, and toilets. This is because, unlike the earlier two rounds, slum households could no longer be identified from the housing structure as concrete walls have become the most common feature in Dhaka city. Subsequently, slum households that were easily identifiable due to their thatched and/or corrugated iron (CI) sheet roof and wood/CI sheet walls in the 1990s were no longer so easily visible in most cases.

CHANGING SLUM IDENTIFIERS

Over time, housing conditions in Dhaka city have changed remarkably. At the time of the first round of survey conducted in 1991, we could easily distinguish slums from non-slum households by their (mostly) bamboo roofs and temporary (*kutcha* and semi-*pucca*) structures. In the late 1990s, bamboo roofs were replaced by CI sheets for slums, and in some cases, concrete roofs, and temporary types of houses became rare. At the time of the survey in 2010, the aggressive expansion of high-rise buildings transformed Dhaka's landscape into vertical structures. Simultaneously, we found it extremely difficult to identify slum households as temporary and semi-permanent housing structures became less visible and more concentrated in fewer pockets of Dhaka.

This does not mean that slums do not exist in Dhaka city. We have identified some 'traditional' slums in Shahidnagar, Sweeper's Colony in Motijheel and certain parts of Alambagh in Jurain built with CI sheet roofs and walls. Rather, it indicates that instead of relying solely on housing structure, it is prudent to explore access to shared modes of basic amenities as an identifier for slum households. To do this, however, we had to go inside the house and investigate whether the household had exclusive access to basic amenities such as gas, water, and toilets, or whether these amenities were shared with other families. This intrusion was not always welcomed and was also time consuming.

CHANGING WARD BOUNDARIES

Since the 1990s, wards have been reconfigured and boundaries have changed rapidly. We have tried to capture this by presenting and comparing the boundaries between the 1988–89 and 2008–09 electoral rolls (Table 1.2). Our comparison shows that not only were the sample wards

Table 1.2 *Mahallas*/Communities under Sample Wards in the 1989–90 and 2008–9 Electoral Rolls, 2011 Census, and *Mahallas* Surveyed in 2010

Sample Wards	Electoral Rolls (1989–90)	Electoral Rolls (2008–09) and 2011 Census	Mahallas/ Communities Surveyed in 2010
Mirpur	Ward #4: Agriculture Workshop, Section 6, Block A and D, Section 6, Block C, Water Tank, Section 7, Nayabari, T & T Office and Mirpur Police Station.	Ward #7: Mirpur Section-2 (Block A-F), Section-2 (Block-New-A, Block-Cha and Block G), Section-6 (Block-A and Block-B). Ward #7 (Part): Alobdi, Rupnagar, Shialbari	Ward #7: Mirpur Section-2 (Block-A-E, Block-Cha, Block-G-H) Ward #7 (part): Rupnagar
Jurain	Ward# 48: West Jurain, Karimullar Bagh, Kuli Bagan, Balur Math, Munshibari, Alambagh.	Ward# 90: Karimullah Bagh, Postogola (part), Army Camp, Alam Bagh, West Jurain	Ward #90: Alambagh, Karimullah Bagh, Postogola (part), West Jurain
Purana Paltan	Ward# 64: Inner Circular Road, Purana Paltan, Naya Paltan, Bijoy Nagar, Drainpar, Fakirapur Water Tank, Arambagh, Baitul Mukarram, GPO, PWD Staff Quarter, Rajarbagh Police Hospital and Shanti Nagar.	Ward# 36: Baitul Mukarram, Bijoy Nagar, BB Avenue, Chamelibagh, Guliatan, Naya Paltan, Purana Paltan, Rajarbagh Police Hospital, Rajarbagh, Shanti Nagar Ward# 31: (part of Motijheel) Gupibagh, Kamlapur Railway Station, Kamlapur Railway Hospital, North Kamlapur, South Kamlapur	Ward #36: Bijoy nagar, Chamelibagh, Gulistan, Naya Paltan, Purana Paltan, Shantinagar Ward #31: Gupibagh (part), North and South Kamlapur Railway Station Ward #33: Sonali Bank Colony

		Ward #33: Bank Colony, Motijheel Colony, T & T Colony	
Lalbagh	Ward# 25: T and T Officers' Quarter, Home Economics Collage, Eden girls collage hostel, Agrani school, Paschim Palashi Barrack, Azimpur Girl's High School, Azimpur Estate, Etim Khana, Rasul Bagh and BC Das Road.	Ward# 60: Jagannath Saha Road, Rajnarayan Dhar Road, Shahid Nagar. Ward# 62: Azimpur Road (Part 1 & 2), Azimpur Estate East, North and South, Azimpur Gorosthan Area, BC Das Road, Dhakeshwari Road, Eden Girls College and Hostel, Home Economics College and Hostel, Palashy second Market, Palashy East and West, Rasulbagh, South Nilkhet Municipal Market	Ward #60: Shahid Nagar Ward #62: Azimpur Road (Part 1 & 2), Azimpur Estate East, North and South, Azimpur Gorosthan Area, BC Das Road, Dhakeshwari Road, Eden Girls College and Hostel, Home Economics College and Hostel, Palashy second Market, Palashy East and West, Rasulbagh, South Nilkhet Municipal Market

Source: Compiled from various electoral rolls, BBS (2012a), and Afsar (1995).

renumbered but their boundaries were also changed, and/or extended or reconfigured under the 2008–09 electoral rolls.

HIGH MOBILITY OF URBAN HOUSEHOLDS

During the sampling process and survey, one of our major problems was the high mobility of the households, particularly in the case of slum households. For example, in Lalbagh and Shahid Nagar, within a span of three years (the gap between the time when the electoral rolls were prepared and the time of the survey) around 50 per cent of the sample households had moved out. Hence, we had to draw more reserve

Box 1.1 Additional Reserve Samples for Purana Paltan and Lalbagh

For Purana Paltan and Lalbagh, we needed to draw an additional 450 reserve samples due to problems of:

- no clear demarcation for households in slum areas;
- restricted access to high-rise apartments in areas such as Shantibagh, Naya Paltan, and Chameli Bagh; and
- non-availability of adult members and or the whole family in the stipulated address due to job-related reasons and overseas migration.

samples in addition to those we drew originally. Considering the risk of high mobility, we initially drew twice as many reserved samples as the required sample size. Thus, along with 150 households for each ward, we had another 300 reserve samples, and the size of the reserve samples was even larger for Purana Paltan and Lalbagh (Box 1.1).

Therefore, to cover 150 households in each ward, we drew 700 samples. Eventually, we ended up surveying 636 households but retained 600 sample households, keeping consistency with the earlier two rounds of survey. Further, to have representation of the households in which women were the heads, we decided to draw 20 per cent of women voters out of the total voters. We assumed that these women were the main and/or major income earners for their households. However, we ended up having 10 per cent of the women voters as the heads of the households because a large majority of the women voters were neither the main bread earners, nor were they the major income/remittance recipients in their families.

TYPES OF INFORMATION COLLECTED

To generate information on the sources of income and the pattern of its utilization, we tried to ensure consistency with the questionnaires used in the earlier surveys. For similar reasons, we also collected information on demographic and socio-economic variables, including age and gender composition of the households, levels of education, employment status and types of occupation of the household members as well the heads of the households, and migration status of the household heads and spouse (Appendix 2).

To explore rural–urban linkages, we asked questions about, for example, distance to main services and institutions such as schools, hospitals, and banks in migrants' birthplaces. We also collected information on access, quality, and equity of urban services such as gas, electricity, and water, sources of procurement and mode of use—shared or private—quality and ownership of dwelling, and the values and attitudes of the head of the household and the spouse regarding women's empowerment, in the same way as in the previous surveys. In addition, considering the rapid changes that Dhaka city has undergone over time, we used both quantitative and qualitative approaches to focus on the nuances of migration decision-making factors and processes, and the dynamics of urban labour market.

In addition to the survey, we have also used qualitative information generated through FGDs and in-depth interviews of workers from different sectors. Our major purpose was to generate understanding regarding the nuances of the migration decision-making process, the types of help migrants received in the process of their settlement, including coping with the work situation, occupational mobility, and capturing dynamism involved in the process of occupational changes (Appendix 2). Also, FGDs were directed to identify factors as well as processes that influenced occupational changes and generate insights on possible outcomes together with occupational hazards and training needs necessary for narrowing the gap between top-down urban policies and needs-based policies for poor people in urban areas. Accordingly, four FGDs were conducted with hawkers and small-shop owners, and transport, construction and garment factory workers. To ensure meaningful discussion in which each member could participate fully, eight members were selected from each sector based on their availability and willingness. Except in the case of garment factory workers, all participants were male.

To elaborate on issues and findings generated through FGDs, particularly highlighting the types of life and livelihood changes resulting from migration, and the coping strategies that migrants adapted to face those changes including occupational hazards, we conducted eight in-depth interviews of two workers from each of these sectors (Appendix 2). In this process, three female workers were interviewed—one each from the RMG and construction sectors, and one female hawker—to highlight the gender perspective. Accordingly, their male counterparts were also interviewed for each of these sectors. However, given that the transport sector is still male-dominated, we interviewed one rickshaw puller and one auto-rickshaw driver. All respondents were informed about the purpose of the study and their verbal consent was obtained before the interview. All information was kept anonymous and confidential. We altered their names in the discussion of findings from qualitative information for the purpose of confidentiality.

The research was sponsored by and conducted from the erstwhile RED, BRAC, Dhaka. The study team comprised both the authors, with the late Mahabub Hossain as advisor and Rita Afsar as the principal investigator together with Mahfuzur Rahman as the data analyst. It is important to mention here that both the authors were involved in the first and second round of surveys conducted from BIDS that provided the baseline data used in this book.

Limitations

In this book, we did not cover the floating population who constitute an important segment of the urban poor population. Given that BRAC has already conducted an in-depth study on the floating population of Dhaka city almost at the same time as this study, we did not duplicate but rather focused on the areas that needed attention. However, it is important to note that the household-based survey data collected for the book may not necessarily prove the most appropriate tool to cover all different categories of the workforce or to capture the dynamism of the urban labour market. For example, the domestic service sector is increasingly becoming more contractual, compared with the traditional mode of having permanent domestic help sheltered at home. Subsequently, those women who offered domestic service for few hours to more wealthy households could not be covered in the survey. On the other hand, those who offered this service from a slum household often did not report the service they provided for few hours, possibly as a matter of prestige as this occupation is not very well-respected in the society.

Similarly, on-site labour supplied for construction and cleaning services largely remained outside the purview of this study, which we supplemented with the help of focus group discussions with, and in-depth interviews of, the occupational groups. This has implications, particularly for female labour force participation rates, although we tried to address the gaps by identifying the sources of income and heads of expenditure.

STRUCTURE OF THE BOOK

This book is organized into nine chapters. After this introductory chapter, which outlines the rationale and purpose of the book, highlighting the three compelling questions and major themes to address them and details of the data sources and method used, Chapter 2 provides a brief overview of Dhaka's demographic transition. It compares Dhaka with other megacities across the world to understand its current challenges and potential to achieve prosperity and inclusivity. It shows clear trends of fertility decline for slum women and the demographic transition in Dhaka city. It analyses population changes in the study communities over time, why and how these changes have occurred, and what trends are emerging in this process that need policy attention. These demographic trends and patterns are compared with the Ward level data from the 2011 Population and Housing Census wherever it was available to help readers understand population changes in the broader context. The question of fertility decline, particularly for women in slum households, is examined with different hypotheses drawing on relevant theories related to the demographic transition and the demographic dividend. Accordingly, we have identified the factors contributing to the changes and analysed outcomes.

Chapter 3 examines whether the causes and context of migration to Dhaka have changed over time since the early 1990s. This chapter focuses on rural–urban connectivity and analyses trends in migration motivation and emerging themes as well as establishes links into structural factors and development scenarios at migrants' birthplaces. This is done to answer contextual issues related to question one: is the poorer segment of urban population that migrates with dreams for better lives and livelihoods benefitting from positive economic trends? Especially, in the context of the declining trends in poverty, which we estimated from the incidence and trends in regional poverty using the 2010 HIES data and the improved level of physical and social infrastructure development at migrants' birthplaces from our 2010 survey, the importance of this analysis becomes clear. These broader contexts are then linked with household decision-making processes and migrants' agency with the help of FGDs and in-depth case studies of migrants. Side by side, it also explores selectivity factors and whether these factors are changing over time, while analysing factors and processes contributing to these changes along with identifying emerging trends. In the light of differential 'gender roles, asymmetric social and gender relations', migrants' gendered backgrounds are considered, while providing causal explanation for migration (Afsar 2011a).

To address better livelihoods aspect of the first question, Chapter 4 examines whether migrants have been able to realize their aspiration for better livelihoods by migrating to Dhaka. It provides a detailed analysis of the respondents' occupational patterns, trends, and changes at different points in time—before migration, immediately after migration, and finally the current occupation at the time of the survey. The book confirms structural changes in the economy with the waning of the number of agricultural workers among migrants, and the increase in those employed in the services, construction and transport sectors, prior to migration to Dhaka as revealed from our 2010 survey data. Therefore, we compared these changes with the findings generated from the first two rounds of survey data and examined the labour market dynamics from the demand side in this chapter. It also addresses some pertinent questions related to the scope for shared prosperity for an average urban resident such as how long it took them to secure a job, whether it involved any cost, their level of job satisfaction, how long they continued with the same job, and whether they got an opportunity to switch to more rewarding jobs.

Chapter 5 analyses the changes in the human capital composition of the labour force, trends and changes in asset base, and livelihoods of respondents, and examines the level and composition of income for different occupational groups. It also identifies the determinants of household income with the help of a multivariate regression model using household-level data. Alongside, it examines distribution of income over time together with changes in the degree of inequality and estimates contribution of different sources of income to income inequality with the help of the Gini decomposition analysis. It also measures poverty lines for the moderate and extreme poor and shows notable decline in the incidence of moderate and extreme poverty in 2010. Also, it estimates changes in the incidence, intensity, and severity of poverty and identifies the correlates of poverty for Dhaka city to answer the concern raised in the first question regarding whether the poorer segment of urban population is benefitting from positive economic trends.

Chapters 6 and 7 focus on quality of life and sustainability issues by examining whether the respondents' access to and quality of basic amenities such as housing, water and sanitation, gas and electricity, and human capital endowment and formation have improved over time. This understanding is important to address the concerns raised by the second and third questions: are these benefits sustainable in the long run? Have these benefits brought qualitative changes creating scope for this group to have a stake in the city's growing prosperity like their non-poor counterparts? The book draws attention to substantial improvement in slum dwellers' access to basic amenities and enrolment rates at the primary and secondary levels over time, as well as paradigm shifts in the disease patterns. Chapter 7 examines the types of changes in morbidity rates and disease patterns, and the factors contributing to these changes. We have then assessed quality of health by analysing treatment-seeking behaviour of men and women from different cross-sections, and whether the determinants of good health are changing over time. Major environmental debates on rapid urbanization related to shortage of housing, water, sanitation, air quality, and gendered impacts are also presented in these two chapters. Especially, the focus was on the context in which urban girls and women experience gender-based disadvantages in performing gendered roles that can lead to a vicious cycle of low education, low employment or low-paid jobs, low income, high morbidity, mortality, and poverty (Uteng 2011; Tacoli 2012; Tacoli and Satterthwaite 2013; Chant 2013; 2014; Afsar 2016c). Accordingly, we have prepared a gendered progress card over time on morbidity pattern, health-seeking behaviour, enrolment rates at different levels, educational attainment, drop out rates, labour force participation rates and types of occupation, rate of return from education, age of marriage, and fertility rates (women only) for different cross-sections in Chapters 2, 7, and 8. The factors that are conducive to positive changes and those which hamper progress are also identified in this process.

Given that emancipative values[10] constitute the key cultural component of a broader process of human empowerment including women's empowerment, Chapter 8 examines some pertinent theories of social change by analysing attitudinal changes associated with urban living such as attitudes of migrants towards gender division of labour, women's higher education, and participation in the labour market. It also assesses whether, how, and to what extent gender and generational relations are redefined and impacted in relation to migration by analysing gender roles, attitudes, and aspirations regarding major institutions and practices including marriage, divorce, dowry, and inheritance that govern gender relations. Side by side, it presents the actual situation of the members of these families on each of these accounts to examine whether there is a consistency between what they think and what they practice. In this process, it identifies the factors that are conducive towards progressive attitudes and practices, and those which impede progress, which is important to answer the third question related to qualitative changes necessary for creating scope for the poorer segment of urban population to have a stake in the city's growing prosperity like their non-poor counterparts.

The ninth and final chapter recapitulates and reflects on what we have presented in all previous chapters. Also, it prepares a report card by highlighting major findings covering each of the themes discussed earlier to address the three compelling questions by identifying changes and their concomitant implications along with major issues from a policy development perspective. It highlights the progress made in the 20-year period and the gaps and challenges that we identified from the analysis of the longitudinal data. Opportunities and challenges are then discussed critically through policy lenses. This policy analysis, aided by policy road maps from SDG and the New Urban Agenda as well as lessons from better practice analysis across the globe, helped us to recommend appropriate measures and strategies to make Dhaka a more prosperous, sustainable, inclusive, and liveable city. Finally, it presents concluding remarks.

NOTES

1. Historically, urbanization has been associated with economic and social transformation reflected in greater geographic mobility, lower fertility, longer life expectancy, higher levels of literacy and education, better health, greater access to basic amenities and social services, poverty reduction, and economic development. Research shows that the cost of delivering basic services is cheaper by 30 to 50 per cent in large cities compared with sparsely

populated areas (McKinsey Global Institute 2011). However, without adequate infrastructure and right policy approach for equitable sharing of benefits and prosperity, rapid and unplanned urban growth can threaten sustainable development leading to urban sprawl, high income disparity and polarization between the rich and poor, environmental degradation, and unsustainable production and consumption patterns (UN 2015c).

2. For an excellent review, see Osmani (2015) and Osmani and Sen (2011).

3. See 'The Future We Want', available at: http://www.un.org/en/sustainablefuture/ (accessed on 26 December 2016).

4. In brief, these goals are: Goal 1. End poverty; Goal 2. End hunger; Goal 3. Good health and well-being; Goal 4. Quality education; Goal 5. Gender equality; Goal 6. Clean water and sanitation; Goal 7. Affordable and clean energy; Goal 8. Decent work and economic growth; Goal 9. Industrial innovation and infrastructure; Goal 10. Reduce inequalities; Goal 11. Sustainable cities and communities; Goal 12. Responsible consumption and production; Goal 13. Climate action; Goal 14. Life below water; Goal 15. Life on land; Goal 16. Peace, justice, and strong institutions; Goal 17. Partnership for the goals.

5. Based on the first two rounds of survey data, authors estimated that per capita income of Dhaka city dwellers grew by 6 per cent while the Gini index also increased from 0.37 to 0.51 (Hossain, Afsar, and Bose 1999). The contribution of the urban sector to the country's GDP doubled from 37 per cent to 60 per cent between 1990 and 2010, and Dhaka's contribution to GDP was estimated at 36 per cent (Muzzini and Aparicio 2013).

6. For example, the urban bias theory (UBT) which argues that the countryside in the developing world remained poor and impoverished due to bias in political structure and system causing distortions in price (such as agricultural goods) and unbalanced growth (Bates 1982; Lipton 1997). The new economic geography (NEG) contests urban bias on the ground of economies of scale, increased productivity and efficiency, and the cross-cutting nature of rural–urban boundaries, nature and interests (see, for example, Varshney 1993; 1995; Skeldon 1997a; 1997b; Satterthwaite 2004; Jones and Corbridge 2010).

7. See Awumbila, Owusu, and Kofi Teye (2014); Suttie, and Vargas-Lundius (2016); Tacoli, McGranahan, and Satterthwaite (2015); and McKay and Deshingkar (2014) for a nuanced debate on migration, poverty, and development linkages based on empirical evidence.

8. The demographic dividend is the economic growth potential that may result from a decline in a country's mortality and fertility, and subsequent change in the age structure of the population, in which the number of people belonging to the working-age population (15 to 64) is larger than those who are not considered as working-age population (14 and younger, and 65 and older).

9. We have witnessed a high mobility problem, which we have discussed later in this section.

10. Emancipative values combines an emphasis on freedom of choice and equality of opportunities, which involves priorities for lifestyle liberty, gender equality, personal autonomy, and the voice of the people. For details, please refer to World Value Survey, available at: https://en.wikipedia.org/wiki/World_Values_Survey#cite_note-FOOTNOTEWelzelInglehart201043.E2.80.9363-9 (accessed on 22 October 2016).

2 Rapid Urbanization and Population Changes in Dhaka City

The Demographic Dividend

In this chapter, we provide an overview of Dhaka city, its urbanization trends, and concomitant outcomes in terms of CPI, which we compare with other megacities across the world to understand its current challenges and potentials to achieve prosperity and inclusivity. Also, we introduce readers to the study communities, analyse changes in these communities, and sample population over a 20-year period. This provides a contextual framework necessary to understand the demographic patterns, trends, and changes in the sample population between 1991 and 2010. We have also compared our findings with the Ward level[1] data from the 2011 Population and Housing Census (BBS 2012a) wherever it was available to understand population changes in the broader context. Particularly, we examined why and how family size is becoming smaller and its implications for different cross-sections in terms of fertility decline and the demographic dividend. The demographic characteristics of a household provide important information that helped us to assess the livelihood system of Dhaka city over time in the subsequent chapters.[2]

AN OVERVIEW OF DHAKA'S RAPID TRANSITION TO A MEGACITY

Evolved as a Hindu trading centre and having a chequered history of political importance and commercial prosperity as a provincial capital, Dhaka emerged as a capital of the new nation of Bangladesh with an approximate area of 104 sq. km and around 1.7 million population in 1974.[3] It is the oldest, largest, and the only megacity of the country with an estimated 15 million and 18 million population in 2010 and 2015 respectively, and with a steady share of one-third of the urban population.[4] While its share of urban population has remained steady at one-third since the 1990s, it comprised one-tenth of the total population in 2010, which has increased from around 7 per cent since the 1990s.

Ever since the country's independence, Dhaka's growth has been spectacular. Between 1974 and 1990, Dhaka's population almost quadrupled to 7 million with an annual average growth rate at 9.2 per cent, which was one of the highest across the world. In 2000, when it first became a megacity with its population reaching 10 million, the growth rate came down to less than half at 3.6 per cent (during 1990–2000) but gradually increased to 4.1 per cent and 3.7 per cent (during 2000–10 and 2010–15) respectively—still very high compared with many other mega cities (UN 2018). There was also a significant expansion of its administrative boundaries while the rate of natural increase has been falling due to declining fertility, which we have analysed later. High concentration of RMG factories,[5] business, banking, finance, insurance and other corporate sectors, head-quarters of government, development partners, NGOs, services sector, colleges, universities and technical institutes, and hospitals contribute to migration pull for the rich and poor alike for better employment and greater income opportunities.

Urban population growth has played a more important role in the urbanization of Bangladesh between 1950 and 2000 (which contributed 86 per cent to the increase) and is likely to do so between 2000 and 2050 (by contributing 78 per cent) as per the United Nations (2013). Migration and reclassification of urban areas, therefore, are the major components of urban growth for Dhaka city compared with natural increase of population. Contribution of migration and reclassification is estimated to have contributed 65 per cent of the urban population growth between 2001 and 2011, compared with 35 per cent by natural increase (Jones, Mahbub, and Haq 2016). This pattern and trend of urban growth is consistent with China, Nigeria, and Indonesia. However, it differs from other countries such as India, Pakistan, the Democratic Republic of Congo, and the Philippines, in which increase in the urban population between 1950 and 2000 was triggered equally by overall population increase and urban growth (United Nations 2013).

DHAKA AND OTHER MEGACITIES: A COMPARISON

A comparison of Dhaka's demographic trends with most megacities of the developing countries across the world (Table 2.1) shows that in 1990, with 7 million people, Dhaka was behind all cities except Lagos, Nigeria, and Kinshasa, Democratic Republic of the Congo—two cities in Africa—and the size of its population was the same as Karachi and Beijing. Its population has more than doubled since 1990 and reached 15 million in 2010, surpassing not only the two African cities but also overtaking Karachi, Kolkata, Manila, Jakarta, and Beijing. By 2030, Dhaka is predicted to become the fourth largest city in the world with a population of 28 million and surpass all other megacities except Delhi, Beijing, and Tokyo (UN 2018). Clearly, Dhaka's population growth rate has been higher compared with many of these cities between 1990 and 2010 and will have the third-highest rate after Lagos and Kinshasa between 2010 and 2030. Dhaka's population density is also the highest, compared to all its comparators (43,500 per sq. km).

Except for Kinshasa and Karachi, all megacities are characterized by a larger share of working age population—between two-thirds and four-fifths, compared with children and older people. Historically, cities have always attracted able-bodied people, a trend that is still valid with other indicators of the demographic transition. These include the degree of balance maintained between the adult population and the growth of children and ageing population depending on fertility level and the maturity of urbanization process among other factors. From that perspective, Dhaka can be classified to be at the post-intermediate stage of urbanization with faster increase in the rate of urbanization and has already started reaping benefits from the demographic transition. Accordingly, the share of adult population more than doubled (65 per cent), compared with children (30 per cent), and a very small proportion of older people (5 per cent),

Table 2.1 Population Characteristics of Dhaka and Selected Megacities

Mega City	Population (million)			Growth Rate (/year)		Population Composition (%)			Density/ Km^2 2010	CPI*
	1990	2010	2030	1990–2010	2010–2030	0–14	15–64	65+		
Dhaka	7	15	28	3.9	3.3	30	65	5	43,500	0.633
Delhi	9	22	39	4.6	2.9	25	71	4	12,100	0.635
Mumbai	12	18	25	2.0	1.6	22	72	6	32,400	0.694
Kolkata	11	14	18	1.2	1.3	26	69	5	12,200	NA
Karachi	7	13	20	3.1	1.7	37	60	3	23,400	NA
Manila	8	12	17	2.1	1.7	31	66	3	15,300	0.723
Jakarta	8	10	13	1.1	1.3	24	73	3	9,500	0.769
Beijing	7	13	23	3.1	2.9	9	80	11	5,500	0.799
Shanghai	9	20	33	4.1	2.5	9	80	11	6,100	0.826
Lagos	5	10	21	3.0	3.8	32	65	3	14,500	0.496
Kinshasa	3	9	22	4.1	4.6	46	51	3	19,900	NA
Sao Paulo	15	20	24	1.8	1.1	22	71	7	7,500	0.757
Mexico City	16	20	24	1.1	0.9	25	68	7	9,700	0.709

Note: *CPI= City Prosperity Index, prepared by UN-Habitat by combining productivity, quality of life, infrastructure, environment, and equity-related indicators (for details, see UN-Habitat 2013).
Source: Authors' estimates from UN (2018), UN (2015a), UN-Habitat (2013), and McKinsey Global Institute (2011).

which is the same as Kolkata and not too different from Delhi (4 per cent) and Mumbai (6 per cent) (Table 2.1).

In general, we can see that the population structure of the cities can be roughly correlated with the CPI (UN-Habitat 2013). However, what matters most is the right policy and governance framework to turn the gift of the demographic transition to sustained economic growth and city's prosperity by focusing on equity and social inclusion, institutional and regulatory framework, and adequate investment on productivity, quality of life, infrastructure development and environmental sustainability.[6] Using 'hub' and 'spoke' matrix, the United Nations Human Settlement Programme (UN-Habitat) constructed CPI with these five dimensions—productivity, quality of life, infrastructure development, environmental sustainability, and equity and social inclusion as the 'spokes'. The 'hub' at the centre of the 'wheel of prosperity' brings together the urban power functions (such as public authorities, laws, regulations, institutions, urban planning, civil society, trade unions, and NGOs) associated with the five 'spokes'.

Therefore, the CPI measures the status of cities together with outcomes of government policies and actions that can help to identify the good policies, practices, and actions. For example, Shanghai and Beijing were among the top three achieving cities, which indicates that in these cities the five spokes are well-connected having relatively strong institutional and legal framework, although Beijing is going through a stage of consolidation of these frameworks and agencies. Note that these are also the cities with the largest share of adult population.

For Dhaka, on the contrary, there are serious governance issues that are structural, functional, financial, and social. Instead of a simple and clear-cut institutional arrangement with adequate power and resources, the current system of urban government is complex, chaotic, hierarchical, and highly inefficient. Planning, infrastructure, and basic services are delivered by a mix of central and local government, national (a total of 22 ministries) and 51 special purpose agencies (GOB 2015a) that have limited resources, weak administrative capacity, little coordination, and no citizen accountability.[7] Subsequently, it represents a weak connection among the spokes to deliver better policy outcomes in relation to shared prosperity due to weak and unambiguous institutional and regulatory framework, inadequate investment in public goods, and lack of pro-poor social programmes. We expect that background information provided regarding the demographic, contextual, structural, and CPI for Dhaka in relation with other megacities of the developing countries will help readers to better understand the population dynamics in the communities that we have studied over time and presented in the following paragraphs.

POPULATION CHANGES IN THE COMMUNITIES STUDIED

Population of the study wards had increased remarkably since 1991 (Table 2.2). Drawing on the 2011 Census, we found that among the four wards Purana Paltan and Lalbagh experienced more than doubling of their respective populations, while the increase was recorded at more than three-quarters (80 per cent) and two-thirds (68 per cent) respectively for Jurain and Mirpur. The population of Dhaka Metropolitan Area (which has been reclassified to include other urban area and economically integrated rural environs) more than doubled from around 7 million to 15.4 million between 1991 and 2011. Other urban areas mainly included five sub-districts (*upazilas*) and 17 unions adjacent to the DCC having urban characteristics.[8] Not surprisingly, therefore, since 2001, approximately 5 million new residents or at least a 50 per cent of people were added to its population, and accordingly, Dhaka's population rose from just under 10 million to more than 15 million people over the decade.[9]

However, it should be noted that the population of the sample wards are strictly not comparable over time because of the reconfiguration and reclassification of urban areas in the mid-2000s. In 2011, the number of thanas (police districts) in Dhaka city almost trebled compared with 1991 (from 14 to 41). Numerically, wards did not change much (from 90 to 92) although their boundaries and composition changed substantially with addition or creation of 124 more mahallas (localities) since 2001 (from 731 to 855). Moreover, as noted in the previous chapter, to keep consistency with the earlier rounds, we have surveyed parts of other adjacent wards, which contributed to the large increase in the ward population.[10]

However, contrary to the overall population trend, our longitudinal data shows decline in absolute population for the sample households

Table 2.2 Basic Demographic Characteristics of the Study Communities in 1991 and 2010

Variables	**Mirpur**		**Purana Paltan**		**Lalbagh**		**Jurain**	
Reference Year	**1991**	**2010**	**1991**	**2010**	**1991**	**2010**	**1991**	**2010**
Total Population	53,564	90,282	45,810	92,221*	33,863	75,815*	36,537	66,637
Sample Population	801	728	814	702	843	768	879	798
Sample HHs	150	150	150	150	150	150	150	150
Family Size	5.3	4.8	5.4	4.7	5.6	5.1	5.9	5.3
Area of Ward (km^2)	23.31	NA	2.59	NA	3.89	NA	4.53	NA
Population Density	2,299	Na	17,687	NA	8,705	NA	8,066	NA
Sex Ratio	119	113.5	153	103.8	114	120.2	123	125.5

Note: *Population of Purana Paltan and Lalbagh are not strictly comparable with that of 1991 because of the inclusion of additional wards in 2010.
Source: Compiled and computed from Afsar (2000) and BBS (2012a) and based on authors' estimates from BRAC third-round urban poverty survey, 2010.

between 1991 and 2010. Population of Mirpur, Purana Paltan, Lalbagh, and Jurain was 728, 702, 768, and 798 in 2010, compared with the corresponding population of these wards—801, 814, 843, and 879 respectively—in 1991. It shows that the sample population has been declining by 9 per cent for each of these wards except for Purana Paltan, where the decline was higher—14 per cent—between 1991 and 2010.

We also found that family size has become smaller, varying between 4.8 (Purana Paltan) and 5.3 (Jurain) in 2010, compared with 1991 when the average size varied between 5.3 (Mirpur) and 5.9 (Jurain), although the number of households surveyed in both years remained identical (150 for each ward). Decrease in absolute population together with that of the family size highlights an unmistakable trend of fertility decline for the sample households, which we have analysed in the next section.

SMALLER FAMILY SIZE, FERTILITY DECLINE, AND THE DEMOGRAPHIC TRANSITION

The child–woman ratio (CWR) (number of under five children per 100 women aged between 15 and 49 years), an indicator of current fertility, is estimated at 27.8 for all study areas which is much smaller compared to the corresponding figures (47 and 39, respectively) in 1991 and 1998 (Hossain, Afsar, and Bose 1999). However, the CWR estimated at 29.5 each for Mirpur and Jurain from the 2010 survey data, was relatively higher compared to that of Purana Paltan (26.4) and Lalbagh (24.9). It may be reiterated that wards have been reconfigured and boundaries changed rapidly in the last 10 years, which can explain this anomaly.

Unlike the previous two rounds, when the Drainpar bostee, one of the largest squatter settlements, was there in Purana Paltan, there were no slum or squatter settlements in this ward at the time of the survey in 2010. Hence, we included Kamlapur from the neighbouring Ward No. 60 (although it falls under Motijheel Thana) to have cross-sectional representation from slum households. Similarly, a part of Shahidnagar, which mainly represents slums, was added to have adequate representation of low-income households from Lalbagh, as discussed in the previous chapter. On the other hand, Mirpur and Jurain, the two lower-middle-class areas, have retained their characteristics to a great extent since the 1990s despite some changes that occurred because of reconfiguration of the ward boundaries in 2010. However, effects of these changes are expected to be smaller compared to the changes in the other two wards (Purana Paltan and Lalbagh).

The CWR is estimated at 33.6 and 25.3 for the sample households from slum and non-slum respectively in 2010. Compared with 1998 and 1991, the CWR for the slum women almost halved (declined by 44 per cent and 54 per cent, respectively) (Figure 2.1). Arguably, the length of settlement period in Dhaka might have influenced fertility behaviour among different categories of migrants. Further, the CWR is estimated at 23.8, 28.1, and 36.4 for non-migrant, long-term, and recent migrants, which tends to support the hypothesis.[11]

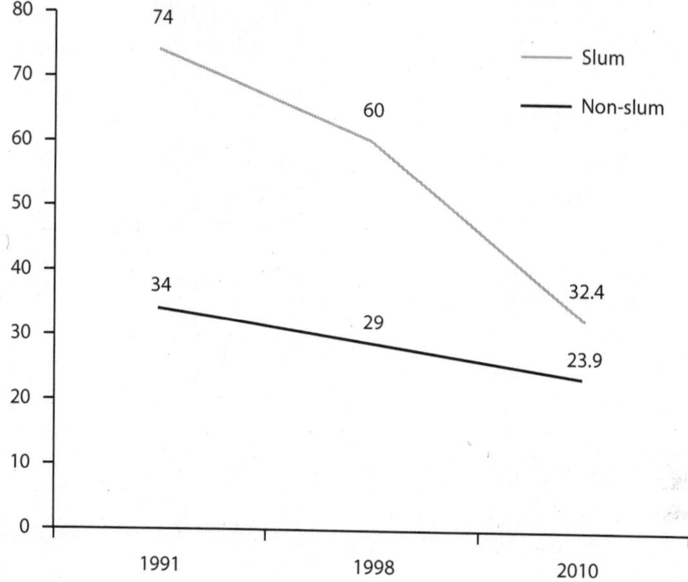

Figure 2.1 Child–Woman Ratio for Slum and Non-slum Women of Eligible Age, 1991–2010

Source: Authors' estimates from the three repeat surveys.

During the same period, the CWR for the women in non-slum households also declined by 13 per cent and 25 per cent respectively. Rapid decline of fertility in Dhaka's slum in recent years compared to that of non-slum is consistent with the Bangladesh Urban Health Survey (BUHS) 2013 report (NIPORT et al. 2014). Although the decline was greater for the women in slum households, it should be noted that the CWR for the women in non-slum households was substantially lower—less than half—compared with slum women in the 1990s. Therefore, it is not surprising that the rate of decline was smaller for them than their counterparts from slum households. What is important to note is that the difference in the CWR for the households in slum and non-slum has been narrowed down dramatically from 118 per cent to 33 per cent over almost two decades, suggesting a clear case of sustained fertility decline across the board.

The 2011 Demographic and Health Survey (DHS) data shows that the total fertility rate (TFR) in the urban areas was 2.0, while it was 2.5 and 2.3 in the rural areas and the country as a whole. Compared with 1999–2000, when the TFR was 2.5 in urban areas and 3.3 at the national level (NIPORT, Mitra and Associates, and ICF International 2013), it not only shows sustained decline but also demonstrates its high achievement, as the rate is the lowest in comparison with countries of similar levels of poverty (Hayes and Jones 2015). The 2013 report of BUHS (NIPORT et al. 2014) shows that the TFR has come down under replacement level—1.9 in urban areas, 1.7 and 2.0 for urban non-slum and slum, respectively.

Our survey shows that over 80 per cent of the eligible couples (aged between 15 and 49 years) were current users of modern contraception in 2010, irrespective of their level of education, income quintile, and slum and non-slum residence (Table 2.3). It should be noted that the contraceptive prevalence rate was higher for the eligible women from

Table 2.3 Percentage Distribution of the Eligible Couples from Sample Households by Selected Characteristics and Methods of Contraception Used, 2010

Eligible Couples by Categories	Modern Method	Safe Period/ Abstinence	Do Not Use	All (No.)
Slum	82.5	2.8	14.7	143
Non-slum	80.4	1.0	18.6	194
All	81.3	1.8	16.9	337
Spouses' Education				
Senior/Higher	78.0	1.6	20.3	123
Secondary Completed				
Primary	84.6	2.0	13.4	149
None	80.4	4.3	15.2	46
Top Quintile	81.8	0.0	18.2	44
Fourth Quintile	75.4	2.9	21.7	69
Third Quintile	83.8	0.0	16.2	74
Second Quintile	76.0	2.7	21.3	75
Bottom Quintile	89.3	2.7	8.0	75

Source: Authors' estimate from BRAC third-round urban poverty survey, 2010.

the lowest income quintile, and this is consistent with the fact that the contraceptive prevalence rate for Dhaka's slum is higher compared to that for other income groups or in non-slum households (NIPORT et al. 2014).

Arguably this supports W.B. Arthur and G. McNicoll's (1978) hypothesis regarding poverty driven fertility decline for Bangladesh although partially, given that there is greater decline in urban than rural areas. Clearly, the argument by J. Cleland, J.F. Phillips, S. Amin, and G.M. Kamal (1994) about improved access to contraception to the rich and poor alike appears to be more appealing, particularly as we found that most of the respondents (nearly 90 per cent), irrespective of their socio-economic backgrounds, depended heavily on private shops as the major source of procurement of contraception. Spread of girls' education at the primary and secondary level from slum households, as we shall see in Chapter 7, also explains this trend.

SMALLER FAMILY IN SLUM THAN NON-SLUM HOUSEHOLDS: FACTS AND FACTORS

The average size of slum households was 4.5 with 2.3 male and 2.2 female members in 2010. Size of the non-slum households was larger with 5.3 members on average—2.8 male and 2.5 female members. Recent migrants had the smallest household size with 4.1 members compared with those of the long-term and non-migrant households, each having 5.1 members on average.

From the trends in size and composition of the sample households (Table 2.4), we can say that the average size of the households declined over time from 5.5 in 1991 to 4.9 in 2010—a reduction of about 11 per cent. Size of the household declined almost at the same rate for both slum and non-slum residents. For non-slum residents, the household size declined from 5.9 in 1991 to 5.3 in 2010—a decline of 10 per cent. For slum residents, the size declined from 5.0 to 4.5—at the same rate of 10 per cent. The reduction in household size over this period was mainly due to reduction in the number of children. The number of children declined by 23 per cent over 1991–2010. The rate of decline was slower for slum residents (17.4 per cent) than for non-slum residents (24 per cent).

Table 2.4 Size (Average Number of Members) and Composition of the Households, 1991 and 2010

Composition of Members	Slum		Non-slum		Dhaka City	
	1991	2010	1991	2010	1991	2010
Heads	1.0	1.0	1.0	1.0	1.0	1.0
Spouses	0.9	0.9	0.9	0.9	0.9	0.9
Children	2.3	1.9	2.9	2.2	2.7	2.1
Immediate Family Members	4.2	3.8	4.7	4.1	4.6	4.0
Other Relatives	0.8	0.6	1.1	1.2	1.0	1.0
Household Size	5.0	4.5	5.8	5.3	5.6	4.9

Source: Authors' estimate from the three repeat surveys.

FAMILY COMPOSITION MATTERS

Despite slower decline in the number of children, the average size of the households in slum was lower than that of non-slum. Lower size of households in slums was mainly due to fewer relatives living in these households, compared with households in non-slum. It also indicates that poverty discourages people from providing shelter to other relatives who migrate to Dhaka in search of better job opportunities or for studies and other purposes that have been examined in the next chapter.

While slum households were predominantly composed of immediate family members (98 per cent) and very few relatives (2 per cent), both relatives and non-relatives (mainly domestic help) made up 4 per cent of the total population for non-slum households. One major reason for households in slums having mainly immediate family members was greater prevalence of nuclear families (65 per cent) than joint or extended types of families (35 per cent) (Figure 2.2). In contrast, the proportion of joint or extended types of families (45 per cent) was larger in non-slum households, although nuclear families comprised the majority (55 per cent).[12]

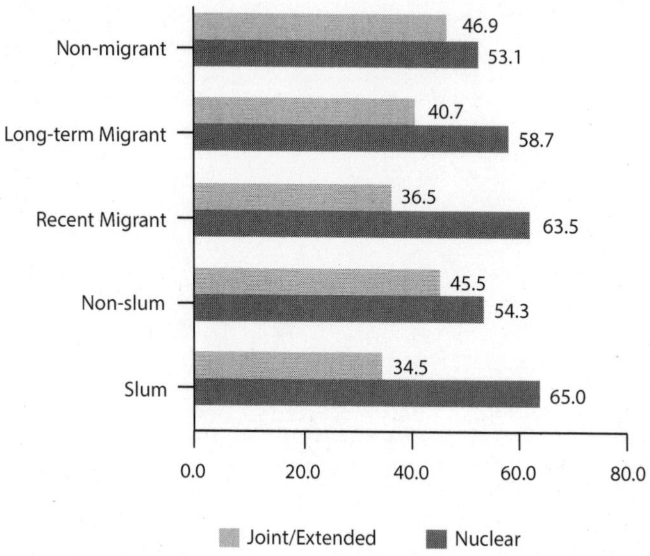

Figure 2.2 Distribution of Categories of the Sample Households by Type of Family

Source: Authors' estimate from BRAC third-round urban poverty survey, 2010.

Not surprisingly, therefore, a little over half (52.4 per cent) of the households in slum were composed of between three and four members, compared to 40 per cent for those in non-slum (Table 2.5). Households in non-slum, on the contrary, were twice (9 per cent) or even three times (12.2 per cent) more likely to have between seven and eight plus members than slum households (4.5 per cent and 4 per cent each). Further, nearly one-tenth of the households in non-slum (7 per cent) had nine or more members compared with barely 2 per cent for those in slum.

Along with a decrease in the number of children, there is also an increase in the size of adult members. As analysed later, the average number of working age members (aged 15–64 years) more than doubled compared to that of children; however, it was relatively smaller in slum (2.9) than non-slum (3.8). Accordingly, the dependency ratio has become smaller over time.

Table 2.5 Percentage Distribution of the Sample Households by Number of Members and Slum and Non-slum Residence, and Migratory Status

Types of Households	1 Member	2 Member	3 Member	4 Member	5 Member	6 Member	7 Member	8+ Member
Slum	0.5	7.0	17.0	35.5	19.5	12.0	4.5	4.0
Non-slum	0.5	2.3	15.0	25.3	22.0	14.0	9.0	12.2
Recent Migrant	2.7	9.5	31.1	27.0	18.9	5.4	2.7	5.4
Long-term Migrant	0.0	3.3	14.2	24.9	23.8	14.5	8.5	10.4
Non-migrant	1.3	2.5	11.9	38.1	16.3	14.4	7.5	9.4
All Households	0.2	3.8	15.7	28.7	21.2	13.3	7.5	9.5

Source: Authors' estimate from BRAC third-round urban poverty survey, 2010.

THE DEMOGRAPHIC TRANSFORMATION: MORE ADULTS THAN CHILDREN AND OLDER MEMBERS

Slum households were marked by relatively young population with children (aged below 15) constituting one-third, and youth (aged 15–24 years) and young adults (aged 25–39 years) each comprising almost one-fifth of the population (Figure 2.3). Of the remaining population, almost one-fifth (17.6 per cent) were aged between 40 and 59 years, and older people (60 years and over) constituted less than 5 per cent (3.7 per cent). The proportion of adult members has increased by almost 10 per cent between 1991 and 2010 (from nearly 55 per cent to almost 64 per cent). With 71 per cent of the population in non-slum being adult members, compared with 72 per cent in 1998, the growth rate for those in non-slum can be described as steady, although it comprised the largest category since the late 1990s (Figure 2.4).

Age–sex distribution of the members of recent migrants' families almost mirrored the population composition for slum households. In contrast, there is a striking resemblance in the population composition between the long-term and non-migrant households on the one

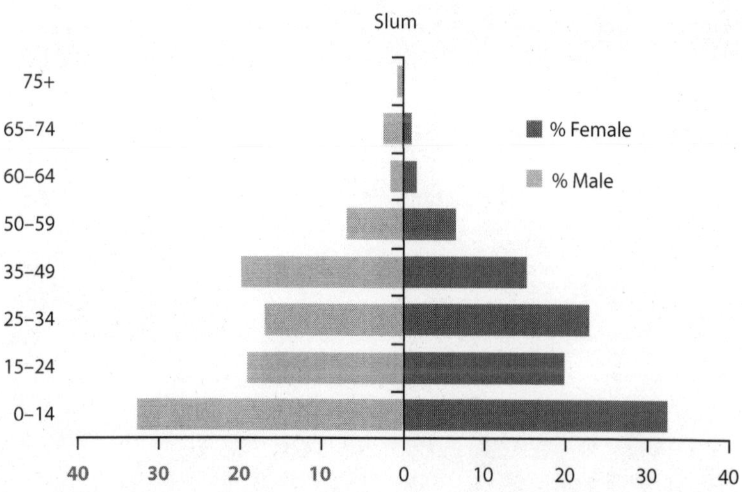

Figure 2.3 Age–Sex Pyramid for the Sample Slum Population, 2010

Source: Authors' estimate from BRAC third-round urban poverty survey, 2010.

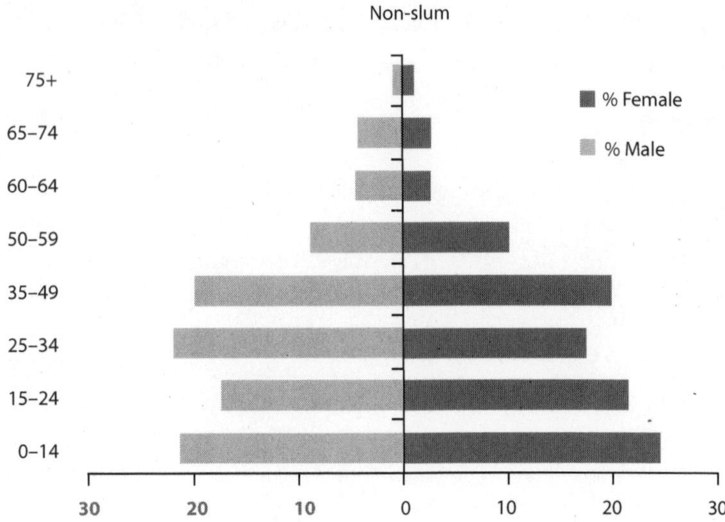

Figure 2.4 Age–Sex Pyramid for the Sample Non-slum Population, 2010

Source: Authors' estimate from BRAC third-round urban poverty survey, 2010.

hand, and non-slum households on the other. This is not unexpected given that many recent migrants (58.4 per cent) lived in slums, while the opposite holds for long-term and non-migrant households, with the majority (65.3 per cent and 73.4 per cent, respectively) living in non-slum households.

Children comprised around one-third of the total population for recent migrant households, compared with around one-quarter for each of long-term and non-migrant households. In contrast, the proportions of mature adults (aged between 40 and 59 years) and older people (aged 60 years and over) have been larger for the latter groups (37 per cent each), compared to the age cohorts from recent migrant families (26 per cent). There are also marked differences in the proportion of older population in slum and non-slum households (Figures 2.3 and 2.4). The proportion of older people in non-slum households was more than twice larger (8.1 per cent), compared to slum households (3.6 per cent). Increasing and larger share of active age members, fertility decline, and small share of older people clearly signal the demographic transition over time, which is particularly encouraging for slums as this is nothing new but a persistent trend for non-slum households.

Over time, the share of the older people in the total urban population has also increased steadily. Compared with 1991, their share almost doubled. Steady increase in the older population can also be supported by the HIES data (BBS 2011a). In 2010, older population in urban areas was 5.8 per cent compared with 5.0 per cent in 2005, indicating gradual increase in the longevity of life over time, as discussed in the introductory chapter.

MORE GENDER BALANCE IN POPULATION STRUCTURE: WOMEN'S INDEPENDENT MIGRATION MATTERS

The sex ratio was higher for the households in non-slum (112.4) compared with slum (109.2), indicating a preponderance of men over women in the overall age structure. However, the overall sex ratio often masks the marked difference in the gender composition of the slum and non-slum population found for specific age groups.

For slum households, the sex ratio was more even for 15–39 age group (101) compared with all other age groups, especially for older people (175) and those aged between 40 and 49 years (126.8), as seen in Figure 2.5. While there was little difference in the gender composition of older people in non-slum (sex ratio being estimated at 173.8), for children (0–14) and mature adults (aged 50–9) the sex ratio was more balanced in non-slum (98.4 and 96, respectively), compared with slum households (109.4 and 114.3, respectively).

These findings are consistent with the trends in the sex ratio for Dhaka city since 1991. Research shows lower sex ratio for the youth (15–24) and young adults (25–39) from urban poor agglomerations of Dhaka city due to young women's independent migration as garment factory workers (Afsar 2000: 123). High sex ratio for the mature adults can be explained by the fact that with longer stay in Dhaka, migrants are more likely to settle better and bring their families and relatives. Thus, on an average there was a larger number of male adults aged between 40 and 49 years (2.7) than female cohorts (2.3) in slum households.

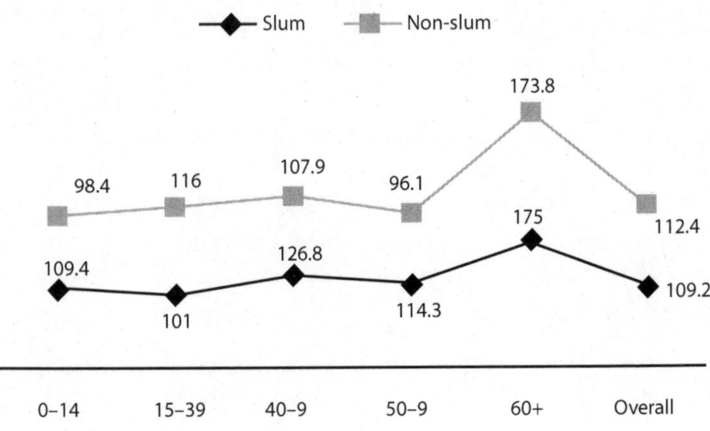

Figure 2.5 Sex Ratio for Different Categories of Respondents by Age Group

Source: Authors' estimate from BRAC third-round urban poverty survey, 2010.

The overall sex ratio for the sample migrant households has also become more even from 116 to 114 between 1991 and 2010. Compared with 1991, high peaks in the gender distribution shifted from 40 to 49 years and consolidated at 50–9 years for long-term migrants in 2010 mainly due to family composition and age gap between the head and spouse, which is discussed later. Recent migrants retained the high sex ratio for the 40–9 age bracket during the same reference period, and gender differential was the highest for older people for all categories of migrants in 2010 (Figure 2.6).

Highly masculine sex ratio for mature adults and older people may be supported by the types of families. The Index of Dissimilarity (I_D) computed for recent migrant and the total urban and rural population was 12.3 and 14 showing hardly any difference between these groups.[13] Further, the value of the I_D has not change since the 1990s. It tends to suggest that less than 10 years of stay in Dhaka city may not be sufficient to bring about demographic changes (Table 2.6). Therefore, it is important to analyse the types of family across different categories of migrants and non-migrants to examine its impact in the gender composition for different age groups and family size.

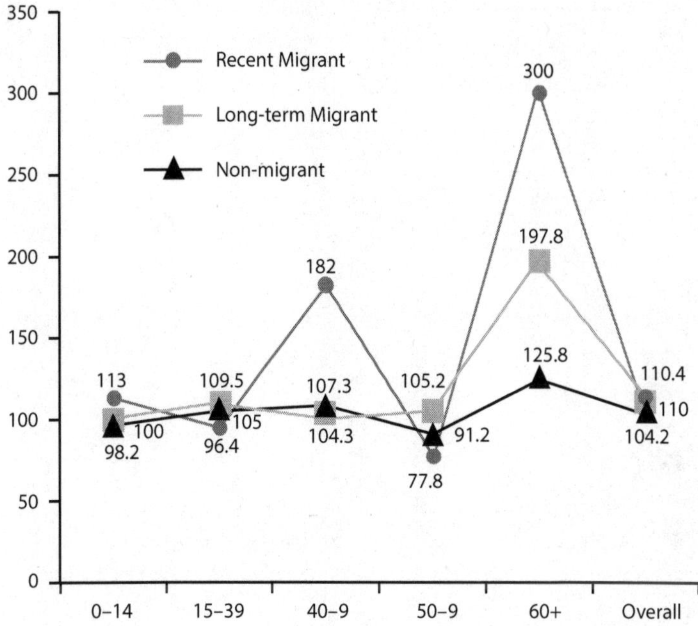

Figure 2.6 Sex Ratio for Categories of the Sample Migrant Population by Age Group

Source: Authors' estimate from BRAC third-round urban poverty survey, 2010.

After controlling for age, we found predominance of joint and/or extended types of families over nuclear families among both migrants and non-migrants aged over 60 years. Almost two-thirds and three-quarters of long-term and recent migrants as well as non-migrant cohorts had joint and/or extended type of family. Greater prevalence of the joint or extended types of families over nuclear families tends to suggest larger number of male than female members, which can be supported by the gender composition of the older members. There were 8.1 per cent of older men, compared to 5.8 per cent of the older women among the sample households, with gender difference being estimated at around 4 per cent for migrants, compared to just over 1 per cent (1.5 per cent) for non-migrants.

Women members were younger than men as reflected in their average and median age—27.7 and 25 years—compared respectively with that

Table 2.6 Dissimilarity Index for Recent Migrant, Urban, and Rural Population, 2010

Age Groups	Recent Migrant R1 %	National N1, %	R1 – N1	Urban U1 %	R1 – U1	Rural R2 (%)	R1-R2
0–4 years	10.4	10.3	0.1	9.4	1	10.6	0.2
5–9 years	12.4	12.3	0.1	10.7	1.7	12.9	0.5
10–19 years	14.6	21.6	7	21.4	6.8	21.7	7.1
20–29 years	23.2	16.7	6.5	18.5	4.7	16.5	6.7
30–39 years	20.2	13.6	6.6	15.2	5	13	7.2
40–49 years	10.1	10.8	0.7	11.8	1.7	10.4	0.3
50–59 years	5.2	7	1.9	7.1	1.9	6.9	1.7
60–64 years	2	2.6	0.6	2	0	2.8	0.8
65+ years	2	4.8	2.6	3.8	1.8	5.2	3.2
I_D 2010			26.1/2 =13		24.6/2 =12.3		27.72/ =13.9
I_D1991	14			12	12		

Source: Authors' estimate from BRAC third-round urban poverty survey, 2010; BBS (2011a); and Afsar (2000).

of 29.5 and 27 years for men. The proportion of older women (65 years and over) was almost half (3 per cent) compared with men (5 per cent). Note that gender differential was greater for the households in non-slum than slum. The median age of female and male members in slum was 23 and 24 years respectively compared with 29 and 26 years respectively for those in non-slum households. However, age-differential between the head and the spouse was even greater compared to members across all categories (Figure 2.7).

The spouses on average were almost 10 years younger than the heads. Thus, while the average age of the male heads in slum and non-slum households was 40 and 50 years respectively it was estimated at 31 and 40 years respectively for their spouses (Figure 2.7). The difference in the median age between the heads and the spouses was six and ten years respectively for recent and long-term migrants (Figure 2.7). Age difference between migrants and their spouses, together with types of families, contributed to a greater imbalance in the sex ratio for the older people among migrants, particularly recent migrants, compared to that of non-migrants.

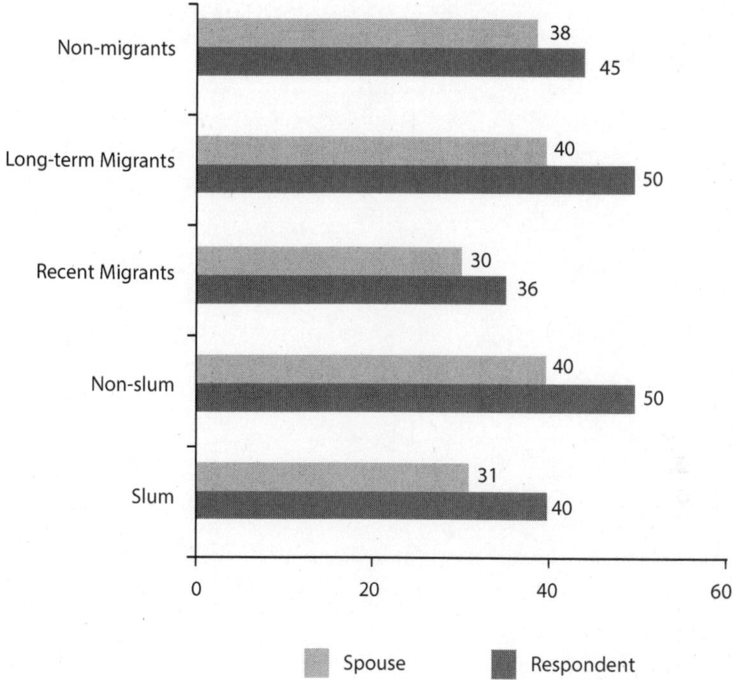

Figure 2.7 Median Age of the Respondents and Spouse by Different Categories

Source: Authors' estimate from BRAC third-round urban poverty survey, 2010.

MATURITY OF MIGRATION PROCESS: RISING AGE AT MIGRATION

To examine age selectivity for the sample migrant population, we have used the I_D to facilitate inter- and intra-group comparison. The I_D computed for the recent and non-migrant population was nine showing a small difference between the two groups. However, the value of I_D becomes 25.8 or almost trebled indicating a significant age difference between the heads of families in the two groups (Table 2.7). This is not surprising given that around 40 per cent of the heads from recent migrant families were aged between 15 and 34 years, compared with less than 17 per cent for non-migrant cohorts at the time of the survey.

Table 2.7 Age Structure (Figures are Percentage of Total) and Median Age of the Heads from Migrant and Non-migrant Households at Destination

Age Group	Recent Migrant (R_1)	Long-term Migrant (L_1)	Non-migrant (N_1)	R_1-N_1	L_1-N_1
15–24	8.2	8.1	0.6	7.6	7.5
25–34	31.1	8.2	16.3	14.8	8.1
35–44	32.4	27.3	28.8	3.4	1.5
45–54	14.9	28.1	27.5	12.6	0.6
55–64	8.2	23.0	18.8	10.6	4.2
65+	5.4	12.8	8.1	2.7	4.7
Median Age	33	45	40		
I_D				51.7/2 =25.8	26.6/2 =13.3

Source: Authors' estimate from BRAC third-round urban poverty survey, 2010.

In contrast, the proportions of heads aged between 45 and 64 years doubled for non-migrants (46.3 per cent) and long-term migrants (51.1 per cent), but almost halved (23 per cent) for recent migrants. Clearly, it suggests age selective migration and predominance of youth and young adults among recent migrants, compared with non-migrants and long-term migrant cohorts.

On the other hand, the mean age at the time of migration for the respondents was 19 years, which increased to 28.9 years for recent migrants and dropped to 19.4, 18, and 14.7 years, respectively, for those whose length of stay in Dhaka ranged between 10 and 20, 20 and 30, and over 30 years. As a result, a majority of the long-term migrants (60.1 per cent) was under 20 at the time of migration, compared with 25.8 per cent for recent migrants (Table 2.8). Further, in sharp contrast to a quarter of long-term migrants, none of the recent migrants was aged below 10 years at the time of migration.

Note that in 1991, 36.6 per cent of the respondents had migrated to Dhaka within the preceding ten years. The proportion of recent migrants declined to 20 per cent and 16.8 per cent, respectively, in 1998 and 2010 indicating maturity of the migration process (Afsar 1999; 2000). Also, note that the median age for recent migrants had

Table 2.8 Respondents' Age at the Time of Migration by Age Group and Migratory Status

	Short Migrant		Long Migrant		Total	
Age at the Time of Migration	**N**	**%**	**N**	**%**	**N**	**%**
<10 years	0	0	85	23.2	85	19.3
10–19 years	19	25.7	135	36.9	154	35.0
20–29 years	27	36.5	108	29.5	135	30.7
30–39 years	16	21.6	29	7.9	45	10.2
40–59 years	9	12.2	9	2.4	18	4.1
60+ years	3	4.1	0	0	3	0.7
All	74	100.0	366	100.0	440	100.0

Source: Authors' estimate from BRAC third-round urban poverty survey, 2010.

increased by almost four years from 21 to 25 years between 1991 and 2010, reinforcing our argument regarding maturity of migrants and rising age at the time of migration. Arguably, however, the rising age of migrants and more importantly the declining proportion of recent migrants can also be interpreted as indicators of the lower incidence of out-migration from rural areas, as revealed by M. Hossain and A. Bayes (2009) based on their panel data generated from a study of 32 villages in the country.

From the age-profile, we can assume that a sizeable proportion of the long-term migrants have migrated to accompany their parents, spouse, and/or other relatives at the time of migration. Our findings show that on the one hand, the proportion of those who migrated as an accomplice of parents or their husband and/or other family members, or neighbours and friends had almost doubled for all categories of migrants in 2010 compared to 1991 (Figure 2.8). On the other hand, the incidence of accompanied migration was greater for the longest-term migrants (who migrated to Dhaka for more than 30 years) in 2010 compared to recent migrants (migrated to Dhaka less than 10 years ago)—36.1 per cent and 10.8 per cent, respectively—supporting the assumption.

In 1991, the comparative figures were 19 per cent and 3.7 per cent, respectively. It indicates that the age at migration is increasing over time, which is directly or indirectly related to the increasing trend of

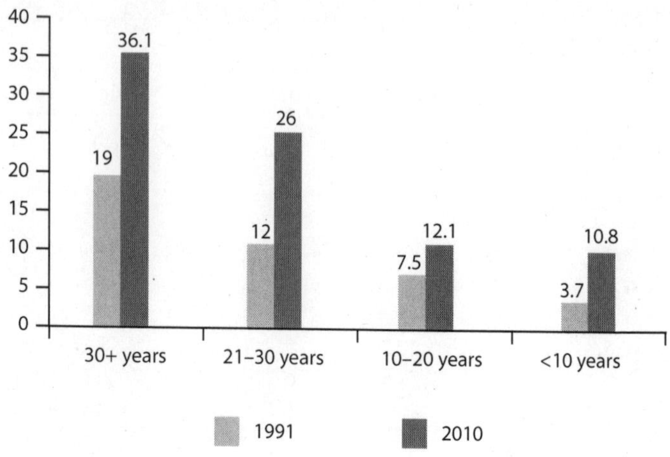

Figure 2.8 Trends in Accompanied Migration for Categories of Migrants in 1991 and 2010

Source: Authors' estimate from the repeat surveys.

independent migration among recent migrants, compared with long-term migrants. However, increased incidence of accompanied migration over time also tends to suggest that migration to Dhaka is largely adopted as a family strategy for betterment of the entire family, which is possible due to the support from the more established social networks of friends and relatives. We have discussed this in subsequent chapters. With the increasing age of migrants and the concomitant maturity of the migration process along with fertility decline, we can expect improvement in the dependency ratio and better economic condition of the migrants, which we have analysed in the next section.

SMALLER THE DEPENDENCY RATIO HIGHER THE DEMOGRAPHIC DIVIDEND FOR NON-SLUM HOUSEHOLDS

The demographic dependency ratio is estimated at 53 and 38.2 for slum and non-slum households respectively meaning that there were two dependents for every adult member (aged between 15 and 64 years)

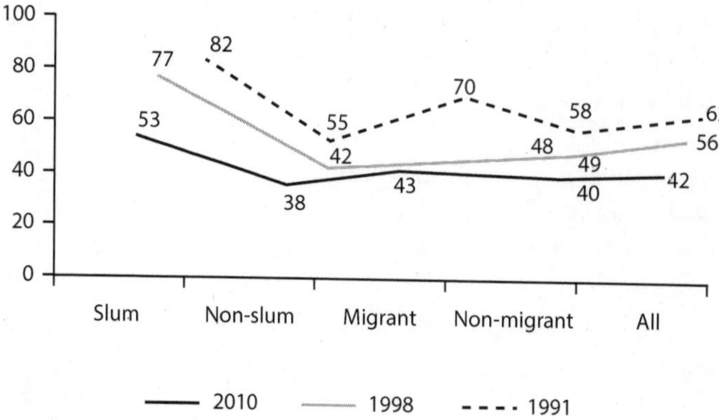

Figure 2.9 Trends in Dependency Ratio for Categories of Sample Households

Source: Authors' estimates from the repeat surveys.

from slum household, compared with two dependents for every five adult members for those in non-slum (Figure 2.9). Clearly, the dependency ratio is higher for slum households compared with that of non-slum because of the relatively larger proportion of children and smaller proportion of active age members in the slum households, compared with those in non-slum, as discussed earlier.

However, HIES estimate (BBS 2011a) shows that the dependency ratio for urban population is higher—55.1—compared particularly with the sample non-slum population. Given that proportion of older people (65 years and over) barely exceeded 1 per cent and 5 per cent for the sample households in slum and non-slum respectively this is an outcome of relatively larger representation of children in slum households (32.5 per cent) than that for non-slum households (23 per cent). Similarly, a larger proportion of children (more than 40 per cent) as reported in the HIES data for urban households compared with the sample households explains the difference between the two sets of data.

The dependency ratios are estimated at 48.3 and 42.1 for recent and long-term migrants respectively. As argued earlier, the share of children in the population generally marks the difference in the dependency ratio for migrant groups. Subsequently, it should be noted that there were 45 and 36 children for 100 adult members of working age in the case of recent and long-term migrants respectively. Compared with 1991, when the proportion of children to working age population was 60 per cent, we could observe marked improvement in the child dependency ratio over time. Also, it is not unexpected to find that the rate of decline in the dependency ratio was the highest for migrant group (38 per cent), followed by slum (35 per cent) and non-slum households (31 per cent) between 1991 and 2010, given that migrants are considered to be the change agents.

However, the rate of decline continued to be high for slum households between 1998 and 2010 (at the time of the second- and third-round survey), which is higher compared to other sample households. Decline in the proportion of children from more than 40 per cent in 1991 and 1998 to a little over 30 per cent in 2010 has contributed to the sustained rate of decline. These findings clearly reinforce the trend of fertility decline as argued at the beginning of this chapter along with the changes in the age composition of population and increasing maturity of migrants. Decline in the demographic dependency ratio corresponds to lower economic dependency or higher employment rates for adult members, especially male members, compared with 1991. In 1991, the rate of employment was 65 per cent and 15 per cent, respectively, for male and female members (Table 2.9). Apart from gender, there are

Table 2.9 Employment and Unemployment Rate for the Active Age Members (15–64 years) by Gender, Slum and Non-slum, and Migratory Status, 1991 and 2010

Active Age	**Employed in 1991**		**Employed in 2010**		**Unemployed in 1991**		**Unemployed in 2010**	
Members	**Male**	**Female**	**Male**	**Female**	**Male**	**Female**	**Male**	**Female**
Migrants	63.3	15.8	79.0	20.1	5.8	2.9	2.3	2.2
Non-migrant	71.6	14.1	76.6	14.0	7.1	4.1	6.6	3.5
Slum	81.2	25.4	91.0	26.6	10.8	4.8	3.0	2.8
Non-slum	59.4	11.8	73.8	15.5	4.3	2.5	3.8	2.4

Source: Afsar (1995) and authors' estimates from BRAC third-round urban poverty survey, 2010.

variations in the employment rate for the members of slum and non-slum, and migrant and non-migrant households.

BENEFITS OF THE DEMOGRAPHIC DIVIDEND ARE NOT GENDER NEUTRAL

Both employment and unemployment rates were highest for the male and female members of slum households but lowest for those in non-slum households compared to other categories. This gap in the employment rate can be explained by a larger proportion of students in both non-slum (35.5 per cent) and migrant households (29.6 per cent), compared with that of slum households (7.8 per cent). In 2010, we found that the rate of employment increased to 78.4 per cent and 18.5 per cent for the male and female active age members, while the proportions of unemployed and students almost halved—at 3.5 per cent and 13.7 per cent, respectively (Table 2.10). The employment gains were more pronounced for both male and female members of migrant households, followed by that of non-migrant households, particularly male members. However, changes in the employment rate since 1991 have been most comprehensive and impressive for the members of short-term migrant households, compared with other categories.

Increase in the women's employment rate as identified in our survey is modest and not fully consistent with the exiting literature that highlights an increased female labour force participation rate along with accelerated economic growth since the 1990s (Rahman and Islam 2013). However, compared to the Labour Force Survey (LFS) 2010 data (BBS 2011b) for urban areas, the male employment rate in our survey was slightly higher (76.5 per cent), but it was much lower (34.5 per cent) for female members. However, our definition of employment rate was different compared to that used in the LFS data. The LFS defined economically active population or labour force as persons aged over 15 years, who are either employed or unemployed during the reference period of the survey (preceding week of the day of enumeration). It excludes the categories of disabled and retired person in the labour force, income recipient, full-time housewife, student, beggar, and other person/s who did not work for pay or profit for at least one hour during the reference week.

Table 2.10: Distribution of Members Aged 15–64 Years from Sample Households by Employment Status

Types of Household	Employed		Housewife		Student		Not Working		Total	
	N	%	N	%	N	%	N	%	N	%
Short Migrant (up to 10 Years)										
Male	95	88.8	0	0	9	8.4	3	2.8	107	50.9
Female	31	30.1	65	63.1	6	5.8	1	1.0	103	49.1
All	126	62.7	65	31.0	15	7.1	4	1.9	210	100
Long Migrant (More Than 10 Years)										
Male	555	77.5	0	0	117	16.3	44	6.1	716	52.9
Female	118	18.5	398	62.5	98	15.4	23	3.6	637	46.7
All	673	49.7	398	28.7	215	15.9	67	4.9	1,353	100
Non-migrant										
Male	232	76.6	0	0	38	12.5	33	10.9	303	51.3
Female	40	14.0	199	69.8	28	9.8	18	6.4	285	48.7
All	272	46.2	199	33.8	66	11.2	51	8.7	588	100
Slum										
Male	274	91.0	0	0	17	5.6	10	3.3	301	51.6
Female	75	26.6	186	66.0	9	3.2	12	3.9	282	48.4
All	349	59.8	186	31.9	26	4.5	22	3.8	583	100
Non-slum										
Male	609	73.8	0	0	146	17.7	70	8.5	825	52.6
Female	115	15.5	476	64.1	121	16.3	31	4.2	743	47.4
All	724	46.2	476	30.3	267	17.0	101	6.4	1,568	100

Source: Authors' estimate from BRAC third-round urban poverty survey, 2010.

Unlike the LFS, we have included members aged 15–64 years who were either working or receiving income from investment such as rent or remittances, but like the LFS we have excluded housewives, students, unemployed, retirees, and people with disability from the employed category (Tables 2.8 and 2.9). Arguably, however, while methodological issues help us to understand the differences, they are not enough to explain such low employment rates as found in the case of female members from non-slum and non-migrant households. Rather it can be related to their income situation given that both categories fall in the highest income brackets. Accordingly, a U-shaped relationship between economic growth and women's employment, in which women's employment tends to decline in the initial stage of development but increase afterwards (Boserup 1970; Schultz 1990), can help explain the lower employment rates for these groups. The possibility that women of these families might have internalized the stereotype of gender role can also explain their lower employment rate. Whether and to what extent women have internalized the social norms will be examined in Chapter 8.

Moreover, while demand generated by the city's ever-expanding construction and transport sectors absorbs men with low skills and medium level of education (secondary or high school graduates), working women with similar level of skills or education had limited options. Like India's urban trend, we found a U-shaped or, more accurately, V-shaped relationship between women's education and employment, indicating a higher participation rate for women with very high and very low levels of education compared to secondary or high school graduates (Figure 2.10). This trend becomes clearer from Figure 2.11 that shows Z and V-type curves for working women from slum and non-slum households respectively.

Clearly, despite experiencing the rapid urban transformation, there is limited proliferation of job opportunities in Dhaka city for women with secondary/high school level education. Women with low levels of education from slum households were mainly engaged in RMG sector that grew from around 6 per cent annually between 1995 and 2000 to 11.5 per cent during 2005 and 2010, generating around 3.5 million employments of which nearly two-thirds (62 per cent) were filled in by women (Lopez-Acevado and Robertson 2012). However, research shows that DCC's share of all formal employment generated by RMG

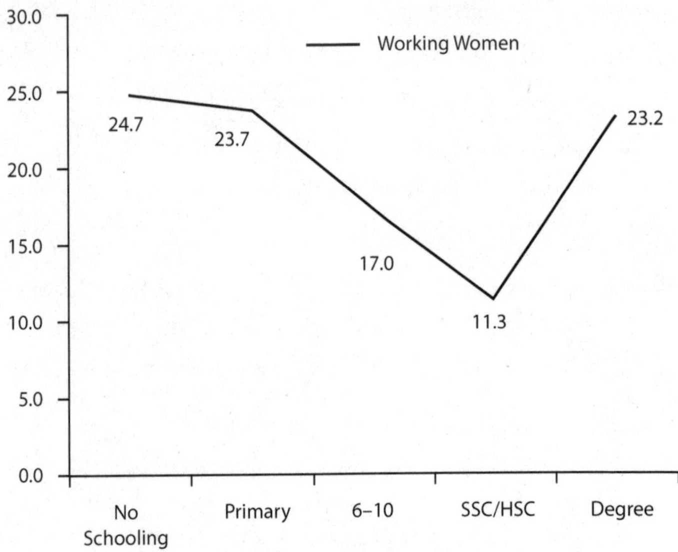

Figure 2.10 Distribution of Working Women by Level of Education

Source: Authors' estimate from BRAC third-round urban poverty survey, 2010.

industry has declined from one-half to one-third between 2001 and 2009 (Ellis and Roberts 2015). Clearly, this has implications for workers, particularly unskilled labour and more so for women, as they now require to commute peri-urban instead of central areas (Chandrashekar and Sharma 2014). Lack of a safe and efficient public transportation system is also one of the factors affecting women's declining employment trend. Except for some opportunities created by the private sector, domestic services remained the second largest employer of the poorer women. Job opportunities are also skewed for women from non-slum households as only better educated women have been pulled into better paid jobs created by the public or private services or as professionals.

Also, occupational patterns of the working women also amply demonstrate the 'missing middle' syndrome of the demand and skills shortage as a part of demand side story (Figure 2.12). However, the presence of women entrepreneurs such as tailors, owner-operators of boutique, sewing, or cottage industries presents a promising trend. It

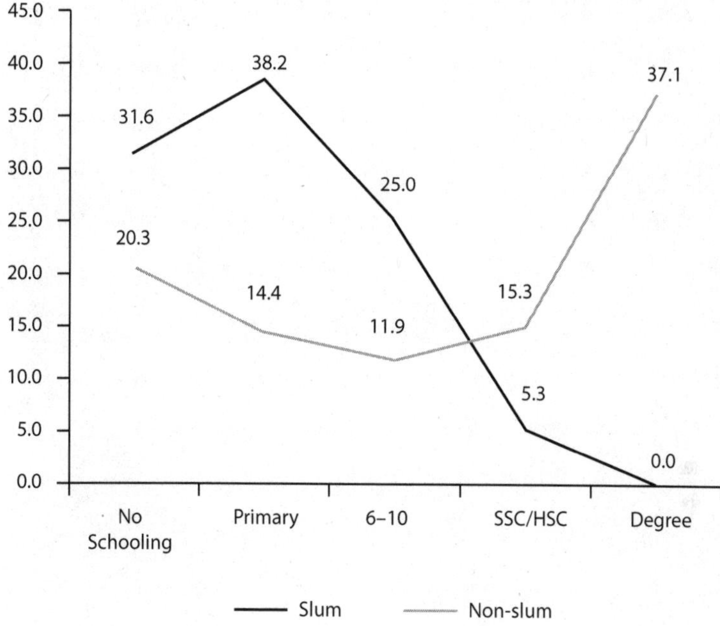

Figure 2.11 Distribution of Working Women from Slum and Non-slum by Level of Education

Source: Authors' estimate from BRAC third-round urban poverty survey, 2010.

is important to probe deeper into the occupational trends and patterns over time, particularly the scope for occupational mobility, which we do in the next chapter. Here we have focused mainly on the supply-side factors to identify barriers such as women's reproductive roles to explain their lower employment rate. This is because marital status and the number of young children had been identified as the determinants of women's labour force participation along with other factors such as land ownership, assets, education, and wage (Khandker 1988; Rahman 2006; Bridges, Lawson, and Begum 2011).

The age-specific employment rate shows that the men's employment rate was lowest for those aged 15–24 years as the bulk of them were students except for those in slum households, and generally all men aged over 35 years were employed. For women on the other hand, two distinct patterns emerge for the poor and non-poor groups. The

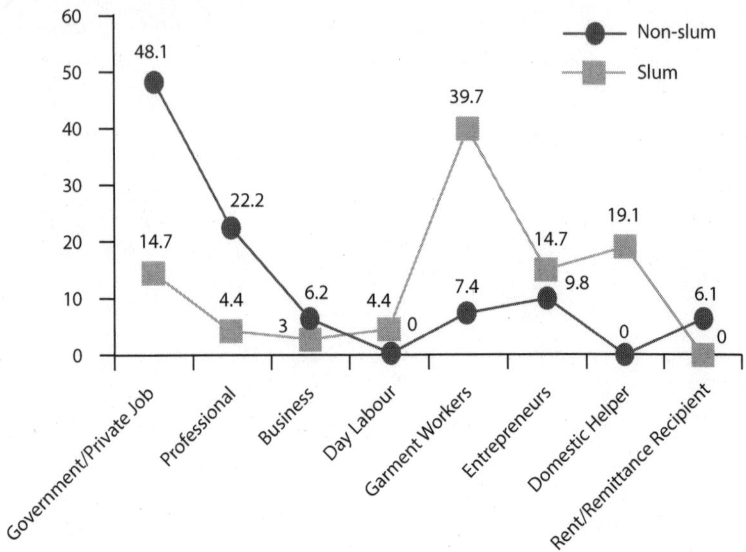

Figure 2.12 Occupational Patterns of Working Women from Slum and Non-slum

Source: Authors' estimate from BRAC third-round urban poverty survey, 2010.

rate of employment was higher for the younger and older women from slum and recent migrant households (Table 2.11). The opposite holds for the women members from non-slum, long-term, and non-migrant households. Among these groups, the rate increased for those aged between 35 and 54 years. Clearly, we need to examine how women's reproductive role is affecting their employment as well as affordability issues.

Although the majority (75.6 per cent) of the working women were married, the proportion varied for those from slum (67.2 per cent) and non-slum (82.7 per cent) households. One-fifth (20.5 per cent) and over one-tenth (11.7 per cent) of the working women were never married or divorced/widowed in slum households. As they entered the labour market early and continued till they grew old due to economic and family necessity, this trend of economic participation by both ever-married and never-married women from slum is not very difficult to comprehend. The higher participation rate in economic

Table 2.11 Age-Specific Employment Rates for Sample Men and Women Representing Different Cross Sections

Age Group	Slum	Non-slum	Recent Migrant	Long-term Migrants	Non-migrant
			Men		
15–24 years	77.8	32.3	66.7	45.9	39.7
25–34 years	92.5	84.4	97.1	85.7	84.0
35–44 years	100	95.5	96.3	97.2	96.8
45–54 years	100	96.6	100	96.9	97.4
55–64 years	95.5	87.4	100	92.9	77.1
			Women		
15–24 years	28.6	10.2	32.3	13.4	13.2
25–34 years	25.5	16.9	32.5	21.2	11.9
35–44 years	24.4	20.1	22.2	22.8	17.3
45–54 years	25.0	23.8	5.9	25.6	21.4
55–64 years	45.5	9.2	42.9	12.2	9.4

Source: Authors' estimate from BRAC third-round urban poverty survey, 2010.

activity by the currently married women from non-slum households was facilitated by domestic helpers who were hired and/or sheltered by these households. From our survey, we found 50 domestic helpers working in those households. This brings us back to the discussion of childcare and affordability issues which we have attempted to answer with the help of changes in the income situation for different cross-sections over time.[14]

On an average, the employed women had 0.1, 0.2, and 0.3 children aged 0–4 years, 5–9 years, and 10–14 years, respectively. Gradual increase in the number of children aged over five years indicates that women generally waited for their children to start primary school before taking up a job. However, there are variations, particularly for the working women from slum and recent migrant households as they have more children in the 0–4 years (0.2 and 0.3, respectively) and 5–9 years (0.4 each) age groups (Figure 2.13). As discussed earlier, both categories of women coming largely from the poorer economic backgrounds participated more out of necessity. It also highlights the need for good quality, safe, and affordable institutional childcare facilities for working women in Dhaka city, which is acutely short in supply.

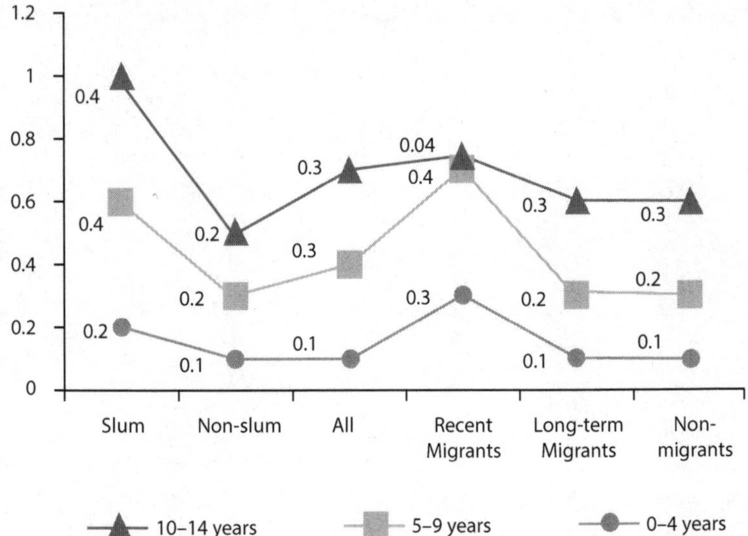

Figure 2.13 Average Number of Children by Age Group and Categories of Ever-Married Working Women

Source: Authors' estimate from BRAC third-round urban poverty survey, 2010.

INCOME GROWTH: A MATTER OF LENGTH OF STAY IN DHAKA, EDUCATION, AND OCCUPATION

Per capita income of the sample households in 2010 was estimated at Tk. 124,338 or US$ 1,772, with slum and non-slum breakdown estimated at Tk. 43,459 (US$ 619) and Tk. 157,138 (US$ 2,239), respectively. Note that per capita income for slum households was only 28 per cent of that of non-slum households. However, the gap in per capita income between slum and non-slum households has improved (from 19 per cent to 28 per cent) between 1998 and 2010.[15] Further, compared with 1998, the growth in per capita income has been impressive—62.7 per cent for all households (from US$ 1,089). In fact, the growth in income is more remarkable for slum households (96 per cent) compared with that for non-slum (58.1 per cent). Upward trend in the income data is consistent with fertility decline and the demographic changes analysed earlier.

Now the question is how and to what extent migrant households gained from the income growth over time. From the initial estimates, we find that the gains from migration is larger for those who migrated to Dhaka less than 10 years ago, compared with those whose stay in Dhaka city ranged between 10 and 20 years, 21 and 30 years, and over 30 years. Per capita income for each of these groups is estimated at US$ 1,657.2, US$ 1,242.5, US$ 1,568.5, and US$ 1,891, respectively. Arguably, a combined income of both male and female members might have contributed to higher income of the recent migrant households compared with that of the other two migrant groups.[16] On the other end of the higher-income spectrum are the migrants who have stayed for more than 30 years in Dhaka city. For these households, per capita income (US$ 1,891) is equivalent to more than 80 per cent of the income for those in non-slum.

Clearly, the study indicates that the income growth in Dhaka city has been impressive over time and it may require not less than 30 years to reap benefits from migration, which we have elaborated in the next two chapters by examining characteristics of migrants and their occupational patterns at different phases of migration—before coming to Dhaka, immediately after coming to Dhaka, and at the time of the survey. This trend is consistent with the second-round survey data (Figure 2.14).

Regarding the patterns and trends of income growth in the study wards, the findings are impressive and consistent with the demographic trends presented earlier in this section. Per capita income estimated for the study wards was US$ 1,892.2, US$ 2,151.1, US$ 1,449, and US$ 1,405 for Mirpur, Purana Paltan, Lalbagh, and Jurain, respectively, in 2010. The income growth trebled and doubled in Mirpur compared with the per capita income in 1991 and 1998, respectively, showing high growth on a sustained basis, while for Purana Paltan per capita income has been the highest since 1991. Notwithstanding the lowest per capita income, compared with that of other wards, the growth rate for Jurain has been highest as it grew at the rate of more than 7 per cent per year between 1991 and 2010 and between 1998 and 2010 (244.8 per cent). Note that the average income estimated for Purana Paltan and Mirpur were higher compared to that of all sample households (ranging between 24.7 per cent and 9.7 per cent, respectively).

We have identified the determinants of urban income and examined income distribution pattern over time in Chapter 5. However, it is

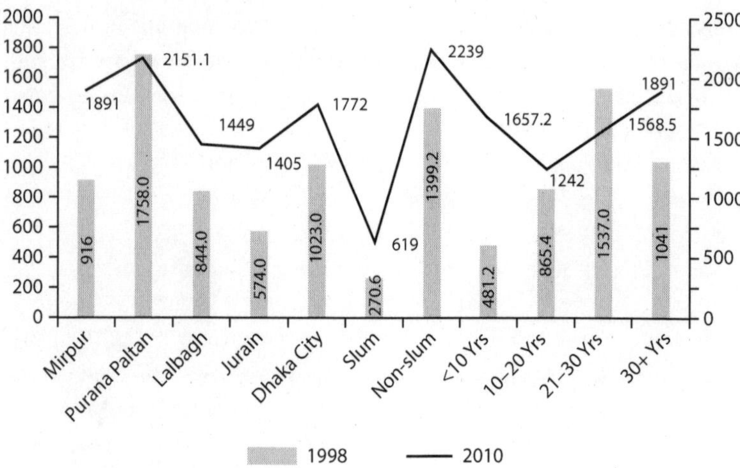

Figure 2.14 Average Per Capita Income for Sample Households by Categories (US$)

Note: The data for 1998 has been plotted along the y axis on the left side and the data for 2010 has been plotted along the y axis on the right side.
Source: Authors' estimates from the repeat surveys.

important to note that both Mirpur and Purana Paltan had the larger share of recent migrants and a lower share of non-migrants, and a greater concentration of the heads with high school– and tertiary-level education (around 60 per cent each) compared with the other two wards (43 per cent and 21 per cent, respectively, for Lalbagh and Jurain).[17] It indicates the importance of migration and education and the resilience of migrants and spread of education, which we have examined in the next chapter.

NOTES

1. In the urban administrative hierarchy, wards occupy an 'intermediate position between thana and the smallest unit mahalla' (Afsar 1995). For a more detailed account of Dhaka's evolution, see Afsar (2000), Dani (1956), and Ahmed (1986).

2. For example, a country may lack natural resources and non-land assets, but a developed human resource base can lead to prosperity. In contrast, a resource-rich country can have a high dependency ratio and challenges to meet

expenses related to consumption and for human capital development such as education and health care.

3. The first census of independent Bangladesh was conducted in 1974 due to the nine-month long liberation war with Pakistan. In the context of the genocide that killed approximately 3 million people and led to massive damage and destruction all over, it was not possible to conduct census in 1971 when it gained independence.

4. Note that here we have used UN estimates for Dhaka Metropolitan Area for the sake of consistency and comparability with other megacities across the globe. However, we have used 2011 Census data from BBS because it provides ward level statistics for analysing population changes in the next part of this section.

5. However, it should be noted that the garment factories are moving out of the city core into its peri-urban areas resulting in a declining share of all formal jobs generated by the industry for DCC (Ellis and Roberts 2015), which we discuss later in this chapter and in Chapter 9.

6. Each of these dimensions is measured with the help of a range of indicators including income, investment, employment, trade, savings, education, health, infrastructure, housing, air quality, carbon emission, the Gini index of income, consumption, access to services, and infrastructure. For details, see UN-Habitat (2013) report.

7. We have analysed the governance issues in detail in Chapter 9, while discussing policy implications emerging from the major findings presented in this book.

8. The sub-districts are—Bandar (Kadamrasul), Gazipur Sadar, Keraniganj, Narayanganj Sadar, and Savar (BBS, available at: http://www.citypopulation.de/php/bangladesh-dhaka.php [accessed on 5 February 2016]).

9. According to the 2011 Census, the population of Dhaka Statistical Metropolitan area was 14,543,124 in 2011 (BBS 2012a). However, BBS is notorious for underestimation and the 2011 census, particularly the City Corporation areas suffered from under-enumeration. Existing estimates suggest that undercount in the 2011 census ranged from 3.8 per cent in rural areas to 5.3 per cent in urban areas (Cox 2012). This makes comparison between 1991 and 2001 census data with 2011 census difficult.

10. Data for the ward level population (or total population as shown in Table 2.1) was computed from the 2011 Population and Housing Census webpage.

11. However, this is not fully reflected in the CPR. The rate of use of modern contraception was higher for both recent migrants (85.2 per cent) and non-migrants (87.5 per cent), compared with long-term migrants (around 80 per cent).

12. A nuclear family is composed of a married couple living with their dependent children. A joint family is composed of two married couples along with children and/or single adult family members ever married or unmarried. An extended family on the other hand is composed of one married couple living along with children and/or single adult family members ever married or unmarried.

13. The I_D represents the proportion of persons in a population who should be redistributed in age groups to achieve identical distribution. The value of the I_D can be between 0 and 100 per cent with high value denoting higher level of difference.

14. A detailed analysis of the changes and determinants of urban income including income distribution and poverty has been presented in Chapter 5.

15. Note that in 2010, the currency conversion rate obtained from the Bangladesh Bank showed that US$ 1 was equivalent to Tk. 70.17, compared with approximately Tk. 48 and Tk. 40, respectively, in 1998 and 1991.

16. As discussed earlier, employment rate was highest for the female members of recent migrant households compared with the other cross-sections.

17. Note that the per capita income for non-migrants is estimated at US$ 1,541.2.

3 Migration and Rural–Urban Connectivity

The Need for Reconstructing New Theoretical Approaches

Migration research in Bangladesh is largely concentrated in the push–pull and rural–urban dichotomy debate. This is despite the country's rapidly changing landscape which blurs the divide between rural and urban spaces due to increasing interactions and interdependencies in terms of capital, goods, information, knowledge, people, technological innovations, services, and more. Also, there is ample evidence that internal migration plays an important role by providing opportunities for poor households to escape poverty, and in transforming rural and urban spaces (Afsar 2000, 2005; Awumbila, Owusu, and Teye 2014; Jones, Mahbub, and Haq 2016). In the context of structural change in the country's economy in which the service sector is becoming more dominant followed by industry from a predominantly agrarian economy, the Seventh Five-Year Plan emphasizes strengthening of economic transformation. The plan also aims to reduce rural–urban divide by increasing diversification and boosting activity base of rural economy (GOB 2015c). Against the background of connectivity between spaces, structural transformation of economy, and growing integration of national and regional economy, we will focus on the rural–urban dynamics of migration in this chapter. Given that migration is a complex, multi-dimensional, and dynamic process, it is important to understand the context and causes that influence migration motivations and whether they are changing over time.

Going beyond the push–pull debate, the chapter recasts migration theories by considering migrants' intrinsic qualities—their self-confidence, hopes, aspirations, and resilience—and blending broader structural and institutional forces with migrants' agency and aspiration. It unbundles the contexts and conditions that influenced migration motivations by estimating district-level poverty and the level of physical and social infrastructure development at migrants' birthplaces to generate a better understanding of migration, space, and poverty as well as development nexus. We have also examined whether these factors are changing over time, while simultaneously identifying emerging trends and theoretical approaches to provide adequate explanation for these trends.

DETERMINANTS OF MIGRATION TO DHAKA

Persistence of Employment Pull and Better Income Opportunity

From our analysis of the reasons for migration to Dhaka city, employment-related reasons, whether it was in search of any job and/or better job, and job transfer emerged as the dominant motivating factor for all, irrespective of migration status and type of residence—slum or non-slum in 2010 (Table 3.1).

Dhaka's centrality in the country's economic growth and development and greater job opportunities remained the major source of attraction for migrants, compared with other cities or towns. Accordingly, there is a secular increase in Dhaka's share of urban population from one-fifth in 1960 to one-quarter (26.7 per cent) in 1980 and almost one-third since 2000.[1] In contrast, the corresponding share of Chittagong, the second largest city, has been 14.4 per cent, declined to 11 per cent during 1980–2000 and further to 7 per cent since 2010 (UN 2018).[2] Most of the head offices of corporate sector, government departments, business houses, NGOs, major consulting firms, educational institutions, and hospitals are located in the capital. It also houses all major manufacturing industries including garment, textile, printing and dyeing,

Table 3.1 Distribution of Respondents by Categories and Reasons for Migration, 1991–2010

Respondents	Job-Related	Education-Related	Family-Related	Disaster/Crisis	Altruism/Self-respect	Others	Total (No.)
			2010*				
Slum	65.6	0.6	20.2	4.9	8.6	0	163
Non-slum	52.0	12.6	25.6	2.2	6.6	0	277
Recent Migrant	68.9	2.7	10.8	5.5	16.2	0	74
Long-term Migrants	54.6	9.3	26.2	2.7	7.1	0	366
All Migrants	57.0	8.2	23.6	3.2	7.9	0	440
No Education	58.4	0	20.8	10.4	10.4	0	77
Primary	53.8	0	24.4	6.4	15.4	0	78
Secondary	63.4	0	30.5	1.2	4.8	0	82
SSC/HSC	56.8	10.5	27.2	0	5.3	0	95
Degree	53.7	24.1	16.7	0	5.6	0	108
			1998				
Slum	65.3	0	16.7	11.7	NA	7.4	162
Non-slum	57.3	18.7	18.7	0.7	NA	6.7	150
Permanent Migrant	60.8	8.9	8.9	6.4	NA	6.1	312
Temporary Migrant	41.2	5.9	5.9	47.1	NA	0	17
All Migrants	59.8	8.8	8.8	8.5	NA	5.8	329

(Cont'd)

Table 3.1 *(Cont'd)*

Respondents	Job related	Education Related	Family Related	Disaster/ Crisis	Altruism/ Self-respect	Others	Total (No.)
			1991				
Slum	70.4	3.5	15.4	3.5	NA	7.1	169
Non-slum	57.1	32	7.9	0.7	NA	2.3	303
Permanent Migrant	62.6	22.5	10.5	1.7	NA	2.7	484
Temporary Migrant	90	8	1	0	NA	1	110
No Education	70	4.7	18.8	4.7	NA	1.9	106
Primary	62.1	14.9	16.7	1.3	NA	5.4	74
Secondary	75	17.3	1.9	3.8	NA	1.9	52
SSC/HSC	64.9	19.3	11.4	0	NA	4.4	114
Degree	49.3	45.7	4.3	0	NA	0.7	138
All Migrants	67.7	19.8	8.7	1.3	NA	2.4	594

Source: Authors' estimate from BRAC third-round urban poverty survey, 2010; Afsar 2000 and Afsar 1999.

ceramic, press and publication, leather and footwear, pharmaceutical, food processing and beverage, cosmetic, and automobile industry.[3] Side by side, there is rapidly expanding real estate, transport and construction sectors, informal services together with formal services such as financial, accounting, information technology, education, health and community development, as well as peddlers, hawkers, and small businesses.

A large body of literature based on urbanization and growth of Dhaka city has already identified employment-related reasons as the major motivating factor in the process of rural–urban migration (Afsar 1999; 2000; Chaudhury 1980; Hugo 1991; Ishtiaque and Ullah 2013; Islam 2005; World Bank 2015). It is argued that pull of greater income and better employment in urban areas compared to rural areas attract poor people to migrate to cities (Afsar 2000; Hossain 2001; Hossain, Afsar, and Bose 1999; Islam 2006; Nabi 1992; Ullah 2004). On the other hand, recurrence of natural disasters, which cause food crisis and scarcity of work in rural areas (Herrmann and Svarin 2009) push people to migrate. Generally, however, there is a consensus that the economic factors—high employment and income-earning opportunity—in the urban centres are the major driving forces for rural–urban migration in Bangladesh (Afsar 2000; Bhuyan, Khan, and Ahmed 2001; Chaudhury 1980; Hossain 2001; Huq-Hossain 1996; Ishtiaque and Mahmud 2011; Islam 2006; Stoeckel, Chowdhury, and Aziz 1972). This view is also reinforced from the third-round survey data which clearly demonstrates that migration to Dhaka city is mainly directed to earn more income and/or in search of and/or to improve livelihood options and opportunities. Also, it reaffirms that the major reasons for migration to Dhaka city have remained consistent since 1991. However, there are some variations, reordering, and (re)emergence of issues as analysed later. The other important motivations for migration that emerged from the survey (given in Table 3.1) have been discussed in subsequent paragraphs.

Education-Led Motivation for Migration Remained Class Driven

Table 3.1 shows that education-related motivation for migration is higher among the better-off and more educated migrants, compared with the poorer and less educated respondents. This class differentiation in the response pattern has also been observed in 1998 and more so in

1991. However, the skewed response pattern which was attributed to the higher level of illiteracy among the younger migrant respondents, in contrast to the highly educated older migrants in 1991, could no longer be supported by the third-round survey data. This is because in 2010, among those who migrated for higher studies, more than one-quarter and two-thirds had higher secondary- and degree-level education, except for a solitary respondent who had no formal education.[4]

However, education-related migration has declined over time which can be attributed to the spread of education including educational facilities in rural areas, which is one of the contributing factors to the country's notable progress in enrolment rates over time. As discussed later in this chapter (Table 3.5), an overwhelming majority of the respondents reported to have both primary and secondary schools within a radius of less than 1 km of their birthplaces and colleges within less than 5 km. Accordingly, the country has made remarkable achievements in education. Between 1990 and 2012, enrolment rates at the primary level increased by 40.6 per cent (from 65 per cent to 95 per cent), doubled at secondary level (from 22 per cent to 44.7 per cent), and adult literacy rate increased by 57.1 per cent (from 35 per cent to 55 per cent) (World Bank 2014).

Similarly, there is remarkable improvement in the level of education of the respondents over time. In 1991 and 1998, nearly one-quarter of the respondents (22 per cent and 27 per cent, respectively) had no formal education, compared with less than one-fifth (17.5 per cent) in 2010. In contrast, respondents with tertiary qualification almost trebled to nearly 25 per cent in both 2010 and 1998, from 7.8 per cent in 1991. Further, the proportion of respondents having secondary and high school-level education increased by 15 per cent and 7 per cent, respectively (28.2 per cent and 24.8 per cent in 2010, compared to 1998).

Therefore, both proliferation of schools and colleges in rural areas and improved level of education of the respondents support our arguments regarding the declining trend in education-related migration over time. In contrast, disaster-related motivation for migration together with the aspiration and confidence to re-establish and recover from losses, family-oriented migration and altruism, as well as freedom and desire to live with respect and dignity have, over time, assumed greater importance as motivating factors for the poorer migrants and those with no or low education, compared to other groups.

Weakening of Push and/or Distressed Migration

Table 3.1 also highlights disaster-led migration in the response pattern since 1991 although in varying proportion. Bangladesh is vulnerable to recurrent natural disasters due to its geographic location and climatic risks.[5] Since independence, it has faced at least one major natural disaster such as severe flooding, cyclones, storms, and tornadoes each year and is at the top of the global climate risk index.[6] Migration due to environmental hazards is not new. However, with increasing research on climate change, the concept of environmental refugee came in vogue, and there is greater acknowledgement of disaster-led migration. For example, R. Reuveny (2007) found that 20–30 million people from Gansu and Ningxia provinces migrated to urban centres in China during the 1980s and 1990s due to floods, land degradation, desertification, and water scarcity from his analysis of cross-country climate change-induced migration. G. Bryan, S. Chowdhury, and A. Mobarak (2013) on the other hand found 'puzzling low migration' from Rangpur, a famine-prone north-western region of Bangladesh. The difficulty to isolate disaster-led migration from the employment-related response has also been argued in a few studies (Afsar 2000).

Our survey, however, has generated some insights into the context and condition in which disaster-led migration becomes more distinct in the response related to migration motivation. For example, in 1998 nearly half of the temporary migrants and little over one-tenth of the respondents from slum households migrated due to floods or riverbank erosion that had swept the country, which was much higher compared with either 1991 or 2010.[7] From a year-by-year analysis of reasons for migration, we found that disaster-led migration becomes more distinct in the response pattern when the survey is conducted immediately in the aftermath and/or during the time of the crisis. Moreover, this narrative came mainly from temporary migrants who migrated from Jamalpur to Jurain in 1998 (Afsar 1999).

It can also be argued that the likelihood for temporary and/or seasonal migration increases during disaster and lean season. For example, from their survey of 1,600 households in Northwest Bangladesh, I.M. Hossain, I.A. Khan, and J. Seeley (2003) found that one-fifth (19 per cent) of households, across all wealth groups, migrated in the lean agricultural season. Similarly, R. Kuhn (2000) had argued that loss of homestead land due to flood did not necessarily lead to migration in Matlab thana, from where people take up permanent migration only when their social ties are weak and the family has no labour to participate in seasonal migration.

NEED FOR CONSIDERING MIGRANTS' INTRINSIC QUALITIES IN EXPLAINING MIGRATION MOTIVATION

Among the other push factors, economic hardship, lack of work opportunity, lack of capital and/or assets, and credit facility in the areas of origin featured prominently as motivations for migration. However, it should be noted that in their push migration narratives, respondents expressed their hopes and aspirations to recover from the losses and start a new life rather than despair and helplessness. Following Arjun Appadurai, it can be argued that 'the poor, no less than any other groups in society, do express horizon in choices made and choices voiced' (2004: 68).

In other words, it is important to recognize that rural poor also have dreams, aspirations, and self-confidence and they often do not consider migration as a strategy for survival only. It is important to emphasize on these aspirational drivers such as to re-establish and/or to recover the losses over and above the *push* side of the narratives that would have concentrated only on the *losses* incurred due to flood, riverbank erosion, and other natural calamities and/or loss in business, loss of land or income, and/or death of the main bread earner (see, for example, Hassan Mia's case as illustrated in Box 3.1).

Similarly, Madan did not lose his spirit despite having a heavy debt burden on his shoulder and facing several challenges due to natural disaster and market competition between handicrafts and mass-produced plastic goods. It was also driven by pull factors such as to earn more income, getting business opportunity, and free housing. Therefore, based on our findings, we underscore the need to uplift push-related migration from a vulnerability framework to a hope, aspiration, and resilience domain while acknowledging the co-existence of negative externalities of environmental vagaries and other health- and wealth-related losses.

Box 3.1 Migrants' Resilience and Self-confidence Can Be Overlooked in 'Their Narratives' about Recovering from Losses by Earning More Income

Hassan Mia (37 years of age) narrated his story of circular migration in which he migrated to and from Dhaka with the aspiration to recover losses in his business and re-establish his career. When he first migrated to Dhaka, he worked in a grocery store with the help of his maternal uncle. After working there for ten years, he saved Tk. 50,000 and left for his village as he had little chance of owning a grocery store in that amount of money. Upon returning, he used his savings to expand the small piece of cultivable land that his family possessed and worked with his father to increase their farm production. He was doing well but soon lost his interest as a part of their land was inundated by flood water in 2004.

Once again, he migrated to Dhaka not only to recover from the loss, but also with the hope of owning a grocery store. He brought with him Tk. 150,000, which his father gave him by leasing out their cultivable land. He was also successful in buying his own store with the help of a few suppliers with whom he established good connections during his last visit to Dhaka. However, owning a store did not turn out to be as profitable as he expected. Rather, he incurred losses because he could not stop people from buying goods on credit. He eventually sold his shop in Dhaka and returned to the village, borrowed money from a usurer, and set up a grocery store there. However, there too he could not make enough money as the level of transaction in the village was low. Therefore, once again he decided to migrate to Dhaka and this time without any capital but hoping to recover from losses and re-establish his career. With the help of his friend Munna, he secured a job in the construction sector.

Madan Kumar (aged 32 years) was a labourer in a *chingri gher* (prawn farm) in a village in Satkhira district. Every year during the rainy season, the farm was inundated by rain water and hence, there was no work. In this lean period, he used to make bamboo baskets, a skill he acquired as a part of his family tradition. He borrowed Tk. 5,000 in 2005, to invest in this business from a local money lender with a high interest rate of Tk. 750 per month. However, there is not much demand for bamboo baskets these days as people use plastic boxes in place of traditional bamboo products. Clearly handicraft products such as bamboo furniture and baskets face tough competition from the cheaper goods produced en masse by machines such as plastic boxes. As he did not make enough money from his business to pay off the interest, he wanted to leave the village for Dhaka to earn more income.

GENDERED DIMENSION OF MIGRATION MOTIVATION: INDEPENDENCE AND TO LIVE WITH DIGNITY

From our FGDs with women garment factory workers, the need to 'live with dignity and self-respect' has emerged as a new gendered dimension in the hope, aspiration, and resilience framework of migration, particularly in context of marital breakdown and dowry-related push. Case studies of Shukhi and Jhuma, working in the RMG sector at the time of the FGD, demonstrates why it is also important not to lose sight of women's resilience and agency aspects even though poverty or dowry-related push may appear to be dominant triggers (Box 3.2).[8] Shukhi was bold enough to take the decision to migrate and work in a garment factory in Dhaka in search of dignity and respect amidst all the humiliation that she experienced in relation to the high demand for dowry placed by the prospective groom's family for her marriage.

Shukhi and Jhuma's story unfolds that the grip of social evil such as dowry has become strong, penetrating deep in the society, particularly among the lower echelons of society causing havoc in the lives of girls and their families. However, Jhuma's story also highlights that the line between the push from dowry and pull of altruism is very thin, and in real-life situation, push and pull factors do not necessarily operate in isolation but often work together as the motivating factors for migration. Thus, we have observed that Jhuma, who developed a complex due to her dark complexion, which she considered a major barrier in the way of her own and her younger sisters' marriages, migrated to Dhaka to enhance the prospects for her sisters' marriage. Her job in the garment factory elevated her status to an earning member in the family, which in her opinion had relieved her father from the worry of arranging her marriage.

It should be noted that the 'male household heads often considered women's income from RMG factory as supplementary to family's income and to enhance the prospect of marriage for unmarried women' (Afsar 2011: 396). However, from the accounts of women RGM factory workers of Dhaka city, N. Kibria (2001) has identified the themes of altruism and sacrifice for the family's betterment, while N. Kabeer

Box 3.2 Migration Motivation: Gendered Dimensions

> Bhai, pet er daye Dhakai ashchhi, izzat niye banchtey chai, shokh kore Dhakai ashinai. [Migrated to Dhaka not for 'bright light' but to make a living with self-respect and dignity.]
>
> —Shukhi

Shukhi (aged 23 years) was born in a joint family, which consisted of a married brother, sister-in-law, parents, and two young sisters in Narail, a district in south-western Khulna Division. She was about to get married. Unfortunately, the prospective groom's family asked for a cash payment of Tk. 50,000 as dowry. Paying such a huge amount of money was a big challenge for her family as they did not have enough resources on which to rely. They had only two options—either to sell their only piece of cultivable land to arrange for dowry and starve or say 'no' to the marriage. Her brother was reluctant to sell the land, while Shukhi was often cursed and mistreated by her sister-in-law, who considered her a burden to the family. To get rid of this mental torture, Shukhi migrated to Dhaka along with other friends and through migration she achieved liberty and peace of mind ('ami swadhinata ar manosik shanti phirey payechi').

Similarly, Jhuma (aged 22 years) who was the eldest daughter in a family of five members with two younger sisters, suffered from an inferiority complex arising from her dark complexion. She considered herself a burden on her family, particularly on her father whose income was too little to pay for her dowry, and for whom it was a moral obligation to marry her off first before arranging marriages for her fair-complexioned younger sisters. However, given the high demand in the marriage market for brides with fair complexion and ability to pay dowry, prospects for Jhuma's marriage were slim. Therefore, she decided to migrate to earn a living by working in a garment factory in Dhaka, thus relieving her father of the constant worries of arranging her marriage—another dimension of altruism.

(2001) has established women's agency at the centre to explain women's experiences in the process of joining factory work.

It can be argued that motivation to live with dignity and self-respect, which emerged from our third-round survey, can help expand the feminist framework of 'autonomy of migration' (Mezzadra 2004) and/or women's agency (Kabeer 2001). It demonstrates that 'migration decision-making is far too complex to be narrowed down by the simple calculation of wage differentials or economic determinism' (Afsar 2011: 395). Also, in stark contrast to the structural determinism of push factors and vulnerability framework that depicts hopelessness and despair only, it brings migrants' resilience, hopes, and aspirations at the forefront. Therefore, elsewhere Afsar (2016a: 5–6) argued that whether push or pull,

> the decision to migrate is largely influenced by the psychological traits of migrants that are often overlooked in the existing literature. Ambition and self-confidence need to be considered important traits of migrants in general, and particularly, poorer migrants that encourage them to take the risk.
>
> What is more important to note is their confidence in their own ability to earn higher incomes through migration which they believed to have transformative potential necessary to change one's situation. This conviction helped them to be resilient and ambitious, irrespective of their age, gender, education, skills and the most severe economic circumstances with no resources to bank on.

The declining trend in push migration can also be supported from the empirical evidence generated by the village-level studies.[9] Based on a longitudinal study of 62 villages, M. Hossain and A. Bayes (2009) found that there was a significant decline in the incidence of inter-district migration (from 72 per cent to 52 per cent) between 1998 and 2008, and the incidence of wage labour dropped from 35 per cent to 11 per cent during the same period. Arguably, these trends suggest weakening of the push and/or distressed migration, which they considered as an outcome of technological progress in rural areas that helped boost productivity and income prospect for the rural poor. More than that, this is an outcome of structural change in economy enhanced largely by remittances of migrant workers due to which more non-farm employment is available in rural areas in housing, construction, and trading sectors. Occupational patterns of migrants prior to migration, which we have analysed in the next chapter, showed waning of agricultural workers, while those employed in the services, construction, and transport sectors, and those who were students increased over time. This is also related to the declining rate of poverty at migrants' birthplaces, which we have discussed later in this chapter.

ALTRUISM AND FAMILY MATTERS GAINING PROMINENCE

As a corollary to the weakening trend in push migration, we found that family-oriented migration, altruism, and pull-dominated migration have emerged as distinct response patterns of migrants over time. In 2010, nearly one-quarter of the respondents migrated in the process of family-led migration as accomplices of parents, siblings, and spouse, compared with less than one-tenth of the respondents either in 1998 or in 1991. Further examination of the survey data (2010) unfolds that nearly half of these respondents were children (below 10 years) at the time of migration and an almost similar proportion were youth (aged between 15 and 24 years). Subsequently, nearly three-quarters of them were accompanied by their parents and siblings, and the remaining one-quarter migrated along with other family members, friends, and relatives. This pattern is symptomatic of out-migration by the second generation, which can be supported by the village-level panel data. Hossain and Bayes (2009) found that sons and daughters comprised nearly three-quarters of the out-migrant members, compared with around three-fifths in 1998. During the same period, the incidence of migration by the household heads reduced significantly from one-quarter to 2 per cent.

Between one-tenth and less than one-fifth of the respondents, particularly those with no and/or low level of education (between 10 per cent and 15 per cent) and recent migrants (16 per cent), came to Dhaka to provide financial assistance to their family, enhance their family income, earn better income, and contribute to their family's betterment along with the aspiration to 're-establish' their livelihoods. Altruism as a reason for female garment factory workers' migration to Dhaka city has been critically discussed by Kibria (2001). Altruism per se has not been focused on much in the literature on urbanization partly because the issue is often subsumed under the typical migration debate of rural–urban wage differential and/or accorded lesser priority by feminist scholars who dealt more elaborately with gender differentials to explain how reasons for women's migration has been treated differentially by male and female respondents.

Undoubtedly, rural–urban or home and host country wage differential has always provided impetus to both internal and international migration. The gap between rural–urban wages that prompted Sarwar

Box 3.3 Typical Pull Factors in Migration Motivation

> Dhaka'ay amagor kajer sujog beshi ar mojuri o dwigun. [Dhaka provides ample work opportunity and, as wage, what we receive is double of what we earned in our villages.]
>
> —Sarwar

Sarwar (aged 30 years) made this comment at the discussion session with the construction sector workers. Large wage gap between Dhaka and his natal village encouraged him like most other participants of the discussion to migrate to Dhaka. As a construction sector worker from Satkhira, a district under Khulna Division in the south-west part of Bangladesh, his wage was Tk. 170 per day, and was even lower (Tk. 130) for his friend who worked as a *jogal/jogan* or helper. He also found it hard to find employment all-round the year as people neither find it profitable nor have enough money to make large-scale investment in rural areas, be it for the real estate business or manufacturing. He migrated to Dhaka with the help of Tajul, a family friend and started working for Tk. 300 per day as a labourer in the booming construction sector.

Similarly, Abdul Razzak (aged 39 years) was inspired to migrate to Dhaka from Munga village in Rangpur district in the northern part of the country after he discovered that his neighbours who worked as rickshaw pullers in Dhaka city used to return home with Tk. 5,000–6,000 as cash in hand. Obviously, it was a lot of money as he could hardly manage to earn Tk. 3,000 after working hard as a farm labourer for the whole month. The possibility of earning and making more money in Dhaka city attracted him towards the capital.

and Abdul Razzaque, construction and transport sector workers, respectively, to migrate to Dhaka bears a testimony to its importance (Box 3.3). However, the recent trends in wages show that for construction workers—both helpers and carpenters—wages were higher in Narayanganj town (Tk. 243 and Tk. 375) and Chittagong city (Tk. 226 and Tk. 312) in 2010–11, compared to Dhaka (Tk. 207 and Tk. 300, respectively) (BBS 2012b). It is important to examine whether internal migration has increased in these cities/towns, which suggests an important area for future research.

Our study has also added a new dimension to the spatial wage differential debate. In Chapter 5, we found significant increase in wages for several occupation groups in Dhaka city between 1998 and 2010 of which most notable was that of the domestic workers. This can be related to the increase in the real wages in agricultural sector, generating greater opportunities for employment in the low paid industrial jobs. Accordingly, the market for domestic services and other low-skilled jobs has become stretched creating greater demand for these services compared with the 1990s.

FAMILY AND SOCIAL NETWORKS: ENABLERS AND PROVIDERS IN THE MIGRATION AND SETTLEMENT PROCESS

However, what is more important to note is that without the established networks of friends and family members at the place of destination that mediate the process of migration and settlement by providing necessary information, help, and support, whatever be the migration motivation, it would have never been realized. The role of social networks has been amply demonstrated in the migration literature (Afsar 1999; 2000; Hugo 1992, 1994; Majumder, Mahmud, and Afsar 1996; Putnam 2000). Increasingly, migration decision-making has been acknowledged as a complex process, multi-layered and multi-dimensional, encompassing not purely economic consideration, but also a livelihood strategy in which the role of family members, and friends and neighbours becomes critical. More than 40 per cent of the respondents highlighted the important role played by their family members in the migration decision-making process (Table 3.2).

Table 3.2 shows that accompanied migration is predominantly a matter of decision by the whole family. Family's role in the decision-making process becomes critical when migration is geared towards higher studies and driven by aspiration to 're-establish' themselves. This is because migrants require resources, support, and commitment from their families to set priority and strategy and the necessary backup services prior to, during, and after migration. For example, Hasan Mia's case study shows that his aspiration to own a grocery store in Dhaka was enlivened by his father's decision to lease out their cultivable land and invest the money to help facilitate Hasan's decision to migrate (Box 3.1).

Table 3.2 Distribution of Respondents by Reasons for Migration and Sources That Contributed to the Decision-Making Process

Reasons for Migration	Self		Family	
	No.	%	No.	%
Job-Related	205	74.8	102	37.2
Push Factor	18	62.1	14	48.3
As Accomplice to Family	6	5.8	103	99.0
Financial Assistance to Family	66	79.5	34	41.0
Get Rid of Family Feud	7	63.6	4	36.4
Higher Study	34	54.0	42	66.7
Pull Factor	15	68.2	11	50.0
All	254	57.7	186	42.3

Note: Total does not tally to 100 per cent as we have considered multiple responses.
Source: Authors' estimate from BRAC third-round urban poverty survey, 2010.

However, family's role may vary in different types of push migration as illustrated from Rahim Mondal and Alim Miah's experiences (Box 3.4). In the context of disaster-led push that shook Rahim Mondal's economic base and made him more self-conscious, his family

Box 3.4 Stigma, Shame, and Lack of Respect for Work in Rural Areas as Motivation for Migration

Rahim Mondal (aged 30 years) belonged to a well-off family in Kishoreganj district under Dhaka Division in central Bangladesh. His father owned two hectares of land approximately and they hired workers to work in their farm. Due to the massive floods in 1998 and 2004, they lost their land and Rahim who discontinued his studies found it humiliating to look for a job in the village. Whenever he talked to people about a job, they asked him why a boy from a landed family was looking for a job and he felt humiliated telling the same old story of his family's misfortune to everyone. Therefore, together with his family, he took the decision to migrate alone to Dhaka to escape humiliation and earn money to help his family recover from the shock of the natural disasters. After coming to Dhaka, he started working in a construction site with the help of his close friend from the same village. However, he did not tell his family that he works as a construction worker as he thinks it will bring shame to the family.

Hasina Begum (aged 45 years) migrated from Rampasha village in Faridpur district to Dhaka to work with respect and dignity. She lived happily with two children and her husband, who was a peasant owning a small piece of cultivable land. Her husband died in 2002 and her son took over the land, which he cultivated himself for a while. Soon after he got married and along with his wife he moved to live with his in-laws in a neighbouring village in 2004. Although he leased out their cultivable land, it did not provide any maintenance cost to Hasina Begum. In order to survive with her young daughter Rumana (14), Hasina Begum had little option but to work as a domestic help for a local well-to-do family. However, her income was hardly enough for herself and her daughter. Moreover, she also felt shy to work as a domestic help in the same village where everyone knew her and often sympathized with her ill-fate, which had servitude in store for her despite her having a *jowan pola* (a young and strong son) and a piece of cultivable land.

In order to escape such a humiliating situation and work in an environment of anonymity and self-respect, she finally migrated to Dhaka with her cousin Leila who used to work in a garment factory and had come to the village on leave. Both Hasina and Rumana were working, respectively, as a hawker and an operator in a garment factory at the time of the interview. They earned on average Tk. 5,000 per month which according to Hasina was enough to make her happy.

Alim Miah (aged 27 years) was the eldest son in his family and his father was a farmer having over one hectare of land in Haripur village, Mymensingh district, located in the northern part of Bangladesh. His father wanted him to study and pursue a professional career. However, after completing high school (HSC), Alim Miah was in a dilemma regarding his career. On one hand, he realized that he earned more respect from the local people due to his educational attainment, compared to how he was perceived when he was simply a *chashar chele* (son of a peasant). On the other hand, he did not want to continue studies because his results were not promising. He neither had a sense of belongingness to his farming family nor could he comfort himself with a professional career because he did not want to study further. Amidst this confusion he started taking drugs and alcohol under the influence of his peer groups. Some family friends cautioned his parents about his newly picked up habits. His father was worried and soon contacted his cousin in Dhaka. He made necessary arrangements for Alim's migration with the help of the cousin, as a strategy to productively engage and rehabilitate him. At the time of the interview, Alim Miah was working as a hawker in Baitul Mukarram shopping area.

lent support to his decision to migrate as a strategy compatible with his self-respect. On the other hand, Alim Miah's story unfolds gradual intrusion of drugs in rural areas, and the migration decision was adopted both as a face-saving protective measure not only to regain family reputation but also to rehabilitate and protect younger generations from the ill effects of drug use.

Nuances and the multiple dimensions of migration, we found, corroborate the sociological and anthropological studies in India (such as Gardner and Osella 2003; de Haan and Rogaly 2002; Shah 2006) that move beyond 'push and pull' analyses and tend to view migration as a complex process combining structure and agency. Further, illustrations from the in-depth interviews that we conducted with male and female RMG and construction sector workers and hawkers as well as male transport-operators can help to elaborate this point.

MIGRATION IN SEARCH OF ANONYMITY AND PRODUCTIVE ENGAGEMENT

From in-depth interviews, we learned that often migration occurs in search of self-respect, anonymity, and respect for work, and to rehabilitate and refrain young family members from drug use, which may not necessarily be identified with either push or pull motivation but may operate under both and/or beyond by transcending the boundaries. Pushed by dire necessity, Hasina Begum, for example, took up the work of a domestic help (Box 3.4). While the income was low in her village, this was not the sole consideration behind her migration to Dhaka city. She was looking for dignity and anonymity, none of which was possible to get in a rural setting where everybody knew her and her past and sympathized with her for her ill fate despite her having a jowan pola (a young and strong son) and a piece of cultivable land. Hence, she decided to migrate to Dhaka.

While escaping social constraints at home was also observed notably in case of women in India (Gardner and Osella 2003), we found that men too (say, for example, Rahim Mondal) can find it humiliating to look for work in their own village. For both men and women, if they happen to descend into poverty from belonging to well-to-do family due to sudden shock, it is difficult to seek work in their natal villages.

However, marriage and dowry are the other factors for women that contribute to social constraints at home, which they want to escape and challenge by adopting migration as a means to re-establish them with dignity as illustrated from Shukhi and Jhuma's case. Rahim Mondal's story illustrates a situation in which self-respect pervades by transcending the disaster-led push boundary and altruism-driven pull. Other pull factors such as everlasting aspiration for recovery from loss and better livelihoods together with migrants' resilience and self-confidence are illustrated from Hasan Mia's case.

DEMONSTRATION EFFECTS MOTIVATE MIGRANTS, WHETHER INTERNAL OR INTERNATIONAL

Abdul Razzak's experience on the other hand highlights the importance of demonstration effect (ability to generate savings in this case by low-paid workers such as rickshaw pullers) in exacerbating migration to Dhaka city (Box 3.3). His migration to Dhaka city questions G. Bryan, S. Chowdhury, and A. Mobarak's (2013) hypothesis that a migrant does not know in advance his suitability for employment such as whether he would be trusted by a rickshaw owner to operate as a driver, which makes incurring the cost of migration risky. His hypothesis can also be contested on the ground of social networks that help migrants with information and other support related to employment and settlements both before and after migration, which is amply demonstrated in this study and in our earlier studies (Afsar 1999; 2000; 2003).

In Bangladesh, discourses regarding the ways to improve livelihoods of rural poor often fail to fully contextualize rural–urban links in broader framework being largely embedded in an 'isolated sectoral perspective' of rural and urban (Afsar 2005: 4). Instead, Bangladesh can take advantage of the synergies to reduce both urban and rural poverty (Garrett and Chowdhury 2004). It is argued that rural–urban linkages are important for poverty alleviation and sustainable rural development and urbanization. M. Cali and C. Menon (2013) demonstrated that the poverty-reducing impacts of rural–urban linkage occur through consumer connections, remittances, changing rural land-to-labour ratio, and non-farm employment. Domestic trade, adequate and efficient infrastructure, and agricultural growth are the backbone of mutually beneficial rural–urban relationships (Fan, Chang-Kan, and Mukherjee 2005; Rosenthal 2000; Tacoli 1998; 2003). Increasingly, however, the importance of rural–urban links is recognized in the national and international policy forums for several purposes. For example, the Agricultural and Rural Convention 2020 highlights it for sustainable and inclusive growth and development (Dower 2013), while Global Monitoring Report (2013) reinforced the importance of the rural–urban linkages for poverty reduction. Accordingly, the Government of the People's Republic of Bangladesh accorded priority to the Agricultural and Rural Convention 2020 for paying special attention to the rural–urban linkages for inclusive and sustainable growth and development (Dower 2013).

To explore the rural–urban linkages and assess how migration motivation is influenced by the local setting of the community in which migrants are located (Findley 1987: 89), we have examined the level of infrastructure development and poverty in the migrants' areas of origin. Research shows that extent of accessibility to infrastructure such as paved road, electricity coverage, and mechanized transport has significant inverse association with poverty (World Bank 2005). Generally, development of infrastructure has indirect and/or multiplier effects on poverty reduction. For example, to attain economic growth through enhancing agriculture and manufacturing sectors, it is important to ensure an efficient transport and communication system for the mobility of labour, capital and raw material, and for production, distribution, marketing, export, import, and tourism. The country's Seventh Five-Year Plan aims to reduce rural–urban divide by increasing diversification and strengthening activity base of rural economy for increasing productivity and structural transformation (GOB 2015c).[10] The plan endorses the importance of transport and communication through infrastructure development and multi-modal transport system for growth and competitive environment. In the past, the country's Poverty Reduction Strategy Paper (PRSP) has also accorded high priority to infrastructure development as one of the means to achieve pro-poor growth (GOB 2005).

MIGRATION, RURAL POVERTY, AND DEVELOPMENT

Migration to Dhaka city occurred from almost all parts of Bangladesh with larger representation from the south, central, south-east, and north-eastern districts, compared with the western part of Bangladesh.[11] Table 3.3 shows that the majority (85 per cent) of the respondents were hailed from 27 out of 64 districts. Keeping consistency with the past trend, the old greater districts of Barisal, Comilla, Dhaka, and Faridpur

Table 3.3 Distribution of Respondents by Categories and Major Districts from which Migration Occurred to Dhaka City in 2010

District of Origin	Slum	Non-slum	Recent Migrant	Long-term Migrants	All (No.)	All (%)
Barisal	9.8	6.1	8.1	7.7	33	7.5
Bhola	4.9	1.1	4.1	2.2	11	2.5
Pirojpur	1.8	2.9	4.1	2.2	11	2.5
Jhalokathi	1.8	1.4	1.4	1.6	7	1.6
Patuakhali	3.7	0.7	1.4	1.9	8	1.8
Comilla	6.1	4.7	1.4	6	23	5.2
Chandpur	4.9	5.1	2.7	5.5	22	5
Brahmanbaria	1.2	1.4	2.7	1.1	6	1.4
Noakhali	3.1	5.1	5.4	4.1	19	4.3
Lakshmipur	1.8	2.5	2.7	2.2	10	2.3
Feni	0.6	2.5	1.4	1.9	8	1.8
Dhaka	1.8	1.4	2.7	1.4	6	1.4
Narsingdi	0.6	2.2	0	1.7	7	1.6
Narayanganj	1.2	1.8	0	1.9	7	1.6
Manikganj	1.2	1.4	0	1.6	6	1.4
Munshiganj	8.0	12.6	2.7	12.6	48	10.9
Mymensingh	3.1	2.5	5.4	2.2	12	2.7
Kishoreganj	1.2	1.4	1.4	1.4	6	1.4
Pabna	1.2	2.2	2.7	1.6	8	1.8
Sirajganj	1.2	1.4	1.4	1.4	6	18.4
Jamalpur	2.5	0.7	0.0	1.6	6	1.4
Tangail	1.2	4.3	4.1	2.5	14	3.2
Jessore	2.5	0.7	5.4	0.5	6	1.4
Faridpur	1.2	2.5	5.4	1.4	9	2
Gopalganj	1.8	2.9	2.7	2.5	11	2.5
Madaripur	5.5	4	1.4	5.2	20	4.5
Shariatpur	13.5	6.9	8.1	9.5	41	9.3

Note: Each of these districts represents more than five respondents. Names of old districts are given.

Source: Authors' estimate from BRAC third-round urban poverty survey, 2010.

remained the major districts from which migrants to Dhaka originated (representing over 60 per cent of the respondents), particularly for the poorer migrants, which corroborates the existing literature including our first two rounds of survey (CUS 1990; Majumder, Mahmud, and Afsar 1996, Afsar 1999; 2000).

Within these greater districts, a few had emerged as important source districts based on the numerical strength of migrants. For example, Munshiganj (Dhaka) and Shariatpur (Faridpur) districts were the most common birthplaces as each contributed nearly 10 per cent of the migrants to Dhaka. Barisal retained its importance as the third largest migrant source district and Comilla ranked fourth followed by Madaripur (Faridpur) and Chandpur.[12]

Top birthplaces of the respondents from slum and non-slum households are not very different, but the ranking varied. For example, top ranking birth districts for slum dwellers are Shariatpur (13.5 per cent), Barisal (9.8 per cent), Munshiganj (8 per cent), Comilla (6.1 per cent), and Madaripur (5.5 per cent), while 4.9 per cent of the slum dwellers hailed from Bhola and Chandpur each and for non-slum dwellers are Munshiganj (12.6 per cent), followed by Shariatpur (6.9 per cent), Barisal (6.1 per cent), Chandpur (5.1 per cent), Comilla (4.7 per cent), and Tangail (4.3 per cent). However, in relative terms there are some differences. For example, there is greater migration from Barisal, Bhola, Patuakhali, Jamalpur, Jessore, and Shariatpur to slum, compared with non-slum. Except Jessore, all these districts fall in the river erosion zone.[13] In addition, Bhola and Patuakhali are part of the cyclone prone region, while Jamalpur, Faridpur, Shariatpur, and Madaripur are in the flood prone region (BBS 2015). It shows that migration to Dhaka mainly occurred from districts prone to natural disasters, particularly in larger proportion for slum dwellers.

On the other hand, a relatively larger proportion of non-slum dwellers were hailed from Noakhali, Feni, Munshiganj, Narsingdi, and Tangail districts than those from slum households. Except Narsingdi and Munshiganj, these districts are also prone to natural disasters such as cyclone, tornado, and river bank erosion (BBS 2015). District based differential is more prominent between the long-term and recent migrants. Unlike the long-term migrants (those who migrated to Dhaka 10 years previously or more), a fewer recent migrants (who migrated to Dhaka less than 10 years previously) hailed from Munshiganj and

Madaripur, while they had larger representation from Jessore, Faridpur, Mymensingh, and Pirojpur. However, in order to examine whether environmentally hazardous districts are also lagging regions in terms of poverty, infrastructure, and economic development, we have estimated district-based poverty and levels of physical and social infrastructure development at migrants' birthplaces. In the following paragraphs, we have analysed the results from these estimates.

Declining Trend in Poverty in All Major Birthplaces of Migrants at Varying Rates

It should be noted that there is a serious paucity of district-based estimates of poverty and economic growth, which makes it difficult to relate the trends in migration with the broader context of regional poverty.[14] Using Head Count Ratio (HCR) based on consumption-expenditure threshold, we measured poverty at the regional level (old districts) from the 2010 HIES data (Table 3.3 and Figures 3.1 and 3.2). Table 3.4 shows that over time the incidence of poverty has declined steadily for almost all districts, particularly between 1999 and 2010 (the period that almost corresponds with the second-round and the current survey).

The pace of decline has been high for seven districts—Noakhali, Kushtia, Chittagong, Dhaka, Bogra, Tangail, and Patuakhali (average annual rate of decline ranging between over 5 per cent and 10 per cent). Among the remaining districts, a majority experienced a moderate decline, which was greater than 2 per cent but less than 5 per cent, and these districts were: Mymensingh, Rajshahi, Jessore, Faridpur, Pabna, Dinajpur, Rangpur, and Sylhet. Deceleration rate has been slow for Barisal (2 per cent) and Comilla (1.5 per cent); the only two districts that recorded slight increase in poverty were Jamalpur (0.4 per cent) and Khulna (0.2 per cent).[15] Therefore, we can say that the major birthplaces of the respondents experienced decline in poverty over time although the rate varied as these districts were almost equally distributed between high and medium pace of poverty decline, followed by those with low rate of decline.

However, migration to slum occurred from some of the districts that experienced slow rate of decline and/or increased level of poverty (such as Barisal and Jamalpur), while other birthplaces such as Patuakhali, Jessore, and Shariatpur experienced rapid and medium rate of decline.

Table 3.4 Incidence of Poverty (Head Count Ratio) for Different Regions in Bangladesh, 1995–2010

Greater Districts	Poverty Incidence (Head Count Ratio)				Annual Average Rate of Decline (%)		
	1995	1999	2005	2010	1995–2005	1999–2010	2005–2010
Barisal	0.647	0.500	0.440	0.400	−3.44	−2.01	−1.58
Patuakhali	0.531	0.406	0.692	0.228	2.44	−5.11	−16.89
Comilla	0.546	0.431	0.285	0.366	−5.74	−1.48	4.26
Noakhali	0.176	0.461	0.351	0.144	6.48	−10.04	−13.80
Dhaka	0.211	0.433	0.214	0.185	0.13	−7.44	−2.40
Mymensingh	0.613	0.549	0.479	0.348	−2.22	−4.06	−5.19
Pabna	0.474	0.468	0.533	0.350	1.07	−2.61	−6.77
Jamalpur	0.603	0.499	0.626	0.522	0.34	0.41	−2.98
Tangail	0.294	0.465	0.372	0.243	2.16	−5.73	−6.85
Jessore	0.417	0.425	0.511	0.299	1.87	−3.15	−8.54
Faridpur	0.601	0.526	0.402	0.373	−3.59	−3.08	−1.24
Khulna	0.409	0.421	0.551	0.428	2.75	0.15	−4.12
Chittagong	0.367	0.418	0.315	0.143	−1.38	−9.29	−12.33
Khagrachari/	NA	NA	0.332	0.164			−11.09
Bandarban	NA	NA	0.607	0.257			−13.35
Dinajpur	0.623	0.390	0.533	0.304	−1.41	−2.24	−8.93
Rangpur	0.708	0.519	0.574	0.405	−1.89	−2.23	−5.65
Bogra	0.324	0.459	0.432	0.203	2.65	−7.15	−11.83
Rajshahi	0.411	0.417	0.446	0.277	0.75	−3.65	−7.63
Kushtia	0.399	0.348	0.245	0.110	−4.34	−9.94	−12.49
Sylhet	0.526	0.400	0.338	0.243	−3.94	−4.43	−5.35

Source: Deb et al. (2008); authors' estimates from HIES data (BBS 2011a); and BRAC third-round survey data, 2010.

By contrast, there was a rapid decline in the incidence of poverty in the districts of origin of the respondents from non-slum such as Dhaka, Noakhali, and Tangail. This is not fully unexpected in the light of two important facts and/or trends—the 'East–West Divide' theory and construction of Jamuna bridge—and other important developments, which we have discussed later.

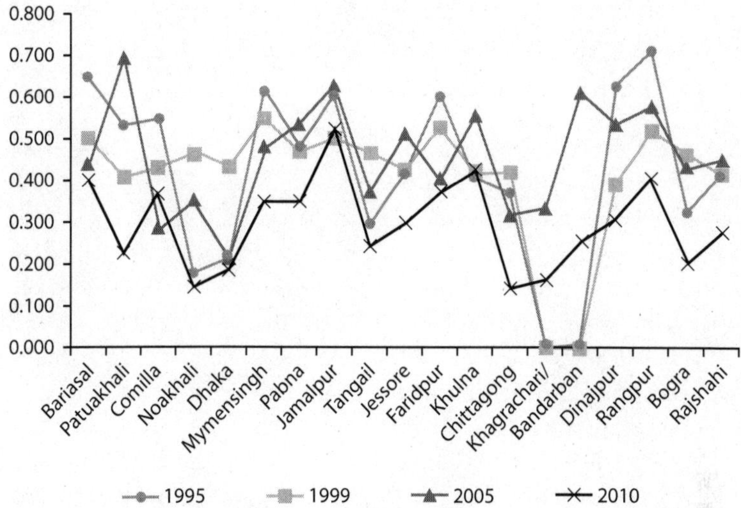

Figure 3.1 Trends in Regional Poverty in Bangladesh, 1995–2010

Source: Deb et al. (2008); authors' estimates from HIES data (BBS 2011a); and BRAC third-round survey, 2010.

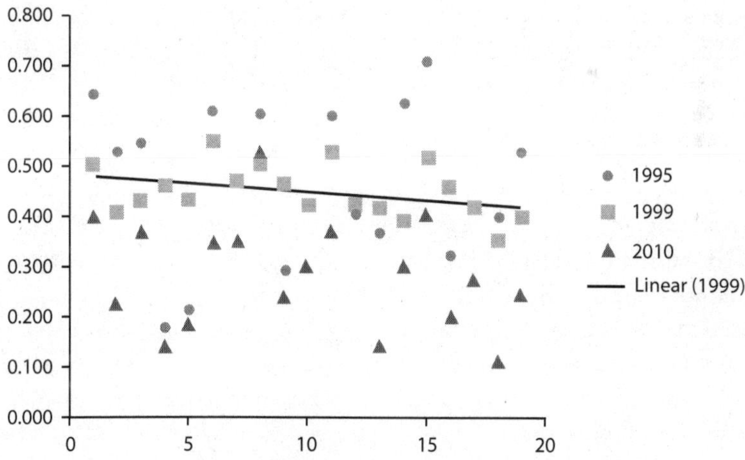

Figure 3.2 Trends in Regional Poverty with Linear Trend Line since 1999

Source: Deb et al. (2008); authors' estimates from HIES data (BBS 2011a); and BRAC third-round survey, 2010.

STRADDLING OF 'EAST–WEST' DIVIDE RESULTING FROM INFRASTRUCTURE DEVELOPMENT AND POVERTY REDUCTION STRATEGIES

First, the 'East–West Divide' or the theory on regional gap in Bangladesh has been well-established. The 'West' is comprised of the administrative divisions and districts thereof that lie across the western side of Jamuna river and are known as lagging region, while those falling on the eastern side of the same river constitute the 'East' or leading region. Among the districts mentioned earlier, Barisal, Jamalpur, Jessore, and Patuakhali, from which some of the slum dwellers migrated are part of the 'West', and Dhaka, Noakhali, and Tangail, from which some of those from non-slum hailed, are the eastern districts. Historically, the West was ecologically vulnerable and economically backward, which is also supported by the HIES data showing that it lagged behind the 'East' in terms of all major development and welfare indicators.

Second, our estimates on district-level poverty from the 2010 HIES data highlights some important positive trends with faster rate of poverty deceleration in some districts of the western regions such as Pabna, Bogra, and Rangpur, compared with Jamalpur, for example, in the East between 2000 and 2010. Research shows that urbanization, migration, policy support including construction of Jamuna bridge and building roads and other infrastructure, and poverty alleviation measures such as safety nets and proliferation of micro-finance institutions are the major contributing factors in narrowing down the gap between the two regions.[16]

This positive trend corroborates our findings on the weakening of push migration supported by out-migration trends from rural areas (Hossain and Bayes 2009), and our earlier arguments that push and pull factors are not isolated or exclusive but rather coexist, and that migration of the rural poor does not necessarily occur from the most impoverished districts only (Afsar 2000). Further, it brings to the forefront the importance of analysing relations between various 'socio-spatial' levels and multiple factors affecting migration decisions and strategies and combining structure and agency framework to understand the complexity of migration decision-making process.[17] As Robert Skeldon has argued, it is often 'not absolute poverty as such that is significant in accounting for migration but whether people feel that they are poor'

(Skeldon 2003: 4). However, without contextualizing migration in the overall regional development scenario, it is imprudent to single out trends in poverty decline or increase as the push factor.

Existing literature on migration highlights a positive correlation between out-migration and high performance of the agricultural sector (Afsar 2000; Fan, Chang-Kan, and Mukherjee 2005; Findley 1987; Mohan and Thottan 1988). The level of growth of agriculture and the share of non-farm households in a district have been identified as significantly correlated to the overall growth of the district (Deb et al. 2008). However, in the same study, the authors (Deb et al. 2008) found no strong relationship between growth in GDP, agricultural growth, and poverty reduction suggesting that it is difficult to explain the trend in poverty by growth factor. Role of remittances in poverty reduction, non-farm employment generation, and ultimately cementing, diversifying and boosting rural economy is amply demonstrated in the literature (Afsar 2005; Cali and Menon 2013; UN-Habitat 2016). The importance of migration and remittances is acknowledged in the Sixth and Seventh Five-Year Plan (GOB 2015c).

Undoubtedly, explaining regional development by linking growth and poverty is complex because of the multiple dimensions and layers involved along with historical antecedents and contextual specificity. While acknowledging the complexity, B. Sen (2005) identified mechanization of agriculture, urban dynamism along with inequality and human capital as the plausible factors explaining variations in regional growth. A review of regional variation by the Planning Commission (GOB 2008; 2015c) highlighted that compared to the more developed regions, the lagging regions were more dependent on agriculture and less industrialized, had received less allocation of the Social Safety Net Program (SSNP) and Annual Development Program (ADP) funds, and had lower levels of infrastructural facilities such as paved roads, transport and communication, and electricity and gas. In the Seventh Five-Year Plan the government has also added lower rate of overseas migration from the lagging regions as one of the major reasons for their under development (GOB 2015c).[18]

On the other hand, World Bank (2015; 2009) and Sen et al. (2014) focused on the role of policy interventions along with migration and urbanization as the important factors in narrowing down regional disparity. There is an impressive body of literature that relates migration with the level of infrastructure development such as paved road, electricity, and cheap and mechanized mode of transportation (GOB 2015c; Hugo 1981; Kols and Lewison 1983; Mantra 1981; Scott 1977; Udall 1981; World Bank 2009; 2015). The role of infrastructure in increasing agricultural productivity, labour wages, and reduction of poverty has also been underscored in some of the empirical studies (such as Ahmed and Hossain 1990; Canning and Bennathan 2007; Fan et al. 1998; Jalan and Ravallion 2002).

Given that access to paved road is often considered as key to employment generation, channelling marketing and information, income and assets generation, and social development (Hossain and Bayes 2009; Sen and Ali 2005), we used distance from migrants' birthplace to paved roads to measure the level of infrastructure development. A regression analysis by the World Bank (2009) shows that travel time as a proxy for access to markets and to urban centres is an important correlate of poverty in rural Bangladesh. 'Per capita expenditure is significantly lower for a rural household when it is located in a community better connected to markets, after controlling for household characteristics and the (unobserved) effects of being located in a particular district' (World Bank 2009: 82). Clearly, it lends support to our approach of using distance (which serves as a reasonable proxy of travel time) as an indicator for the level of infrastructure development. A.K.M.F. Rahman (2005) also found positive impacts of road infrastructure on poverty reduction through creating job opportunities in the transport sector, and contributing to the growth of markets, transforming biweekly *haats* to the Growth Centre Markets and rural hubs by increasing business and small trade.[19]

Similarly, in the context of multidimensionality involved in measuring development and progress, respondents' access to other facilities such as markets, educational institutions, hospitals, banks, and NGO offices is also assessed by measuring the distance between these institutions or services and the respondent's birthplaces.[20] Accordingly, highly developed districts are classified as those in which more than 50 per cent of the respondents had access to any of these facilities at a distance of less than 1 km, while for the same proportion of respondents a distance of less than 5 km and greater than 5 km has been classified as indication of medium and low level of development. A matrix table (Table 3.5) is presented below to generate an understanding on the level of development of the major districts of out-migration.

Table 3.5 Level of Development of the Major Districts of Origin of the Respondents

District of Origin	Paved Road	Bazaar	Primary School	Secondary School	College	Hospital	Bank	NGO Office
Barisal	Medium	High	High	High	Medium	Medium	Medium	Medium
Bhola	High	High	High	High	Medium	Medium	Medium	Medium
Pirojpur	High	High	High	High	Medium	Medium	Medium	Medium
Jhalokathi	High	High	High	Medium	Medium	Medium	Medium	Medium
Patuakhali	Medium	High	High	Medium	Medium	Medium	Medium	Medium
Comilla	High	High	High	High	Medium	Medium	Medium	Medium
Chandpur	High	High	High	High	Medium	Medium	Medium	Medium
Brahmanbaria	High	High	High	High	Medium	Medium	Medium	High
Noakhali	High	High	High	High	Medium	Medium	Medium	Medium
Lakshmipur	High	High	High	High	Medium	Medium	Medium	Medium
Feni	High	High	High	High	Medium	Medium	Medium	Medium
Dhaka	High	High	High	High	Medium	High	Medium	High
Narsingdi	High	High	High	High	Medium	Medium	Medium	Medium
Narayanganj	High	High	High	High	Medium	High	High	High
Manikganj	High	High	High	High	Medium	Medium	Medium	Medium
Munshiganj	High	High	High	High	Medium	Medium	Medium	Medium
Mymensingh	High	High	High	High	Medium	Medium	Medium	Medium
Kishoreganj	Medium	High	High	High	Medium	Medium	Medium	Medium
Pabna	High	High	High	High	Medium	Medium	Medium	High

(Cont'd)

Table 3.5 (*Cont'd*)

District of Origin	Paved road	Bazaar	Primary School	Secondary School	College	Hospital	Bank	NGO Office
Sirajganj	Medium	High	High	High	Medium	Medium	Medium	Medium
Jamalpur	Medium	Medium	High	High	Medium	Medium	Medium	Medium
Tangail	High	High	High	High	Medium	Medium	Medium	Medium
Jessore	Medium	High	High	High	High	Medium	Medium	Medium
Faridpur	High	High	High	High	Medium	Medium	Medium	Medium
Gopalganj	Medium	High	High	High	Medium	Medium	Medium	Medium
Madaripur	Medium	High	High	Medium	Medium	Medium	Medium	Medium
Shariatpur	High	High	High	Medium	Medium	Medium	Medium	Medium

Source: Authors' estimate from BRAC third-round urban poverty survey, 2010

BETTER CONNECTIVITY AND BOOST IN SOCIAL AND PHYSICAL INFRASTRUCTURE DEVELOPMENT AT MIGRANTS' BIRTHPLACES

Table 3.5 shows that most of the birthplaces (districts in this case) of the respondents were well connected to primary and secondary schools, local markets, and paved roads. However, road connectivity was neither too strong nor too weak for Barisal, Patuakhali, Gopalganj, Madaripur, and Jessore in the South and South-West and Kishoreganj, Jamalpur, and Sirajganj in the North-Central and North-Western parts of the country. Some of these districts such as Barisal, Jamalpur, and Kishoreganj are part of lagging region (GOB 2015c). Clearly, there has been a huge expansion of paved road networks and schools over time which is consistent with the country's important achievements in the social sector, particularly enrolment rates at the primary and secondary level and even the overall literacy rate.[21]

However, for a country like Bangladesh which is covered by wide networks of rivers and their tributaries, access to paved road alone is not sufficient to indicate connectivity. Subsequently, we found that many respondents used mechanized transport such as bus and launch as the major modes of communication between Dhaka and their birthplaces. Between 66 per cent and over 90 per cent of the respondents from Barisal, Bhola, Patuakhali, Pirojpur, Jhalokathi, and Chandpur used launches as the mode of communication. Birthplace groups including Feni, Jamalpur, Mymensing, Noakhali, and Pabna also used inter-district train services.

So far as colleges, banks, and other institutions or services are concerned, medium level of connectivity in the case of many of the respondents may not necessarily allow us to categorize their birthplaces as part of the lagging region, particularly when we take the demand and supply situation into account. Among the birthplaces, Narayanganj and Dhaka followed by Pabna and Brahmanbaria are the top achievers as these districts scored high ranks in terms of the respondents' access to many of these facilities (which ranged between five and seven). Fourteen districts which secured high scores for four basic facilities such as paved road, local market, and schools (both primary and secondary) may be considered above average from the perspective of infrastructure development, while Jamalpur, Madaripur, and Patuakhali emerged as under achievers because of their medium ranking, except for primary and/or secondary schools. Therefore, our study reaffirms that migration to Dhaka city does not necessarily occur from the most lagging region only and/or the lagging regions have made some progress, with the exception of Jamalpur and Madaripur. This is also consistent with the district-level poverty trends (Table 3.4) analysed earlier, reinforcing our argument regarding the importance of infrastructure development for poverty reduction.

Whether and in what conditions can migrants realize their aspirations, self-respect, and dream of improving their (family included) situations and livelihoods has been examined in the next chapter as a part of the compelling question raised in the Introduction. With the help of the respondents' occupational patterns at different stages of migration—prior to migration, immediately after migration, current occupation at the time of the survey, and if there is any intermediate job undertaken between post-migration and current occupation—we examined the question of occupational mobility and better livelihoods. This helps unbundle the transformative potential of migration in changing or improving the migrants' situation and establishing the link between migrants' dominant motivation for migration and outcomes, which is often missing in the existing literature.

NOTES

1. Except for 2010 and 2015, when the share of Dhaka's population is estimated to be lower, around 27 per cent, UN projections suggest that it will peak up again in 2030 by reaching 33.1 per cent (UN 2018).
2. Clearly, the gap between the two cities not only increased over time but is also projected to grow further.
3. As indicated in Chapter 2, RMG factories have increasingly shifted from the city core to peri-urban and adjacent districts (Ellis and Roberts 2015).
4. However, level of education of the respondents represents their current educational level, hence, it may not be of much use as we do not have data on the level of education at the time of migration given the difficulties associated with the recall method, and also the questionnaire was very lengthy.
5. Increasingly, it is argued that the climatic risks faced by poorer countries have been exacerbated due to the excessive carbon emission by the more developed countries.

6. Please see, 'Global Climate Risk Index 2015. Who suffers most from the extreme climate events?' available at: https://germanwatch.org/sites/germanwatch.org/files/publication/10333.pdf (accessed on 26 August 2019).

7. However, one may raise question regarding 1991 when there was a severe cyclone in the country, and yet this was not reflected in the migration motivation-related responses. This may be partly related to the fact that the survey was not conducted immediately after the cyclone. However, it is also observed that among the disaster-led migration, flood had received relatively larger attention in the existing literature, compared to cyclone, draught, and other types of calamities. Clearly, there is a need for more research on the impacts of different types of disasters in the migration pattern.

8. It may be reiterated that to generate insights into the dynamics of rural–urban migration and occupational mobility, we have conducted FGD with different occupational groups such as construction, transport and garment factory workers, and hawkers.

9. We have also discussed how structural changes in economy influenced migration motivation in Chapter 5.

10. Despite that, there is no clear vision for broader national urban development policy that could reap benefits from rapid urbanization for equitable distribution to bridge the gap between rich and poor and across geographical divide. This we have discussed in Chapter 9.

11. Seldom there is migration from south-east, north-west, and north-eastern districts to Dhaka. Districts from which migration did not occur are Bandarban, Khagrachari, Joypurhat, Kurigram, Thakurgoan, and Sunamganj.

12. For the sake of consistency, the names of old or greater districts are used in the study, although old districts were reorganized in 1984 as a result of the decentralization process in the country.

13. Riverbank erosion is a perennial problem in Bangladesh. Heavy monsoon generally transports large amounts of sediment from the Himalayan mountains to the sea through the delta of Bangladesh. These fine soils lack resistance capacity to the flowing water and can be easily transported and deposited. Subsequently, the country faces huge risk of riverbank erosion from the large rivers, which can exceed 1 km per year causing severe damage including erosion of agricultural lands and assets of floodplain dwellers.

14. A recent study by Sen et al. (2014) on 'East–West Divide' provides an insightful analysis of regional development and welfare based on HIES data for administrative divisions only.

15. Between 1995 and 2005, districts were almost equally divided between those in which there was a decline in the incidence of poverty and those which experienced an increase. However, it is disturbing to observe that some of the districts with high rate of annual average increase in poverty fell in a

completely reverse pattern of poverty deceleration between 1999 and 2010. Both the scattered diagram and line graph suggest a consistent pattern over time if 2005 data is taken out of the equation. Being laden with too many outliers, it is difficult to accept the 2005 poverty estimates and, hence, we used 1999 and 2010 poverty measures.

16. For a detailed analysis and statistical evidence, see World Bank (2009) and Sen et al. (2014).

17. Some of these approaches include interdisciplinary dialogue as envisaged by Massey et al. (1998), Favell (2008), and Castles (2008); 'political economy' (Freeman and Kessler 2008; Collinson 2009), a combination of the new economics of migration with network theory (Skeldon 1997a) or a livelihoods approach with 'relational' political economy approach (Collinson 2009), and establishing greater interconnections between the causes and consequences of migration (Stark 1991; de Haas 2008).

18. Official estimate suggests that on an average 1,372 people from 15 most lagging districts migrated overseas for employment in 2010, compared with 33,896 people from the top 15 non-deprived districts (GOB 2015c).

19. This is based on an evaluation of the Asian Development Bank (ADB) funded Southwest Road Network Development Project (SRNDP) under the Roads and Highways Department (RHD). Please see Rahman (2005) for a detailed discussion, available at: http://www.adbi.org/files/2005.07.18.cpp.infrastructure.poverty.bangladesh.pdf (accessed on 3 October 2016).

20. Research also highlights that school completion rate is dependent on the extent of paved road in the district and proximity to a bus station (Rahman 2005). However, we are fully aware that this assessment cannot be considered comprehensive and/or adequate to measure district-level development. However, it is done to help generate insights into the indirect effects of growth such as via public spending on social and physical infrastructure (Anand and Ravallion's empirical study in 1993 may provide a useful reference).

21. Adult literacy rate (persons aged 15 years and over) increased from 35.3 per cent to 59.8 per cent between 1991 and 2010 (BBS 2011a), and the net enrolment rate for primary school cohorts (6–10 years) has reached more than 90 per cent for boys and girls.

4 Migration and Occupational Changes

Dreams and Realities of Better Livelihoods

In the previous chapter, we observed that the search for livelihood and/or better employment and income remained the prime motivation for migration to Dhaka since 1991. Obviously, the pertinent question that arises is whether migrants can achieve their goals and realize their aspirations for better livelihood, as raised in the Introduction. In this chapter, we address this compelling question by examining migrants' occupational patterns, trends, and changes at different points in time, which include before migration, immediately after migration to Dhaka, and current occupation at the time of the survey, and by comparing the findings of this round with those from the previous two rounds of surveys.

We have supplemented and complemented survey findings by in-depth interviews and FGDs with different occupational groups to generate understanding of the strategies that poorer migrants adopt to compete in the urban labour market and to identify the factors and conditions that help enhance occupational mobility or lead to stagnation. Side by side, the respondents' level of satisfaction with the current job and plans for job change have been assessed to identify conditions necessary to realize the motivations and aspirations for better livelihoods, more self-respect, and brighter future.

CHANGES IN OCCUPATIONAL PATTERNS: MOBILITY AND STAGNATION

As discussed in the previous chapter, over time there has been an improvement in the poverty situation in the respondents' birthplaces, and most of these villages are well-connected to the district headquarters and/or nearest towns or cities through developed infrastructure such as paved roads, local markets, and schools in varying degrees. In the context of such overall improvement, we have highlighted the weakening of distress-led migration to Dhaka from rural areas. It can also be argued that migrants in general and even the poorer migrants were likely to be less dependent on agriculture as a means of livelihood. They can now afford to wait for better employment and remain unemployed or continue their studies prior to migration, compared to the previous surveys.

Agriculture Sector No Longer Remained the Largest Employer of Rural Migrants

An analysis of the occupational pattern of the respondents from slum households shows that the agriculture sector no longer remained the largest employer of the poorer migrants prior to migration. In contrast to around half of the slum dwellers (48.6 per cent) who worked as agricultural labourers in 1998 prior to migration, the proportion reduced drastically to 5 per cent in 2010 (Table 4.1). Even for the respondents from non-slum, the decline was significant (from 17 per cent to 5 per cent). While the macro-level employment trend of the country supports the declining share of the agriculture sector it is still large, generating 40 per cent of employment for men aged 15 years and over, and 47 per cent of the total employment (BBS 2011b).

However, the share of agriculture in the country's GDP has declined significantly over time. For example, in 1995, the agriculture sector generated more than 60 per cent of the total employment and contributed 50 per cent to GDP. Over time, its contribution to GDP declined significantly to 20 per cent and 16 per cent respectively in 2011 and 2014 (BBS 1996; 2012b; GOB 2015a). However, its share in the country's total employment is still large but declining gradually to 50 per cent and 45 per cent respectively during these reference years (BBS 1996; 2012b; GOB 2015a). During 1990–2011, the share of industry and

Table 4.1 Distribution of Respondents from Non-slum and Slum by Types of Their Occupation Prior to Migration to Dhaka City, 1991–2010

Occupation before Migration	1991				1998				2010			
	Slum		Non-slum		Slum		Non-slum		Slum		Non-slum	
	N	%	N	%	N	%	N	%	N	%	N	%
Service	11	7.6	64	20.9	5	2.9	44	15.0	5	3.1	32	11.6
Business	12	8.3	20	6.5	18	10.4	16	5.4	8	4.9	17	6.1
Self-employed Entrepreneurs	2	1.4	1	0.3	0	0	0	0	4	2.5	1	0.4
Skilled Labour	1	0.7	1	0.3	1	0.6	3	1.0	9	5.5	5	1.8
Un/Semi-skilled Labour	5	3.5	3	1.0	9	5.2	2	0.7	42	25.8	4	1.4
Agriculture	50	34.7	21	6.9	84	48.6	50	17.0	8	4.9	13	4.7
Shop/Home/Property	0	0.0	0	0.0	0	0	0	0	0	0	1	0.4
Remittance/Transfer/Gift	4	2.8	0	0.0	0	0	0	0	0	0	1	0.4
Unemployed	4	2.8	4	1.3	13	7.5	42	14.3	27	16.6	24	8.7
Housewife	1	0.7	8	2.6	0	0	0	0	11	6.7	13	4.7
Children/Adolescent	11	7.6	17	5.6	26	15.0	32	10.9	22	13.5	24	8.7
Not Working	32	22.2	27	8.8	7	4.0	3	1.0	0	0	0	0
Student	11	7.6	140	45.8	10	5.8	102	34.7	27	16.6	142	51.3
All	144	100	306	100	173	100	294	100	163	100	277	100

Source: Authors' estimate from BRAC third-round urban poverty survey, 2010; BIDS first and second-round surveys, 1991 and 1998.

services sectors to GDP increased from 24.3 per cent to 28.4 per cent and 47.8 per cent to 52.9 per cent respectively (World Bank 2012).

Changes in the structure of economy are driven by multiple factors such as remittances, rural–urban linkages, and poverty alleviation measures among others. Subsequently, there is greater expansion of the non-agricultural sector both in terms of employment generation and its contribution to GDP, which has been discussed in a large body of economics and development literature.[1] Here it is sufficient to say that such changes are also reflected in the occupational patterns of rural migrants.

Construction and Transport Sectors Generating More Employment for Rural Poor

Construction and transport sectors emerged as the major employer of the respondents both in 1998 and 2010 (Table 4.1), which is also consistent with the country's overall employment growth pattern. Almost one-third of the respondents from slum households were employed mainly as unskilled or semi-skilled labourers (25.8 per cent), and a few (5.5 per cent) as skilled labourers such as bus, truck or auto-rickshaw drivers, carpenters, and electricians, mostly in these two sectors.[2] This shows more than a five fold increase compared to the first two rounds of our survey when only a small number or proportion (4 to 6 per cent) were engaged in the similar occupations. Countrywide employment generated by the construction sector more than doubled from 1.2 million to 2.6 million from 1999–2000 to 2010, with an annual average growth rate of 7.8 per cent (BBS 2011b). Contribution of the construction sector to GDP had also increased from 5.9 per cent in the 1990s to 8.4 per cent in 2010 (GOB 2011). Rural–urban linkage and remittances are among the major drivers behind the rapid expansion and growth of the construction and transport sectors. Evidence shows that construction and repair/extension of home constitute the second largest expense for rural households next to food and clothes from the remittances sent by overseas migrant workers (Siddiqui 2003). Similarly, in urban areas, remittances are used to build high-rise buildings, shopping malls, and several establishments, which create formal and informal job opportunities in the urban areas for rural migrants (Chowdhury 2014).

Although the construction sector's contribution to GDP was not as large as the professional services (17.8 per cent) and the other sub-sectors such as wholesale and retail trade (14.8 per cent) and transport, storage, and communication sectors (10.7 per cent), yet it is considered a 'dynamic' source of growth in Bangladesh since the 1990s. This is because with massive increase in the real estate and commercial enterprises, the value addition from construction and its significant contribution to the creation of employment for the skilled, semi-skilled, and unskilled labour increased faster than the overall GDP (GOB 2011). The potential for future growth in this sector should be noted, particularly in the context of growing income, remittances, private investment, and urbanization.

Rising Number of the Unemployed and Students before Migration

However, respondents' employment in the retail and wholesale trade, services, and manufacturing sectors prior to migration was small and not consistent with either rural or the country's overall employment trend.[3] Employment in the services sector had declined over time for respondents from both slum and non-slum households, while that of trade almost halved for slum dwellers but remained steady for those from non-slum prior to migration. Rather, there was a large increase in the number of the unemployed and students, particularly for respondents from slum households, which is not only distinct compared to previous occupational patterns but also suggests increased accessibility to education and improved affordability of migrant households over time. The unemployed were predominantly adolescents or youth, and most migrated to Dhaka for employment-related reasons (Table 4.2).

Note that among the respondents from non-slum, the proportion of the unemployed prior to migration was lower than those in slum households. However, more than half of the respondents from non-slum households (51.3 per cent) were students before migrating to Dhaka (Table 4.1). The presence of students has always been larger among the respondents from non-slum than that of slum households. In 1991, almost half of the respondents from non-slum households were students (45.8 per cent) and only a fraction (1.3 per cent) unemployed. However, the proportion of unemployed increased (14.3 per cent and 8.7 per cent respectively) in the next two survey rounds (1998 and 2010), while students comprised the largest but fluctuating proportion (34.7 per cent

Table 4.2 Profile of Respondents from Slum and Non-slum, Who Were Unemployed or Students Prior to Migration

	Unemployed from Slum		Students from Non-slum	
Age Group (Years)	**Number**	**Per Cent**	**Number**	**Per Cent**
Profile				
<10	4	14.8	28	19.7
10–29	23	85.2	107	75.4
30 and Over	0	0	7	4.9
All	27	100.0	142	100
Reasons for Migration				
Employment-Related	20	74.1	71	50.0
To Accompany Family	4	14.8	31	21.8
Financial Assistance to Family	6	22.2	25	17.6
Pull Factors	3	11.1	6	4.2
Higher Studies	0	0	53	37.3
Other	1	3.7	5	3.5
Average Education	27	3.4	142	12.5

Source: Authors' estimate from BRAC third-round urban poverty survey, 2010.

and 51.3 per cent, respectively). The proportions of students (16.6 per cent) and the unemployed (16.6 per cent) doubled for slum households (5.8 per cent and 7.5 per cent, respectively) during the same period.

The fluctuating proportion of students among the respondents from non-slum households over time can be explained by the fact that many students were also unemployed. Subsequently, half of the respondents, who were students at the time of migration, migrated for employment-related reasons (50 per cent), followed by those who migrated in pursuit of higher studies (37.3 per cent). Also, one in five of these students were below 10 years of age at the time of migration and, hence, it is not surprising that they mainly migrated to accompany their parents and other family members (Table 4.2).

Note that the propensity of migration by students was twice as large in the case of long-term migrants (42.1 per cent), as compared to recent migrants—those who migrated to Dhaka less than 10 years ago (20.3 per cent). Further, while none of the recent migrants came to Dhaka as children, a little over one-tenth (12.6 per cent) of the long-term migrants came to Dhaka when they were children. However, irrespective of their year of arrival, around 12 per cent of the respondents were unemployed, which supports our earlier argument of greater accessibility to the education and other development services/institutions and affordability of the respondents.

It should be noted that the average level of education of the respondents from slum doubled to 4.1 years from 2.3 years in 1998. In the context of substantial improvement in adult literacy rate and net primary enrolment rates at primary and secondary levels, as discussed earlier, this finding is not surprising. Subsequently, whether it reflects that the poorest of the poor are not migrating to Dhaka can be debated. While village level studies (Hossain and Bayes 2009) found a declining trend in internal migration, it is important to explore how this declining trend is affecting different classes and what are the factors that deter them from migrating. It can be reiterated that we did not cover the respondents from squatter settlements in this round and hence, the danger of the non-inclusion of the poorest of the poor in the sample cannot be totally ignored. However, results of census of slum areas and floating population by BBS (2015a) clearly shows considerable improvement in the rate of literacy (for people aged 7 years and over) in 2014—32.7 per cent, compared with 14.7 per cent in 1997. Also, for the same age group close to half (around 45 per cent) had primary level of education—more than double compared to 1997 when only 20 per cent had the same level of education.

CHANGING OCCUPATIONAL PATTERNS IMMEDIATELY AFTER COMING TO DHAKA

Consistent with the structural change in the economy as discussed earlier, we can assume that immediately after coming to Dhaka both students and the unemployed had made inroads to the expanding construction and transport sectors. Also, those engaged as unskilled and/or semi-skilled labourers, running petty trade and employed in informal services have found more rewarding opportunities with the passage of time by acquiring skills, even though informal, or by investing more capital. We assessed these assumptions by comparing respondents' first job immediately after coming to Dhaka with what they had prior to migration, which also helped us to identify occupational changes and emerging trends (Table 4.3 and Figure 4.1).

Transport and Construction Sectors: Major Employers of Poorer Migrants in Dhaka

From a comparative analysis of the occupation patterns prior to and immediately after migration to Dhaka (Table 4.3), we found that by providing employment to mainly skilled and semi-skilled or unskilled labourers of agriculture and non-agriculture sectors, the unemployed and students, transport and construction sectors became the largest employers of slum dwellers (45 per cent). This pattern has not changed since 1998, but how far it has become an established norm needs to be studied further. However, the composition of un/semi-skilled labourers has become more diversified over time. For example, in addition to rickshaw/van/cart pullers, there are also rickshaw/van/cart makers and porters in the transport sector. Similarly, there are day labourers, earth-digging labourers, and helpers in the construction sector in this category. The skilled category comprises drivers of mechanized and/or motorized vehicles (such as auto-rickshaw); carpenters, electricians, head labourers or labour suppliers, and workers of RMG sector and linked industries.

Therefore, we can say that by generating job opportunity for both skilled and/or unskilled and semi-skilled labourers, they became the stepping stone to urban life, particularly for the poorer migrants. Importance of these two sectors can easily be understood from the city's growing traffic congestion and the vertical expansion of buildings and establishments. From macro-economic perspective, research shows that annual growth rate of the real estate, renting and business services by 3.3 per cent between 2001–02 and 2009–10, contributed to the huge expansion of the construction sector in Dhaka city. Real estate alone contributed 7 per cent to the country's overall GDP (REHAB 2012). Official estimates show that together with storage and postal services, transport sector's contribution to GDP was 10.72 per cent in 2010–11 and the annual growth rate was 5.7 per cent (Ministry of Finance 2012).

NO UNEMPLOYED, FEW HOUSEWIVES, AND FEWER STUDENTS AFTER MIGRATION

Consistent with our assumptions, we found that both the construction and transport sectors were the stepping stones for the poorer migrants.

Table 4.3 Distribution of the Respondents from Slum by Occupational Patterns before and Immediately after Migration

Pre-migration	**Service**		**Business**		**Self-Employed Entrepreneurs**		**Skilled Labour**		**Un/Semi-skilled Labour**		**Not Working**		**All Respondents**	
Occupation	**No.**	**%**	**No.**	**%**	**No.**	**%**	**No.**	**%**	**No.**	**%**	**No.**	**%**	**No.**	**%**
Service	3	60.0	2	40.0	0	0	0	0	0	0	0	0	5	100
Business	2	25.0	3	37.5	0	0	2	25.0	1	12.5	0	0	8	100
Self-Employed Entrepreneurs	2	50.0	0	0	2	50.0	0	0	0	0	0	0	4	100
Skilled Labour	3	33.3	2	22.2	0	0	4	44.4	0	0	0	0	9	100
Un/Semi-skilled Labour	3	7.1	3	7.14	8	19.0	3	7.1	25	59.5	0	0	42	100
Agriculture	2	25.0	0	0	0	0	4	50.0	2	25.0	0	0	8	100
Unemployed	5	18.5	5	18.5	3	11.1	6	22.2	8	29.6	0	0	27	100
Students	9	33.3	5	18.5	6	22.2	2	7.41	5	18.5	0	0	27	100
Housewife	3	27.3	0	0	2	18.2	0	0	3	27.3	3	27.3	11	100
Children/Adolescent	5	22.7	4	18.2	4	18.2	5	22.7	3	13.6	1	4.5	22	100
All Occupation after Migration (Col.)	37	22.7	24	14.7	25	15.3	26	16	47	28.8	4	2.5	163	100

Source: Authors' estimate from BRAC third-round urban poverty survey, 2010.

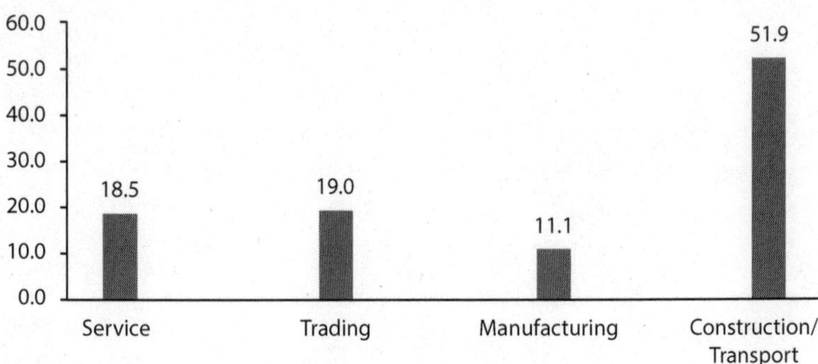

Figure 4.1 Distribution of Respondents from Slum Who Were Unemployed Prior to Migration, by Occupation Patterns Immediately after Migrating to Dhaka

Source: Authors' estimate from BRAC third-round urban poverty survey, 2010.

Together they employed over half of the unemployed (52 per cent), followed by the services (19 per cent) and retail and wholesale trading (18 per cent) sectors (Figure 4.1). In total, one-third of the slum dwellers who were unemployed prior to migration managed to acquire skills after migration and became self-employed entrepreneurs and skilled labourers in manufacturing and linked industries in the supply chain and in the construction and/or transport sectors. Students were mainly engaged in the services (33 per cent) and manufacturing (22 per cent) sectors and in trading activities (19 per cent), underscoring the importance of education in opening doors for more rewarding occupations after migration. Amongst the housewives, three-quarters took up jobs in the services, construction, and RMG sectors and the remaining one-quarter continued as housewives.

INCREASING DEMAND FOR PRIVATE SERVICES

Employment generated by the services and wholesale and retail trading sectors for the respondents (22.7 per cent and 14.7 per cent) also remained compatible with the trend found in 1998. In the services sector, there is an increasing demand for private services such as cook, night guard, and house tutor whether for newly constructed apartments and/or trades and commercial establishments. Most of these types of services are provided by poorer migrants. However, the proportions of the self-employed entrepreneurs such as tailor, TV/fridge/mobile phone/computer and motor mechanics, laundry man, barber, and cobbler, along with skilled labourers of the manufacturing and the related industries/services linked to the supply chain almost doubled (from 8.6 per cent to 15.3 per cent) in 2010 compared to 1998, which is consistent with the national pattern.

Contribution of the manufacturing sector to the total employment had increased from 10 per cent to 12 per cent between 2001 and 2010, while its share to the country's total GDP also increased from 15.6 per cent to 17.9 per cent during the same period (GOB 2012). Clearly, growth of the RMG sector and its dominance in the export market (contributing 77 per cent of the total exports) was the key factor that raised the manufacturing sector's performance. Poorer migrants' entrance into the manufacturing sector and their becoming self-employed entrepreneurs indicates improvement in their skills after migration. However, the question is not only regarding the improvement of entry-level skill sets but also to what extent it has been improved to secure a more rewarding job. This we have examined with the help of migrants' current occupational patterns after shedding light on different aspects of jobs that they got immediately after coming to Dhaka.

SELF-EMPLOYED ENTREPRENEURS: OPPORTUNITY TO ACQUIRE SKILLS

Almost one-tenth (8.6 per cent) of migrants managed to acquire skills after migration and became self-employed entrepreneurs compared to barely 1 per cent before migration. Similarly, there was a two-and-a-half times increase in the proportions of the skilled labourers of the construction and transport sectors (from 3.1 per cent to 7.9 per cent, respectively), indicating an improvement in the level of skills of respondents after migration.

These changes in the employment pattern of migrants tend to suggest the scope for inter-sectoral mobility and, to some extent, upward mobility for poorer migrants immediately after coming to Dhaka (Table 4.3). We have also assessed how long migrants, in general, and poorer migrants had to wait to secure their first job after migration, and whether finding more skilled jobs required longer time and/or money. Further, we have highlighted whether sources who helped them in the procurement of jobs remained the same over time or if they differed for the respondents from non-slum and slum households in the following section.

MIGRANTS' SOCIAL NETWORK: MAJOR PROVIDERS AND ENABLERS

Most of the respondents from slum (85 per cent) received help either from their family members and/or friends and neighbours in procuring these jobs (Table 4.4) compared with less than two-thirds (63.5 per cent) of the respondents from non-slum households. Most of the poorer migrants who were employed as skilled labourers (96.2 per cent), self-employed entrepreneurs (92 per cent), and in the services sector (89.2 per cent) received help mainly from their family members, followed by friends and/or neighbours and co-workers. Types of help they had received included information about the job, initial hands-on training, and introduction with the employers, an opportunity to borrow rickshaws, auto-rickshaws, and other work implements such as sewing machine in the case of RMG sector workers for practice (see Box 4.1). Going beyond employment, social networks of family members and friends contributed to enhance the overall well-being of migrants such as by helping in the rehabilitation process of migrants who use drugs through productive engagement, collective bargaining to settle wages, and lending money to cushion exigencies arising out of work-related accidents or lack of work (Box 4.1).

However, high-skilled jobs such as mason in the construction sector required experience of working with another mason, which was not possible without a longer duration of stay in Dhaka and, more importantly, having close acquaintance with an experienced mason, which was not an easy option for many migrants working in the sector. Other jobs such as machine operator in the RMG factory and/or car or bus mechanics also required time, hands-on-training, and even money, which respondents often tried to manage with the help from their family, friends, and/or neighbours.

Table 4.4 Distribution of Respondents from Slum and Non-slum by Types of First Job in Dhaka and Sources Who Helped in Securing the Job

First Job in Dhaka Slum Dwellers	None/Self		Family/ Relative		Friend/ Neighbour		Others		All Respondent	
	No.	%	No.	%	No.	%	No.	%	No.	%
Service	4	10.8	23	62.2	6	16.2	4	10.8	37	100
Business	7	29.2	11	45.8	6	25.0	0	0	24	100
Self-employed Entrepreneurs	2	8.0	14	56.0	8	32.0	1	4.0	25	100
Skilled Labour	1	3.8	17	65.4	5	19.2	3	11.5	26	100
Un/Semi-skilled Labour	7	14.9	19	40.4	15	31.9	6	12.8	47	100
Not Working	4	100	0	0	0	0	0	0	4	100
All Occupation	25	15.3	84	51.5	40	24.5	14	8.6	163	100
Non-slum	No.	%	No.	%	No.	%	No.	%	No.	%
Service	60	36.1	78	47	19	11.4	9	5.4	166	100
Business	13	24.1	39	72.2	1	1.8	1	1.8	54	100
Self-employed Entrepreneurs	1	7.7	8	61.5	4	30.8	0	0	13	100
Skilled Labour	1	11.1	6	66.7	1	11.1	1	11.1	9	100
Un/Semi-skilled Labour	1	11.1	4	44.4	3	33.3	1	11.1	9	100
Not Working	25	96.2	1	3.8	0	0	0	0	26	100
All Occupation	101	36.5	136	49.1	28	10.1	12	4.3	277	100

Source: Authors' estimate from BRAC third-round urban poverty survey, 2010.

Box 4.1 Social Networks Act as Referral and Help in Productive Engagement, Collective Bargaining, and Lending Money at Times of Crunch

Social networks of family, friends, or co-workers acted as a referral for migrants in their new workplace. Saidur Rahman (54 years) was a rickshaw puller from Sherpur thana who came to Dhaka to earn more money with the help of his cousin's husband, Moshtaq, who was a rickshaw puller. Because of his close acquaintance with the garage owner, Moshtaq managed to secure a rickshaw for Saidur on lease which enabled him to learn the skill of rickshaw pulling, which is needed in order to navigate the streets and alleyways of Dhaka city. Without a reference, however, garage owners do not lend rickshaws.

Social networks helped in the rehabilitation process of drug users by providing help for their active engagement, such as information and assistance to set up a business. For example, Alim Miah (aged 27 years) was transferred to Dhaka from Mymensing district by his parents with the help of his cousin mainly for rehabilitation after he started taking drugs and alcohol. His cousin, Manowar used to sell garments at the Baitul Mukarram hawkers' market. First, he brought Alim along to the market and created a space beside his own for Alim to sell his product, which is very important in the context of intense and fierce competition over scarce space. Also, he shared tips of the trade, such as how to attract customers and the location of wholesale markets from where he could buy cheap garments.

Social networks helped in collective bargaining for adequate wage and working conditions. During the FGD with construction sector workers, Madan Kumar (32 years) told us that migrants like him who seek jobs in the construction sector formed groups at the haat (weekly bazaar) near Purabi Cinema, Mirpur, where buyers come to look for construction labourers. He and his group members knew each other as they were all from Satkhira district and lived in the same village. They selected Jainal Mia as their leader because of his long experience in this sector (12 years) and his ability to negotiate with buyers.

Generally, once a buyer makes the offer, the onus is on the leader to ask the buyer about the nature of work, and the rate and mode of payment. Payment is settled through a process of negotiation and bargaining and upon reaching an agreement, the contracted labourers start working at the agreed work place. Madan Kumar also confided that the minimum rate at which they accepted an offer was Tk. 270–80 for the day. He also cited an example of solidarity and compassion of his team members. He recollected how the previous year, due to work-related injury, he was unable to go for work for a few days. His team members completed the unfinished work on his behalf as per the contract and offered him money for treatment. His team members also lent him money which helped him survive for a few days when he first joined the construction sector and was not getting any work offer from the buyers at the haat.

LONGER WAITING PERIOD FOR MORE REWARDING JOB

On an average, the respondents spent 3.7 months to secure employment in Dhaka's labour market, which was reduced to three months for slum dwellers (Figure 4.2). However, the number of days spent also varied depending on the types of occupations (Table 4.5). For procuring easy-entry jobs such as unskilled or semi-skilled workers in the construction and/or transport sectors, nearly half (44.6 per cent)

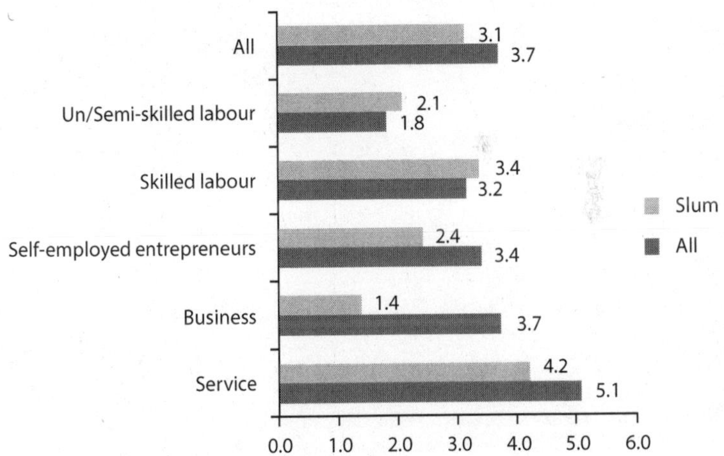

Figure 4.2 Distribution of All Respondents (Migrants) and Respondents from Slum by the Types of First Jobs in Dhaka and Average Waiting Period (Months) to Secure the Job

Source: Authors' estimate from BRAC third-round urban poverty survey, 2010.

Table 4.5 Distribution of All Respondents from Slum by Types of First Jobs in Dhaka and Number of Days They Waited to Secure the Job

First Job in Dhaka	<7 Days		7–29 Days		30–99 Days		100–365 Days		366+ Days		Total	
All Migrants	**No.**	**%**	**No.**	**%**	**No.**	**%**	**No.**	**%**	**No.**	**%**	**No.**	**%**
Service	57	28.1	30	14.8	63	31.0	39	19.2	14	6.9	203	100
Business	15	19.2	18	23.1	30	38.5	12	15.4	3	3.8	78	100
Self-employed Entrepreneurs	10	26.3	14	36.8	11	28.9	1	2.6	2	5.3	38	100
Skilled Labour	9	25.7	11	31.4	9	25.7	5	14.3	1	2.9	35	100
Un/Semi-skilled Labour	25	44.6	15	26.8	13	23.2	2	3.6	1	1.8	56	100
Agriculture	0	0	0	0	1	100	0	0	0	0	1	100
Not in Labour Force	29	100	0	0	0	0	0	0	0	0	29	100
All Migrants	145	33	88	20	127	28.9	59	13.4	21	4.8	440	100
Slum Dwellers	**No.**	**%**	**No.**	**%**	**No.**	**%**	**No.**	**%**	**No.**	**%**	**No.**	**%**
Service	6	16.2	6	16.2	15	40.5	8	21.6	2	5.4	37	100
Business	6	25	5	20.8	11	45.8	2	8.3	0	0	24	100
Self-employed Entrepreneurs	6	24	10	40	8	32	0	0	1	4	25	100
Skilled Labour	7	26.9	7	26.9	8	30.8	3	11.5	1	3.8	26	100
Un/Semi-skilled Labour	21	44.7	13	27.7	10	21.3	2	4.3	1	2.1	47	100
Agriculture	0	0	0	0	0	0	0	0	0	0	0	0
Not in Labour Force	4	100	0	0	0	0	0	0	0	0	4	100
All Slum Dwellers	50	30.7	41	25.2	52	31.9	15	9.2	5	3.1	163	100

Source: Authors' estimate from BRAC third-round urban poverty survey, 2010.

of the respondents spent less than a week, and for over one-quarter (26.7 per cent), the average waiting period was less than a month. By contrast, between one-fifth and one-quarter of respondents employed in other industries such as services, trading, and as skilled labourers in the transport and construction sectors as well as RMG and allied industries waited for less than a week. Almost half waited even longer—between one month and one year, exempting self-employed entrepreneurs.

Although only 5 per cent of the respondents waited for more than a year to secure their first job in Dhaka, they were largely represented by the service sector employees (two-thirds and two-fifths for all migrants and slum dwellers respectively), compared to other occupational groups (Table 4.5). Subsequently, the average waiting period was longest—five months—for those who were employed in the services sector and shortest for unskilled labourers (1.8 months), compared to other occupational groups who spent more than three months on an average.

Trend in the waiting period for the first job for migrants in general was similar to what we found in the case of those from slum households with one major exception. Nearly half (45.8 per cent) of the slum dwellers managed to own businesses within a period ranging between seven days and less than a month after coming to Dhaka, while the other half did so in a month but less than 100 days. However, among all the respondents who owned businesses, almost one-fifth (19.2 per cent) waited between 100 days and even a year or more to start their first enterprise. Subsequently, the average waiting period was shortest—1.4 months—for small business owners including hawkers, followed by unskilled labourers (2.1 months) in slum, but increased to 3.7 months for all respondents engaged in trading (Figure 4.2).

By contrast, the average waiting period was the longest for procuring jobs in the services sector (4.2 months for slum dwellers) and over one-fifth (21.6 per cent) waited between 100 days and more than a year. For procuring jobs in the other sectors, very few respondents had to wait for so long (Table 4.5).

Longer Waiting Period for the First Job Signals Migrants' Greater Affordability

The waiting period was shorter in 1998 when half of the respondents from slum procured their first job in less than a week after migration, and three-quarters did so within a month. However, the longer waiting period in 2010 does not necessarily indicate squeezing of job opportunities for poorer migrants. Rather the types of jobs they availed after migration (Figure 4.3) suggests expansion of opportunities for more skilled jobs compared to 1998, and greater affordability of the migrants to wait longer for a better job (as argued earlier).

In 2010, almost one-fifth (16 per cent) of the respondents who settled in slum made in-roads straight to skilled labour (for which they had to wait longer—more than three months on an average to acquire skills). However, it shows that the opportunity for procuring skilled jobs in the construction and transport sectors has been four times greater in 2010 compared with 1998 (4 per cent). Similarly, the opportunity for self-employment as entrepreneurs doubled (from 8.4 per cent to 15.3 per cent), while the proportions of unskilled or semi-skilled labour decreased by more than 10 per cent and those not actively engaged in the labour force were halved.

Apart from the expansion of job opportunity and significant improvement in the level of education of the poorer migrants since 1991, it is difficult to ascertain what contributed to poorer migrants' gradual entry

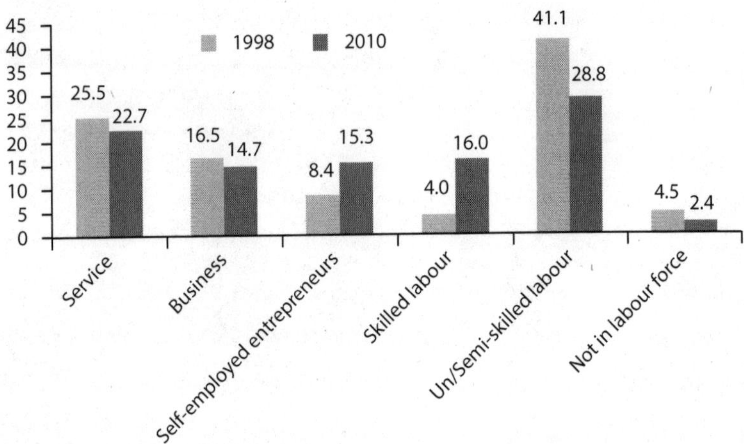

Figure 4.3 Distribution of the Respondents from Slum by First Job after Coming to Dhaka in 1998 and 2010

Source: Authors' estimate from BRAC third-round urban poverty survey, 2010.

to more skilled jobs in the absence of data on the level of education prior to migration. With the help of data on the amount of money migrants brought at the time of migration, we have explored if it helped to increase their affordability to wait longer to avail better employment opportunity. Also, we have used the findings from the FGD and in-depth interviews with different occupational groups to illustrate the types of help they received in order to improve their skill levels to some extent such as from helper to machine operator in a garment factory and/or rickshaw puller to auto-rickshaw driver. However, as mentioned earlier, high skilled jobs such as mason in the construction sector requires capital and apprenticeship, none of which are easy to obtain for a poorer migrant. Therefore, it draws attention of the policymakers and planners in the government, non-government, or private sectors for programmatic intervention to facilitate apprenticeship and other hands-on vocational training for the urban poor, which we discuss in the concluding chapter.

Migrating with Capital: A Common Strategy

Two-thirds of the respondents from slum and non-slum households (65 per cent and 68.2 per cent, respectively) brought money at the time of migration, although the size of the capital was different for each group. The variation was based on their capacity, largely facilitated by the types of occupation they were engaged in prior to migration particularly in the case of respondents from non-slum (Table 4.6). Their capacity to bring money along was also influenced by the types of support they received from their social networks of family and friends. However, for larger amounts of money, migrants were dependent mainly on their own incomes and/or savings (Figure 4.4). By contrast, smaller amounts were funded by family members and/or borrowed from friends.

The amount of money brought by a respondent was estimated at Tk. 4,972 (US$ 71) on an average with those from non-slum bringing Tk. 7,142 (US$ 101.8), more than six times larger than the average for slum dwellers: Tk. 1,103 (US$ 15.7). Respondents who owned businesses migrated with the largest sum of money—Tk. 26,516 (US$ 377.9) on an average. For slum dwellers, those who were employed in the services sector, the average size of the capital was three times larger (US$ 48.7), while it was five times larger for business owners (US$ 506.1), and almost double in the case of those who were unemployed (US$

Table 4.6 Distribution of Respondents from Slum and Non-slum Who Brought Money at the Time of Migration by Average Amount and Types of Occupation

Pre-migration Occupation	Slum	Mean		Non-slum	Mean		Total	Mean	
	No.	Tk.	US$	No.	Tk.	US$	No.	Tk.	US$
Service	5	3,420.0	48.7	31	10,400.0	148.2	36	9,430.6	134.4
Business	6	1,028.3	14.7	17	35,511.8	506.1	23	26,516.1	377.9
Self-employed Entrepreneurs	3	900.0	12.8	1	500.0	7.1	4	800.0	11.4
Skilled Labour	9	916.7	13.1	3	2,116.7	30.2	12	1,216.7	17.3
Un/Semi-skilled Labour	33	1,234.9	17.6	3	866.7	12.4	36	1,204.2	17.2
Agriculture	6	1,633.3	23.3	12	2,138.3	30.5	18	1,970.0	28.1
Unemployed	16	932.5	13.3	17	13,855.9	197.5	33	7,590.0	108.2
Housewife	8	331.3	4.7	7	7,557.1	107.7	15	3,703.3	52.8
Children/Adolescent	2	750.0	10.7	1	300.0	4.3	3	600.0	8.6
Student	18	724.2	10.3	97	1,029.2	14.7	115	981.5	14.0
Total	106	1,102.6	15.7	189	7,141.8	101.8	295	4,971.8	70.9

Source: Authors' estimate from BRAC third-round urban poverty survey, 2010.

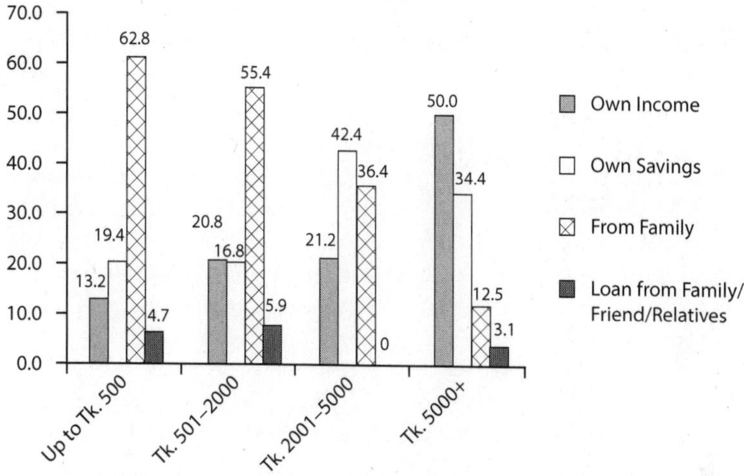

Figure 4.4 Distribution of Respondents Who Brought Money at the Time of Migration by the Sources Who Financed Them and the Amount of Money

Source: Authors' estimate from BRAC third-round urban poverty survey, 2010.

197.5) among non-slum dwellers. Clearly, it reflects better capacity of those who were engaged in the services sector prior to migration. For students, however, it indicates mainly a cautionary measure to fend for themselves during their waiting period.

While more than three-quarters of respondents brought smaller amount ranging up to Tk. 500 (44 per cent) or between Tk. 500 and Tk. 2,000 (34 per cent), for less than one-quarter (22 per cent), the size of the capital varied between Tk. 2,001 and over Tk. 5,000 at the time of migration. An overwhelmingly large majority of respondents (between 63 per cent and 84 per cent) who brought larger amount (Tk. 2,001–5,000) did so from their own incomes and savings. Family members and friends, on the other hand, financed a large majority (67 per cent and 61 per cent, respectively) of those who brought smaller sums of money (Tk. 500 and/or Tk. 501–2,000).

None of the slum dwellers brought over Tk. 5,000 and for most of them the size of the capital ranged up to Tk. 500 (48.1 per cent) or over Tk. 500 but up to Tk. 2,000 (39.6 per cent). With such a small amount

Box 4.2 Amount of Money Migrants Bring Along Influence Their Job Selection

FGDs with different occupational groups revealed that the participants who managed to migrate with capital ranging from Tk. 5,000 to Tk. 10,000 (US$ 71.25–142.51), immediately took up trading as hawkers on the streets as they did not have to pay rent for trading. For example, Ramzan Ali (aged 39 years), who migrated to Dhaka 19 years ago, used to drive a van in Bhanga, Faridpur, prior to migration. His cousin who owned a small business in Dhaka asked Ramzan to join his business. Subsequently, Ramzan sold his land for Tk. 4,000 (US$ 57) and invested in his cousin's business after migrating to Dhaka. By contrast, participants who did not have or could not bring any capital were mainly employed as rickshaw pullers, day labourers in construction, or helpers in the RMG sector.

of money, the question naturally arises whether they got any leverage in Dhaka's labour market apart from, of course, in their post-migration settlement process. Box 4.2 presents how money migrants bring along can influence their job selection.

Money Helps the Poorer Migrants to Sustain and the Non-poor to Reap Better Benefits from Job Search

From the data presented in Table 4.7, it is difficult to find any systematic relation between the size of the capital and types of job they secured after migrating to Dhaka. At the most we can say that the cash in hand might have helped a significant proportion (ranging between one-third and one-half) of poorer migrants to survive as they waited for between a month and more than three months to procure jobs in the services, business, and manufacturing sectors, or acquire skills to be self-employed as entrepreneurs (Table 4.7). However, respondents from non-slum households who brought large sums of money reaped the benefit of more rewarding jobs from investment in business and education after migration, as we shall see in the detailed analysis of determinants of incomes in the next section. Here we have focused on incomes from current jobs briefly to examine whether it influences duration in the same job or job satisfaction.

By comparing respondents' current occupations and how and to what extent these are different from their first jobs after coming to Dhaka, we

Table 4.7 Distribution of Respondents from Slum Who Brought Money at the Time of Migration by the Amount of Money and Types of Occupation after Migration

Occupation after Migration	Up to Tk. 500		Tk. 501–2,000		Tk. 2,001–5,000		All Slum Dwellers	
	No.	%	No.	%	No.	%	No.	%
Service	8	36.4	10	45.5	4	18.2	22	59.5
Business	8	47.1	6	35.3	3	17.6	17	70.8
Self-employed Entrepreneurs	10	55.6	6	33.3	2	11.1	18	72.0
Skilled Labour	8	50.0	7	43.8	1	6.3	16	61.5
Un/semi-skilled Labour	16	50.0	13	40.6	3	9.4	32	68.1
Not Working	1	100.0	0	0.0	0	0.0	1	25.0
Total	51	48.1	42	39.6	13	12.3	106	65.0

Source: Authors' estimate from BRAC third-round urban poverty survey, 2010.

have examined their options and the scope for upward and inter-sectoral mobility in the city's job market. We have also examined the reasons for sustenance and discontinuity in the first job, their levels of satisfaction with the current job, and whether they wanted to change their current job in the future with the help of quantitative and qualitative analysis.

INTER-SECTORAL AND UPWARD MOBILITY, JOB SATISFACTION, AND JOB CHANGE

We found that the average duration in the first job after migration differed for slum and non-slum residents, and it also depended on the types of occupations (Table 4.8). On an average, the respondents from slum have been continuing with the same job for 10 years since migrating to Dhaka, and the duration increased to 15.2 years for those from non-slum. This differential may not be surprising considering that the proportion (37.8 per cent) of the respondents from non-slum, who were in the same job for over 20 years, was more than double compared to that of slum (17.8 per cent) households.

Table 4.8 Distribution of Respondents from Slum and Non-slum by Duration in the Occupation They Secured after Migrating to Dhaka and Types of Occupation

	Up to 1 Year		2–4 Years		5–9 Years		10–19 Years		20+ Years		Total	
Occupation	**N**	**%**	**N**	**%**	**N**	**%**	**N**	**%**	**N**	**%**	**N**	**%**
Slum												
Service	2	5.4	5	13.5	10	27.0	13	35.1	7	18.9	37	100
Business	2	8.3	5	20.8	8	33.3	4	16.7	5	20.8	24	100
Self-employed Entrepreneurs	7	28.0	4	16.0	5	20.0	6	24.0	3	12.0	25	100
Skilled Labour	3	11.5	7	26.9	3	11.5	6	23.1	7	26.9	26	100
Un/Semi-skilled Labour	8	17.0	10	21.3	14	29.8	8	17.0	7	14.9	47	100
Not in the Labour Force	4	100	0	0	0	0	0		0	0	4	100
Total	26	16.0	31	19.0	40	24.5	37	22.7	29	17.8	163	100
Non-slum												
Service	5	3.0	29	17.5	26	15.7	37	15.7	69	41.6	166	100
Business	0	0	3	5.6	3	5.6	20	37.0	28	51.9	54	100
Self-employed Entrepreneurs	1	7.7	5	38.5	2	3.7	2	15.4	3	23.1	13	100
Skilled Labour	0	0	3	33.3	3	33.3	2	22.2	1	11.1	9	100
Un/Semi-skilled Labour	0	0	3	33.3	1	11.1	3	33.3	2	22.2	9	100
Agriculture	0	0	0	0	0	0	1	100	0	0	1	100
Not Working	25	0	0	0	0	0	0	0	0	0	25	100
Total	31	11.2	43	15.5	35	12.6	65	23.5	103	37.2	277	100

Source: Authors' estimate from BRAC third-round urban poverty survey, 2010.

Longer Duration in the Same Job Signals Stability and Security

Longer duration in the same job can be an indication of stability and security. With more than 10 years of formal education, it is obvious that the respondents from non-slum had greater options to secure more stable jobs than their counterparts from slum households, who had only four years of schooling on an average. Nearly two-thirds (62.5 per cent) of the respondents from non-slum had either a university degree (35.5 per cent) or completed senior secondary and/or high school (27 per cent), compared to less than one-tenth (8.5 per cent) from slum who had equivalent qualification at the secondary or high school level.

Business Owners, Government Officers/Professionals/ Managers, and Skilled Workers Enjoy Greater Job Stability

Those who owned businesses or were employed in the services sector were more likely to continue with the same occupations for longer—for almost 20 years (19.6 and 16.8 years, respectively)—compared to other occupational groups from non-slum that migrated to Dhaka (Figure 4.5). Almost 9 out of 10 who owned businesses continued for over 20 years (51.9 per cent) or between 10 and 19 years (37 per cent). The proportions with similar duration in services sector were 41.7 per cent and 15.7 per cent, respectively. However, services sector also provided an opportunity to more recent entrants into the job market, being the largest employer of respondents from non-slum households. Thus, there were more than one-third of respondents in services sector (36.2 per cent) who had been in their first job for less than 10 years, which was more than three times higher than those owning business (11.2 per cent) with the same duration.

Among slum dwellers, skilled labourers had the longest duration in their jobs in Dhaka—12.5 years on an average, compared with 11.3 and 9.6 years for those employed in the services sector or who owned businesses. Unskilled or semi-skilled labourers and self-employed entrepreneurs had been in their respective jobs for nine years on average. Job security is undoubtedly an important issue, but for the poorer migrants what appear to be more important are their option to change to more rewarding jobs and the ability to acquire skills and accumulate capital for better income and decent work environment. This is because

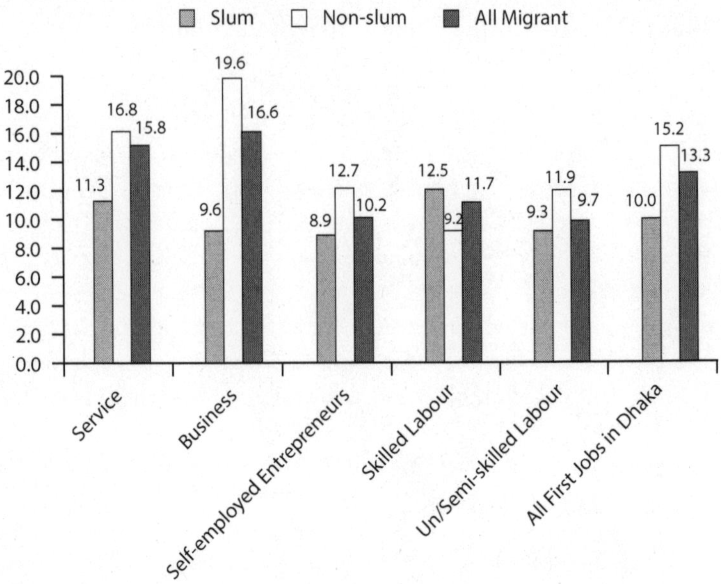

Figure 4.5 Distribution of Respondents from Slum and Non-slum by Average Duration in the First Job in Dhaka

Source: Authors' estimate from BRAC third-round urban poverty survey, 2010.

services and trade sectors have different hierarchical contours for different classes.

For example, the highly educated or skilled respondents from non-slum households occupied mainly the upper and middle echelons of government service as professionals such doctors, engineers, lawyers, teachers, and bureaucrats; or tax consultants, managers, directors, or chief executive in the corporate sector, and public or commercial banking and other financial services. Others with lower levels of education or skills were represented in the lower ranks and profiles such as officers and clerks in public and private sectors and were even self-employed as house tutors or freelance consultants or running private coaching centres.

Poorer migrants made in-roads mainly to the informal services such as midwife, paramedic, and guard or night guard, and procured jobs in a shop or establishment which were run by private individuals or small companies. Similarly, respondents from non-slum households who owned businesses were mainly industrialists, contractors, or running big business, while those from slums were small shopkeepers, hawkers, and owners of small cottage industry.

Slum Dwellers' Increased Prospect for More Skilled Jobs with Longer Length of Stay in Dhaka

By comparing respondents' first job in Dhaka with their current job at the time of the survey (Table 4.9), we find that the opportunity to switch to more skilled jobs increased for slum dwellers. The proportion engaged as unskilled or semi-skilled construction and/or transport sector workers declined by 34 per cent at the time of the survey as some of them (16.2 per cent) moved upwards within the same sectors to skilled occupations such as drivers, mechanics, skilled construction sector workers, head labour, and labour suppliers by acquiring skills and establishing connections. A few others (8.1 per cent) either joined as skilled labour in the RMG sector and became self-employed entrepreneurs or made in-roads to the services sector (8.1 per cent).

Although the services sector continued to be the largest employer of migrants, the number of employments generated by this sector has declined by 18 per cent (from 203 to 166). This is because one-quarter (26 per cent) of those who were previously engaged in services started their own business, followed by those who joined as skilled and un/semi-skilled workers in the transport and construction sectors, while fewer still depended either on rental property for income or became too old to work.

The retail and wholesale business sector expanded significantly—by 73 per cent—compared to the number of jobs that it generated at the time of migration, which is good news. Apart from the employees from the services sector who now owned their business, as mentioned earlier, some of the skilled and un/semi-skilled labourers also started their small enterprises (26 per cent). Box 4.2 gives insight into how they generated capital to own business and the types of problems they had in running the businesses they owned.

Employment situation of the poorer respondents who lived in slum households did not differ much from the above trends except that employment in the services sector remained almost the same,

Table 4.9 Distribution of Respondents (Migrants) by Their First Job after Migration and Current Job at the Time of Survey

First job in Dhaka	Service		Business		Self-employed Entrepreneurs		Skilled Labour		Un/Semi-skilled Labour		Not Working		All Current Jobs (Col.)	
All Current Jobs (Col.)	N	%	N	%	N	%	N	%	N	%	N	%	N	%
Service	148	89.2	4	2.4	5	3.0	3	1.8	5	3.0	1.0	0.6	166	100
Business	33	26.0	60	47.2	9	7.1	8	6.3	17	13.4	0.0	0	127	100
Self-employed Entrepreneurs	1	5.3	2	10.5	15	78.9	0	0	1	5.3	0.0	0	19	100
Skilled Labour	3	10.3	1	3.4	1	3.4	16	55.2	8	27.6	0.0	0	29	100
Un/Semi-skilled Labour	3	8.1	2	5.4	3	8.1	6	16.2	23	62.2	0.0	0	37	100
Agriculture	1	33.3	0	0	0	0.0	0	0	0	0	1.0	33.3	3	100
Shop/Home/Property	2	50	0		0		0		0		2	50	4	100
Remittances/Transfer/Gift	0		0		0		0		0		2	100	2	100
Housewife	1	3.4	0	0	4	13.8	0	0	2	6.9	22	75.9	29	100
Not Working	11	45.8	9	37.5	1	4.2	2	8.3	0	0	2	4.2	24	100
Current Jobs (Col.)	203	46.1	78	17.7	38	8.6	35	7.9	56	12.7	30	6.8	440	100

Source: Authors' estimate from BRAC third-round urban poverty survey, 2010.

while the number of those who became self-employed entrepreneurs halved from 25 to 12 as some of them started their own business (24 per cent), while a few of them also joined construction or transport sectors. The number of those who owned small businesses and/or were hawkers almost doubled from 24 to 43 (Table 4.10). Also, those who were unemployed or housewives immediately after migration mainly became self-employed entrepreneurs after acquiring skills or started petty trading or working as unskilled labourers at the time of the survey.

By contrast, less than half of the respondents who were employed as un/semi-skilled labourers (47 per cent) after migration to Dhaka continued in the same occupation. Of the remaining 53 per cent, more than half (28 per cent) started their business, while more than one-quarter (15 per cent) were employed as skilled labourers in the construction, transport, and manufacturing sectors or became self-employed entrepreneurs. Note that the employment opportunities for unskilled labourers have been expanded by 50 per cent as half of those in the respective occupations had switched over to other jobs over the course of time. The case studies of Saidur and Shukhi presented in Box 4.3 sheds lights on how they managed to acquire skills over time with the help of their neighbours and friends—Jabbar and Pari—who offered informal on-the-job training.

Greater and More Diversified Job Opportunities for Poorer Migrants Over Time

A comparison of the respondents' current employment patterns at the time of second and third-round survey in 1998 and 2010 indicates (Figure 4.6) that job opportunities for poorer migrants have been expanded in the services sector by 27 per cent but declined in the business sector by 6.5 per cent. However, increase in the number of skilled workers in the construction, transport and manufacturing sectors and opportunities for self-employment by 84 per cent, and reduction of unskilled or semi-skilled workers by 41 per cent can be considered the most impressive achievements over time. With the expansion of employment opportunities in these sectors, occupations have been diversified and slum dwellers stepped into the new upper-level positions such as labour suppliers, head labourers, electricians in the construction sector, and/

Table 4.10 Distribution of Slum Dwellers by Their First Job after Migration and Current Job at the Time of the Survey

First Job in Dhaka	Service		Business		Self-employed Entrepreneurs		Skilled Labour		Un/Semi-skilled Labour		HW/NW		Total	
	No.	%	No.	%	No.	%	No.	%	No.	%	No.	%	No.	%
Service	27	73.0	3	8.1	0	0	3	8.1	3	8.1	1	2.7	37	100
Business	3	12.5	16	66.7	2	8.3	0		2	8.3	1	4.2	24	100
Self-employed Entrepreneurs	3	12.0	6	24.0	9	36.0	2	8.0	2	8.0	3	12.0	25	100
Skilled Labour	2	7.8	5	19.2	0	0	13	50.0	6	23.0	0	0	26	100
Un/Semi-skilled Labourers	3	6.4	13	27.6	1	2.1	6	12.8	22	46.8	2	4.2	47	100
Not Working	0		0		0		0		0		4	100.0	4	100
Current Job (Col.)	38	23.3	43	26.4	12	7.4	24	14.7	35	21.5	11	6.7	163	100

Note: HW = housewife; NW = not working

Source: Authors' estimate from BRAC third-round urban poverty survey, 2010.

Box 4.3 Friends and Neighbours Provide Informal Hands-on Training

Social networks helped migrants upgrade skills. Saidur Rahman (34 years) was a rickshaw puller for five years, during which he developed a friendship with his neighbor Jabbar, an auto-rickshaw operator. Rickshaw pulling being arduous, he wanted to switch over to a less strenuous but more rewarding job. Jabbar helped Saidur by providing hands-on-training in auto-rickshaw driving during the night, and procuring a driver's license and an auto-rickshaw on lease. Saidur mastered the skill of driving an auto-rickshaw in the busy and narrow lanes of Dhaka after a year of practicing at night.

Similarly, Shukhi who started her career as a helper in a garment factory upgraded her skills by learning machine operation informally from her friend, Pari, who was an operator in a garment factory. The job in the factory helped Shukhi survive in Dhaka, but she was highly dissatisfied and demoralized as she had to endure relentless verbal abuse from the supervisor for making even the smallest of mistakes. In this stressful situation, Pari came to her rescue by offering her training in machine operation informally. In this way Shukhi learned machine operation. Eventually, she quit the factory after procuring an operator position in another factory which offered her a better income, matching an operator's scale (Tk. 4,500–6,000 or around US$ 65–85 per month), which the factory where she started her career was not paying despite the progression in her skill level.

or TV/fridge/computer/mobile phone repairers or motor mechanics, laundry men, midwives, cooks, and night guards.

Better and More Diversified Job Opportunities Do Not Necessarily Ensure Job Satisfaction

However, the issue is not only the provision of better and more diversified job opportunities but also whether the respondents were satisfied with their current job. Nearly two-thirds of the respondents who were employed in the services sector (64 per cent) or owned business (60 per cent) were more satisfied with their existing jobs than other occupational groups (Table 4.11). By contrast, most of the un/semi-skilled labourers reported either dissatisfaction (40.5 per cent) or moderate satisfaction (40.5 per cent) with their current occupation, and they were predominantly from slum households (97.3 per cent). We have also observed that dissatisfaction among a significant proportion (26.3

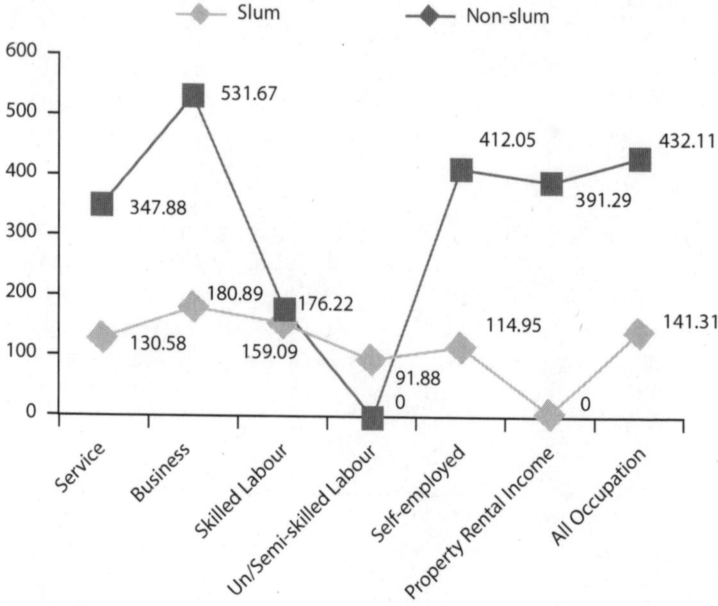

Figure 4.6 Monthly Income of the Respondents from Slum and Non-slum by Current Occupation (US$)

Source: Authors' estimate from BRAC third-round urban poverty survey, 2010.

per cent) of self-employed entrepreneurs, while skilled labourers were almost equally divided between those who expressed satisfaction (44.8 per cent) or moderate satisfaction (51.7 per cent) with their job situation.

HIGHER EDUCATION, SKILLS TRAINING, AND CONDUCIVE WORK ENVIRONMENT INFLUENCE JOB SATISFACTION

From Table 4.11, we can say that higher the level of education, greater is the level of satisfaction. Similarly, more slum dwellers expressed moderate satisfaction (45.5 per cent) and dissatisfaction (19.9 per cent), and the opposite holds for the respondents from non-slum households (26.6 per cent and 3.5 per cent, respectively). Similarly,

Table 4.11 Distribution of Respondents by Categories and Level of Satisfaction in the Current Job

Current Occupation	Highly Satisfied		Satisfied		Moderately Satisfied		Dissatisfied		Total
	No.	%	No.	%	No.	%	No.	%	No.
Service	12	8.5	79	56.0	39	27.7	11	7.8	141
Business	7	5.6	68	54.0	47	37.3	4	3.2	126
Self-employed Entrepreneurs	0	0	8	42.1	6	31.6	5	26.3	19
Skilled Labour	0	0	13	44.8	15	51.7	1	3.4	29
Un/Semi-skilled Labour	0	0	7	18.9	15	40.5	15	40.5	37
Agriculture	0	0	1	50.0	0	0	1	50.0	2
All	19	5.4	176	49.7	122	34.5	37	10.5	354
<5 Years in the Same Job	2	5.0	20	50.0	13	32.5	5	12.5	40
5–9 Years in the Same Job	0	0	27	42.2	24	37.5	13	20.3	64
10–19 Years in the Same Job	2	1.8	55	48.7	43	38.1	13	11.5	113
20–39 Years in the Same Job	14	10.9	70	54.3	39	30.2	6	4.7	129
40+ Years in the Same Job	1	12.5	4	50.0	3	37.5	0	0	8
All Duration	19	5.4	176	49.7	122	34.5	37	10.5	354
Slum	0	0	53	35.1	68	45.0	30	19.9	151
Non-slum	19	9.4	123	60.6	54	26.6	7	3.5	203
All Respondents	19	5.4	176	49.7	122	34.5	37	10.5	354
Recent Migrants	0	0	31	48.4	21	32.8	12	18.8	64
Long-term Migrants	19	6.6	145	50.0	101	34.8	25	8.6	290

(Cont'd)

Table 4.11 (*Cont'd*)

Current Occupation	Highly Satisfied		Satisfied		Moderately Satisfied		Dissatisfied		Total
	No.	%	No.	%	No.	%	No.	%	No.
All Migrants	19	5.4	176	49.7	122	34.5	37	10.5	354
No Education	0	0	17	27.4	35	56.5	10	16.1	62
Primary	2	3.3	27	44.3	20	32.8	12	19.7	61
Secondary	1	1.4	32	45.1	30	42.3	8	11.3	71
SSC/HSC	5	6.8	42	56.8	23	31.1	4	5.4	74
Degree	11	12.8	58	67.4	14	16.3	3	3.5	86
All Levels of Education	19	5.4	176	49.7	122	34.5	37	10.5	354

Note: Respondents not in the labour force and those who derive income from rent/remittances are excluded.
Source: Authors' estimate from BRAC third-round urban poverty survey, 2010.

dissatisfaction was higher among recent migrants (18.8 per cent) in comparison to long-term migrants (8.6 per cent). However, it is difficult to find such direct bearings from duration in the current job. While it may not be possible to pursue the highest level of education for everybody, but the options for skills development and on-the-job training need to be actively considered by the employers and service providers of public and private sectors, which will help raising the level of satisfaction, productivity, and the scope for value addition.

Consistent with their level of dissatisfaction, we found that more unskilled or semi-skilled labourers of the transport, construction, and RMG sectors, followed by the self-employed entrepreneurs wanted to change their jobs in the future, compared to other occupational groups (Table 4.12). From the case studies presented in Box 4.2, we can identify health risks and hazards associated with the unskilled occupation in transport, construction, and RMG sectors as important factors influencing their response pattern along with better working conditions and conducive work environment.

For the unskilled or semi-skilled labourers and self-employed entrepreneurs, dissatisfaction with rather than duration in the current job appears to influence their decision to change jobs in the future. Whether

Table 4.12 Distribution of Respondents by Plans for Changing Occupation and by Average Duration in the Current Job

Current Job	Wanted to Change Job (%)	Average Duration (Years)	Did Not Want to Change Job (%)	Average Duration (Years)	All Respondents
Service	14.2	10.7	85.8	17.4	141
Business	15.1	11.5	84.9	16.7	126
Self-employed Entrepreneurs	42.1	16.0	57.9	17.5	19
Skilled Labour	24.1	10.0	75.9	19.0	29
Un/Semi-skilled Labour	51.3	12.2	48.6	15.6	37
Agriculture			100	9.6	2
All	20.6	11.8	79.4	17.1	354

Source: Authors' estimate from BRAC third-round urban poverty survey, 2010.

they would be able to change their jobs would depend on a number of factors such as labour market demand, capital, skills, and appropriate programmatic intervention to enhance their skills and capital formation. By contrast, among the skilled labourers, one-quarter who expressed a desire to change their current job had an average duration of 10 years in the job, which is almost half the duration of those who did not want to change their occupation. Similarly, most of the respondents employed in the services sector and those owning businesses did not want to change occupation and had longer duration in the same job than those who wanted to change.

Longer Duration in the Same Job: Freedom, Flexibility, and Better Income Matters

At the time of the survey, nearly half of the respondents (49 per cent) including slum dwellers (45 per cent) were continuing in the same job that they procured after migration to Dhaka. As per Table 4.13, propensity to continue in the same job was highest (65.4 per cent) for those who owned a business, were employed in the services sector (45.8 per cent), or worked as skilled labourers (45.7 per cent). The prospect is lowest for the self-employed entrepreneurs (36.8 per cent) and unskilled or semi-skilled labourers (37.5 per cent) to continue in the same job. Better job opportunities and/or owning a business were the major reasons for leaving the first job, which applied to all respondents including the slum dwellers, indicating that even poorer migrants have opportunities for better employment. Whilst income is one of the indicators of a better job (Figure 4.7), case studies (Box 4.4) revealed that respondents often preferred more flexible and decent jobs rather than the repressive ones, irrespective of income.

Respondents owning business earned the highest monthly income (US$ 531.67 and US$ 180.89 from non-slum and slum households respectively) compared to other occupational groups (Figure 4.6). Self-employed entrepreneurs and those who derived incomes from property and rent were the second and third largest income earners, followed by the service holders, while skilled labourers fall in the lowest income bracket among the respondents from non-slum households. For slum dwellers, on the contrary, the unskilled or semi-skilled labourers were the lowest income earners, followed by

Table 4.13 Distribution of All Respondents and Slum Dwellers by Reasons for Leaving the First Job in Dhaka, Types of Occupations, and Mean Duration in the Job

All Respondents Reasons for Leaving (%)	Service	Business	Self-employed Entrepreneurs	Skilled Labour	Un/semi-skilled Labour	All Respondents	Mean Duration (Years)
Term Over/Sacked	10.8	2.6	7.9	0.0	3.6	6.6	23.1
Dissatisfaction/Loss	6.9	12.8	18.4	20.0	10.7	10.0	5.9
Family/Sickness	3.0	2.6	10.6	0.0	1.8	2.9	14.5
Retirement/Old Age	4.9	5.1	0.0	0.0	0.0	3.2	30.7
Better Job/Own Business	28.1	10.3	26.3	34.3	42.9	25.2	6.1
Still Working	45.8	65.4	36.8	45.7	37.5	48.6	17.0
Others	0.5	1.3	0.0	0.0	3.6	3.4	4.2
Total	100.0	100.0	100.0	100.0	100.0	100 (440)	13.3

(Cont'd)

Table 4.13 (*Cont'd*)

Slum Dwellers/ Reasons for Leaving (%)	Service	Business	Self-employed Entrepreneurs	Skilled Labour	Un/semi-skilled Labour	All Slum Dwellers	Mean Duration (Years)
Term Over/Sacked	5.4	8.3	8.0	0.0	4.3	4.9	11.2
Dissatisfaction/Loss	13.5	16.7	24.0	23.1	12.8	16.6	5.6
Family/Sickness	8.1	4.2	12.0	0.0	2.1	5.0	9.5
Retirement/Old Age	0.0	0.0	0.0	0.0	0.0	0.0	0.0
Better Job/Own Business	24.3	16.7	20.0	30.8	36.2	26.4	4.7
Still Working	48.6	50.0	36.0	46.2	42.6	44.8	15.2
Others	0.0	4.2	0.0	0.0	2.1	2.5	9.1
Total	100.0	100.0	100.0	100.0	100.0	100 (163)	10.0

Source: Authors' estimate from BRAC third-round urban poverty survey, 2010.

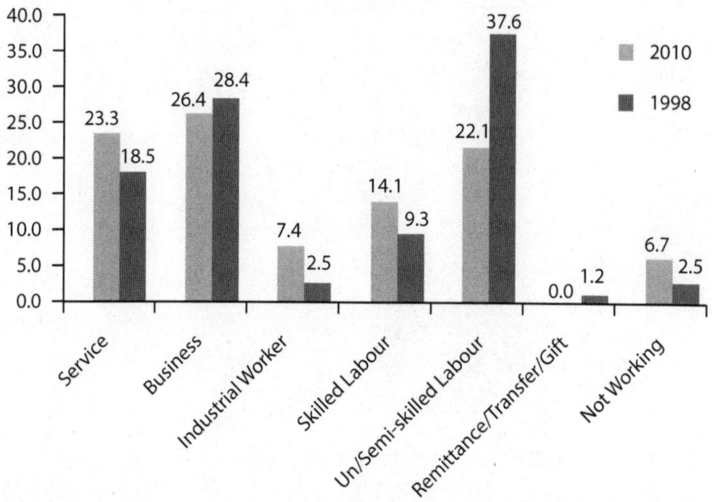

Figure 4.7 Distribution of Respondents from Slum by the Types of Employment at the Time of Second- and Third-Round Surveys, 1998 and 2010

Source: Authors' estimate from the repeat surveys.

the self-employed entrepreneurs, while skilled labourers were the second highest income earners.

The search for a better life and livelihood does not stop with migration. Rather it is a continuous process. This continuity is reflected in the entire spectrum of occupational mobility that we have analysed so far. Therefore, in addition to the duration in the same job, we also examined the prospect for job change. We found that slum dwellers started earlier (after 4.7 years on an average in the same job) to look for better opportunities, compared with six years for all respondents. As expected, those who looked for better jobs were mainly unskilled or semi-skilled labourers, followed by skilled labourers and employees of the services sector, in comparison to other occupational groups; and those owning a business were least likely to do so. In changing jobs, push factors such as loss in business, health hazards, and sickness played an important role.

Box 4.4 Better Income, Freedom, and Flexibility Matters

Higher income is widely acknowledged as an important motivating factor for changing occupation. Going back to Ramzan Ali's case, we found that from his independent business, he earned only Tk. 100 per day (US$ 1.4), while the co-boarders of his mess (boarding house) earned more—Tk. 200–50 per day (US$ 2.8–3.6) by pulling rickshaw. His friends secured a vehicle for him from the same garage owner who employed them and trained him for 10–15 days. Once he became familiar with the roads and fares, he started pulling rickshaw. Similarly, apart from his sickness, Rafiq Miah (28 years) was not happy about the salary that he received from the RMG factory which was less than Tk. 2,000 per month (US$ 28.5 per month or less than a dollar per day) despite working all day and night. In contrast, as a day labourer in the construction sector, he was earning Tk. 300 (US$ 4.3) per day at the time of the FGD in 2010.

Flexibility in the working conditions has also influenced job selection and sustenance. For example, FGD participants from the construction sector told us that the freedom of choosing and leaving the job provided an added incentive for joining the sector. They found the RMG sector to be most repressive as it lacked flexibility and freedom. Some of them described the RMG sector as 'regimental', while others considered it 'abusive'.

Push Factors: Loss in Business, Health Hazards, and Sickness Influence Job Change

Push factors such as dispute, loss in business, health hazards, and sickness can lead to dissatisfaction and job change (Box 4.5). Dissatisfaction and/or loss in the existing business was the second most important reason for quitting the first job. Self-employed entrepreneurs, skilled

Box 4.5 Dispute, Loss in Business, and Health Issues Influence Job Change

Dispute, loss of income, and theft were identified as major factors that induced job change. Ramzan Ali's case for example, reveals that after working together for some time, he and his cousin got entangled in a dispute on the question of transparency related to profit. As a result, Ramzan Ali started his own separate business but could recover only a part of his investment (Tk. 25,000 or US$ 356.3) from his cousin. Jewel's (35 years) case illustrates that a loss in business can prompt job change. He started a shoe store in Gulistan by investing TK. 300,000 (US$ 4,275.3), which he accumulated from his father and father-in-law as dowry for his marriage. Due to lack of care and proper attention, he experienced huge losses in the business and eventually was left with Tk. 50,000 (US$ 712.6). At this critical time, Rajib, a hawker who used to sell his goods sitting at the corner of the street right next to his store helped him re-establish himself as a street hawker.

Health hazards and sickness can lead to dissatisfaction and job change. Initially, after migration, Madan Kumar (32 years) was employed as a rickshaw puller with the help of his brother-in-law. However, he could not master the vehicle well and had several accidents. Due to injuries in his head, shoulder, and legs from a major accident, he decided to change his occupation. He then switched over to the construction sector as a day labourer with the help of his cousin.

During an FDG, rickshaw pullers told us that they did not want to continue in the same occupation for long as it was physically arduous. Abdul Hamid (52 years) said that he had to take painkillers and gastric medication daily to recover from the chronic headache and aches and pains caused by rikshaw pulling. He wanted to drive an auto-rickshaw, which he considered more rewarding and less demanding physically. On the other hand, Nuru Molla (29 years) did not want to work in the transport sector anymore. After pulling rickshaw or driving an auto-rickshaw for another five years, he wanted to save enough money to receive computer training and start a business.

Another illustration of sickness-induced job change emerged from Rafiq Miah's (28 years) case. He initially secured a job in a garment factory as a helper with the support of a neighbour from his natal village. After working for a few months, he contracted jaundice (hepatitis B infection) due to the excessive heat inside the factory and a lack of hygienic toilet facilities, and he eventually left that job. With the help of a construction worker from his own village, he managed to secure a job at a building site as a construction worker. However, the construction sector is also full of risks. Jainal Mia (41 years) for example, was injured while carrying bricks on his head and climbing up the building site. The bricks dropped causing injury to his foot for which neither did he receive compensation nor was he able to recover the costs incurred for his treatment.

labourers, and business owners were relatively more dissatisfied with their jobs, compared to public or private sector employees or unskilled workers. This apparently contradictory finding in which a smaller proportion of unskilled labourers left their jobs on the ground of dissatisfaction can be explained partly by their shortest duration in the same job, as discussed earlier. From the case studies, however, we found that dissatisfaction was higher among this group because they perceived a lack of opportunities to acquire skills and capital and a lack of availability of enough suitable jobs in the market as major constraints to enhancing their income and/or job prospect, compared to other occupational groups (Box 4.5).

Case studies also highlighted that unskilled labourers such as rickshaw pullers and helpers in garment factories had changed or wanted to change their occupation mainly on grounds of health and physical arduousness. The garment sector is also notorious for lack of flexibility, unhealthy work environment, and abusive behaviour of supervisors experienced by helpers and/or operators when they made mistakes. However, the construction sector is also not devoid of risks and problems. Working in the construction sector involves carrying heavy loads of sand and bricks up the buildings and/or on unfinished roofs with bare feet and bare head, which is very risky and requires skill, balance, and caution. In the context of Bangladesh, where lack of compliance of building codes and health insurance is widespread and injured workers are seldom compensated, occupational hazards are high in the construction sector.

In conclusion, we may say that over time job opportunities for the poorer migrants in the construction and transport sectors has expanded significantly. There is also an improvement in the skill levels of migrants which helps to enhance their upward mobility within these sectors and also creates self-employment opportunities. However, job opportunity does not always positively co-relate with job satisfaction. More unskilled or semi-skilled labourers and self-employed entrepreneurs expressed dissatisfaction with their current job. Further, the level of education appears to influence the level of satisfaction.

NOTES

1. See, for example, World Bank, BIDS, and Centre for Policy Dialogue (CPD) publications.

2. For the tables in this chapter, we have used skilled and un/semi-skilled labourers instead of transport and construction sectors because we believe this would be helpful to understand changes and occupational mobility.

3. Between 1995–96 and 2009–10, employment generated by the industry sector doubled from 10 per cent to almost 20 per cent, while the same for the services sector grew significantly from around a quarter to more than one-third (BBS 1996, 2011b; Raihan 2012).

5 Dynamics of Livelihoods, Income, and Poverty

Scope for Shared Prosperity

Bangladesh has made significant progress in poverty reduction over time. The HCR of poverty has declined from 58 per cent in 1990 to 32 per cent in 2010. The rate of decline has been faster for urban (45 per cent to 21 per cent) than rural areas (from 61 per cent to 35 per cent) (BBS 2011a; GOB 2005). It is generally perceived that with migration of landless and asset-less rural population to cities, poverty has been transported from rural to urban areas and inequality in income distribution has worsened. In this chapter, we have analysed the trends and changes in asset base and livelihoods of slum and non-slum households and examined the level and composition of income and employment along with real earnings for different occupational groups. With the help of a multivariate regression model, we have analysed the determinants of household incomes. We have also examined distribution of income over time, the incidence of poverty along with changes in the degree of inequality, and factors contributing to the changes in income distribution. Understanding generated in this process helped us address the first of the compelling questions laid out in Chapter 1: Is the poorer segment of the urban population that migrates with dreams for better lives and livelihoods benefitting from positive economic trends?

LABOUR FORCE, OCCUPATIONS, AND EARNINGS

Detailed information on the labour force and occupation is not available from the first-round survey in 1991. Therefore, we have compared the information from our second and third-round surveys conducted in 1998 and 2010 for this section.

Overall Improvement in the Incidence of Child Labour but Not for Boys

The incidence of child labour is indicated by the proportion of children aged between 10 and 15 years engaged in income-earning activities.[1] In 1998, the incidence of child labour was quite high—11.3 per cent, 14 per cent for boys and 7.8 per cent for girls (Table 5.1). The rate was much higher for slum households—26 per cent and 20 per cent for boys and girls, respectively. Data from 2010 survey shows a marked improvement in the situation, compared to 1998. The proportion of child labour was estimated at 7.2 per cent for Dhaka city—10.2 per cent of boys and 3.5 per cent of girls. The situation has not improved much for boys from slum households as almost one-quarter of them (23 per cent) were engaged in income earning activities in 2010, although girls' participation declined substantially to less than one-tenth (8 per cent).

Table 5.1 Labour Force Participation Rate by Gender and Age Group for Slum and Non-slum Households, 1998 and 2010

Age Group	Slum		Non-slum		Dhaka City		
Year 1998	**Male**	**Female**	**Male**	**Female**	**Male**	**Female**	**Total**
10–15 Yrs	25.8	20.3	7.3	1.5	14.0	7.8	11.3
16–30 Yrs	82.0	27.9	52.9	9.5	59.7	14.8	38.1
31–64 Yrs	96.7	39.2	94.7	23.1	95.3	27.2	63.4
16–64 Yrs	90.0	33.0	61.8	16.1	77.1	20.7	50.3
Year 2010							
10–15 Yrs	22.7	7.5	2.7	1.1	10.2	3.5	7.2
16–30 Yrs	86.6	26.2	56.5	9.8	65.2	15.6	39.1
31–64 Yrs	100.0	23.2	89.5	15.5	92.4	17.1	57.3
16–64 Yrs	93.4	24.6	64.5	14.5	80.2	16.7	44.8

Source: Authors' estimate from BRAC third-round urban poverty survey, 2010.

This positive trend can be attributed to improved school attendance for girls compared to that for boys, as discussed in Chapter 7. In that chapter, we have argued that growing employment opportunity for girls in RMG factories in and around Dhaka that require basic education and/or above was one of the triggers that encouraged parents to send girls to schools. Also, with sustained decline in fertility, there is less need for engaging girls to look after younger siblings. Further, parents might have considered prospects for girls' marriage given that eligibility improves in the marriage market for better educated girls, compared with those with less or no education.[2] However, in the absence of any financial support for slum children from municipal areas, the opportunity cost for sending children to school remains very high for poor households who would prefer to use the male children to augment the family's meagre income rather than sending them to school.

Decline in Female Labour Force Participation

The labour force participation rate for adult members has declined from 50 per cent in 1998 to 45 per cent in 2010. This can be attributed mainly to declining female labour force participation rate as the rate has increased for male members. The participation rate for female members has reduced from 21 per cent in 1998 to 16.7 per cent in 2010. The trend is similar for both slum and non-slum households. Reduced participation of women can be an outcome of more young adults attending higher secondary schools and colleges. The decline is more pronounced for older women compared to young adults.[3] With the help of regression analysis, we have identified high gender disparity in wages and remunerations later in this chapter, which we believe deter women from participating in the labour market. Older women, on the other hand, tend to withdraw from the labour market with improved economic conditions of their families.

STRUCTURAL CHANGES IN EMPLOYMENT

A Shift from Public to Private Services for Male Workers

For male earners, major occupational shift has occurred from public to private services and from formal to informal business during 1998–2010 (Table 5.2). Nearly 35 per cent of the male earners were engaged in

Table 5.2 Changes in the Occupational Distribution of Employed Workforce by Gender, 1998 and 2010

Occupation	All Workers		Male Workers		Female Workers	
	1998	2010	1998	2010	1998	2010
Public Service	20.9	8.6	21.3	7.6	19.3	17.8
Private Service	13.1	24.8	13.6	24.0	11.1	28.0
Professional Job	6.8	2.8	6.2	2.8	9.7	2.5
Formal Business	21.0	15.0	23.3	17.4	9.7	1.3
Informal Business	11.9	19.4	11.4	22.3	5.8	3.8
Industrial Worker	10.1	19.2	7.2	15.5	25.1	37.6
Manual Labour	16.2	10.2	17.0	10.4	19.3	9.0
Total	100.0	100.0	100.0	100.0	100.0	100.0

Source: Authors' estimate from BRAC third-round urban poverty survey, 2010.

various services in 1998, which had declined marginally to 33 per cent in 2010. However, the rate declined substantially from 21 per cent to 8 per cent for those employed in formal services. Note that the deficit was compensated by the growing and expanding employment in informal services, generated by business enterprises, hotels and restaurants, and real estate including the high-rise apartments. The proportion of those employed as professionals (such as doctors, engineers, and lawyers) has almost halved from 6 to 3 per cent. In contrast, the rate of employment for industrial labour more than doubled from 7 per cent in 1998 to 15 per cent in 2010. Such an increase can be attributed to the expansion of the garment industry, which is highly labour-intensive, and employs girls in large proportions, generating around 3.5 million jobs in 2011 (Lopez-Acevado and Robertson 2012).

Proportional Increase in Industrial Workers and Decline in Domestic Workers among Female Earners

For female earners, major increases are noticed in the proportions of industrial workers from 25 per cent to 38 per cent (for less educated women), and for those in private services, from 11 per cent to 28 per cent (for higher-educated women). In contrast, there was a significant decline in the proportion of domestic workers from 19 per cent to only 9 per cent during the same reference period.

Similar Occupational Patterns for Male and Female Workers in Slum

As expected, occupational distribution of adult members from slum households is different compared with those from non-slum. Male workers living in slums were mainly employed as industrial workers (27 per cent), followed by those in informal business (27 per cent), wage labour (26 per cent), and private services (16 per cent). Compared with 1998, employment opportunities for industrial workers doubled (from 13 per cent) but declined for those in private services (from 23 per cent) and halved for manual-based wage labour (from 35 per cent).

Female workers were mainly employed as industrial workers (62 per cent), wage labour (19 per cent), followed by those in private services (15 per cent) in 2010. Compared with 1998, the rates doubled for industrial workers (from 34 per cent) and increased for those engaged in informal business (from 12 per cent) and private services (from 10 per cent). In contrast, the proportion of women employed as wage labour, mostly as domestic helpers, halved (from 38 per cent), indicating that with increase in family income, female workers are moving out from low-paid derogatory jobs.

Educational Backgrounds Influence Occupational Patterns

It should be noted that occupational patterns of workforce are generally influenced by their educational backgrounds, which obviously is expected. From the information about educational background (years of schooling, see later in this chapter), we find that the least educated workers were employed mostly in manual labour–based occupations such as construction labourers, rickshaw pullers, and van drivers, and daily wage–based miscellaneous occupations. Those who have completed primary level or dropped-out from secondary schools were employed as industrial workers (such as in the garment industry), other transport operations (such as car and bus drivers), informal business that required small amount of capital (such as roadside retail stores), and low-paid services in the private sector. Those who obtained high school certificates or have university degrees were employed in formal business, government service, or in professional jobs such as doctors, engineers, lawyers, and teachers.

Migration-Induced Occupational Changes

As mentioned earlier, a large proportion of urban households are migrants. To capture occupational changes of workforce in the households that occurred as a result of migration, we have cross-examined pre- and post-migration occupation for those who migrated to Dhaka in the last five years (Table 5.3).[4] Note that migrant workers were mostly engaged in agriculture, or were students or unemployed prior to migration in 1998. Over time, the incidence of migration of workers engaged in agriculture at the place of origin has waned, while those who migrated to Dhaka for higher studies has increased substantially. The proportion of people who were unemployed prior to migration was relatively low (15 per cent in 2010) and remained almost unchanged over time. After migrating to Dhaka, major occupations of the most recent migrant households were services (42 per cent), business (32 per cent), and skilled (11.6 per cent) and unskilled labour (10.5 per cent) in 2010. The occupational patterns and trends of these households are consistent with what we have presented in the previous chapter.

Several implications can be drawn from the findings. It should be noted that migration reduces unemployment to a significant extent

Table 5.3 Changes in Occupations due to Migration, 1998 and 2010

Occupation	Occupation Prior to Migration		Present Occupation	
	1998	2010	1998	2010
Agriculture	39.4	13.8	nil	nil
Business	11.8	9.4	36.3	32.0
Service	11.9	16.5	28.6	42.0
Skilled Labour	1.5	5.6	13.5	11.6
Unskilled Labour	4.9	7.2	15.1	10.5
Student	12.4	27.1	nil	nil
Unemployed	16.2	14.9	nil	nil
Others	1.9	5.5	6.5	3.9

Source: Authors' estimate from BRAC third-round urban poverty survey, 2010.

(from 15 or 16 per cent to none). Clearly, a substantial proportion of migrants who come to Dhaka as unemployed or for higher studies do not return to rural areas as they find jobs in services, industries and business, and in manual labour–based occupations. Similarly, many of those who come from agricultural backgrounds migrate to Dhaka city with surplus generated from agriculture to set up formal or informal business. Only a small proportion engaged in unskilled and semi-skilled jobs after migration that require low levels of education and provides low levels of earnings. These findings endorse our earlier arguments (Chapter 3) that pull of greater economic opportunities in Dhaka compared with rural areas are more important drivers for migration to Dhaka city than the push factors.

Information that we have collected on the reasons for migration reaffirms this hypothesis (for details, see Chapter 3). The respondents were asked to provide three reasons for migration in order of importance. In 1998, the reported reasons in order of importance were 'in quest of a job' (52 per cent), 'unemployed in the place of origin' (28 per cent), 'on-the-job transfer' (14 per cent), and 'displaced because of river erosion' (11 per cent). Reasons offered by migrants in 2010 were 'to find a job or in quest of better job' (76 per cent), 'financial assistance to the family members in the place of origin' (23 per cent), 'to accompany the husband' (11 per cent), 'for higher study' (9.4 per cent), and 'river bank erosion' (4 per cent). Clearly, it shows the growing importance of economic pull and weakening of push factors such as unemployment in rural areas and loss of land due to river bank erosion.

CHANGES IN EMPLOYMENT RATE AND AGE OF WORKERS

As noted earlier, mostly adult male members participated in income-earning activities. In 1998, women constituted 21 per cent of the income-earning members. In 2010, the ratio further reduced to 17 per cent. Arguably, women's participation was largely poverty driven and they worked long hours in low-paying jobs to augment household incomes. With increase in household incomes, some women withdrew from the labour market and/or reduced their working hours, a manifestation of the backward-bending supply curve of labour.

The average age of a male workers has remained almost the same—39 years for both periods (1998 and 2010). However, the average age varies significantly across different occupations (Table 5.4). Occupations in which younger people were employed included industrial workers, drivers of mechanized vehicles such as buses, trucks and private cars, private services, and construction workers. These are also the fast-growing occupations, as noted earlier.

Increased Average Age of Male Workers in Both High- and Low-Paid Jobs

Age of the workers has increased substantially in manual labour–based occupations such as rickshaw or van driving (non-mechanized vehicles) and domestic helpers on the one hand, and professional jobs on the

Table 5.4 Average Age, Years of Schooling, and Income (at 2010 Prices) of Male Workers, 1998 and 2010

Occupation	Age (Year)		Schooling (Year)		Income per Month (Tk.)		Growth (Per Cent per Year)
	1998	2010	1998	2010	1998	2010	
Government Service	43	46	12	12	14,502	20.230	2.8
Private Services	32	36	7	11	6,148	16,844	8.4
Professional Job	41	46	15	15	28,154	43,487	3.6
Formal Business	40	41	11	11	45,550	44,135	−0.3
Informal Business	40	38	4	7	8,424	12,744	3.4
Industrial Worker	33	30	5	6	4,098	5,768	2.8
Construction Worker	36	33	3	4	6,158	7,082	1.2
Rickshaw/Van Puller	36	41	1	2	5,749	7,053	1.7
Car/Bus Driver	32	33	5	5	10,609	11,077	0.4
Domestic Helper	35	41	0	0	1,234	4,069	9.9
Rent Receiver	61	55	10	12	16,849	29,585	4.7
All Earners	39	38	8	9	18,552	25,296	2.6

Source: Authors' estimate from BRAC third-round urban poverty survey, 2010.

other at the top end. It indicates that the younger workers are moving out of these arduous jobs or are not attracted to these occupations, which is not surprising. However, what is a matter of concern is the high average age of male workers, particularly in the case of professional jobs that are well paid and critical for a country's prosperity. Presumably, many young doctors and engineers are migrating overseas for better income and opportunities for professional development. From the household-level out-migration data, we found that of the male members who migrated out of house more than two-thirds (68 per cent) went overseas mainly for better-paid jobs and higher studies in the year preceding the survey.[5] Therefore, it is important to create better opportunities for brain circulation and brain exchange to offset the effects arising out of brain drain with the migration of young professionals.[6]

Higher the Level of Education, Greater the Income

Average years of schooling for male earners has increased only marginally from eight to nine years. However, like age, there are significant variations in educational attainment across occupations. The average level of education has been highest for professionals such as engineers, doctors, lawyers, and teachers. The level of earnings for this group is also one of the highest, next to those running formal business, whose average level of education is lower than the former. It may not be incorrect to say that business owners earn more compared to other occupational groups due largely to entrepreneurship skills and investment of physical capital in business rather than human capital endowment per se.

Those who are employed in government or private services are also relatively better educated compared to other occupational groups. It should be noted that the level of schooling has increased substantially since 1998 for those who are employed in private services. With implementation of structural adjustment policies (SAP) since the late 1980s, private services such as banking, insurance, and real estate expanded rapidly, creating more employment opportunities for better educated workers.

Unlike their male counterparts, average years of schooling increased for female earners from six to eight years (Table 5.5). We have noted the highest improvement in education for women workers engaged in business and private services. After attaining higher level of education,

Table 5.5 Average Age, Years of Schooling, and Income (at 2010 Prices) of Female Workers, 1998 and 2010

Occupation	Age (Years)		Schooling (Years)		Income/ Month (Tk.)		Growth (Per Cent per Year)
	1998	2010	1998	2010	1998	2010	
Public Sector Service	40	44	12	15	11,882	21,929	5.1
Private Services	33	35	5	11	4,158	11,811	8.7
Professional Job	40	36	16	16	9,919	18,750	5.3
Formal Business	37	38	7	12	17,272	45,002	8.0
Informal Business	38	40	2	8	6,140	13,000	6.3
Industrial Worker	25	27	4	5	2,828	4,360	3.6
Construction Worker	28	25	0	2	1,730	2,583	3.3
Domestic Helper	35	41	0	0	923	1,723	5.3
Rent Receiver	42	42	7	7	14,125	33,000	7.1
All Earners (Number)	36	34	6	8	6,165	11,384	5.1

Source: Authors' estimate from BRAC third-round urban poverty survey, 2010.

women (those who want to participate in the labour market) have moved into these occupations. Renting out properties and business also yield highest level of earnings for women. It should be noted that these sectors also experienced highest growth in earnings.

Whether male or female, the level of education is very low for those working as industrial workers, in informal business, and for manual labour–based occupations such as domestic helpers, construction labourers, and transport workers. The least educated are employed in these occupations. These are also the lowest paid jobs in the market.

Highest Income Growth from Private Services, Rental Income from Properties, and Domestic Service

The highest growth in income accrued from services in the private sector, rental income from properties, and in domestic service. Increase in the earnings from the domestic service is surprising. It can be an outcome of the increase in real wages in the agricultural sector, generating greater opportunities for employment in low paid industrial jobs. Accordingly, the market for domestic services and other low-skilled jobs has been tightened. Also, the income from business has declined in real terms over 1998–2010 indicating greater competition in the market, with movement of capital and labour to urban areas and from the higher end of farm business in villages to invest in urban business respectively.

The rate of earnings in domestic service has also increased substantially for women engaged in such low-paid work that is often considered a 'vulnerable job' by the International Labour Organisation (ILO 2009: 48) as there is 'no social protection, basic rights or voice at work'. Arguably, availability of employment as RMG factory workers and construction labour provided women an opportunity to move out of low-paid jobs, creating shortage of workers in the market, which in turn has increased wage rates in those occupations.

Income Growth Is Higher for Female than Male and so Is Gender-Based Income Disparity

For female workers, the average growth in earnings has been 5.1 per cent per year, almost double that of male workers (2.6 per cent). However, it should be noted that on average women workers earned less than half (45 per cent) of what was earned by male workers and the gender-based income disparity increased over time (from 33 per cent in 1998).

INCOME, POVERTY, AND GROWTH: SOME METHODOLOGICAL ISSUES

Estimates on household income generated by asking questions on income and expenditure are often debated mainly due to quality issues. The non-sampling errors in such data can be significant despite supervising data collection process at a reasonable level. For example, surveys can miss out income from some informal household activities of members such as selling eggs, making paper bags, and sewing (can be both income generating and/or expenditure saving), particularly for slum households. Similarly, the respondents may not be able to recall the expenses incurred in running a business, particularly informal business which is one of the major economic activities in urban areas. Surveys can also miss out on income earned through corrupt practices such as rent seeking by misusing power that has grown over time and become a common practice in the public sector.

Collecting information on food and non-food expenses, and savings in different savings instruments (including fixed deposits) and acquisition of consumer durables and ornaments can be a better way of estimating incomes. However, information on savings and assets including gold jewellery can be 'sensitive', which respondents prefer to hide rather than share. Therefore, we chose not to collect information on consumption expenditures and savings. Accordingly, we had to depend on the information on duration of employment and average monthly income of household members for estimating income. This is supplemented by additional information on gross income and expenses incurred on business enterprises run by the household and the rent received from properties, including from land owned in rural areas and transfers such as remittances from family members or relatives.

There is another methodological issue that we addressed to ensure consistency and compatibility in the income data. This relates to the use of the proper deflator to convert estimates of current income at the time of survey in constant prices (real values) to estimate growth rates over the survey periods. To address this issue, we used the GDP deflator (GOB 2015a), which increased by 54.5 per cent during the 1991–8 period, 82.1 per cent during the 1998–2010 period, and 181.3 per cent during the 1990–2010 period. The deflators were used to convert household incomes at nominal prices estimated for the year of survey into constant 2010 prices. We then used average size of the households for each survey period to estimate per capita income at constant prices and then converted it into US dollars using the exchange rate for 2010.[7]

GROWTH OF INCOMES

In this process, we have estimated the average household incomes for Dhaka from the 1991 survey at Tk. 99,515—Tk. 32,348 for slum and Tk. 133,098 for non-slum households (Table 5.6). A slum household thus earned 24.3 per cent of the income earned by those from non-slum. However, income disparity between slum and non-slum becomes larger—28.1 per cent—in the case of per capita income. The average household size was 5.56 in 1991. Therefore, at nominal price, we have estimated per capita income at Tk. 17,898. The exchange rate at that time was Tk. 32.92 per US dollar and, hence, per capita income at the prevailing exchange rate was equivalent to US$ 544 in 2010. Also, using the GDP deflator that increased at a higher rate than the exchange rate and converting 1991 income at 2010 constant prices, we have estimated per capita income for Dhaka city at US$ 718 (Table 5.6).

From the 2010 survey data, we have estimated average household income for the residents of Dhaka city at Tk. 616,718. As indicated in Chapter 2, average household size became smaller—4.96—compared to 1991. Therefore, per capita income was Tk. 124,338 or US$ 1772 at the 2010 exchange rate. The income for slum household was estimated at Tk. 190,783 and per capita income at Tk. 43,459 (US$ 619), almost 23 per cent of the income of non-slum household and 27.6 per cent on a per capita basis. The income disparity remained substantially high between slum and non-slum households and hardly changed over the last 20 years (1991–2010).

Table 5.6 Level and Growth of Household and Per Capita Income for Slum and Non-slum (at Constant 2010 Prices), 1991 to 2010

	Slum	**Non-slum**	**Dhaka City**
Household Income (at 2010 in Tk.)			
1991	90,995	374,405	279,936
1998	106,190	558,757	407,902
2010	190,783	829,686	616,718
Per Capita Income (at 2010 in Tk.)			
1991	18,090	64,331	50,348
1998	22,169	99,423	76,386
2010	43,459	157,138	124,338
Per Capita Income (at 2010 in US$)			
1991	258	917	718
1998	316	1417	1,089
2010	619	2239	1,772
Growth Rate (Per Cent Per Year)			
1990–1998	2.9	6.2	6.0
1998–2010	5.6	3.8	4.1
1990–2010	4.5	4.8	4.7

Source: Authors' estimate from BRAC third-round urban poverty survey, 2010.

Higher Income Growth in Slum Reduced Slum–Non-slum Income Inequality

Table 5.6 shows that the average growth rate of per capita income in US dollar terms was 4.7 per cent per year between 1991 and 2010, marginally lower for slum households (4.5 per cent) compared with those for non-slum (4.8 per cent). However, between the first and second rounds of survey (1991 and 1998), the growth rate for non-slum doubled in comparison to slum households. It contributed to an increased inequality in the income distribution during this period. In contrast, during 1998–2010, the growth rate reversed, which reduced income inequality to some extent.

The main factor behind the slowdown of income was the sluggish growth of incomes from business due to greater competition and from public services as salaries were not adequately adjusted with the rate of inflation. On the other hand, the income from manual labour such as rickshaw and van driving, domestic service, and construction labour increased at a faster rate due to the rapid increase in rural wages over the last decade. To attract manual workers from rural areas, employers had to offer higher wages in industrial enterprises for such labour. A larger proportion of slum dwellers also found higher employment opportunity in informal trade and retail stores in markets and road side that required small amount of capital.

SOURCES OF INCOME

To study changes in the sources of household incomes, we classified occupations of earning members into five groups based on the resource base of the households. The first group includes households that depend on manual labour for livelihoods, such as domestic helpers, construction labourers, and rickshaw and van drivers. These occupations require low-level skills that could be acquired through apprenticeships with little education and/or physical capital. The second category includes occupations that require some education, such as workers employed in the garment and other industries and the services sector. The third category includes all kinds of services that require investment in education. In other words, it includes officers and employees in the government and/or private services, private business, and the self-employed professionals who acquired technical and/or tertiary qualification such as engineers, doctors, lawyers, and university teachers. All types of trade, business, and industrial enterprises are included in the fourth category. This group requires investment of financial resources as well as at least high school or tertiary-level education and personal aptitude to become an entrepreneur. The fifth category includes households that depend on the rents from property such as land or houses and/or remittances sent by members working abroad. This group has made prior investments in property and education or training of members for acquisition of skills that could be marketed abroad.

Trade and Business, and Manual Labour–Based Occupations: The Highest and Lowest Contributor to Household Income

Changes in the sources of income and their contribution to household income can be viewed in Table 5.7. In 2010, nearly half (46.7 per cent) of the household income generated from trade or business, one-quarter (25.9 per cent) from services, and another one-fifth (20.5 per cent) from property and remittances. Manual labour–based occupations accounted for only 7 per cent of the total income, although it comprised nearly 20 per cent of the labour force. It shows great disparity in the earnings of the illiterate or semi-literate labour force compared to those who have

Table 5.7 Changes in the Share (Per Cent) of Different Sources of Household Income for Slum and Non-slum, 1991, 1998, and 2010

Sources	Slum			Non-slum			Dhaka City		
Year	1991	1998	2010	1991	1998	2010	1991	1998	2010
Services	12.9	6.8	18.5	47.7	30.4	26.8	42.3	24.0	25.9
Business	24.4	33.3	34.5	38.6	54.3	48.3	38.6	54.3	46.7
Wages/ Industry	12.2	12.7	13.1	2.7	2.1	2.7	3.2	2.1	2.6
Wage Labour	47.4	44.3	28.1	nil	nil	nil	5.3	6.4	4.3
Rent/ Remittances	3.1	2.8	5.8	11.0	13.2	22.2	10.6	13.2	20.5
Total	100	100	100	100	100	100	100	100	100

Source: Authors' estimate from BRAC third-round urban poverty survey, 2010.

invested in education or accumulated physical capital through savings and investment.

There has been an erosion in income from services throughout the period, with its contribution declining from over two-fifths (42.3 per cent) to one-quarter (25.9 per cent) between 1991 and 2010, while that from manual labour remained stagnant at around 3 per cent. In contrast, the income from the rent and transfers almost doubled (from 10.6 per cent to 20.5 per cent). Note that the annual growth in income was highest for the property owners (22 per cent) and lowest (5.3 per cent) for those engaged in services.

Clearly, the contribution of income from manual labour and rent and transfers have created notable slum and non-slum differentials. For example, in 2010 slum households derived 28 per cent of the income from manual labour and another 13 per cent of the income was earned by the workers employed in manufacturing and other industries. The corresponding figures for non-slum households were 0 and 2.7 per cent respectively. In contrast, while the share of income from rent and transfers was 22.2 per cent for non-slum households, it was only 5.8 or lowest for slum dwellers, compared to other sources.

However, one-third of the income for slum households originated from business, mostly from informal business (self-employment with small amount of capital), and almost one-fifth from services. The contributions from both these sources have increased since 1991. Note that these two were also the major sources of income for non-slum households. However, since 1991, while the contribution of the services sector has declined significantly by 20 per cent, that from business increased by 10 per cent.

DETERMINANTS OF INCOME AND INCOME INEQUALITY

To determine the relative contributions of different factors to the changes in household income, we constructed a multivariate regression model using the household level data. We assumed that the income earning capacity of a household depends on the number of earning members, investment in education (measured by the number of years of schooling of the employed member), and cumulative investment made in fixed assets necessary to the formation of physical capital. We have differentiated physical capital, which mainly connotes ownership of the accumulated property such as land and housing, from capital formation that results from investment in industry, trade, and other business. While the last category of capital depreciates in value over time, the first two categories are subjected to capital gains if the price of property and land increases over time.

Other factors considered in the model are gender of the household head (a dummy variable with value '1' for female-headed households), residence of the household (a dummy variable with value '1' for slum dwellers), and another dummy variable with value '1' representing the households receiving remittances from family members and/or relatives working abroad. We also included a location dummy to account for the random fixed effects. A generalized least square (GLS) model was applied using the household serial number as weights. The regression was estimated using the 'robust' estimator of the statistical package, Stata.[8] The estimated parameters and results are reported in Table 5.8.

Return from Education Much Lower for Female Than for Male Workers

From the model's estimation (Table 5.8), we can say that more than 70 per cent of the variations in household incomes across the sample is explained by the variables included in the model. The value of regression coefficients shows that a male worker in 2010 contributes at the margin Tk. 98,707 per year to the household income, which reduces to Tk. 58,019 for a female earner. Clearly, there is a considerable gender disparity in the earnings of the household members, with female workers receiving 41 per cent less income compared to male workers. Assuming a six-day working week as the duration of employment, the daily earnings of the workers is estimated at Tk. 316 (US$ 4.44) for male workers and Tk. 186 (US$ 2.61) for female workers. For each year of education, a male worker earns an additional Tk. 27,000 compared to only Tk. 1,455 for a female worker.

However, the value of this coefficient is statistically insignificant. Nonetheless, the low return on education for female workers contributes to the low participation of women in the labour market, which we have discussed earlier. Subsequently, it may not be wrong to assume

Table 5.8 Determinants of Income: Estimates of Regression Coefficient, 1998 and 2010

Explanatory Variables	1998 Survey			2010 Survey		
	Regression Coefficient	T-Value	Level of Significance	Regression Coefficient	T-Value	Level of Significance
Property	0.032	4.38	0.000	0.021	2.14	0.033
Business Capital	0.189	6.36	0.000	0.142	2.68	0.008
Male Worker	60,732	3.86	0.000	98,707	4.74	0.000
Female Worker	20,416	−0.56	0.578	58,019	1.30	0.193
Education of Head	8,661	2.65	0.008	27,303	4.36	0.000
Education of Spouse	73	0.04	0.965	1,455	0.23	0.816
Female Head	−28,608	−0.64	0.525	−46,344	− 0.74	0.460
Remittances/Income Transfer	299,684	2.58	0.010	253,130	2.15	0.032
Dummy Slum	−77,682	−3.22	0.001	−173,215	−4.06	0.000
R-Square	0.71			0.78		

Source: Authors' estimate from BRAC third-round urban poverty survey, 2010.

that many educated women prefer to be housewives to provide better care for their children rather than directly participating in income generating activities.

The rate of return from accumulation of property is estimated at only 2.1 per cent per year and has declined from 3.2 per cent estimated from the 1998 survey data. It reflects appreciation of the value of property over time. The return on physical capital is estimated at 14.2 per cent in 2010, which is lower than 18.9 per cent estimated for 1998. It indicates that over time competition in this type of investment has increased with more entrepreneurs migrating and capital being transferred from rural to urban areas.

With other resource endowments remaining constant, a female-headed household earned Tk. 46,344 (7.8 per cent) less income than a male-headed household in 2010. The coefficient is, however, statistically insignificant. A slum household earned about Tk. 173,215 (22 per cent) less than that of a non-slum. The slum–non-slum income disparity has not changed much since 1998 (when the difference was 23 per cent). For both years, the value of the coefficient was statistically significant.

With a member working overseas and sending remittances, a household's income increased to nearly Tk. 253,000. The real value of income earned from remittances was, however, lower compared to that of 1998. However, it should be noted that only a few of the households in Dhaka city (almost one-tenth) had a member working overseas and sending remittances. In contrast, the incidence of overseas migration occurred in 9 out of every 10 rural households (Romano and Traverso 2016; Hossain and Bayes 2009).

Inequality and Poverty

To examine changes in the degree of income inequality, we have first ranked the sample households on the scale of per capita income as a measure of economic standing of the household and then estimated income shares of different groups. Our estimates from the 1998 survey (Table 5.9) show highly skewed distribution of urban incomes. The bottom 25 per cent of households owned only 5 per cent of the total income, and the bottom 50 per cent only 15 per cent. At the other end of income scale, the top 10 per cent of households owned 42 per cent of income, while the top 25 per cent owned 67 per cent. The Gini ratio for concentration of per capita income was estimated at 0.51 for the sample households, which is considered extremely high compared with the concentration of rural income (Hossain and Bayes 2015).

Moderation in Income Distribution between 1998 and 2010

It should be noted that between 1991 and 1998, there was a drastic deterioration in the distribution of urban incomes (Table 5.9). Share of income for the bottom 50 per cent declined from 25 per cent to 16 per cent during this period. In contrast, the share of the top 10 per cent of households increased from 28 per cent to 42 per cent, while the top 25 per cent experienced a 20 per cent increase (from 47 per cent to 67 per cent) during 1998. Subsequently, the Gini income index increased from 0.37 to 0.51.

However, with the Gini income index estimated at 0.48 in 2010, we observed some moderation in income distribution between 1998 and 2010, although the level of income disparity remained at a high level (Table 5.9). Accordingly, there has been an increase in the share of income by middle 40 per cent (from 30.8 per cent to 33.1 per cent). In contrast, share of income for the top 10 per cent of households has declined from (41.9 per cent to 37.8 per cent).

To estimate contributions of different sources of income to inequality in income distribution at the household level, we conducted a Gini

Table 5.9 Changes in the Distribution of Income (Per Cent Share of Household Income), 1991–2010

Rank of the Household in Per Capita Income Scale	1991 Survey	1998 Survey	2010 Survey
Bottom 40 Per Cent	17.0	11.3	12.6
Middle 40 Per Cent	39.5	30.8	33.1
Ninth Decile	16.0	16.3	16.4
Top 10 Per Cent	27.5	41.9	37.8
Top Five Per Cent	17.2	30.6	25.5
Concentration Coefficient (Pseudo-Gini)	0.37	0.51	0.48

Source: Authors' estimate from BRAC third-round urban poverty survey, 2010.

decomposition analysis. Accordingly, we have estimated the concentration coefficient of income by ranking households on a per capita scale, not by sources of income as indicated earlier. Therefore, with the help of the 'pseudo-Gini coefficient', we have estimated the concentration coefficient of different sources of income. By multiplying the share of income from each of the sources to the estimated pseudo-Gini coefficient, we estimated the share of that source to the concentration pseudo-Gini coefficient in the total household income. The results of the analysis are presented in Table 5.10.

Note that the pseudo-Gini coefficient is negative for incomes from manual labour and industrial labour indicating that the incomes from these sources are distributed in favour of the low-income households. The highest inequality in distribution of income are contributed by incomes from property and business, with the value of concentration coefficient exceeding 0.60. The degree of inequality from these sources of income has not changed much since 1998. On the other hand, the concentration ratio of income from services has declined from 0.51 in 1998 to 0.40 in 2010. This suggests a better distribution of income from services, and its benefits are transferred from high to middle and low-income households. Investment in education is thus an equalizing factor in income disparity, given that education of those employed in this sector is higher compared with other sectors, as discussed earlier (Tables 5.4 and 5.5).

Table 5.10 Contribution of Different Sources of Income to Income Inequality, 1998 and 2010

Sources of Income	Share (%) of Household Income		Concentration Ratio (Pseudo Gini)		Contribution of the Source to Pseudo Gini	
	1998	2010	1998	2010	1998	2010
Manual Labour	6.4	4.3	−0.21	−0.42	−0.015	−0.018
Industrial Labour	2.1	2.6	−0.33	−0.26	−0.007	−0.007
Services	24.0	25.9	0.51	0.40	0.122	0.104
Business	54.3	46.7	0.60	0.58	0.325	0.271
Rent/Transfer	13.2	20.5	0.64	0.63	0.084	0.130
Total	100	100	0.51	0.48	0.51	0.48

Source: Authors' estimate from BRAC third-round urban poverty survey, 2010.

Households' Income from Services and Trade and Business Moderates Income Inequality but Worsens if Derived from Property

Based on the Gini decomposition analysis (Table 5.10), we estimated that in 2010 trade and business contributed to nearly 56 per cent of the income inequality index, followed by 27 per cent and 22 per cent from property and services respectively. It should also be noted that incomes accrued to households from services and trade and business contributed to moderation of income inequality in 2010 compared to 1998, while that from property further worsened income inequality.

Higher Concentration of Physical Capital in Fewer Hands: The Main Factor behind Income Inequality

The main factor behind acute inequality in urban incomes is the high concentration in resource base, particularly in terms of physical capital (Table 5.11). In 1998, the bottom 40 per cent in the per capita income scale controlled only 7 per cent of the total value of fixed assets, which increased almost five fold (30.7 per cent) for the top 5 per cent. The value of Gini concentration ratio for the ownership of capital was estimated at 0.57 and 0.61 in 1998 and 2010 respectively. Clearly, the

Table 5.11 Changes in the Concentration of Education and Physical Capital

Per Capita Income Scale	Schooling of Earners		Investment on Education		Value of Fixed Assets		Investment in the Year	
	1998	2010	1998	2010	1998	2010	1998	2010
Bottom 40%	21.4	25.5	15.1	14.3	6.9	6.1	2.2	2.0
Middle 40%	49.1	45.8	41.4	46.5	35.4	32.0	18.0	12.1
Ninth Decile	12.6	13.2	16.5	18.5	18.2	14.6	14.4	46.3
Top 10%	16.9	15.5	24.0	20.7	39.5	47.3	65.4	39.7
Top 5%	7.5	8.1	13.8	12.8	30.7	38.5	55.0	13.8
Concentration Coefficient	0.23	0.19	0.39	0.36	0.57	0.61	0.79	0.74

Source: Authors' estimate from BRAC third-round urban poverty survey, 2010.

ownership of capital is becoming further skewed indicating even more inequality, mainly an outcome of increasing control by the top 10 per cent (from 39.5 per cent to 47.3 per cent) and top 5 per cent (from 30.7 per cent to 38.5 per cent), while share in the value of fixed assets declined for the bottom 40 per cent (from 6.9 per cent to 6.1 per cent).

The share of the top 5 per cent of households in investments on assets made in 1998 was 55 per cent, while the bottom 40 per cent had a meagre share of 2 per cent, and the middle 40 per cent had only 18 per cent. The value of the Gini investment index is staggeringly high—0.79. Note that in 2010, there was a secular decline in the share of investments for almost all income groups. Despite that, the value of the concentration coefficient only comes down moderately to 0.74, which can be attributed mainly to the massive increase in the share for ninth decile (from 14.4 per cent to 46.3 per cent).

Investment in Education Has the Greatest Potential to Reduce Income Inequality

With the concentration ratio estimated at 0.23 for schooling of earners in 1998, which had declined further to 0.19 in 2010, we can say that the human capital is less unequally distributed than the ownership of physical capital. However, the inequality has been growing, as shown by the higher concentration ratio for the current investment in the education of children (0.39 and 0.36 respectively), in comparison to the concentration ratio that is estimated for investment on schooling of the working members. Unless positive action is taken to reverse the situation by providing better access to capital and education for lower income groups, income equality is likely to worsen further.

DETERMINANTS AND INCIDENCE OF INCOME POVERTY

The scarcity of income to satisfy basic needs is the most widely used measure of poverty, often called income poverty. Increasingly, however, academic discourse points to the limitations of the measurement of income poverty and highlights the importance of measuring non-income dimensions of poverty (UNDP 2012). We have presented access, equity, and quality issues involved in some of these non-income dimensions of poverty such as health, education, and basic services in the next two chapters (6 and 7) of this book. In this chapter, we have focused on the measure of income poverty and the changes over time in this indicator.

Income poverty is determined in reference to a 'poverty line' that estimates the minimum income necessary to live a decent life, and then estimating from income distribution data the proportion of households living below this poverty line (Foster and Thorbek 1984; Ravallion and Sen 1996). This process is referred to as the 'head-count' measure of poverty (incidence of poverty). The other measures of income poverty are the poverty gap index (intensity of poverty) and the squared poverty-gap index (severity of poverty). In this section, we will mainly focus on the head-count index given that it is well understood by general readers.

The poverty line is estimated by taking a normative food basket with minimum requirement of different food items needed to have a balance diet to live a healthy life. For Bangladesh, a normative food basket is provided by the Food and Agriculture Organization (FAO) considering the age–sex distribution of the population and their activity levels (Hossain and Sen 1992; Khan 1976; Muqtada 1986). The basket allows a total of 842 grams of food per person per day that would provide 2,120 calories to an adult equivalent person.

Poverty Line Estimates for Dhaka City

For estimating the poverty line, we have valued the price of each item of food as per its retail price in Dhaka city in the reference year of survey. This estimate provides the income needed to consume a normative food basket. However, keeping in mind the importance of non-food expenditure to meet other necessities—housing, clothing, education, and healthcare, we provide allowances for these items also. Estimates from the 2010 HIES survey data (BBS 2011a) show that urban households at the margin of poverty spend about 40 per cent of their total expenditure on non-food necessities. This provision is added with the food expenditure to estimate the poverty line.

Another concept that gained popularity in the contemporary development discourse is the term 'extreme poor' or '*hata daridra*' in Bengali.[9] In simplest terms, these are households that cannot even meet the minimal daily requirement of 1,800 calories for each member from their incomes. To measure extreme poverty, we have adjusted the normative food basket with full provision for cereals (rice and flour) and vegetables, half (50 per cent) provision for pulses, oils, vegetables, sugar, and spices, and no provision for fish and animal products. This adjusted basket would provide 1,800 calories to a person per day. The food basket is valued as per the retail prices of food items in Dhaka city to derive an estimate of income that can buy 1,800 calories of food. We also added another 40 per cent to cover expenses of other non-food necessities mentioned earlier.

In this way, we estimated the amount of income needed to access the normative food basket for an average Bangladeshi to maintain a healthy and productive life at Tk. 49.57 per day at the prevailing market prices in Dhaka city in 2010 (Table 5.12). The poverty line expenditure after adjusting for the cost of other basic needs is estimated at Tk. 82.61 (US$ 1.16) per person per day, which is equivalent to Tk. 30,104 (US$ 423) per person per year. A household with a per capita income below this level is termed as poor. The poverty line for extreme poverty is estimated at Tk. 42.60 (US$ 0.60) per person per day or Tk. 15,549 (US$ 218) per year.

Table 5.12 Estimates of Poverty Line, Moderate and Extreme Poverty, 1991–2010

Indicators	Moderate Plus Extreme Poverty			Extreme Poverty		
	1991	**1998**	**2010**	**1991**	**1998**	**2010**
Expenditure on Food (Tk. per Person per Day)	14.66	18.68	49.57	10.43	13.29	25,56
Expenditure on Other basic needs (Tk. per Person per Day)	24.43	31.13	82.61	17.38	22.15	42.60
Poverty Line Income (Tk. per Person per annum)	8,920	11,360	30,104	6,344	8,056	15,549
Poverty Line (US$ per Person per annum)	271	250	423	192	177	218

Note: Estimated by costing a normative food basket containing 2,112 and 1,850 calories respectively.

Source: Authors' estimates based on the second-round (BIDS) and third-round (BRAC) survey data, 1998 and 2010.

Faster Increase in Cost of Living for the Extreme Poor

Compared with the poverty line estimates for 1998, the cost of living for the poor households had increased by around 8.1 per cent per year, higher than the rate of inflation (5 per cent) during 1998–2010. For the extreme poor, the cost of living has increased by 5.5 per cent per year. It can be argued that faster increase in the cost of living for poor households caused mainly by rapid increase in cereal prices after the food crisis in 2007–08, as they spend a higher proportion of income on food compared with that of non-poor. Also, due to supply of pulses and animal products not keeping pace with the growth in demand, there was a huge increase in the prices of these products, which has influenced the cost of living for poor.

Notable Decline in the Incidence of Moderate and Extreme Poverty Over Time

The head count index for households with income levels below the poverty line shows that in 1991, 42 per cent of the population in Dhaka city was poor—the incidence more than doubled (87 per cent) for slum households but halved for (27 per cent) non-slum (Table 5.13). The HCR had declined substantially by 2010 with the proportion of poor declining to 20 per cent in Dhaka city—37 per cent for slum dwellers and only 3 per cent for non-slum. There is also a marked improvement in the incidence of extreme poverty. It has declined from 27 per cent in 1991 to only 3 per cent in 2010.

For slum dwellers, the rate of decline has been very impressive, from 69 per cent in 1991 to 28 per cent by 1998 and further to only 7 per cent in 2010. Our findings are consistent with the poverty estimates of BBS (2011a) for urban areas. According to BBS, the incidence of poverty for urban areas had declined from 43 per cent in 1991–92 to 35 per cent in 2000 and further to 21 per cent in 2010. The incidence of extreme poverty had declined from 44 per cent in 1991–92 to 38 per cent in 2000 and further to 7.7 per cent in 2010. Except for extreme poverty, these figures are similar to our estimates (Table 5.13). Arguably, the incidence of extreme poverty is higher in other cities of Bangladesh compared with what we estimated for Dhaka.

Table 5.13 Changes in Incidence, Intensity, and Severity of Poverty, 1991–2010

Poverty Indicators	Slum Residents			Non-slum Residents			Dhaka City		
Head Count Index (%)	**1991**	**1998**	**2010**	**1991**	**1998**	**2010**	**1991**	**1998**	**2010**
Moderate and Extreme Poverty	87.3	51.3	34.5	25.7	4.3	3.0	41.7	29.7	20.0
Extreme Poverty	68.8	29.4	7.5	6.7	2.0	nil	27.4	11.1	2.5
Poverty-Gap Index (%)	28.9	21.0	10.1	4.2	1.5	0.9	11.2	7.8	4.1
Squared Poverty-Gap Index (%)	12.7	13.9	3.4	1.5	0.8	0.2	4.7	4.2	1.3

Source: Estimated by applying the poverty line on the data for income distribution for the surveys.

Faster Income Growth from Manual Labour–Based Occupations Improved Severity of Poverty

It should be noted that the index for the severity of poverty increased marginally during 1991–8. It is an outcome of the drastic increase in income inequality noted earlier. During this period, growth in income was substantially lower for slum dwellers compared to non-slum households and inequality in the distribution of business sector income was also very high. However, the trend had reversed during the 1998–2010 period, in which income of slum households grew faster compared with that of non-slum. Similarly, the earnings from lower paid jobs requiring manual labour also increased at a faster rate compared to other occupations. As a result, severity of poverty improved considerably with households at the lower end of the income scale benefitting much from the growing economic prosperity in recent years.

Congruence between Quantitative and Qualitative Measures of Poverty

We have also documented perceptions of the respondents regarding their economic standing, changes in economic conditions, and the drivers of change (Table 5.14). In recent years, such perceptions often carry greater weight in poverty discourse than the objective estimates from survey data because it can be of dubious quality, and the analytical method can also be debated. The findings are reported in Table 5.14 which show that over one-tenth (14 per cent) of households perceived themselves as poor, including 2 per cent who considered themselves as extremely poor. These figures are similar to the results of our objective estimates reported in Table 5.13. However, a large proportion of households considered themselves as non-poor, although they are at the brink of poverty. These households are vulnerable to external shocks such as natural disasters and loss of employment and earnings from the downturn of economic growth. Thus, for a large proportion of households, there is a high risk of moving into poverty due to economic instability.

Economic Conditions Improved for the Majority, but Economic Instability Increased

In the 1998 and 2010 surveys, we also sought the opinion of respondents regarding changes in their economic conditions over the past decade

Table 5.14 Self-perception of Respondents Regarding Their Economic Status, 2010 (Per Cent of Cases)

Economic Status	Slum Households	Non-slum Households	Dhaka City
Affluent	10.5	66.8	48.0
Non-poor but at the Brink of Poverty	50.0	32.5	38.3
Moderate Poverty	34.0	0.7	11.7
Extreme Poverty	5.5	nil	2.0

Source: Authors' estimate from BRAC third-round urban poverty survey, 2010.

Table 5.15 Perceived Changes in Economic Conditions over the Last 10 Years by Respondents (Per Cent of Cases)

Changes	1998 Survey			2010 Survey		
Residence	Slum	Non-slum	Dhaka City	Slum	Non-slum	Dhaka City
Improved a Lot	3	3	3	nil	8	6
Improved Marginally	58	53	55	51	65	60
Unchanged	19	24	23	11	7	8
Deteriorated Marginally	18	20	18	33	19	24
Deteriorated a Lot	2	nil	1	6	1	2
Total	100	100	100	100	100	100

Source: Authors' estimates based on the second-round (BIDS) and third-round (BRAC) survey data, 1998 and 2010.

(Table 5.15). Almost 66 per cent of the households in the 2010 survey reported improvement in economic conditions and 26 per cent reported deterioration. The net change is thus about 40 per cent. The situation is almost similar to what respondents reported in the 1998 survey, when 58 per cent of the households reported improvement in economic conditions, 23 per cent said it remained unchanged, and 19 per cent reported deterioration. The net change was 39 per cent. However, a larger proportion of households in 1998 reported their conditions as stable (23 per cent) compared to those who reported so in 2010 (8 per cent), indicating greater economic instability in the recent period compared with the 1990s.

From the systematic analysis of the poverty situation over time, we found that poverty has declined significantly and income distribution has improved compared with the 1990s. However, the gap between the rich and poor and the men and women persists largely arising from concentration of resource base, particularly ownership of capital becoming more and more skewed. The hope lies with investment in education as income inequality declines with schooling of earners. This brings us to the analysis of quality of life and sustainability matters presented in the next two chapters. Our emphasis is to focus on whether the material gains help in improving migrants' living conditions and human capital development, necessary for a healthy and productive life, and key to sustained development.

NOTES

1. The basic assumption is that a child labourer is a working child who would be better off not working, as it deprives him of his childhood, education, leisure, and his basic human rights as a child.

2. A significant proportion of parents from slum households considered this a reason when we explored their attitudes toward women's education, which we have analysed in Chapter 8.

3. In Chapter 3, we have discussed this declining trend in women's employment in greater details. Note that there is a slight difference in the women's participation rate because in that chapter we defined active age population as those aged between 15 and 64 years to keep consistency with other datasets such as BBS, World Bank, and global literature.

4. Note that Chapter 4 provides a detailed account of occupational changes of migrant heads of households at different stages of migration—before and immediately after migration and at the time of survey. To complete the story, here we have considered the most recent migrants.

5. In contrast, most female members migrated for marriage and/or to accompany their husband or parents while only one-tenth migrated for higher studies or employment-related reasons. The numbers of adult male and female members who out-migrated were 75 and 84, respectively.

6. Brain-circulation describes career paths in which students or workers go abroad to specialize and then return to their country of origin, drawing on the experience they have amassed to secure more advantageous employment conditions. Policies that promote circulation through active diaspora, high-skilled labour and student exchanges, and incentives for retention and return of skilled labour force are considered effective. Refer to Wickramasekara (2002; 2015) and/or Smith (2006) or Robertson (2006) for a good review of relevant policies.

7. As indicated earlier, in 2010, one US dollar was equivalent to Tk. 70.17.

8. Stata is a statistical software package created in 1985 by StataCorp. It is mostly used in research, especially in the fields of economics, sociology, political science, biomedicine, and epidemiology for data management, statistical analysis, graphics, simulations, regression analysis, and custom programming.

9. See, for example, Hulme and Green (2005); BRAC (2004); Sen and Hulme (2006); Ali et al. (2006); and Kabeer (2009).

6 Quality of Life

Shared Modes of Basic Services and Sustainable Development Goals

Access to basic services and supportive infrastructure such as safe water, sanitation, solid waste management, electricity, and housing is essential for health, security, livelihood, and quality of life. Achievement of human development targets relies on these services. For example, access to safe drinking water and sanitation prevents infectious diseases and access to electricity improves health, education, and productivity. It is also argued that with the provision for dependable and reasonably priced basic utilities, urban poverty can be reduced substantially and can lead to achievement of the MDGs (Calderon and Serven 2004). What Calderon and Serven argued in 2004 still applies to SDGs, particularly Goal 11 that calls to make cities inclusive, safe, resilient, and sustainable with the end of the MDG era in 2016.

QUALITY OF LIFE AND SUSTAINABILITY MATTERS

According to the Human Development Report (UNDP 2015), deprivation in the living standards contributed to around half (47.5 per cent) of the overall poverty of Bangladesh in 2007.[1] It indicates that basic services that are essential for a decent standard of living are often unequally distributed across space and among different categories of inhabitants such as poor and non-poor, and men and women. With growing urbanization and migration, cities house an increasing proportion of poor residents. In the last three decades, growth in urban population has been triple of that of rural areas in developing countries (UNDP 2015).

Since 2007, for the first time in history, more people have been living in urban than in rural areas worldwide. However, the housing, water, sanitation, and hygiene infrastructure of many cities have not kept pace with rapid and unplanned urbanization. As a result, urban poor face enormous challenges in their daily lives as they often live in slums and squatter settlements characterized by overcrowding, inadequate basic service, and lack of supportive infrastructure (UN-Habitat 2003).

From the first two rounds of the survey, we found that poor migrants did not have much difficulty in securing a job or better job and improving incomes faster in Dhaka, compared to what they and their families or friends earned in rural areas. The third-round survey reconfirms this finding as we observed in Chapter 5, in which we examined growth and the determinants of income and analysed changes in household income and income distribution patterns for Dhaka city. However, what is important to consider is whether the material improvements help improve the living conditions and human capital development necessary for a healthy and productive life, and are key to sustained development, which we have also raised as the compelling questions in the introductory chapter. We have addressed this question by examining respondents' access to the basic amenities such as improved housing, safe drinking water and sanitation, electricity connections, and piped gas from supply side. More importantly, we highlighted the quality and equity issues, central to meet SDG, and identified types of changes that occurred over a period of 20 years along with the underlying causes.

HOUSING

Housing is one of the basic social conditions that determines the quality of life, welfare of people, and standard of living. According to the UN-Habitat (2012), the location, durability, and resilience of homes, economic activities in housing, and their links with the environmental, social, cultural and economic fabric of communities are factors that influence the daily lives of people, their health, security, prosperity, and well-being, which are necessary for sustainable development. To make cities more inclusive, safe, resilient, prosperous, and sustainable (Goal 11), it is indispensable to improve the living conditions in slums and 'to guarantee the full recognition of the urban poor as rightful citizens, to realize their potential and to enhance their prospects for future development gains' (UN-Habitat 2016: 72).

Research shows that residents from neighbourhoods of concentrated poverty lack the necessary support, services, and opportunities to reach their full potential. Generally, the living condition of Dhaka's residents is appalling as is the case in many other cities in the South Asian region. Against the backdrop of one of the highest growths of urban population (at 3 per cent annually between 1980 and 2011) and the concentration of the densest cities of the world (15 out of top 30) (Demographia 2018), South Asian cities are challenged with stark poverty and inequality. These challenges are manifest in inadequate housing and slum proliferation and increased burden on existing public infrastructure such as electricity, transportation, and water and sanitation facilities (MHHDC 2014).[2]

In 2014, 881 million urban residents, comprising 28 per cent of urban population in the developing world, lived in slum and squatter settlements, which varied greatly by cities and towns (UN-Habitat 2016). Although over time the proportion of slum population declined to half from over 55 per cent to 28 per cent between 1990 and 2014, the absolute number of slum dwellers continues to increase (from 689 million in 1990). It is widely acknowledged that 'slums are the products of failed policies, poor governance, corruption, inappropriate regulation, dysfunctional land markets, unresponsive financial systems, and a lack of political will' (UN-Habitat 2016: 72). Dhaka is one of the fastest growing (3.6 per cent per year since 2000) and among the top most densely populated cities in the world with nearly 43,500 people per square km in metropolitan areas, and faces acute housing shortage, particularly for urban poor population. Accordingly, slums account for 40 per cent of urban population, higher than the South Asian average. According to a BBS census of slum and squatter settlements, there were 25 per cent slums in DCC area compared to 52.8 per cent in 1997 (BBS 2015).[3] Unplanned urban growth, poor quality housing, high cost of living, inadequate basic services, recurring social and political conflicts, high level of vulnerability to natural disasters, poor infrastructure, and unbearable traffic jams influence Dhaka's liveability prospect considerably.[4]

Despite such adversities, Bangladesh has made remarkable progress in meeting several targets of the MDGs such as increasing enrolment at primary schools, lowering the infant mortality rate and maternal mortality ratio, improving immunization coverage, and reducing the incidence of communicable diseases (GOB 2015c). From that perspective, it is important to explore whether quality of life, particularly poor migrants' housing quality and access to basic utilities, improved over time. One of the targets of Goal 11 that calls for 'making city and human settlements inclusive, safe, resilient and sustainable' is to ensure access for all to adequate, safe, and affordable housing and basic services and upgrade slums by 2030 (UN-Habitat 2016).

Rapid Transformation in Housing Quality: *Kutcha* to *Pucca*

Our data shows that housing structure and per capita space availability, particularly for poor migrants, has improved over time. In contrast, the better-off sections of urban residents lost the luxury of large living space with massive and rapid spread of vertical high-rise buildings in the city. Households in slum can no longer be identified by thatched or bamboo structured kutcha (non-permanent) housing, as already discussed earlier in the methodological approach (Chapter1). This is because the bulk of slum dwellers now live in pucca or permanent types of buildings with CI sheet roof and concrete wall and floor (65.5 per cent) or in concrete buildings (16 per cent), and only a fraction (1.3 per cent) in kutcha structures made of CI sheet roof, bamboo wall, and mud floor (Table 6.1). Transformation of the housing condition of slum dwellers is also evident from the Bangladesh Urban Health Survey 2013 (NIPORT, Mitra and Associates, and ICF International 2013).

In stark contrast with 1998 and 1991, when the kutcha structure was the predominant mode of housing for slum dwellers as a small proportion lived in permanent type buildings (17.2 per cent and 13.0 per cent, respectively), it shows a marked improvement in housing quality. While members of non-slum households lived mainly in permanent-type housing, in 2010 concrete buildings became the dominant mode of housing for them (89.3 per cent). This is an important shift compared with 1998 and 1991, when significant proportions (34 per cent and 24

Table 6.1 Distribution of the Sample Households by Slum and Non-slum, and Migratory Status and Housing Structure, 1991–2010

Household	Cement Roof/ Wall/ Floor	C.I. Sheet Roof and Cement Wall/Floor	C.I. Sheet Roof and Wall/Cement Floor	C.I. Sheet Roof and Bamboo Wall/ Mud Floor	Bamboo Roof and Wall/Mud Floor	Others	All Types (#)
2010							
Non-slum	89.3	10.3	0.5	0.0	0.0	0.0	400
Slum	15.0	65.0	7.0	1.5	0.0	11.5	200
All	64.5	28.5	2.7	0.5	0.0	3.8	600
Migrant	62.7	30.2	2.7	0.5	0.0	3.9	440
Non-migrant	69.4	23.8	2.5	0.6	0.0	3.8	160
1998							
Non-slum	65.5	34.0	0.5	0.0	0.0	0.0	404
Slum	3.2	6.5	7.5	61.8	5.4	20.4	196
All	34.0	20.5	4.0	31.5	2.5	7.5	600
Migrant	31.2	18.8	4.9	34.3	3.0	7.9	429
Non-migrant	47.9	28.2	0.0	18.3	0.0	5.7	171

1991							
Non-slum	71.0	24.0	5.0	0.0	0.0	0.0	400
Slum	1.0	12.0	–	41.0	36.0	10.0	200
All	48.0	20.0	1.0	15.0	12.0	4.0	600
Migrant	45.0	19.0	–	17.0	15.0	4.0	484
Non-migrant	58.0	24.0	–	10.0	3.0	5.0	116

Source: Afsar 1999; Authors' estimates from BRAC third-round urban poverty survey data, 2010.

per cent, respectively) of them used to live in houses made of CI sheet roof, concrete wall, and floor (Table 6.1).

Prospects for Living in Concrete Houses Increased with Longer Duration of Stay in Dhaka

Our data also shows duration of stay in Dhaka as one of the factors influencing quality of housing. For example, in 2010, prospect to live in concrete houses had increased by one and a half times in cases where the stay was for over 25 years' duration in Dhaka, compared with those whose duration had not exceeded 10 years (72.8 per cent and 45.9 per cent, respectively). It is important to note that greater access to improved housing for migrants with longer stay in Dhaka had also been observed both in 1998 and 1991 (Afsar 1999; 2000). However, what marks the departure is the remarkable decline in kutcha type houses in 2010. A significant proportion of long-term migrants (21 per cent) and nearly three-fifths of recent migrants (56.7 per cent) used to live in kutcha structures in 1998, which was no longer the case in 2010 (Figure 6.1). Smaller family, greater scope for better livelihoods, and improved income, which we observed in the previous chapters, have contributed to the improvement of poorer migrants' affordability to better housing. Also, it suggests a major shift in housing quality.

Clearly, these changes have profound impact on Dhaka's housing structure that lost traditional character with the expansion of apartment culture in the last few decades (Kamruzzan and Ogura 2007). Multi-storied apartments became popular in the context of unprecedented population growth, and acute shortage of housing supply was exacerbated by the fact that outward horizontal expansion of Dhaka is difficult because of the city being surrounded by a network of rivers. From barely 100 apartments in the mid-1980s the number of apartments rose to 13,300 in 2010, registering a massive growth of 20.7 per cent per year (Seraj 2012). Our analysis of the growth in per capita income for residents of Dhaka at constant 2010 prices (presented in Chapter 5) shows an annual average increase of 4 per cent between 1998 and 2010, which supports increasing affordability of Dhaka residents over time. It is argued that slum owners have improved the quality of housing including basic amenities such as gas, electricity, water, and sanitation facilities to earn more income (Jones, Mahbub, and Haq 2016). However, it is

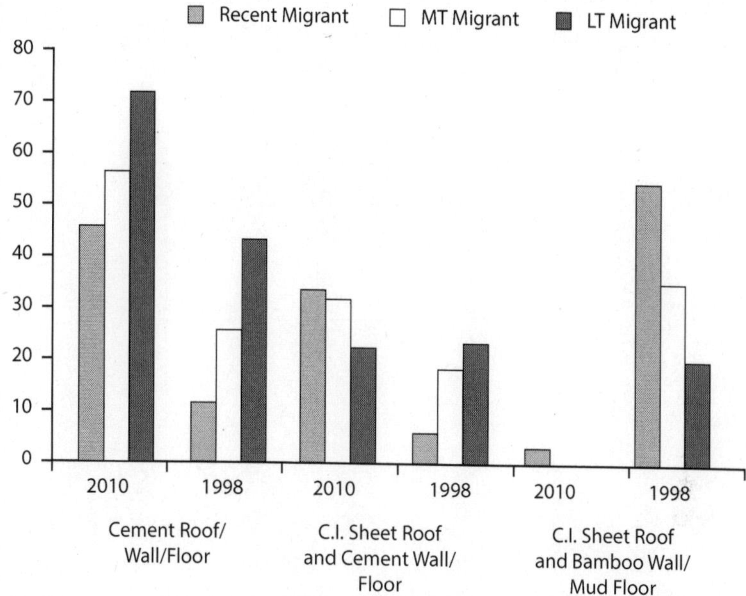

Figure 6.1 Distribution of Migrant Households by Length of Stay in Dhaka City and Housing Structure, 1998–2010

Note: Recent migrants = Migrated to Dhaka less than 10 years ago
MT Migrant = medium-term migrant, who lived in Dhaka between 10 and 25 years ago
LT Migrant = long-term migrant, who lived in Dhaka for 25 years or more
Source: Authors' estimate from the repeat surveys.

important to examine what the increased income can buy in the context of extremely limited and highly skewed land and housing market.

Average Area Increased for Slum Dwellers but Declined for Non-slum Households

The average area of dwelling units for Dhaka residents had declined in 2010, compared with the 1991 level (61.3 and 69 square metres, respectively). However, on a per capita basis, each person in Dhaka now occupies an area of 13.5 square metres, which is larger than what they occupied in 1998 (9.6 square metres) and 1991 (12.3 square metres) (Table 6.2). Increase in per capita dwelling space can be interpreted

Table 6.2 Average Area of Dwelling Unit, Per Capita Space, and Family Size for Slum and Non-slum Households and Migrants and Non-migrants, 1991–2010

Types of Household	2010			1998			1991		
	Family Size	Average Area (m^2)	Space Per Capita (m^2)	Family Size	Average Area (m^2)	Space Per Capita (m^2)	Family Size	Average Area (m^2)	Space Per Capita (m^2)
Non-slum	5.3	86.5	18.4	5.7	91.2	16.0	5.8	97.9	16.9
Slum	4.5	16.5	4.0	5.2	13.8	2.7	5.0	12.5	2.5
All	5.0	63.2	13.5	5.5	52.3	9.6	5.6	69.0	12.3
Migrant	5.0	60.9	13.2	5.5	50.0	9.2	6.2	67.6	12.5
Non-migrant	5.1	69.5	14.4	5.6	61.2	11.2	5.4	75.1	12.1

Source: Afsar (1999); Authors' estimates from BRAC third-round urban poverty survey data, 2010.

mainly as an outcome of significant decline in the family size over time. In 2010, average size of the households in Dhaka was 5.0, compared to 5.5 and 5.6, respectively, in 1998 and 1991. That the families are becoming smaller over time can be supported from the HIES 2010 data (BBS 2011a), as discussed in Chapter 2.[5]

Another interesting trend observed from our third-round survey relates to a gradual decline of dwelling space for non-slum households, even though they also became smaller in size over time (Table 6.2). Average dwelling space for these households squeezed to 86.5 square metres in 2010 from 91.2, and 97.9 square metres in 1998 and 1991, respectively. This can be related to the changing housing pattern culminating in vertically-structured high-rise buildings in the context of increasing population pressure and galloping land price. Based on the Real Estate Housing Association of Bangladesh (REHAB) estimates (2012), we can say that the average price of land in Dhaka city more than trebled between 2000 and 2010 from approximately US$ 489.7 to US$ 1,541.8 per square metre, showing a staggering increase of 214.8 per cent or 12.2 per cent per year.

On the contrary, dwelling space increased for slum dwellers both in terms of average size and on a per capita basis. Average dwelling space has increased by 4 square metres from 12.5 and 13.8 square metres in 1991 and 1998, respectively, to 16.5 square metres in 2010 (Table 6.2). Arguments such as squatters generally occupy larger dwelling space than private slum dwellers can no longer explain this incremental gain (Afsar 1999). This argument lost validity on the ground that over the last decade large and established squatter settlements such as Agargoan and Drainpar bostee had extinguished due to a massive eviction drive by the government.[6] Accordingly, there is massive decline in the proportion of households living in squatter settlements from 42 per cent to a fractional 0.5 per cent between 1998 and 2010.[7] Therefore, the incremental gain in dwelling space can be seen not only as an outcome of smaller family size but also in relation to the changing housing and tenancy arrangements. It also tends to suggest greater affordability of slum dwellers than before.

Rapid Increase in the Number of Tenants and Decline in Owner-Occupied Houses

It should be noted that since 1991, the number of Dhaka residents living in rental accommodation has increased significantly. There was a small difference between the proportions of owners (34.2 per cent) and tenants (37.2) in 1991. This balance was completely lost in 2010 with a rapid increase in the number of residents (57.5 per cent) living in rental accommodation, while those living in owner-occupied houses declined to 30.3 per cent.

The changes in tenancy are more evident for non-slum households in which the number of tenants increased by 39.4 per cent while that of owners declined by 12.4 per cent during the reference period. Although the increase is even higher for slum dwellers as the number of tenants increased by 75 per cent, it is largely an outcome of the massive eviction of squatters mentioned earlier. Accordingly, the proportion living mainly as squatters in public and/or private land has declined remarkably (by 79.3 per cent), while the number of owners remained almost the same (Table 6.3). Slum census data generated by BBS (2014) shows rapid increase in rental tenancy from almost half (48.9 per cent) in 1997 to more than four-fifths (ranging between 73 per cent and 87 per cent for Dhaka North and Dhaka South City Corporation) in 2014, which supports our findings. Similarly, the numbers of tenants increased more rapidly for non-migrants (93.5 per cent) and long-term migrants (53.8 per cent) compared with owners (whose numbers increased by 28.3 per cent for non-migrants and declined by 29.7 per cent for long-term migrants).

Skewed Housing Market and Ownership of Houses

Clearly, it indicates that the distribution of land and housing in Dhaka is becoming more and more skewed. Generally, for all income quintiles, there is a secular increase in the number of tenants (ranging between 44.5 per cent and 71.7 per cent for the top and bottom 40 per cent, respectively). Parallel to this, there is a decline in the number of owners except for the highest income quintile (Table 6.4). Even for the highest income quintile (top 20 per cent in the income ladder), the number of owners did not change much—increased slightly by around 5 per cent between 1991 and 2010. Therefore, as discussed earlier, this indicates that even if there is a significant increase in the per capita income of Dhaka residents, it will not be enough to keep pace with the massive increase in the price of land and/or house. Absence of land/property tax and capital gains tax often play a major role behind the speculative

Table 6.3 Distribution of Slum Households by Length of Migration to Dhaka City and Residential Tenancy

	2010						1998					
	N	Owner	Tenant	Squatter	Others	Mean Area (m^2)	N	Owner	Tenant	Squatter	Others	Mean Area (m^2)
Recent Migrant (<10 Years)	44	0.0	97.7	0.0	2.3	11.7	46	–	67.4	30.4	2.2	11.7
Medium Migrants (10–25 Years)	73	2.7	87.7	1.4	8.2	17.2	68	1.5	57.3	39.7	1.5	12.5
25+ Years	46	6.5	82.6	0.0	10.9	19.7	48	–	33.3	62.5	4.2	15.8
Non-migrant	37	21.6	62.2	0.0	16.2	17.1	34	20.8	45.8	29.2	4.1	17.9
All	200	6.5	84.0	0.5	9.0	16.5	196	3.2	52.1	41.9	2.7	13.8

Note: 'Others' includes government quarter and/or private company accommodation; house built on relatives' land.
Source: Authors' estimate from the repeat surveys.

Table 6.4 Distribution of Sample Households by Tenancy Arrangements and Income Quintiles, 1991–2010

Income Quintiles	Owner		Tenant		Others		All
1991	**No.**	**%**	**No.**	**%**	**No.**	**%**	**No.**
Highest Quintile	55	45.5	41	33.9	25	21	121
2nd Quintile	58	48.3	38	31.7	24	20	120
3rd Quintile	47	39.8	42	35.6	29	25	118
4th Quintile	34	27.9	44	36.1	44	36	122
Lowest Quintile	11	9.2	58	48.7	50	42	119
All	205	34.2	223	37.2	172	29	600
Income Quintiles	**Owner**		**Tenant**		**Others**		**All**
1998	**No.**	**%**	**No.**	**%**	**No.**	**%**	**No.**
Highest Quintile	68	56.7	42	35	10	8.3	120
2nd Quintile	61	50.8	34	28.3	25	21	120
3rd Quintile	39	32.2	47	38.8	35	29	121
4th Quintile	16	13.3	55	45.8	49	41	120
Lowest Quintile	13	10.9	75	63	31	26	119
All	197	32.8	253	42.2	150	25	600
Income Quintiles	**Owner**		**Tenant**		**Others**		**All**
2010	**No.**	**%**	**No.**	**%**	**No.**	**%**	**No.**
Highest Quintile	60	50	50	41.7	10	8.3	120
2nd Quintile	43	35.8	57	47.5	20	17	120
3rd Quintile	38	31.7	66	55	16	13	120
4th Quintile	23	19.2	86	71.7	11	9.2	120
Lowest Quintile	18	15	86	71.7	16	13	120
All	182	30.3	345	57.5	73	12	600

Source: Authors' estimate from the three repeat surveys.

investment in landholdings and real estate, which contributed to a rapid escalation of land prices, especially in major metropolitan cities such as Dhaka and Chittagong (GOB 2015c).

Improved Housing Quality Involves Higher Housing-Related Expenditure

The average annual housing-related expenditure that includes utilities such as gas, water, electricity connection fees, and/or rent was estimated at Tk. 74,736 (US$ 1,065) in 2010, accounting for one-quarter (24 per cent) of all expenditures of Dhaka residents. Housing-related expenditure more than doubled compared to 1998, showing an annual increase of 6.9 per cent during this period (1998–2010). The increase was particularly higher for slum dwellers (11.3 per cent) and short-term migrants (14 per cent) compared to other cross-sections. While on average slum dwellers used to spend Tk. 7,632 (US$ 159) or over one-tenth (12.6 per cent) of the total expenditure on housing in 1998, they spent Tk. 27,711 (US$ 394.9) or one-fifth (19.6 per cent) on this account in 2010. For those from non-slum households, the expenditure doubled from Tk. 46,520 (US$ 969.2) to Tk. 98,248 (US$ 1,400). Clearly it indicates that improved housing quality and other services (which we have discussed later) have come with a high cost, particularly for slum dwellers.

With more than 10 years of stay in Dhaka, the average expenditure on housing increased by 26 per cent, compared with recent migrants who migrated to Dhaka less than 10 years ago. Clearly, it suggests greater affordability by poor migrants to move to better housing over time, as argued earlier (Table 6.1). On the other hand, it also indicates galloping house rent which increased more for the poorer than the better-off sections of Dhaka, bringing the equity issue to the forefront as a policy challenge.

Slum Dwellers' Increased Access to Electricity Connection Through Formal Channel

Access to electricity and cooking gas has increased remarkably, particularly for slum dwellers over time (1991 through 2010) because non-slum households always enjoyed near universal access. In 2010, all households from non-slum and 99 per cent from slum had electricity connection at home (Table 6.5). This is a remarkable achievement in comparison to 1998 and 1991, when 16.1 per cent and 42 per cent of households from slum did not have any electricity connection at all. High coverage

Table 6.5 Distribution of Sample Households by Categories, Electricity Connection, and Formal and Informal Channels of Procurement

Households	Procured through Formal Channel			Procured through Informal Channel			No Connection			All Sources (No.)		
	2010	1998	1991	2010	1998	1991	2010	1998	1991	2010	1998	1991
Non-slum	100.0	99.0	97.0	0.0	1.0	2.0	0.0	0.0	1.0	400	404	400
Slum	98.5	17.2	30.0	1.0	66.7	28.0	0.5	16.1	42.0	200	196	200
All	99.5	72.3	75.0	0.3	21.8	11.0	0.2	5.2	14.0	600	600	600
Migrant	99.8	52.3	72.0	0.2	39.2	11.0	0.0	8.5	17.0	440	429	484
Non-migrant	98.8	83.1	85.0	0.6	12.6	8.0	0.6	4.2	7.0	160	171	116

Source: Authors' estimate from the three repeat surveys.

of electricity connection is also supported by the HIES data that shows 90 per cent of urban households in Bangladesh had access to electricity in 2010 (BBS 2011a). Similarly, the BUHS, 2013 (NIPORT, Mitra and Associates, and ICF International 2013), which shows that 97.8 per cent and 99.5 per cent of households from city corporation slum and non-slum, respectively, had electricity and cooking facility, is also consistent with our findings.

More than access, we consider that the shift in the source of electricity procurement for slum households deserves greater attention. These households now access electricity through legal channel, compared with 1998 when two-thirds procured electricity connection through illegal channel (Afsar 1999), as seen in Table 6.5. While clearing of squatter settlements from illegally occupied public and/or private land explains a large part of this improvement, the remainder can be explained by the changing tenancy arrangements along with housing quality. Given that the bulk of slum dwellers now live as tenants in permanent type of housing, they are entitled to have access to basic services including electricity connection even though on a shared arrangement. As a result, the onus of providing utilities falls on the owners. This is because a proof of residence address is required to acquire all types of utility services including electricity supply through formal channel in Bangladesh. As argued before, in order to earn more income, owners invest in improving housing quality and basic amenities (Jones, Mahbub, and Haq 2016). However, whether and to what extent the owners are following the laws and regulations in procuring these services needs to be examined, which is beyond the scope of this study.

Sharing of Electric Lines by Multiple Tenants Under One Roof

However, during fieldwork, we observed that in areas such as Shahidnagar, 10 to 15 families were living in one house and/or had the same address. Clearly, it highlights that basic services such as gas, electricity, water, toilets, and piped gas lines are shared by all tenants, which is neither new nor uncommon. What draws our attention is the prevalence of subletting to multiple tenants in the same address, which raises the legality issue surrounding this practice. Obviously, it shows the demand for low-cost housing, and until such measures as community or other types of low-cost social housing are provided by the government in partnership with the private and/or not-for-profit sector, entrepreneurs will make inroads to profitable ventures to meet this need, paying little or no attention to legality or ethical issues.

Side by side, we can argue that too many regulations by government can potentially destroy the private low-income housing market.[8] Private developers are often engaged in building low-cost housing as a stopgap measure until they get better value of their land rather than in social responsibility. However, in the absence of either government or not-for-profit sector playing a proactive role to address the acute shortage of low-cost housing, it is important to partner with private developers to maintain a 'delicate balance between social wellbeing and market economy' (Rohekar 2016). Since the informal sector provides for most housing needs, following UN-Habitat (2016), we underscore the need for policies that should encourage informal sector contractors and make them more efficient through training and financing as well as community-led financing for housing and services.[9]

Most Slum Dwellers Now Own Electric Fans and Television Sets

With almost universal access to electricity connection at home in Dhaka, we can expect that poorer migrants' ownership of electrical goods and appliances such as electric fans, televisions, and refrigerators will increase. Ninety-five per cent of residents in Dhaka, irrespective of economic backgrounds, owned electric fan/s in 2010. This contrasts with 1998 when nearly half of the slum dwellers owned electric fans and less than one-quarter had television sets. With three-quarters (76 per cent) of slum households owning television sets in 2010, television can no longer be considered a luxury item for the better-off sections of society given that many electronic goods have become cheaper over time. It is also important to note that with longer stay in Dhaka (exceeding 10 years), purchasing capacity of migrant households tends to increase. While nearly two-thirds (64.4 per cent) of recent migrants owned television sets, the proportion increased to four-fifths (79 per cent) for long-term migrants (Figure 6.2).

Unlike television sets, non-slum households are almost four times more likely to own a refrigerator compared to slum dwellers, clearly sug-

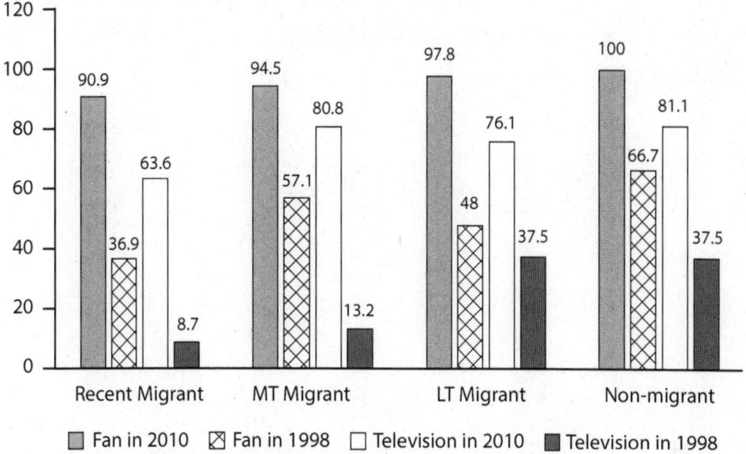

Figure 6.2 Distribution of Respondents by Migration Status and Ownership of Electrical Appliances, 1998–2010

Note: LT Migrant = long-term migrant, MT Migrant = medium-term migrant
Source: Authors' estimate from BRAC third-round poverty survey, 2010.

gesting that price is a deterrent to poorer segments' choice of electronic appliances. However, the propensity to buy a refrigerator doubled for long-term migrants compared to recent migrants indicating increased purchasing capacity of migrants with longer stay in Dhaka city, as argued before.

Improved Coverage of Piped Gas for Slum Dwellers

Like electricity, over time, there is dramatic improvement in slum dwellers' access to piped gas for cooking. Compared with 1998 and 1991, the increase was fourfold from 23 per cent to 93.3 per cent (Table 6.6). Subsequently, their dependence on other cooking materials has declined substantially. For example, dependence on wood and kerosene for cooking had declined by 10 times between 1998 and 2010 (from 51.1 per cent to 5.8 per cent) and on dried leaf and other waste materials by almost 20 times (from 20.4 per cent to 0.9 per cent). Clearly, it suggests that with the change in tenancy arrangements and by acquiring an address, slum dwellers in general are now entitled to access better

Table 6.6 Distribution of the Sample Household by Type of Cooking Arrangements, Types of Residence, and Migratory Status, 1991–2010

Types of Households	Cooking Gas	Wood and Kerosene	Dried Leaf/ Waste Materials	Electric Heater	Others	Total	
						N	%
			2010				
Non-slum	99.8	0.3	0.0	–	–	400	100.0
Slum	92.5	6.5	1.0	–	–	200	100.0
Migrant	97.7	2.0	0.2	–	–	440	100.0
Non-migrant	96.3	3.2	0.6	–	–	160	100.0
			1998				
Non-slum	99.0	0.5	–	0.5	–	197	100.0
Slum	22.6	51.1	20.4	1.6	3.8	186	100.0
Migrant	55.0	28.0	12.8	1.2	3.0	329	100.0
Non-migrant	84.5	9.9	5.6	–	–	71	100.0
			1991				
Non-slum	92.0	5.0	–	1.0	2.0	400	100.0
Slum	23.0	59.0	–	2.0	16.0	200	100.0
Migrant	66.0	26.0	–	1.0	7.0	484	100.0
Non-migrant	81.0	11.0	–	–	8.0	116	100.0

Source: Authors' estimate from the three repeat surveys.

amenities through formal channel which they lacked before. With access to piped gas, poorer women are likely to have more time and better health outcomes compared with the 1990s, which we have examined in Chapter 7.

Telecommunication Becoming Poor-Friendly over Time

The use of telephone was almost universal (99.7 per cent) for non-slum households, and in 2010 slum dwellers were not far behind (86.6 per cent). However, there is a marked difference between the two groups regarding the types of telephone used, which is not unexpected. The bulk (85 per cent) of slum dwellers relied on cell phones as the sole mode of communication. Non-slum households on the other hand enjoyed multiple options. Nearly three-quarters (71 per cent) used cell phones, while a significant proportion (nearly 30 per cent) also had access to land phones (Figure 6.3). High ownership of mobile phones by slum dwellers and those from non-slum is consistent with the BUHS survey data (NIPORT, Mitra and Associates, and ICF International 2013).[10]

High level of cell phone ownership, particularly among the poorer segment of population, can easily be understood in the context of its increasing popularity because of easy accessibility and cheaper deals available from a plethora of competing companies since the mid-2000s. Subsequently, we found that slum dwellers have been using mobile phones for a little over four years compared to non-slum dwellers who have been using mobile phones for seven years on average. Increasing popularity of cell phones is also supported by the HIES data which shows that its use in urban households had almost quadrupled between 2005 and 2010 (from 22.7 per cent to 82.7 per cent) (BBS 2011a).

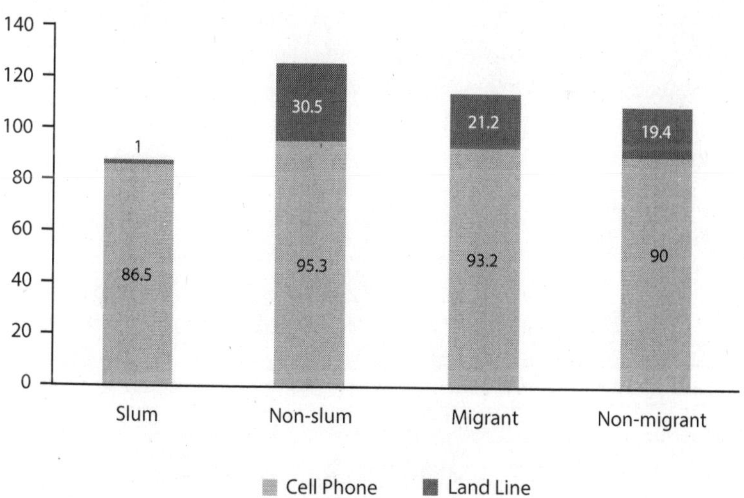

Figure 6.3 Types of Telephones Used by Respondents in Slum and Non-slum Residence, and Migratory Status, 2010

Source: Authors' estimate from BRAC third-round urban poverty survey, 2010.

Sluggish Digital Divide between the Rich and the Poor

However, unlike cell phones, the use of computers has not been revolutionized. The domain of computer use is almost exclusively dominated by the urban elites. As a result, we found that two-fifths (41 per cent) of non-slum households owned computers in 2010, as opposed to only two slum dwellers. Over a period of five years (2005–10), the proportion of households owning a computer in Bangladesh barely increased from 4.9 per cent to 8.6 per cent (BBS 2011a). Digital literacy which is increasingly becoming important for all types of information such as health, employment, income, and government policy is an important area that needs policy focus for better delivery of service and enhancing greater citizens' participation.

Significant Improvement in Tap Water Coverage at Home for Slum Dwellers

Over time, slum dwellers' access to running tap water within the premises increased substantially from less than 10 per cent in the 1990s (1991 and 1998) to 40 per cent in 2010. Subsequently, their dependence on public and/or private sources of water outside home such as Dhaka Water and Sewerage Authority (DWASA) standpipes, public taps, and private taps from neighbouring households and institutions had declined dramatically over time to 4.5 per cent from 22 per cent and 62 per cent, respectively, in 1998 and 1991. Although non-slum households' access to tap water inside the premises has always been high, it increased from 82.3 per cent to 92.2 per cent between 1991 and 2010. Increased coverage of access to the running water can be attributed to changes in the tenancy arrangement, particularly for slum households (Table 6.7). Accordingly, most of the tenants (89 per cent) pay for water facilities as a part of their rent (Arias-Granada et al. 2018).

As a signatory to the SDG, Bangladesh is among the countries committed to providing safely managed water and sanitation to all by 2030. Safely managed water services extend beyond access to a technologically improved water source, guaranteeing need-based availability on users' immediate premises free of contamination. Safely managed sanitation services need to ensure a technologically improved sanitation facility which is not shared with other households and excreta are safely disposed in situ or transported and treated off-site (World Bank 2018).

Table 6.7 Distribution of Sample Households by Sources of Drinking Water, Types of Residence, and Migratory Status, 1991–2010

Type of Households	WASA Line Inside House	WASA Line Outside House	Public / Private Sources	Tube Well	Others	Total N	Total %
			2010				
Non-slum	92.8	1.5	0.5	3.0	2.3	400	100.0
Slum	40.0	41.5	2.0	14.0	2.5	200	100.0
Migrant	75.0	16.5	0.7	5.7	2.0	440	100.0
Non-migrant	75.6	10.0	1.9	12.3	0.8	160	100.0
			1998				
Non-slum	98.5	1.0	–	–	0.5	197	100.0
Slum	9.7	43.0	23.7	19.9	3.7	186	100.0
Migrant	48.6	22.5	15.2	11.9	1.8	329	100.0
Non-migrant	76.1	14.1	12.8	2.8	4.2	71	100.0
			1991				
Non-slum	82.3	2.5	2.4	12.5	0.3	400	100.0
Slum	8.0	18.0	43.5	19.5	11.0	200	100.0
Migrant	56.0	8.1	17.2	14.7	4.3	484	100.0
Non-migrant	63.8	6.0	15.0	15.5	1.7	116	100.0

Source: Authors' estimate from the three repeat surveys.

Major Issues of Water: Irregular Supply and Poor Quality

Despite increased access to running tap water within the premises over time, 44 per cent of the slum dwellers said they draw water from DWASA sources such as standpipes and water tankers outside the household premises, while another 12 per cent depended on tube wells as the major source of drinking water.[11] The proportions of households that depended on shared sources remained significantly high over time.

This is mainly because of the irregular supply of tap water, which is a year-round problem for Dhaka residents that worsens in dry season. Official estimates suggest that DWASA provides water to about 12.5 million people within its service area and can meet about 90 per cent of the total requirements, which is 2,250 million litre per day (MLD) (GOB 2015c). It is already an established practice that well-off households in Dhaka manage their demand for water by digging private deep tube wells illegally, which contributes to depletion of the groundwater table among other problems.[12]

A study conducted by the World Bank (2018: 2) shows that 'people who use piped water on their premise, which is theoretically the best, safest kind, face E. coli contamination more than 80 percent of the time'. Also, urban dwellers are more likely to have access to contaminated sources than rural residents have access to clean water (55 per cent and 45 per cent, respectively). It is an irony that although Dhaka is surrounded by four major rivers and many rivulets, only 12 per cent of the water supplied by DWASA is obtained from these sources, while the bulk (88 per cent) is derived from the groundwater aquafer (DWASA 2011).[13] As a result of over dependence, the groundwater level of the city had dropped by 20 metres between 2000 and 2007 at the rate of 2.8 metres annually, which can further worsen water supply due to dryness of tube wells and rising production cost (Azim Uddin and Baten 2011).

Apart from the problems of water sources, there are some serious risks of pollution related to the intermittent water supply system. It is argued that during non-supply hours when the pressure in the pipes drops, there is a danger that leaked water from faulty joints and holes can be polluted by water from sources such as toilets, septic tanks, and drains and can be sucked back in the pipes contaminating the water (Satapathy 2014). This risk is minimal when the water supply is continuous. Poor water quality together with lack of sanitation and unhygienic conditions can lead to adverse health consequences including diarrhoea and a host of other diseases such as hookworm, malaria, dengue, hepatitis A, hepatitis B, and typhoid. Among the most vulnerable groups are infants, children, pregnant women, seniors, and those living in slum areas, which we have examined in the next chapter.

The above statistics on slum dwellers' reliance on water sources outside the premises has implications on women's time use and energy. It is encouraging to note that over time average distance between water source and slum households has been reduced substantially from 69 metres to less than 10 metres between 1998 and 2010. In their survey of Dhaka slums, Arias-Granada et al. (2018) found that slum dwellers spend just seven minutes to reach water sources. As a result, women's workload is likely to reduce as they are mostly responsible for fetching water and managing household chores with stored water, which is not examined here as it is beyond the scope of the study. However, by examining morbidity rate and disease patterns for different age groups disaggregated by gender, including among adult women in Chapter 7, we have been able to reflect on this aspect, even if only partially.

It is also important to mention that whether it is through access to tap water inside the premise or the public water sources from outside the house, slum households are generally sharing water with more than one family, which also has implications for time use patterns, particularly for women, and health concerns. This is consistent with the BUHS, 2013, which shows that two-thirds of slum households in city corporation areas share their water with 10 or more families (NIPORT, Mitra and Associates, and ICF International 2013).

From Unhygienic to Shared Mode of Private Sanitary Toilets

With regards to slum dwellers' access to sanitary toilets, we found massive improvements over time. There has been a total transformation from unhygienic, such as hanging types of open toilets in the 1990s, to shared mode of private sanitary toilet. Nearly half and three-fifths of slum households used hanging and other types of non-sanitary toilets in 1998 and 1991 respectively (Table 6.8). This trend changed in 2010 with the majority (85 per cent) of slum households predominantly using sanitary toilets which they share with five to six or even more families and the use of unhygienic toilets dropped down to a fraction (0.9 per cent). Unlike water facilities, sanitation facilities are rarely included as part of rent. Accordingly, in their survey, Arias-Granada et al. (2018) found that only 6 per cent paid it as a part of their rent.

However, the shared mode of sanitary toilets does not fall under 'improved sanitation' as defined by the World Health Organization (WHO) and United Nations Children's Fund (UNICEF) Joint Monitoring Programme (JMP) for water and sanitation.[14] To qualify JMP's definition of improved sanitation, toilets must be used only by

Table 6.8 Distribution of the Sample Household by Types of Toilets They Use, Type of Residence, and Migratory Status, 1991–2010.

Households	Sanitary Toilet for Private Use	Non-Sanitary Toilet for Private Use	Common Sanitary Toilet	Common Non-sanitary Toilet	Hanging/ Others	Total	
						No.	%
			2010				
Non-slum	93.3	0.0	6.8	0.0	0.0	400	100.
Slum	8.0	3.0	85.0	3.0	1.0	200	100.
Migrant	62.5	0.7	35.4	0.9	0.4	440	100.
Non-migrant	71.3	1.9	25.6	1.3	0.0	160	100.
			1998				
Non-slum	91.4	–	8.1	0.5	–	197	100.
Slum	4.3	3.8	14.0	29.6	48.3	186	100.
Migrant	43.2	1.5	11.6	15.2	24.3	329	100.
Non-migrant	66.2	2.8	11.3	11.3	29.6	71	100
			1991				
Non-slum	82.0	3.0	3.7	11.3	–	400	100.
Slum	4.5	6.5	2.5	29.5	57.0	200	100.
Migrant	54.0	4.0	21.0	9.0	12.0	484	100
Non-migrant	64.0	5.0	21.0	5.0	5.0	116	100

Source: Authors' estimate from the three repeat surveys.

one household and meet certain design standards that prevent human contact with faeces. Thus 'improved sanitation' does not have any scope to include diversity of shared sanitation that arises from the differential use of shared toilets depending on the types of toilets and types of users. For example, Rheinelander et al. (2015) argued that health and environmental implications are different when a toilet is 'shared between a limited number of households who know each other', compared with a public toilet that is often used by mobile population and institutional toilets such as those in workplaces, markets, schools, hospitals, and community centres. To quote Rheinlander et al. (2015: 3):

> Experiences from Ghana and other sub-Saharan African countries illustrates how household shared sanitation may well fit with culturally acceptable sanitation choices and not necessarily unhygienic. Indeed, household shared sanitation may be the only realistic option that brings people the important first step up the sanitation ladder from open defecation to a basic level of sanitation.

One major factor of Ghana's success in shared sanitation is attributed to the planning of living settlements (Keraita et al. 2013). According to the Ghana Statistical Services (GSS), many Ghanaians (79 per cent) lived in the 'compound houses' in 2008. The compound houses include several households built around a common area or yard in which they share utilities such as water, electricity, and sanitation. The living arrangements of slum dwellers in Dhaka city is similar to 'compound houses' in relation to the shared utilities. However, here, slum dwellers live in premises of one single household in which several rooms are partitioned and/or built in a semi-detached way for rental purposes.

However, whether living in the 'compound houses' or in slums, the need for maintenance and cleanliness is paramount in the context of density per toilet. With the help of a logistic regression model, we have examined the determinants of illness in Chapter 7. Accordingly, we find that those who use non-sanitary latrine and share it with others are likely to suffer most, given the highest negative value of z score (–3.610) and the high statistical significance obtained for this variable. Therefore, the residents of Dhaka city who do not have access to sanitary toilet for private use, proper drainage, and waste disposal facilities are more likely to be sick compared to those having access to improved basic amenities. It is encouraging that over time Bangladesh has achieved almost universal access to safe drinking water. Similar scale of coverage is needed through appropriate policy measures and social movement for 'improving hygienic standards of shared facilities to a level that satisfies and protects users' (Rheinlander et al. 2015: 5). Local government in partnership with private sector can implement measures for collection, disposal, and treatment of faecal sludge. According to the World Bank

(2018), only 2 per cent of faecal sludge is estimated to be treated despite a sewerage connection of 22 per cent, and there is no on-site faecal sludge management system. In the context of its very high population density, poor sanitation increases the risk of spreading faecal pathogens, which can lead to illness (Hathi et al. 2017).

Persistence of Drainage and Waterlogging Problems

Unlike water and toilets, from the 2010 survey data, we do not find much improvement in the conditions pertaining to drainage and waterlogging. This affects both slum and non-slum households, but the extent to which these households are affected varies. More than 80 per cent of slum households experienced the problem of waterlogging due mainly to inadequate drainage facility in 2010. Nearly half of these households have been under the constant threat of water stagnation in low-lying areas such as Jurain, which is easily over-flooded even with little rain. A strikingly similar situation was found in 1998 when the same proportion of slum households were found prone to waterlogging due to rain. Half of the households in Jurain including both slum and non-slum experienced this problem, compared to nearly one-third (29.4 per cent) in Purana Paltan and Kamlapur, one-quarter (23 per cent) in Lalbagh, and less than one-fifth (15 per cent) in Mirpur.

What is also important to note is that almost two-thirds of non-slum households were affected by waterlogging indicating pervasiveness of the drainage problem in Dhaka city (Figure 6.4). Nearly one-quarter of households—13 per cent and 33 per cent from slum and non-slum, respectively—were immune to waterlogging and nearly half of these households (46.5 per cent) were in Mirpur.

Waterlogging in Dhaka city is often considered a consequence of unplanned construction due to rapid urbanization, which encroached, filled-up, and diverted most of the traditional natural waterbodies and storm-water drainage (Mowla and Islam 2013). As a result, smooth flow of water to the outfall rivers has been obstructed, creating severe waterlogging in the city every year during monsoon. Apart from public inconvenience, waterlogging creates serious problems for the infrastructure, economic loss arising from the loss in production and damage of existing property and goods, ecological imbalance, and spread of communicable diseases (Mark and Chusit 2002; Mowla 2005).

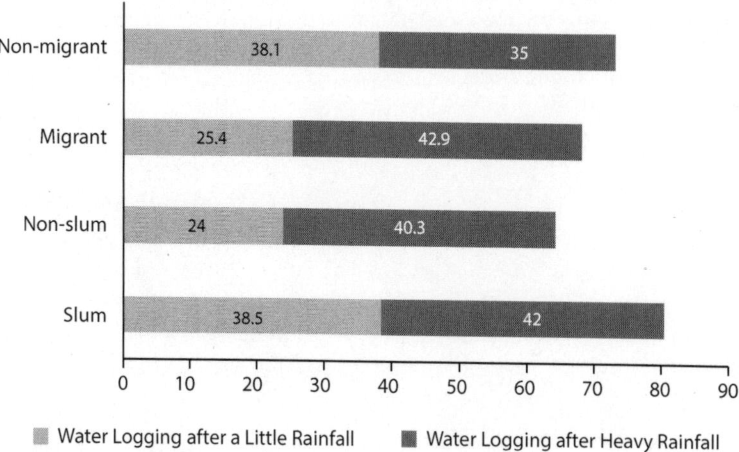

Figure 6.4 Distribution of Respondents by Slum and Non-slum Residence, and Migratory Status; and Extent of Waterlogging Problem

Source: Authors' estimate from BRAC third-round urban poverty survey, 2010.

Given the constant threat of waterlogging faced by a large number of households and the high level of emission of carbon monoxide, it is difficult for the city dwellers, particularly the poorer ones, to reap benefits from improved water and sanitation situation. Therefore, following Alam and Islam (2013), we emphasize the need for effective management and restoration and operation of the natural drainage system to improve the situation through a close coordination among urban authorities and developing partnership between public and private sectors. In the Seventh Five-Year Plan, DWASA targets to ensure water production ratio in which 70 per cent of water will come from surface water and 30 per cent from ground water, increase sanitation coverage from 40 per cent to 60 per cent, and drainage coverage from 60 per cent to 80 per cent (GOB 2015c). However, apart from the need to monitor these targets, DWASA should focus on safe containment, collection, disposal, and treatment as necessary steps to reduce faecal contamination, which we have discussed in Chapter 9. In the next chapter, we have analysed matters regarding quality of life from the perspective of human capital by examining changes, access, and performance indicators together with quality and equity issues to determine the impact of urbanization on health and education of migrants and their family members.

NOTES

1. See Technical note 5 for details on how the Multidimensional Poverty Index is calculated; available at: http://hdr.undp.org/sites/default/files/hdr2015_technical_notes.pdf (accessed on 2 April 2016).

2. South Asian cities have a very high population density. With around 30,000 people per square km on an average, Mumbai is one of the densest cities in the world, followed by Kolkata and Karachi (City Mayors 2007). The proportion of urban population living in megacities with a population of 10,000,000 or more almost trebled in South Asia (from 7 per cent to 18 per cent). Dhaka's growth is astounding because its population grew from 6.6 million in 1990, when it was not even a megacity, to 14.7 million in 2010—its population more than doubled (UNDP 2014; MHHDC 2014).

3. According to the same census, Dhaka accounted for 30 per cent of the total national slum households in 2014 (BBS 2014).

4. Dhaka is ranked the second worst liveable city of the world by the Economic Intelligence Unit's (EIU)'s survey of 140 liveable cities of the world based on five lifestyle indicators—stability, health care, culture and environment, education, and infrastructure. There is little improvement in the city's ranking since the last five years, as it remains among the 10 least liveable cities of the world (http://www.thedailystar.net/country/dhaka-second-least-livable-city-the-world-129154 [accessed on 4 May 2016]).

5. However, the average family size is estimated at 4.6 for Dhaka urban areas in 2010 by HIES, which is smaller compared to our sample households (5.0) but similar to what we found for slum (4.5) (BBS 2011a).

6. Estimates from the United Nations Development Programme (UNDP) suggest that approximately 300,000 people were displaced in 115 forced evictions from the cities of Dhaka, Chittagong, and Dinajpur from 1996 to 2004. At least another 60,000 people were evicted from Dhaka alone between 2006 and 2008 (http://citiscope.org/story/2015/after-painful-eviction-bangladesh-slum-dwellers-start-over-99-year-lease#sthash.GNSGX2Qz.dpuf, accessed on 2 April 2016).

7. Subsequently, the proportion of tenants has increased significantly from 52 per cent to 84 per cent during the same period. However, a small proportion of owners ranging between 6.7 per cent and 3.2 per cent, respectively, between 1998 and 2010 indicates that the prospects for home ownership has always been low for urban poor and does not increase much with longer duration in Dhaka.

8. Please see http://www.youthkiawaaz.com/2016/03/slums-in-dhaka (accessed on 24 April 2016).

9. We have discussed the housing policy issues and options in detail in the concluding chapter (9).

10. Note that the proportions of households from the city corporation slum (92 per cent) and non-slum (98 per cent) areas owning mobile phones was higher in 2013 according to the BUHS, compared with our data. However, the same survey (BUHS) also highlighted a great leap from the 2006 level of ownership when the averages were 20 per cent and 55 per cent, respectively (NIPORT, Mitra and Associates, and ICF International 2013). Clearly, the rapid changes in the level of ownership can explain the difference between the two sets of data given that our dataset represents 2010 figures.

11. Note that DWASA not only supplies water through household connections but also through 1,643 standpipes, 560 deep tube wells, and water tankers.

12. The DWASA estimate suggests that there are also 1,330 and 1,500 deep tube wells (DTWs) that are under operation by private agencies and other unrecognized sources, respectively.

13. These are Buriganga, Turag, and Balu Rivers, and Tongi Khal (canal), Dhanmoni, Gulshan, and Crescent lakes which cover around 10 per cent and 15 per cent of the city's land area (Islam et al. 2010). However, water in these rivers and lakes has already been polluted due to discharge of huge amounts of untreated and municipal waste material. Therefore, it is argued that on the grounds of huge expenses involved in treatment of this water, agencies such as DWASA prefer to depend on groundwater aquifer for drinking water production (Biswas, Mahtab, and Rahman 2010).

14. Shared sanitation is defined by JMP as 'sanitation of an otherwise acceptable type shared between two or more households' (WHO 2014).

7 Impact of Urbanization on Health and Education

Progress and Inter-generational Prospects for Shared Prosperity

The impact of urbanization on health can be both positive and negative. On the one hand, rural migrants who come to urban areas have access to basic urban amenities, improved health care services, better quality of education as well as the scope to acquire higher levels of education, better and diversified employment opportunities, and greater scope for economic development than rural areas. On the other hand, they are exposed to new threats and challenges particularly evident in cities, which include waterborne and other communicable diseases transmitted due to overcrowding and high population density, environmental pollution, non-communicable diseases (cardiovascular diseases, cancers, diabetes, and chronic respiratory diseases), loneliness, depression, stress-related illness, unhealthy diets and physical inactivity, harmful use of alcohol, as well as the risks associated with disease outbreaks. The challenges of urbanization are well acknowledged (UN-Habitat 2016). Accordingly, SDGs emphasize on making cities and human settlements inclusive, safe, resilient, and sustainable (Goal 11) and together with Goal 3, seek to ensure healthy lives and promote well-being for all at all ages by 2030.

As indicated in the introductory chapter, between 1990 and 2017, the value of HDI for Bangladesh improved from 0.387 to 0.608, showing 57.1 per cent increase, which improved its ranking to 136 and placed the country in the medium development category (UNDP 2018). This has been possible mainly due to continuous improvements achieved in social indicators such as life expectancy, arresting under-5 and infant mortality rates, and achieving all-round progress in schooling and education. For example, between 1990 and 2017 under-5 mortality and neonatal mortality rates declined rapidly from 143.8 per thousand to 32.4 per thousand and 64.1 per thousand to 18.4 per thousand, respectively.[1]

In the last two chapters, we observed that poor migrants not only improved their livelihoods and income but also made headways in accessing basic amenities such as improved housing, water, and sanitation although not without some quality and equity issues. Undoubtedly, it is important to explore whether migrants, particularly poor migrants, have enough incentive to spend on health and education: the two important human development indicators that can ensure inter-generational prospect to get out of the poverty trap and secure a rightful claim in the city's growing prosperity. In this chapter, we have examined health status of respondents and their family members by estimating morbidity rates and highlighting disease patterns to assess changes and identify the affected groups, and the factors that are contributing to these changes that are necessary from the policy perspective. To assess quality of health, we have analysed their treatment seeking behaviour, immunization of children, and whether the determinants of good health are changing over time.

Education has always been a driving force behind rural–urban and international migration, particularly for the non-poor segment of population. We have examined how children of migrant families, both rich and poor, are faring over time in Dhaka city, which is the major centre of quality education, by examining changes in enrolment rates of urban poor children, adolescents, and youth group, and gender parity at the primary, secondary, and tertiary levels. We have examined whether the quality of human capital has improved over time by analysing the trends in adult literacy, educational attainment, and per capita expenditure in health and education in this chapter. By examining all these aspects of quality of health and education, we addressed the third compelling question raised in the Introduction: have the income gains, better livelihoods, and improved access to basic services brought qualitative changes creating scope for the poorer segment of urban population to have a stake in the city's growing prosperity like their non-poor counterparts?

CHANGING TRENDS AND PATTERNS OF MORBIDITY

We estimated the overall morbidity rate, defined as the proportion of sick members including members who were chronically sick, during a fortnight preceding the survey to the total household members at 26.3 per cent in 2010, lower compared to our second-round survey in 1998 (34 per cent).[2] This is also lower compared to the proportion of morbid population for Dhaka Division which was 34.7 per cent in 2012 (BBS 2013c). However, the rate varies for different population groups, which we have discussed later.

Morbidity Rate Is Higher for Slum Dwellers and for Women in General

Our survey shows that the morbidity rate is higher for those living in slum households across all age groups compared to that for non-slum. For example, the morbidity rate doubled for children––both boys and girls—in slum compared to that of non-slum households, highlighting the importance of questions regarding equity and access of primary health care that we have analysed later in this chapter. It is also higher for female than male members irrespective of slum and non-slum residence and their age. However, the morbidity rate doubled for women in the prime reproductive age (between 25 and 49 years) in non-slum compared to male cohorts (29.1 per cent and 14.7 per cent, respectively), while for slum dwellers gender difference became larger with increase in age and largest for those aged 60 years and over (Table 7.1).

Fever and Acute Respiratory Infection: Most Common Sickness among Children and Youth

We found that the incidence of fever was most common among the sample population irrespective of age, gender, and slum and non-slum residence. Other major diseases in descending order included diabetes, gastritis/ulcer, acute respiratory infection (ARI), blood pressure, pains

Table 7.1 Morbidity Rate for the Sample Population by Age Group, Gender, and Slum and Non-slum Residence

Age Group	Slum		Non-slum		Total		
Morbidity Rates	**Male**	**Female**	**Male**	**Female**	**Male**	**Female**	**Total**
<5 Years	44.7	42.2	19.7	18.4	28.4	27.3	27.8
5–14 Years	16.8	18.3	14.9	17.4	15.7	17.7	16.6
15–24 Years	11.2	25.0	9.8	11.3	10.2	15.2	12.8
25–49 Years	32.7	44.2	14.7	29.1	19.5	33.7	25.9
50–59 Years	53.1	71.4	47.5	51.5	48.9	55.7	52.3
60+ Years	47.6	75.0	53.1	61.5	52.2	63.6	56.4
All Age Groups	27.8	37.2	21.0	26.9	23.0	30.0	26.3
Chronic Diseases							
<5 Years	0	0	0	1.3	0	0.8	0.4
5–14 Years	0.9	3.2	0.6	2.4	0.7	2.7	1.7
15–24 Years	3.4	7.1	1.5	2.8	2.1	4.0	3.1
25–49 Years	8.2	9.8	7.4	14.4	7.6	13.0	10.1
50–59 Years	18.8	39.3	34.3	39.8	30.5	39.7	35.1
60+ Years	38.1	41.7	42.5	46.2	41.8	45.6	43.1
All Age Groups	6.9	9.6	10.9	13.6	9.7	12.4	11.0

Source: Authors' estimate from BRAC third-round urban poverty survey, 2010.

and aches, rheumatic fever and/or heart disease or chest pain, and diarrhoea (Table 7.2). However, incidence of other major diseases varied by age group and gender. For example, the pattern of sickness was similar for children under-5 and youth (aged between 15 and 24 years), with ARI as the second most common sickness. However, the ordering differed. For example, there was higher incidence of diarrhoea among children than among youth. For youth, on the other hand, gastritis/ulcer was the third most common sickness.

It should be noted that our ranking based on the second-round survey of sickness for children under-5 is consistent with the national pattern of major diseases (BBS 2013c) and the Bangladesh Demographic and Health Survey (BDHS) 2011 survey data (NIPORT et al. 2013) as

Table 7.2 Incidence of Major Sickness by Age Group of Sample Population, 2010

Diseases	<5 Years	5–14 Years	15–24 Years	25–49 Years	50–9 Years	60+ Years	Total
Fever	14.8	9.8	7.2	7.0	7.6	7.1	8.0
Diabetes	0	0	0.2	3.8	21.0	23.7	4.9
ARI	5.2	2.9	2.1	2.2	2.3	1.4	2.4
Gastritis/Ulcer	0.8	0.2	1.0	3.3	5.7	5.7	2.4
Blood Pressure	0	0	0.2	2.2	8.0	9.0	2.2
Aches/Pain	0	0.5	0.2	1.8	4.9	1.9	1.4
Rheumatic Fever	0	0.7	0.7	0.6	2.7	2.8	0.9
Diarrhoea	4.7	0.7	0	0.6	0.7	1.4	0.9
Asthma	0	0.4	0.8	0.8	0.8	1.9	0.7
Kidney Problem	0	0	0.3	0.7	1.9	1.9	0.6
All Major Diseases	25.6	15.3	12.7	23.2	55.7	56.8	24.6

Source: Authors' estimate from BRAC third-round urban poverty survey, 2010.

well as with our previous survey result (Afsar 2004). Our assessment of worsening health conditions among slum dwellers, particularly women and children, being mostly due to communicable and some chronic diseases such as gastritis/ulcer and rheumatic fever, compared to those from non-slum are also consistent with the Urban Health Survey 2006 (NIPORT et al. 2008).

However, we would like to emphasize that the trends and ranking of diseases mainly among children under-5 have been changing over time. Diarrhoea that accounted for 20–30 per cent of acute illness in rural areas in the mid-1990s (Rahman, Hossain, and Sen 1996) is being replaced by fever and ARI both in rural and urban areas. This can be resulting from the improved access to safe drinking water for slum dwellers and general masses on the one hand and deteriorating air, noise, chemical, and other types of environmental pollution in Dhaka city and across Bangladesh on the other. Research shows that lead and particulate matter (PM) concentration in the air is dangerously high in Dhaka city (Begum, Biswas, and Nasiruddin 2010; Mahadi 2010). Factors that contribute to the increased environmental pollution include the lack of adequate regulation of motor vehicles, industrial and commercial sectors, and greenhouse gases generated by burning fossil fuels that are used for electricity generation and household fuel combustion.

Adults and older people suffered from multiple sicknesses due to higher incidence of chronic diseases such as diabetes, cardiovascular diseases, aches and pains, gastritis/ulcer, rheumatic and/or heart disease or chest pain together with fever, ARI, and asthma. The rate of morbidity for chronic illness was much higher amongst adult population aged 25 years and above and highest for older people (aged over 60 years) compared to the younger age group (Table 7.1). Almost one-quarter of the sample population aged 50 years and over reported that they had diabetes, followed by those who had high blood pressure (8.5 per cent) and fever (7.5 per cent) during the last two weeks preceding the survey.

The incidence of gastritis/ulcer and/or abdominal pain and rheumatic fever and/or heart disease or chest pain was higher among adult and older women living in slum households, while adult women from non-slum suffered more from high blood pressure compared to their male cohorts. A study undertaken by Save the Children (UK) on health problems in urban slums of Bangladesh also reported gastric pain, dysentery, skin diseases, diarrhoea, aches and pains, general weakness, jaundice, menstrual problems and anaemia amongst females, and fever, cough, pneumonia, and measles amongst children as the most common health problems prevailing in the country (2009). Trends in the incidence of sickness (Table 7.2) highlight some important changes in the disease patterns over time, which we have presented later.

Increasing Prevalence of Fever Cutting across Age, Sex, and Social Classes

An increasing prevalence of fever cutting across age, sex, and social classes is consistent with what we found in our second-round survey (1998), although then it was high mainly among children and young adults. Incidence of air borne diseases such as ARI and asthma was high across all categories of the sample population, compared to waterborne diseases such as diarrhoea, dysentery, and cholera that are most commonly found among children.

Higher Prevalence of Chronic Diseases among Mature Adults and Older People

Rheumatic fever and/or heart disease or chest pain, diabetes, and high blood pressure have become more common among mature adults and older people in general compared to the 1990s. However, women suffered more from rheumatic fever and high blood pressure compared to men of the same age. This is consistent with the urban prevalence pattern as recorded in the HIES data generated by BBS (2011a) and global sickness trend (WHO 2011).

Higher Prevalence of Hypertension among the Oldest People and High-Income Earners

Prevalence of hypertension was also higher in the oldest, compared to other age groups, which is consistent with the findings in existing literature (Kabir et al. 2005; Khanam et al. 2011) that identify increasing age as a risk factor for hypertension. Prevalence of hypertension was higher among the people belonging to the top income quintiles compared to other income groups, which is consistent with the findings of studies that identified links between cardiovascular risk factors and economic development (Ezzati et al. 2005).

DETERMINANTS OF ILLNESS

To explain the plurality of factors contributing to the morbidity rates and incidence of illness, we have analysed the likelihood of morbidity for the sample population as a function of quality and equity of access to the urban basic services with the help of a logistic regression model. The dependent variable measures sickness for two weeks preceding the survey. We have selected two sets of explanatory variables as measures for quality and equity factors.

Arguably, rapid urbanization can lead to social deprivation and social inequality. The equity factors include socio-demographic variables such as age, gender, education of the spouse, migration status, and income levels, which often constitute the basis for discrimination regarding access to urban services.[3] Given that morbidity rate was higher for both children under-5 and older people aged 50 years and over, we created dummy variables for these two age groups and 0 otherwise. Further, as adult population (aged between 16 and 59 years) also suffered from various chronic diseases such as gastritis/ulcer, rheumatic fever, blood pressure, and diabetes, we created two dummy variables for adult men and women, respectively, while controlling for children and older people to assess if they have greater likelihood of morbidity. A gender dummy was created for women by controlling for men in the context that morbidity was much higher among women compared with men.

Given that with longer stay in Dhaka city the difference in the access to urban amenities tends to diminish between migrant and non-migrant, we created a dummy variable with those who migrated to Dhaka city in the 10-year period at the time of the survey. There is no denying that higher income ensures improved and greater access to health information and services; hence, a dummy variable was created with bottom 40 per cent of the income ladder, controlling for other income quintiles. Considering that women predominantly manage water and sanitation in the household and that the level of education of spouses can potentially influence households' access to urban services (both in terms of physical access and quality), a dummy variable was created with no schooling and primary level dropouts, controlling for other educational qualifications.

To examine whether and to what extent quality of the basic amenities influence good health, we have used indicators for assessing quality of life such as the type of residence (slum and non-slum), types of basic amenities including access to safe drinking water and sanitary toilets for private use, drainage and waste disposal facilities, and the type of fuel used for cooking. As the morbidity rate was higher for slum population, people living in non-slum households were used as a control group. The underlying assumption was that the slum dummy will help capture the correlation between the quality of housing and health outcome, as non-slum dwellers almost inevitably live in relatively better-quality housing compared to slum dwellers. Considering that the members of households using public stand posts and shared modes of water sources and latrines are several times more likely to suffer from waterborne diseases than those having in-house piped water and private sanitary toilet facilities, dummy variables were created for those accessing safe water and sanitary latrines for private use and enjoying an adequate drainage facility and a fixed place for waste disposal.

Results of the logistic regression presented in Table 7.3 confirm many of our assumptions that are highlighted below.

Table 7.3 Results of Logistic Regression Model Predicting Likelihood of Morbidity for Respondents in Dhaka, 2010

Variables	Coefficient	Robust Standard Error	Z	P>Z	95% Confidence Interval	
<5 Years	0.410	0.160	2.570	0.010	0.097	0.723
50+ Years	1.731	0.112	15.440	0.000	1.511	1.950
Female	0.431	0.091	4.730	0.000	0.252	0.609
Education of Spouse (Illiterate and Primary Drop Out)	0.246	0.117	2.100	0.036	0.016	0.476
Working Age Female (15–59 Years)	−0.175	0.055	−3.210	0.001	−0.282	−0.068
Working Age Male (15–59 Years)	−0.106	0.047	−2.230	0.025	−0.198	−0.013
Bottom 40% of Income Quintile	−0.053	0.115	−0.460	0.648	−0.279	0.173
Migrant (up to 10 Years)	−0.081	0.150	−0.540	0.589	−0.375	0.213
Living in Slum	−0.110	0.179	−0.610	0.539	−0.461	0.241
Sanitary Latrine for Private Use	−0.647	0.179	−3.610	0.000	−0.999	−0.296
Safe Drinking Water Inside House	0.034	0.156	0.220	0.827	−0.272	0.341
Adequate Drainage Facility	−0.126	0.107	−1.180	0.237	−0.336	0.083
Adequate Waste Disposal Facility	−0.437	0.606	−0.720	0.470	−1.625	0.750
Using Piped/ Cylinder Gas	0.554	0.610	0.910	0.364	−0.642	1.750
Constant	−1.343	0.294	−4.570	0.000	−1.919	−0.767

Note: Number of observations = 3,065, Wald chi2 = 289.4, Prob>chi2 = 0.000, Log pseudo likelihood = 1,587.359, Pseudo R^2 = 0.925

Source: Authors' estimate from BRAC third-round urban poverty survey, 2010.

Lack of Access to Private Sanitary Toilets Increases the Risk of Morbidity

The residents of Dhaka city who do not have access to sanitary toilet for private use and/or proper drainage and waste disposal facilities are more likely to be sick compared to those having access to improved basic amenities. Particularly, those who use non-sanitary latrine and share it with others are likely to suffer most given they have the highest negative value of z score (−3.610), which is highly significant, statistically. While, over time, Bangladesh has achieved almost universal access to safe drinking water, similar scale of coverage is needed through appropriate policy measures and social movement for improving access to safe latrines for private use by each family.

Children, Older People, and Women have the Highest Risk of Morbidity

Positive signs of the coefficient obtained for the children, older people, and women indicate that the likelihood of morbidity is higher for these groups compared to other age groups and men, and the correlations are highly significant statistically. It highlights the need for especial emphasis on children, women, and older groups in the urban health care strategy. High values obtained from coefficient and *z* score highlights that older people, followed by women and children, have the highest morbidity rate. Negative signs of the coefficient for adult men and women also reinforce greater risks of morbidity for children and older urban population.

The survey questionnaire included questions on the incidence of mortality over the last 10 years. Based on self-reporting of the incidence of mortality over the last 10 years by the respondents, we found that it was higher for children under 5 (8 per cent) and older people, particularly those aged over 65 years (60 per cent), compared to other age groups and across slum and non-slum households. The highest incidence of mortality for older people, which is also higher for non-slum (62 per cent) than slum (50 per cent) households, suggests a real risk of diabetes and cardiovascular disease burden and the need for preventative measures through policy and programmatic intervention. Note that Bangladesh ranks ninth in the age-standardized mortality rate due to chronic diseases among 23 developing countries (Abegunde et al.2007). According to BBS (2007b), half (51 per cent) of the deaths in

Bangladesh are due to non-communicable diseases and other chronic health conditions.

Increased Risk of Morbidity in Households with Spouses Having Low/No Formal Education

Positive sign for spousal education dummy suggests that the likelihood of morbidity increases more for households with spouses who are primary dropouts or have no formal education, and this is also statistically significant. By contrast, the negative sign obtained for migrant dummy indicates that the risk of morbidity increases with increased duration in Dhaka city due to higher prevalence of chronic diseases among older people, non-poor urban dwellers, and long-term migrant household. This draws our attention not only to social deprivation as an issue of urban health but also to the emerging problem of chronic disease burden for non-poor segments of the urban population that require policy intervention (as indicated earlier and also discussed later).

Access to Safe Drinking Water and Gas Pipe Reduces the Risk of Morbidity

We also find positive signs for safe drinking water and type of fuel used, which suggest that with most of the households having access to safe drinking water (Chapter 6), irrespective of slum and non-slum residence, the risk of morbidity is almost equitably spread across the sample population. The same logic applies for the type of fuel used because most of the respondents rely on piped and/or cylinder gas for cooking (as observed in Chapter 6).

Risk of Morbidity Transcends the Rich–Poor Boundary

Negative signs for poor and slum dwellers' dummy groups indicate that the risk of morbidity cuts across rich and poor respondents. Our survey data (Table 7.4) reveals that the morbidity rate does not differ much among different income quintiles. Rather, the morbidity rate for chronic disease is higher for those falling in the higher-income bracket than for the bottom two quintiles. From the pattern of prevalence of disease (Table 7.5), we have observed that poorer respondents (mainly defined as those living in slum households) do not suffer as much from

Table 7.4 Morbidity Rate by Gender and Income Quintiles of Sample Population, 2010

Income Quintile	All Types of Sickness			Chronic Diseases		
	Male	Female	Total	Male	Female	Total
Bottom Quintile	24.9	33.4	29.1	6.8	10.3	8.5
Second Quintile	23.4	31.7	27.3	8.3	8.3	8.3
Third Quintile	25.7	28.1	26.8	12.8	12.9	12.9
Fourth Quintile	17.8	29.2	23.2	7.7	15.7	11.5
Top Quintile	22.5	26.8	24.5	13.0	15.9	14.3
Top 10 Per Cent	17.5	27.7	22.3	10.2	16.8	13.3
All Quintile Groups	23.0	30.0	26.3	9.7	12.4	11.0

Source: Authors' estimate from BRAC third-round urban poverty survey, 2010.

diabetes and cardiovascular diseases as compared to high earning urban dwellers (in non-slum). This is consistent with the Urban Health Survey 2006 (NIPORT et al. 2008) that found a remarkably higher prevalence of non-communicable diseases (NCDs) such as hypertension and diabetes among the richer non-slum populations compared to slum people.

In explaining negative signs for poor and slum dwellers' dummies, it is worthwhile to note the reporting discrepancy between the respondents from poor and non-poor backgrounds in the first place. It is often argued that compared to non-poor, poorer people are likely to have greater tendency to ignore sickness due largely to cultural perception and lack of health education. Also, the nature of the job of respondents can offer some explanations to the negative signs even if partially. As we have observed in Chapters 4 and 5, slum dwellers are largely employed in occupations that require physical labour and, hence, they have greater opportunities for burning calories compared to those living in non-slum households and engaged in occupations requiring minimal energy combustion.

Apart from working conditions, urban environment in general, particularly in Dhaka city, tends to discourage physical activity and promote unhealthy food consumption. The lack of open space in Dhaka city and the threat of mugging and insecurity prevailing in public space, and increasing environmental pollution prevent middle- and high-income groups of city dwellers from walking, jogging, and other outdoor physical activities.[4] Moreover, due to the growing craze for and affordability of Western-style junk food, it has become a part of the food habit for high-income urban dwellers to consume high cholesterol food. Clearly, it underscores the need for health education and wider campaign for more nutritious food. In the context of positive correlation between age and prevalence of diabetes and cardiovascular diseases that are predicted to rise globally along with an increase in ageing population, it is important to examine the implication of the 'diseases of affluence paradigm' for the shifting disease pattern and burden in urban Bangladesh, particularly in Dhaka city (Ezzati et al. 2005).

Therefore, overall, our survey results challenge some of the conventional wisdom. It highlights that the likelihood of sickness can no longer be explained simply by slum and non-slum residence of urban population. Rather, we need to examine the quality of services, particularly access to private sanitary latrine, along with standard demographic variables such as age and gender and the level of education of the spouse. Also, it underscores the growing importance of balanced and nutritious food and physical exercises, and for health education to be considered as an integral part of urban health strategy that should also address safety and security issues.

Modern Allopathy Is the Most Common Mode of Treatment

The residents of Dhaka city mainly sought modern allopathic treatment although from three different sources (Table 7.5). Most went to either MBBS or specialist doctors (47.6 per cent) or to a pharmacy and/or drug seller for treatment (43.8 per cent). Increasingly, however, private hospitals have become popular sources for treatment. Nearly one-fifth (18.9 per cent) of the respondents also went to hospitals, largely private ones, mainly for the treatment of chronic diseases such as diabetes (47.7 per cent) and kidney problem (42.3 per cent), hypertension (27.9 per cent) and rheumatism, and/or heart problem or chest pain (25 per cent). Twice as many older people aged 50 years and over (35 per cent) as adults aged between 25 and 49 years (16.4 per cent) went to hospitals, given that the incidence of chronic diseases was higher among the former (Table 7.1).

Table 7.5 Incidence of Morbidity among Sample Population by Major Diseases, Gender, Slum and Non-slum Residence, and Migration Status

Major Diseases	Male	Female	Slum	Non-slum	Recent Migrant	Long-term Migrant	Non-migrant
Fever	7.6	9.0	13.9	5.9	14.6	7.8	6.8
Diabetes	4.9	5.4	1.9	6.5	0.6	5.2	
ARI	2.5	2.5	8.4	1.9	3.4	2.6	2.0
Gastritis/ Ulcer	2.1	3.0	3.8	2.1	1.3	2.5	3.1
Blood Pressure	1.4	3.2	1.0	2.9	0.3	2.6	2.2
Aches/Pains	1.4	1.7	1.9	1.2	0.3	1.9	0.7
Rheumatism	0.5	1.4	1.3	0.8	0	1.0	1.1
Diarrhoea	0.8	1.0	1.8	0.5	1.7	0.8	0.7
Asthma	0.6	0.9	0.9	0.6	0.6	1.0	0.5
Kidney Problem	0.6	0.6	0.7	0.6	0	0.7	0.7
All Major Diseases	22.3	28.7	31.8	23.0	23.1	26.1	24.8

Source: Authors' estimate from BRAC third-round urban poverty survey, 2010.

Pharmacy and/or Drug Sellers: Main Treatment Providers for Slum Children

Unlike the morbidity patterns, the treatment-seeking behaviours of both men and women did not differ much. Compared to both adult and older respondents, there was a higher propensity to get infants (54.7 per cent), children (56.8 per cent), and young people (58.3 per cent) treated by pharmacies and/or drug sellers, which could be related to the higher prevalence of non-chronic types of diseases (or communicable diseases) among this group that requires instant medical intervention. Simultaneously, affordability and equity issues related to the health services can also be considered in explaining differential treatment seeking behaviour of rich and poor people. For example, three-fifths of slum dwellers (60.7 per cent) relied on pharmacies or drug sellers for treatment instead of other sources compared to those in non-slum (34.3 per cent) households.

According to Jahan et al. (2015) slum dwellers' heavy reliance on this source is mainly due to their inability to pay consultancy fees to qualified private practitioners or bear private hospital charges. Other reasons are proximity from home, short waiting period, and availability of medicine (Jahan et al. 2015). Whether the differential mode of treatment is affecting the health outcome and/or causing greater mortality in slum households compared to non-slum households needs to be explored in future research.

However, research (Goel et al. 1996; Smith 2009) shows that by providing health advice and medicine, pharmacies play an important role all over the world, and particularly in low-income countries. For fever and communicable diseases such as ARI and diarrhoea, many respondents (73.2 per cent and 63 per cent, respectively) approached the pharmacy, while they consulted qualified doctors and/or specialists for aches and pains (73.1 per cent) and chronic diseases such as kidney problem (63.2 per cent), asthma (57.1 per cent), and diabetes (56.6 per cent) as seen in Table 7.5.

A study by the International Centre of Diarrhoeal Disease, Bangladesh (ICDDRB) (2009) reveals that during the 2009 influenza pandemic, 48 per cent of respondents with influenza-like illnesses used pharmacies as their first point of care. According to the 2007 national survey, drug sellers comprised almost one-fifth (16 per cent) of the health care providers in urban areas (Ahmed, Hossain, and Chowdhury 2009).

Our findings regarding the treatment-seeking behaviour of the sample population is partly comparable with the national trend, in which a majority (62.2 per cent) of the respondents seeks treatment from a doctor and only a few (5.2 per cent) go to a homeopath or Ayurvedic doctors (BBS 2013c). We also found that only a few respondents resorted to either traditional treatment such as homeopathy or Ayurveda (3 per cent) or others (1 per cent) such as village quacks or peers (faith healers) notwithstanding their poverty or literacy level. A small proportion of respondents (3 per cent) did not seek any treatment at all when they were sick, which suggests a high level of public awareness among the Dhaka city dwellers regarding the need to seek modern medical intervention to cure illness rather than taking risks with such traditional healers. A similar trend has been observed in the survey conducted by the MRC Mode Limited and FGD among respondents from Kamrangir Char and the catchment slum areas in 2009.

However, the tendency to seek treatment from a pharmacy or drug seller was much higher among the sample population compared to the national average (43.8 per cent and 20 per cent, respectively). In contrast, they were less inclined to go to paramedics and/or health workers (less than 1 per cent) than the national average (9.4 per cent), as seen in Table 7.6. According to HIES data, private for-profit providers are the dominant health care providers in Bangladesh (BBS 2011a). Two-fifths of the people who sought medical care went to drug retailers (pharmacies/dispensaries/shops) irrespective of whether they were trained or not, and a similar proportion (39 per cent) sought care from qualified private providers (BBS 2011a). These qualified private providers include government-employed doctors engaged in private practice.

Improvised Treatment Facilities in the Last Decade: Dominant Perception of Respondents

We have also explored the perception of the respondents regarding improvement in their access to the medical facilities in the years between 2001 and 2010. It is encouraging to note that most (88.7 per cent) perceived considerable improvement in the treatment facility in the last decade, while for a small proportion (3.7 per cent), it has worsened. The response pattern does not change regardless of respondents' slum or non-slum residence or their migration status (Table 7.7). Their perception may partly be justified on the grounds that there are more than 600 hospitals and clinics, mostly private, in Dhaka city (Rahman and Rahman 2010), coexisting with thousands of pharmacies. Although there are only 0.6 hospital beds per thousand people in Dhaka, which is way behind its South Asian neighbours, the highest concentration—close to 50 per cent—of hospitals of the country are in Dhaka.[5]

Also, it is often argued that 95 per cent of health care providers are unregulated, informal, and often lack qualifications in their field (Ahmed, Hossain, and Chowdhury 2009), which casts doubt on the quality of service. One plausible reason for this perception regarding improved health facilities can be related to increase in the incidence of

Table 7.6 Distribution of Morbid Members by Age Group, Gender, Slum and Non-slum Residence, Migration Status, Major Diseases, and Types of Treatment Sought

Age Group	MBBS/Specialist	Hospital	Pharmacy	Traditional	Other	Did Not Seek Treatment	All Types*
<5 Years	39.1	3.1	54.7	3.1	0.0	1.6	101.6
5–14 Years	35.2	6.8	56.8	1.1	3.4	5.7	109.1
15–24 Years	45.8	4.2	58.3	5.6	0.0	2.8	116.7
25–49 Years	46.3	16.4	45.6	4.4	1.7	4.4	118.8
50–64 Years	53.2	33.7	30.0	1.6	0.0	0.5	118.9
65+ Years	64.1	35.9	31.3	0.0	0.0	0.0	131.3
All Sick Members	47.6	18.9	43.8	3.0	1.0	2.8	117.1
Male	47.8	18.1	44.4	3.9	1.4	3.6	119.2
Female	47.4	19.7	43.3	2.2	0.7	2.2	115.4
Slum	37.1	10.7	60.7	3.9	2.1	4.3	118.9
Non-slum	53.4	23.6	34.3	2.4	0.4	2.0	116.1
Recent Migrants	30.7	8.0	66.7	2.7	1.3	5.3	114.7
Long-term Migrant	47.8	22.4	42.4	2.9	1.0	2.4	119.0
Non-migrant	53.1	14.7	38.9	3.3	0.9	2.8	113.7

Major Diseases							
Fever	37.6	5.4	63.2	1.2	2.1	4.5	114.0
Gastritis/Ulcer	49.3	13.3	62.7	2.7	2.7	0.0	130.7
Diarrhoea	48.1	14.8	63.0	3.7	0.0	3.7	133.3
ARI	32.4	16.9	73.2	1.4	0.0	7.0	131.0
Asthma	57.1	14.3	21.4	3.6	0.0	10.7	107.1
Rheumatic/Heart problem	50.0	25.0	42.9	0.0	0.0	7.1	125.0
Aches/Pains	73.1	19.4	29.9	1.5	0.0	0.0	123.9
Blood Pressure	39.5	27.9	60.5	2.3	0.0	2.3	132.6
Diabetes	56.6	47.4	21.1	0.0	0.0	0.0	125.0
Kidney Problem	63.2	42.1	26.3	5.3	0.0	0.0	136.8
All Sick Members	47.6	18.9	43.8	3.0	1.0	2.8	117.1

Note: *Total does not add up to 100 per cent because of multiple responses to questions on both morbidity and types of treatment sought.
Source: Authors' estimate from BRAC third-round urban poverty survey, 2010.

Table 7.7 Respondents' Perception about Their Access to Medical Facilities in 2010, Compared with 2001 by Slum and Non-slum Residence and Migration Status

Respondents' Category	Much Better Than Before		Better than Before		Same		Worse or Worst		Do Not Know		All	
	No	%	No	%	No	%	No	%	No	%	No	%
Slum	28	14.0	151	75.5	17	8.5	3	1.5	1	0.5	200	100
Non-slum	93	23.3	260	65.0	28	7.0	19	4.8	0	0	400	100
All	121	20.2	411	68.5	45	7.5	22	3.7	1	0.2	600	100
Recent Migrants	18	24.3	50	67.6	3	4.1	2	2.7	1	1.4	74	100
Long-term Migrant	71	19.4	249	68.0	34	9.3	12	3.3	0	0	366	100
Non-migrants	32	20.0	112	70.0	8	5.0	8	5.0	0	0	160	100

Source: Authors' estimate from BRAC third-round urban poverty survey, 2010.

treatment and per capita household expenditure on health as a percentage of total expenditure.

Significant Increase in Households' Expenditure on Health

Households' expenditure on health comprised 5.1 per cent of the total expenditure in 2010 on a per capita basis, compared with 1.2 per cent in 1998, and the proportional share was almost the same for both slum and non-slum households (Figure 7.1). This represents an annual average growth rate of 18 per cent on the balance—14.3 per cent and 18.9 per cent, respectively, for slum and non-slum households, during the reference period. Clearly, households' increasing share in health spending can be related to inflation in the cost of health services, particularly diagnostic, and medicine (Sarker et al. 2014). At the same time, it also suggests households' greater incentive to spend on human capital. However, questions arise regarding the efficient and effective allocation of health expenditure and who benefits most, which have been addressed in some of the existing researches.[6] In this study, we have partially covered other aspects such as how the quality of human capital is affecting productivity and economic growth as well as helping to sustain gains from improved income (discussed in Chapter 5).

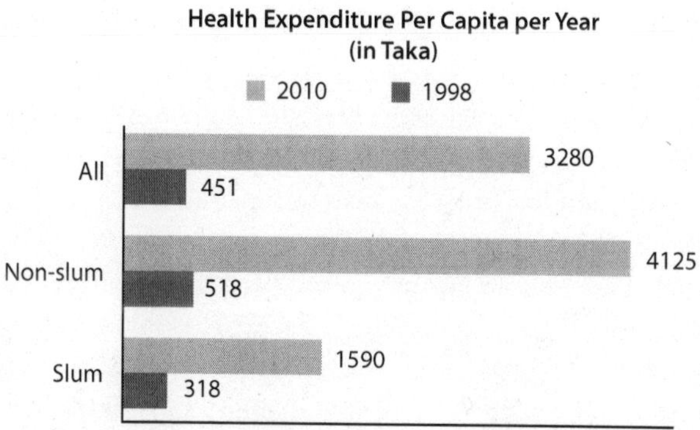

Figure 7.1 Household Health Expenditure Per Capita by Slum and Non-slum Residence, 1998 and 2010

Source: Authors' estimate from repeat surveys.

During the same reference period, the total health expenditure of the country as a percentage of GDP had increased by 2.7 per cent annually from 2.55 per cent to 3.52 per cent. Research shows that a rise in health spending by one percentage point of GDP is associated with 0.6 per cent and 0.5 per cent increase in the under-5 survival rate and annual per capita GDP growth (Baldacci et al. 2004). Bangladesh made considerable progress in meeting some targets for the MDGs, particularly those relating to nutrition, universal primary education, and reducing under-5 mortality. These goals are now part of Goal 3 and Goal 4 with broader scope to ensure healthy lives and promote well-being for all at all ages and inclusive and equitable quality education, and promote life-long learning opportunities for all by 2030, respectively. An urban health survey (NIPORT, Mitra and Associates, and ICF International 2013) shows that the under-5 mortality and infant mortality rates had declined by 30 per cent and 22 per cent, respectively, in urban slums between 2009 and 2013. As a preventative measure, near universal immunization rates achieved in the country can be considered as one of the conducive factors behind this achievement. Therefore, in order to highlight the equity issue, we examined whether the same rate of success is achieved in slum areas.

Rate of Immunization for Children Remained High across the Board

Our survey shows that over 90 per cent (91.1 per cent) of children aged 0–2 years were fully immunized in Dhaka city (Table 7.8). The rate of immunization for children was lower for girls (88.5 per cent) than boys (94.1 per cent) and was the same for both slum and non-slum households. Note that the proportion of immunized children is higher from recent migrant families (94.4 per cent) compared with either long-term (90.1 per cent) or non-migrant families (91.3 per cent). Except for children from the bottom income quintile, the rate of immunization was high for all other income quintiles. The main reasons for the gap in the immunization coverage among different groups of children as reported by respondents included sickness and inability to avail the service due to travel-related reason.

Existing studies focused on the lower rate of immunization among slum-children compared to the urban average and the need for

Table 7.8 Rate of Vaccination for Children Aged 0 and 2 Years by Slum and Non-slum Residence, Migratory Status, Spouse's Education Level, and Income Quintile, 2010

Types of Households	Male	Female	Total	Total (Numbers)		
	%	%	%	Male	Female	Total
Slum	94.1	96.0	95.2	17	25	42
Non-slum	100	91.2	95.5	33	34	67
All	98.0	93.2	95.4	50	59	109
Recent Migrants	100	100	100	10	9	19
Long-term Migrants	96.7	89.7	92.8	30	39	69
Non-migrants	100	100	100	10	11	21
No Education	87.5	100	95.2	8	13	21
Primary/Secondary	100	88.0	93.3	20	25	45
SSC/HSC	100	100	100	16	8	24
Degree	100	100	100	3	9	12
Highest Quintile	100	100	100	7	7	14
Second Quintile	100	100	100	4	8	12
Third Quintile	100	100	100	17	6	23
Fourth Quintile	92.9	84.6	87.5	8	12	20
Bottom Quintile	98.0	93.2	95.4	50	59	109

Source: Authors' estimate from BRAC third-round urban poverty survey, 2010.

developing different strategies to reach marginal groups (Atkinson and Cheyne 1994; Uddin et al. 2009). Our survey, however, tends to suggest that different strategies adopted by the government and the city corporation such as an extension of the Expanded Program on Immunization (EPI) service schedule, training for service providers on valid doses and management of side-effects, and an EPI support group for social mobilization helped reducing slum and non-slum differential. Rather, it draws attention to the intra-group differential and the need for improvised strategies to cover the children from extremely poor families and mobile population.

The overall analysis of the health status of Dhaka city dwellers highlights important changes in the disease patterns for different age groups, men and women, slum and non-slum dwellers, and more-educated and less-educated mothers. The importance of education as a preventative measure can hardly be overemphasized. In the remaining part of this chapter, we have focused on the inter-generational perspective on education-related progress and issues over time.

EDUCATION AND HUMAN CAPITAL DEVELOPMENT

Existing literature amply demonstrated that education is a critical factor inducing the capability to safeguard sustainable development, voicing protest against exclusion, inequality, and injustice necessary for ensuring that the benefits of growth are equitably distributed and thereby reducing inequality between the rich and poor, men and women, and also between generations (Sen 1999; UNESCO 2005). The Education for All Global Monitoring Report estimates that for every single dollar spent on education, between US$ 10 and US$ 15 would be generated in economic growth.[7] Education is vital to escape poverty by developing skills, increasing productivity, knowledge, and capability essential to lead a decent and fulfilling life. Based on the Gini decomposition analysis in Chapter 5, we found that Gini concentration ratio for schooling of earners declined between 1998 and 2010, and was more equitably distributed compared with distribution of the physical capital, which was most skewed. Achieving inclusive and quality education for all reaffirms the belief that education is one of the most powerful and proven vehicles for sustainable development. This goal ensures that all girls and boys complete free primary and secondary schooling by 2030. It also aims to provide equal access to affordable vocational training, eliminate gender and wealth disparities, and achieve universal access to quality higher education.

Of the three composite components of the HDI used by the United Nations, knowledge plays a more vital role compared to the other two components—life expectancy at birth and quality of life in terms of purchasing power parity (PPP). This is because both life expectance at birth and quality of life are indirectly dependent on knowledge. Knowledge consists of adult literacy and the combined ratio of enrolment. It should be noted that adult literacy carries double weight (two-thirds) as compared to the combined enrolment ratio (one-third), and the direct contribution of adult literacy alone to HDI is estimated at around one-quarter (23 per cent).[8]

Improved Adult Literacy Rate

We estimated the rate of adult literacy for the sample population of Dhaka city aged 16–59 years at 81 per cent in 2010—84.1 per cent and 77.4 per cent for male and female populations, respectively.[9] The rate has increased by almost 10 per cent since 1991 from 75.7 per cent and 66.7 per cent, respectively (Table 7.9). However, for mature adult women (aged 45–59 years) the rate of increase was much lower—around 4 per cent—from 61.8 per cent to 64.6 per cent during the same period. Compared with the urban averages for male (75.6 per cent) and female (67.8 per cent) population aged 15 years and above, the rates are higher for the same year (BBS 2013b). This is not unexpected given that Dhaka city is generally ahead of urban areas and the national averages on both economic and social development indicators.

Table 7.9 Age-Specific Rates of Adult Literacy and Education Attainment of the Sample Population, 1991–2010

Education Level	1991				2010			
	16–29 Yrs	30–44 Yrs	45–59 Yrs	Total	16–29 Yrs	30–44 Yrs	45–59 Yrs	Total
Men								
Literate	79.2	74.9	69.2	75.7	87.1	83.8	78.4	84.1
SSC and HSC	35.6	22.2	19.2	27.5	36.0	23.1	23.0	28.5
Degree	7.5	26.3	27.9	18.3	11.7	29.3	32.9	22.7
Women								
Literate	70.4	62.8	61.8	66.7	88.0	71.8	64.6	77.4
SSC and HSC	30.7	20.9	17.6	25.8	36.2	21.3	25.0	28.8
Degree	5.8	10.8	11.8	8.3	11.0	19.3	9.0	13.3
Total								
Literate	74.8	69.3	67.1	71.5	87.6	78.4	71.5	80.9

(Cont'd)

Table 7.9 (*Cont'd*)

Education Level	1991				2010			
	16–29 Yrs	30–44 Yrs	45–59 Yrs	Total	16–29 Yrs	30–44 Yrs	45–59 Yrs	Total
SSC and HSC	33.2	21.6	18.8	26.7	36.1	22.3	24.0	28.6
Degree	6.7	19.1	23.3	13.8	11.4	24.8	21.2	18.2
Slum								
Literate	30.8	26.1	23.1	27.8	69.4	48.7	22.3	53.5
SSC and HSC	2.2	1.8	0.0	1.8	13.5	7.5	2.1	9.3
Degree	0.0	0.0	0.0	0.0	0.0	0.5	0.0	0.2
Non-slum								
Literate	93.0	86.0	79.2	88.1	95.0	90.8	85.5	91.2
SSC and HSC	45.9	29.1	23.9	36.2	45.5	28.5	30.2	36.1
Degree	9.4	26.3	29.9	19.0	16.1	34.9	27.2	25.1
Recent Migrant								
Literate	59.3	46.7	64.3	54.1	86.8	71.8	55.6	76.1
SSC and HSC	13.5	12.9	14.3	13.4	28.9	17.9	18.5	22.9
Degree	6.3	17.7	21.4	11.6	6.0	30.8	22.2	18.6
Long-term Migrant								
Literate	76.6	70.3	71.8	73.4	86.7	78.0	67.5	80.7
SSC and HSC	39.3	21.0	19.7	29.1	38.8	23.5	19.4	30.5
Degree	7.8	21.2	26.1	15.9	12.2	22.8	26.3	18.0
Non-migrant								
Literate	79.8	78.5	47.3	75.2	90.0	82.1	71.5	83.1
SSC and HSC	25.3	29.2	18.4	25.8	32.3	21.5	23.2	26.4
Degree	3.2	11.3	13.2	7.3	11.4	26.7	18.8	18.6

Source: Authors' estimate from the repeat surveys.

Increased Adult Literacy Rate for Slum Dwellers, but the Slum–Non-slum Gap Persists

The progress has been most impressive for slum dwellers as the rate almost doubled from 27.8 per cent to 53.5 per cent between 1991 and 2010, while for those from non-slum it remained steady at around 90 per cent since 1991 (Table 7.9). However, the gap in the adult literacy rate between slum and non-slum is still very high. The rate of increase (38.6 per cent) has been more rapid for younger adults (aged between 16 and 29 years) from slum households compared to other age groups.

Rapidly Increased and Highest Adult Literacy Rate for Young Adults

Among migrant population, the rates of adult literacy were estimated at 76.1 per cent and 80.7 per cent in 2010, respectively, for recent and long-term migrants compared with 83.1 per cent for non-migrants. The rate was highest for young adults aged 16–29 years (87 per cent) for both recent and long-term migrants as well as non-migrants (90.8 per cent). This increase in rate has been rapid, particularly for recent migrants.[10] Rapid increase of literacy rate among the young adult population, particularly from slum and recent migrant families, is consistent with our earlier finding (Chapter 4) regarding the growing numbers of students among migrants to Dhaka, indicating an increase in the demand and spread of education over time.

However, for a nation to progress, we not only need increased number of literate adults but also improvement in the quality of education. What is meant by quality of education is highly debated in the literature.[11] Also, we do not have data to examine the multiple dimensions involved in quality of education such as teaching and learning, assessment methods, support and resources available, and creative and emotional skills. For this study, we have used outcomes of education such as literacy, numeracy, and life skills as proxy of quality, which we believe can be captured partly from educational attainment of the respondents. Accordingly, we have examined the extent to which the adult population has secondary school and/or higher secondary certificates (SSC/HSC) and tertiary qualification, and whether it has changed over time.

Increased High School and Tertiary Qualification Rates for Young Adults Diminished Gender Gap, but Slum and Non-slum Gap Remained

Nearly half of the adults (46.8 per cent) had SSC/HSC and tertiary qualification in 2010, compared with 40.5 per cent in 1991 (Table 7.9). The rates were higher for male (51.2 per cent) than female adults (42.1 per cent), and six-times higher for non-slum (61.2 per cent) than slum cohort (9.5 per cent). However, what is encouraging is that with more young female members (aged between 16 and 29 years) having SSC/HSC and tertiary qualification, the gender gap has diminished for this group over time (47.7 and 47.2 for male and female adults in 2010, respectively, compared with 43.1 per cent and 36.5, respectively, in 1991). Generally, mature adults and older women, aged between 45 and 59 years, and slum dwellers had slightly lower levels of qualifications compared with either youth or young adults.

Parents' Literacy and Non-School Qualifications Increased with Fathers Retaining Higher Levels

Also, it should be noted that both the rate of adult literacy and levels of educational attainment had increased for fathers and mothers in 2010, and the rate of increase was particularly higher for mothers (Figure 7.2). The rates increased from 70 per cent to 77 per cent for fathers and 60 per cent to 73 per cent for mothers between 1991 and 2010. Compared with 45.2 per cent of fathers who had SSC/HSC and tertiary qualifications, the proportion of mothers having the same qualification was lower—35.9 per cent. However, the percentage change since 1991 was higher for mothers (7.5 per cent) than fathers (2.9 per cent). Given that parents' education often acts as a positive trigger, we can assume that children's education will increase reasonably over time, which we have examined later.

CONSIDERABLE NARROWING OF GAPS IN ENROLMENT RATES BETWEEN POOR AND NON-POOR CHILDREN AND ADOLESCENTS

We have noted a rapid progress in school participation for the children aged between 6 and 16 years in Dhaka city over time. Enrolment rate

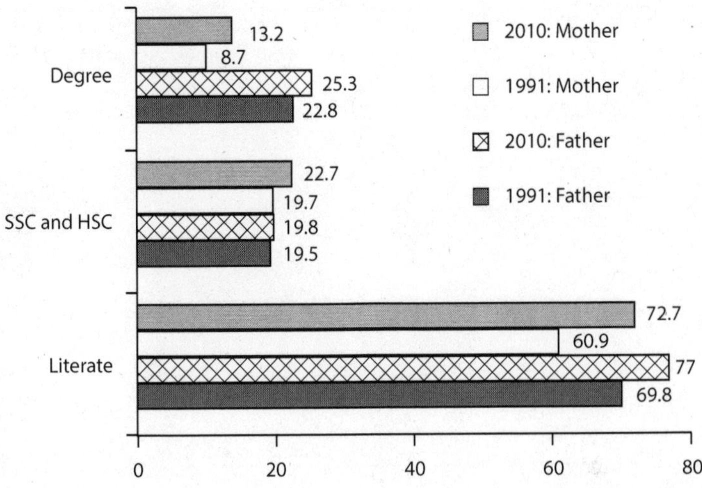

Figure 7.2 Level of Literacy and Educational Attainment of Parents, 1991 and 2010

Source: Authors' estimate from the repeat surveys.

for the primary school age group (6–10 years) increased from 77 per cent in 1991 to 94 per cent in 2010—near universal level (Table 7.10). More importantly, the progress has been faster for children from slum compared to non-slum households, in which enrolment rate was already very high in 1991. In 2010, almost 89 per cent of the primary school age children from slum households attended schools, compared to 51 per cent estimated from our 1991 survey. This shows a remarkable increase by 74.5 per cent or an annual average increase of 3 per cent during the reference period.

Similarly, the participation rate for primary age cohorts from short-term migrant families has been most impressive as it doubled from 46 per cent to 92 per cent. The corresponding rates for those from long-term and non-migrant families were 93 per cent and 97 per cent, showing an increase by 13 per cent and 18 per cent, respectively (from 80 per cent and 89 per cent, respectively) during the same period.

With a 9 per cent increase from 77 per cent to 84 per cent during 1991–2010, progress regarding adolescents' (11–16 years) participation at the secondary level has also been impressive. The rate of increase

Table 7.10 Participation Rate of 6–22 Years' Age Group from Slum and Non-slum, Migrant and Non-migrant Families at Primary, Secondary, and Tertiary Education Levels, 1991–2010

Respondents by Categories	Primary: 6–10 Yrs		Secondary: 11–16 Yrs		Tertiary: 17–22 Yrs	
	1991	**2010**	**1991**	**2010**	**1991**	**2010**
Slum	51.4	88.9	31.6	70.5	7.2	11.4
Non-slum	93.1	97.6	90.1	90.4	64.3	57.5
All Respondents	77.0	94.2	75.8	83.5	48.2	43.7
Recent Migrants	46.5	92.3	54.8	68.2	27.7	32.4
Long-term Migrants	80.3	93.3	80.9	84.2	58.3	49.2
Non-migrants	89.5	97.3	79.5	89.2	21.1	38.2

Source: Authors' estimate from the repeat surveys.

had been most rapid for adolescents from slum households (from 32 per cent in 1991 to 71 per cent in 2010), while it remained steady (at 90 per cent) for the cohort from non-slum. It should be noted that the participation rate was the highest for adolescents from non-migrant families (89 per cent), followed by those from long-term and recent migrant families—84 per cent and 68 per cent. However, since 1991, the rate of increase has been higher for those from recent migrant families (13 per cent) compared with non-migrant (10 per cent) and long-term migrant families (3 per cent).

What is more important to note is that the gaps in enrolment rates between the rich and poor and recent and long-term migrant children and adolescents have been narrowed down remarkably over time. Compared with 1991, there was a fourfold and threefold decline in the slum and non-slum participation rate gaps for age cohorts at the primary and secondary levels, respectively. Similarly, from a 33 per cent gap at the primary level between recent and long-term migrant children, participation rate had almost equalized for the two groups. Further, at the secondary level, it had reduced by 20 per cent (from 36 per cent to 16 per cent) between 1991 and 2010 for the same reference groups. Tremendous improvements in adolescents' enrolment rate suggests that parents living in slums have become more conscious about continuing children's education till secondary level, as employment opportunities in industries (particularly in the garment industry) and informal services has grown over time, as observed in Chapters 4 and 5. It is generally acknowledged that acquiring a lower secondary education is a minimum prerequisite today for young people to gain the foundation skills they need to find decent jobs.[12] We can also argue that graduates from secondary schools have a better scope to be absorbed in these jobs compared to primary school completers or illiterates. As discussed earlier (in Chapter 5), the average level of education for both male and female workers in the private services, informal business, and garment industry increased significantly over time.

Tertiary Enrolment Rate Declined for Young Adults from Non-slum Families, but Slum–Non-slum Gap Persists

However, the changes recorded at the tertiary level are not at all encouraging. The participation rate for young people aged between 17 and 22 years attending tertiary educational institutions had declined from 48 per cent in 1991 to 44 per cent in 2010. This is particularly notable for young people from non-slum households as their participation rate declined by 7 per cent (from 64 per cent to 57 per cent). For the cohort from slum households, it has always been low, although it increased to 11 per cent in 2010 from 7 per cent in 1991, but the huge gap between the two groups persists at the tertiary level.

Tertiary Enrolment Rate for Non-migrant Cohort Increased but Declined for Those from Long-Term Migrant Families

Participation rates for young people from migrant and non-migrant families show two contrasting trends. On the one hand, it has declined for those from long-term migrant families by 9 per cent—from 58 per cent to 49 per cent. On the other hand, the participation rate increased significantly from 21 per cent to 38 per cent for those from non-migrant families, although they still lagged behind their cohorts from long-term migrant families. Unlike these two groups, the rate increased from 28 per cent to 32 per cent for those from recent migrant families during the same period.

Whether such contrasting trends represent growing awareness of the importance on higher education, particularly for young males, among non-migrant families and frustration among the youth from long-term migrant families need to be examined.[13] We have analysed this in Chapter 8 on attitudinal changes.[14] However, it tends to confirm partially that urban internal migrants are generally ahead of non-migrants in human development indicators which K. Harttgen and S. Klasen (2009) validated from 9 out of 16 countries they studied. In addition, it also suggests that all types of migrants are not on the same page and non-migrants are catching up fast with long-term migrants. What contributes to the changes discussed above needs further investigation.

Link between the Increased Enrolment Rates and Per Capita Expenditure in Education

Research shows that household expenditure on education is directly correlated with the educational outcome defined as educational attainment of children of migrant and non-migrant families (Cameron 2012). Analysis of our third-round survey data shows that households' education expenditure on a per capita basis for current students had increased by 4.5 per cent annually across the board over the period between 1998 and 2010 (Figures 7.3 and 7.4).[15] The rate of growth had been most impressive for recent migrant (11.2 per cent) and slum households during the reference period (10.4 per cent). Clearly, this increase in per capita expenditure can be used to explain the rapid improvement in the participation rates for the primary and secondary school age cohorts from these two groups. Accordingly, the amount spent on education by non-slum households which was estimated at seven times higher compared with that of slums in 1998 had been halved in 2010, while the gap in the expenditure between recent and long-term migrant households has more than halved (Figure 7.5).

However, it is intriguing that there is smaller difference between non-migrant and long-term migrant households regarding the education expenditure pattern compared to other categories. Particularly in the context of contrasting trends in education, participation rates were higher for adolescents from non-migrant households in comparison to adolescents from long-term migrant households, but this was reversed for young people at the tertiary level. It indicates that expenditure pattern alone is not sufficient to determine the level of higher education acquired. Accordingly, in the next chapter, we have examined how

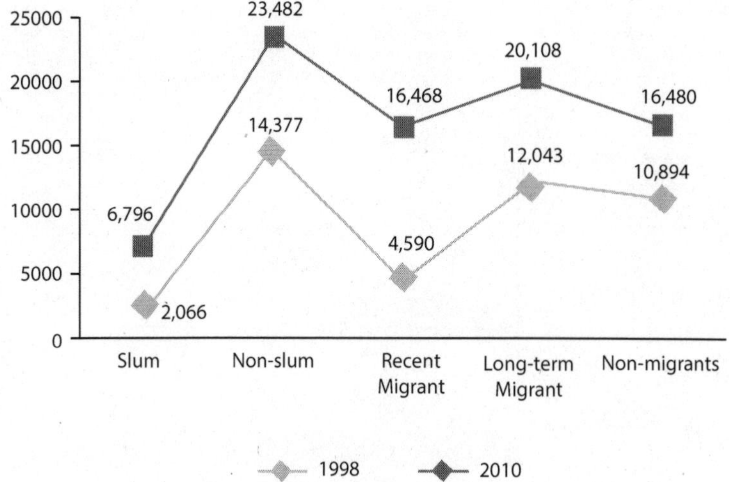

Figure 7.3 Household Annual Per Capita Expenditure on Current Students' Education in Taka for Different Categories of Sample Households, 1998–2010

Source: Authors' estimate from the repeat surveys.

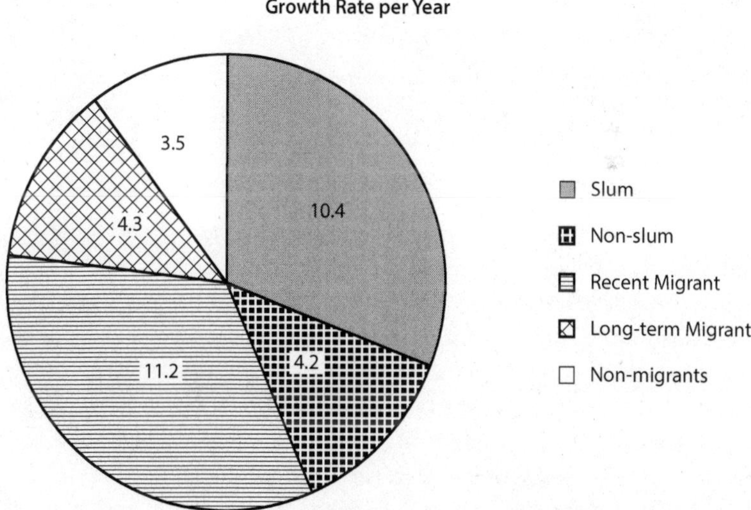

Figure 7.4 Annual Average Growth Rate of Per Capita Expenditure on Current Students' Education for Categories of Sample Households, 1998–2010

Source: Authors' estimate from the repeat surveys.

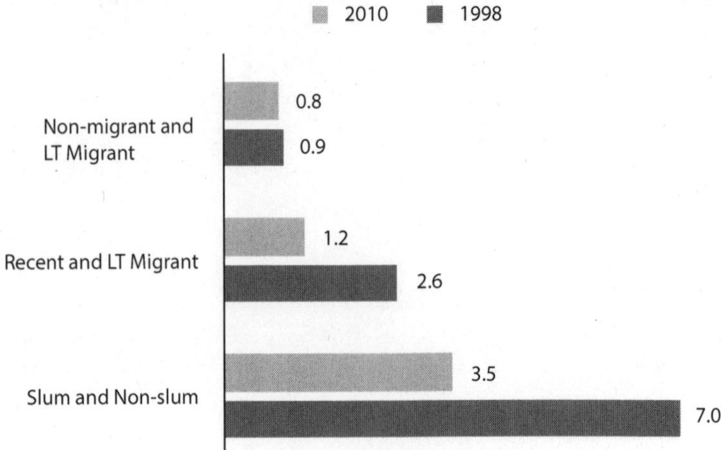

Figure 7.5 Gap in the Per Capita Expenditure on Current Students for Categories of Sample Households, 1998 and 2010

Note: LT Migrant=long-term migrant
Source: Authors' estimate from the repeat surveys.

attitude can influence educational attainments by using a range of indicators such as attitudes towards women's education and aspirations for children's education.

Labour Market Push and Pull Factors behind Declining Tertiary Enrolment Rate

It can be argued that due to the high rate of unemployment amongst the educated workforce in urban areas, the inducement to send young people to college has waned over time for cross-sections. This is true particularly for those from non-slum and long-term migrants' households, whose participation rates have been higher compared to those of other age cohorts. According to the Labour Force Survey Report 2010 (BBS 2011b), unemployment rate is highest in urban areas, particularly for those with HSC or equivalent level certification (17 per cent), followed by engineering or medical degree holders (14.7 per cent) and masters or equivalent qualification holders (11.5 per cent). The corresponding averages for rural areas are 11.3 per cent, 12.3 per cent, and 8.6 per cent, respectively.

Our data also shows that unemployment rate was higher, particularly for young males with a secondary school certificate and a higher secondary certificate (37.5 per cent), although the overall rate of unemployment was low (3.7 per cent for males and 6 per cent for females). Evidence suggests that the rate of youth unemployment is higher when compared with the rate of adult unemployment and tends to rise with educational attainment, which is partly related to family income and largely attributed to the skill mismatch in the labour market.[16]

In contrast, from the supply side, it can be argued that growing job opportunities in the expanding manufacturing and services sectors and increasing pull for overseas migration have also contributed to the decline in participation rate at the tertiary level. As a result, low-performing high-school graduates do not find enough incentive to continue education beyond the secondary level. For example, by analysing out-migration by family members, we found that of the 75 male members, mainly sons and brothers migrated overseas (63.6 per cent), followed by other cities or towns. Almost one-quarter of them was up to 25 years of age with almost three-quarters who had either primary and secondary level or SSC and HSC level education, and two-fifths (41 per cent) of the age cohort did so for employment-related reasons (Table 7.11).

Overall Dropout Rate Declining, but Still High for Adolescent Boys

By estimating the dropout rate from third-round survey data, we found that it remained high for adolescent group at 15.7 per cent, although it halved from 35 per cent since 1998. However, the rates were much higher for boys and girls from recent migrant families (35.7 per cent and 25 per cent, respectively) and those from slum households (34 per cent and 23.5 per cent, respectively). The corresponding averages were the lowest for those from non-slum and non-migrant households—9.3 per cent and 6.9 per cent, respectively (Table 7.12). As reasons for dropping out, almost one-fifth (17 per cent) of the adolescent boys and girls reported that they got a job. For another one-quarter lack of interest to study (25.5 per cent) emerged as an important reason (Figure 7.6). However, poverty was the number one barrier (40 per cent), particularly for girls (61.1 per cent), and this is clearly reflected in the participation

Table 7.11 Distribution of Out-migrating Male Members by Age Group, Level of Education, Reasons for Migration, and Destination

Age (Years)	Level of Education				Reason for Migration			Destination			Total
	None	1–9	SSC/ HSC	Degree	Job	Studies	Others	Overseas	Same City	Other	(No.)
Up to 20	40.0	20.0	40.0	0	10.0	60.0	30.0	60.0	30.0	10.0	10
21–5	8.3	50.0	33.3	8.3	66.7	8.3	25.0	66.7	25.0	8.3	12
26–9	0	26.7	40.0	33.3	53.3	26.7	20.0	66.7	20.0	13.3	15
30+	2.6	26.3	28.9	42.2	73.7	18.4	7.9	71.1	5.3	23.7	38
All	8.0	29.3	33.3	29.3	60.0	24.0	40.0	68.0	14.7	17.3	75

Source: Authors' estimate from BRAC third-round urban poverty survey, 2010.

Table 7.12 Rates for Dropping Out and Never Attending School and the Number of Out of School Children by Age Group, Gender, and Types of Households, 1991–2010

	Drop Out Rate				Never Attended School				Out of School (Number)			
	6–10 Yrs		11–16 Yrs		6–10 Yrs		11–16 Yrs		6–10 Yrs		11–16 Yrs	
	Male	Female	Male	Female	Male	Female	Male	Female	Male	Female	Male	Female
Slum	3.1	0	32.1	23.5	7.8	11.4	1.9	0	7	5	18	12
Non-slum	2.5	0	9.3	6.9	1.3	2.3	0.9	0	2	2	11	6
All	2.1	0	16.8	13.0	4.2	5.3	1.2	0	9	7	29	18
Recent Migrant	4.2	0	35.7	25.0	8.3	0	0	0	3	0	5	2
Long-term Migrant	2.3	0	18.3	12.1	4.6	6.6	0.9	0	6	5	20	12
Non-migrant	0	0	7.0	12.9	0	4.9	2.3	0	0	2	4	4

Source: Authors' estimate from the repeat surveys.

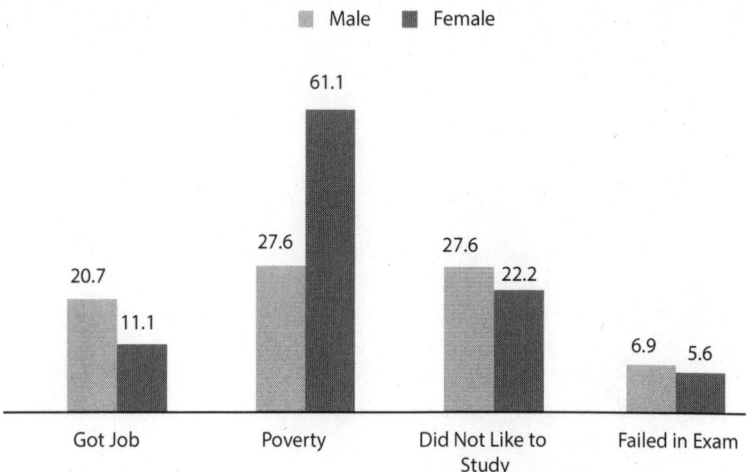

Figure 7.6 Distribution of Out of School Adolescents (11–16 years) by Gender and Reasons for Dropping Out and Never Attending Schools, 2010

Source: Authors' estimate from BRAC third-round urban poverty survey, 2010.

rate at the tertiary level which shows a huge gap between the slum and non-slum age cohorts, as discussed earlier.

Increased Gender Parity at the Primary and Secondary Levels

At the primary level, both boys (93.7 per cent) and girls (94.7 per cent) were participating almost equally in 2010. The highest rate of participation was noted for girls from recent migrant families (Table 7.13), followed by those from slums. For these two groups, the growth in enrolment rates was also higher—109.2 per cent and 59.2 per cent compared to the 13.9 per cent and 6.7 per cent growth rate for girls from long-term migrant households and non-slum households between 1991 and 2010. Note that a similar trend is also observed for boys from slum and recent migrants' households. However, with boys participating at a higher rate, non-migrant households present a contrasting trend, although over time the gender gap has reduced significantly.

Table 7.13 Educational Participation Rates for Primary, Secondary, and Tertiary Age Cohorts by Gender and Respondents' Categories, 1991 and 2010

Respondents by Categories	Primary: 6–10 Yrs.				Secondary: 11–16 Yrs.				Tertiary: 17–22 Yrs.			
	1991		2010		1991		2010		1991		2010	
	M	F	M	F	M	F	M	F	M	F	M	F
Slum	54.5	55.9	89.1	89.0	27.7	40.0	66.0	76.4	7.8	5.2	16.3	8.9
Non-slum	94.0	91.5	97.5	97.7	90.9	94.1	89.8	93.1	72.1	66.3	64.1	52.2
All Households	76.9	76.4	93.7	94.7	75.2	76.4	82.1	85.1	58.3	42.3	49.5	38.4
Recent Migrants	45.0	47.8	87.5	100	66.7	43.8	64.3	75.0	42.1	38.1	46.7	21.1
Long-term Migrants	82.2	82.0	93.1	93.4	79.7	82.1	80.8	87.9	60.8	55.4	53.9	45.0
Non-migrants	86.4	93.8	100	95.1	69.8	90.0	90.7	87.1	31.3	13.6	44.7	31.0

Note: M=male, F=female

Source: Authors' estimate from the repeat surveys.

At the secondary level, however, enrolment rate was higher for adolescent girls (85.1 per cent) than adolescent boys (76.4 per cent), clearly indicating a growing trend of gender parity. In 1991, the girls' participation rate was 82 per cent and that of boys was 75.2 per cent. For cohorts from slum and short-term and long-term migrant families, gender parity was much higher (1.2 each) when compared with other groups. What is important to note is that the gender gap for slum and recent migrant households has been reduced significantly over time. In contrast, a gender differential has emerged for cohorts from non-migrant households as the female enrolment rate declined between 1991 and 2010 while there was a significant increase (29.9 per cent) in the rate of participation for males. However, the rate of participation for girls was highest for cohorts from non-slum (93.1 per cent), followed by those from long-term migrant families (87.9 per cent), slum households (76.4 per cent) and recent migrant households (75 per cent).

Gender Parity Turned to Gender Deficit at Tertiary Level

However, gender parity has turned to gender deficit at the tertiary level since 1991, with female participation rate remaining lower than that of male cohorts over time. The gap was largest for recent migrants (25.6 per cent) due to a declining rate of participation for females in between 1991 and 2010 and a reversed trend for males. For young people from non-slum and long-term migrant households, the rate had declined for both males and females but faster for the latter. The trend was just the opposite for cohorts from non-migrant families, with a much faster increase in the rate of participation for females than males, although a gap remains (Table 7.13).

Given that the propensity to drop out from school starts from 13 years of age, we have examined the rate of marriage for adolescents (13–15 years) and youth (16–22 years) groups for different cross sections and over time. With an exception of a sole girl from the cohort of non-migrant families, none of the adolescent girls were married from the sample households irrespective of slum or non-slum residence and migration status. This is encouraging in the context that Bangladesh has the highest rate of child marriage in South Asia and ranked fourth on the same account globally (Nguyen and Wodon 2012). An increasing prevalence of dowry might have made the law against child marriage ineffective—parents are often motivated to marry their daughters early to reduce the price of dowry (Field and Ambrus 2008). There could be a counter argument on the ground that education is the premium, enhancing the prospect for a girl's marriage.

Higher Rate of Marriage for Young Girls Matters in Their Higher Education

However, on the other hand, the rate of marriage was remarkably higher among young girls aged between 18 and 21 years (43.9 per cent), compared to boys of the same age (2.6 per cent), which explains the gender gap at the tertiary level (Table 7.14). The rates were particularly higher for girls from slum (55.2 per cent) and short-term migrant households

Table 7.14 Rate of Marriage for Married Girls and Boys between 18 and 21 by Slum and Non-slum Residence, Migratory Status, Level of Education of Spouse, and Income Quintiles

Types of Households	2010			1991		
	Male	Female	All	Male	Female	All
Slum	8.6	55.6	33.4	87.2	93.0	90.0
Non-slum	0	38.7	19.5	90.2	91.1	90.6
All	2.6	43.9	23.5	89.3	91.6	90.4
Short-term Migrant	12.5	50.0	35.0	93.3	89.5	91.2
Long-term Migrant	2.7	43.7	23.9	89.6	93.3	91.1
Non-migrant	0	41.7	18.2	86.2	89.1	88.0
None	5.3	55.6	34.8	90.3	96.9	93.7
Primary/Secondary	1.9	42.8	23.4	100	98.6	99.3
SSC/HSC/Degree	0	21.7	9.6	100	100	100
Highest Quintile	0	35.3	15.8	81.3	94.2	88.0
Second Quintile	0	26.1	14.3	89.3	93.1	90.8
Third Quintile	5.0	52.2	30.2	97.4	87.5	92.8
Fourth Quintile	3.4	55.6	23.4	92.6	78.9	86.9
Bottom Quintile	4.0	48.6	30.0	88.9	100	96.9

Source: Authors' estimate from the repeat surveys

(50 per cent), compared to that of girls from long-term (43.7 per cent), non-migrant (41.7 per cent), and non-slum (38.7 per cent) households. Compared with 1991, the rates almost halved for almost all cross-sections. The legal age of marriage for women in Bangladesh is 18 years. However, almost two-thirds (65 per cent) of the women aged between 20 and 24 years got married before the age of 18 in 2011, although the proportion declined from 73 per cent in 1989 (NIPORT, Mitra and Associates, and ICF International 2013).

Note that the trend of reversed gender gap at the secondary-level enrolment rate that was observed for adolescents of Dhaka city in our first-round survey in the early 1990s had become an established trend in 2010. What our study has added to the existing body of knowledge is that the gap between the poor and non-poor children and migrant and non-migrant households regarding educational outcome is narrowing down. This is notwithstanding the fact that metropolitan children, particularly those from slum households, are not covered under the female stipend scheme (FSS). Compared with the urban averages, participation rates are higher (87.9 and 77.5, respectively) for primary and secondary school age cohorts, with girls leading the way (88.9 per cent and 83.4 per cent) compared to boys (86.9 per cent and 72.2 per cent) (BBS 2011a).

A recent study on the economic implications of gender parity by the McKinsey Global Institute (MGI) has estimated that US$12 trillion can be added to global growth by advancing gender equality (2015). With higher gender-parity scores strongly correlating with higher levels of development, such as GDP per capita or the degree of urbanization, the most developed regions of Europe and North America are closest to gender parity, while developing regions of South Asia have the furthest to go. It has particularly underscored that smaller differences in educational attainment between men and women can strongly enhance the status of girls and women, which helps to reduce the incidence of sex-selective abortions, child marriage, and violence from an intimate partner. Although our data clearly supports the declining trend in child marriage, we do not have data to support all these assertions. However, we have discussed women-empowerment issues by analysing attitudinal and aspirational changes in the next chapter to measure how and to what extent gender and generational relations within families are redefined and impacted in relation to migration in the urban milieu.

NOTES

1. Estimates Developed by the UN Inter-agency Group for Child Mortality Estimation (UNICEF, WHO, World Bank, and UN DESA Population Division) at childmortality.org and at infantmortality.org.

2. It should be noted that morbidity rate measured in one short survey generally raises the validity and reliability question as it is generally seasonal in nature.

3. As indicated in the methodology section, the migration status is determined by the length of stay in Dhaka city for those who were not born in Dhaka.

4. Open space is increasingly being captured by the real estate companies, commercial and services sectors, and varied means of transportation plying on the city streets.

5. Corcco Limited, 15 July 2015, 'Innovations to Fill the Gap in Medical Services', Dhaka: JICA, available at: http://www.jica.go.jp/bangladesh/bangland/en/report/543.html (accessed on 10 January 2016).

6. See, for example, Sarker et al. 2014.

7. Blog written by Global Education Monitoring (GEM) on 17 October 2013, available at: https://gemreportunesco.wordpress.com/2013/10/17/we-will-never-eradicate-poverty-without-quality-education-for-all/ (accessed on 15 February 2016).

8. However, in recent years, there are debates regarding the efficacy of human development indicators. For example, it is argued that while literacy helped evaluating progress during the past two decades, almost half of the countries have a literacy rate higher than 95 per cent, and developed countries no longer collect data on basic literacy. Since 2010, adult literacy measure has been replaced with mean years of schooling and measure of the education of children, the gross enrolment ratio has been replaced with a measure of expected years of schooling. For an excellent review, see Klugman, Rodriguez, and Choi (2011).

9. Note that we have excluded persons with no formal education and those who dropped out at the primary level from the definition of literacy.

10. The rates are increased by 27.5 per cent, 10.1 per cent, and 10.2 per cent, respectively, since 1991.

11. A good review of the debates and viewpoints regarding quality of education is available at www.unesco.org/education/gmr_download/chapter1.pdf (accessed on 15 February 2016).

12. Please see the United Nations Organization for Education and Culture report (UNESCO 2012) for a review of the global situation.

13. Note that gender gap is most prominent for non-migrants compared with other groups, as discussed next in this chapter.

14. As we shall see in the following paragraphs on gender parity (Table 7.10), the gender gap in the participation rate is one of the highest for non-migrant families, particularly at the tertiary level.

15. For expenditure, we relied on the 1998 data as we do not have details of expenditure from the 1991 data. Note that the enrolment rate did not vary much between 1991 and 1998.

16. http://www.ilo.org/wcmsp5/groups/public/---dgreports/--dcomm/documents/publication/wcms_212423.pdf (accessed on 27 March 2016). For skill mismatch, see http://us.manpower.com/us/en/multimedia/2011-Talent-Shortage-Survey.pdf (accessed on 15 February 2016).

8 Migration, Modernization, and Social Change

An Inquiry into Migrants' Attitudinal Changes

Urbanization is always associated with innovation, and demographic, social, and economic transformation. Cities often project the image of all that development and modernization entails; hence, their crucial role in every sphere of life cannot be overemphasized. Indeed, civilization has aptly been described as what goes on in cities (Boulding 1963). Many sociologists believed that cities were the only places in which human beings could realize their potentialities to the full. According to the French sociologist Émile Durkheim (1933: 296): 'Great cities are the uncontested homes of progress; it is in them that ideas, fashions, customs, new needs are elaborated and then spread over the rest of the country. ... Minds naturally are there oriented to the future.'

What is social change? Social change can be defined as the alteration of social interactions, institutions, stratification systems, and elements of culture over time. Existing theories identified several causal factors underneath social change which include among others population mobility, social movement, technological innovations, and cultural diffusion.

MIGRATION AND MODERNIZATION

The city has been termed the 'centre of change' (Dwyer 1972) and growth. It is often argued that migrants play an important role in shaping ideas about the societies in which they live. There is widespread evidence that migrants sustain the links between rural and urban areas in all spheres of life. It is believed that urban living is conducive to positive changes of attitudes, aspirations, behaviour, and personal relationships, no matter for how little time migrants have experienced it.[1] It should be noted that women's role is critical in this respect as they preserve and at the same time transmit culture to the next generation.

In the context of dearth of studies in Bangladesh related to migration and its impact on modernization and social change, in this chapter, we have examined whether attitudes and aspirations of the respondents have changed over time using some of the gender and generation indicators. Drawing on the existing literature (Weber 1922; Durkheim 1933; Tonnies 1935; Hoselitz 1957; Parsons 1959; Eisenstadt 1966; Epstein et al. 1967; Gugler and Flanagan 1978; Curran and Saguy 2001), we can assume that in post-industrial societies, there will be strong adherence to a wide range of cultural changes, including a cluster of attitudes such as support for freedom and autonomy and egalitarian attitudes towards gender roles in home, family, and workplace.

Given that emancipative values[2] constitute the key cultural component of a broader process of human empowerment including women's empowerment, we have examined attitudes of migrants towards gender division of labour and women's higher education and participation in the labour market. To understand whether, how, and to what extent gender and generational relations within families are redefined and impacted in relation to migration in the urban milieu, we have examined women's roles, attitudes, and aspirations regarding major institutions and practices such as marriage, dowry, divorce, and inheritance that govern gender relations, often reinforcing social asymmetries' as indices of modernization. In this way, we addressed the compelling question on qualitative changes as a result of migration raised in the Introduction.

We have also assessed migrant women's aspirations for their sons' and daughters' education and marriage, which we have cross-examined by analysing actual practices regarding the trends in the age-specific current marital status and mean age at marriage. This we did to understand the congruence between what respondents said they believed and what they actually practiced and also the extent to which respondents' aspirations are gendered. Side by side, we have also highlighted changes that occurred over time with the help of previous rounds of survey data to establish trends.

GENDER AND GENERATIONAL RELATIONS AND CHANGES

There are many modes of transmission of modern values, attitudes, and aspirations. Human behaviour is largely governed by preferences, beliefs, and norms that are formed partly because of genetic evolution and partly transmitted through generations and acquired through learnings and other forms of interactions. The process in which preferences, beliefs, and norms of behaviours are transmitted through social interactions within and across generations is called cultural transmission. Socialization process is often considered a major vehicle for cultural transmission and the role of marriage is critical in this process. There is no denying that family, particularly the mother, plays an important role in the socialization and changing attitudes and aspirations of her children.[3] According to G.J. Hugo (1991: 30):

> Women at urban destination are more likely than their rural counterparts in the rural origins to work outside of the home and family, work in the formal sector, to be free of personal and other traditional restraints on behavior, etc.

Based on the existing literature, particularly Hugo (1991) and J.A. Jackson (1969), we can assume that migrant women are likely to opt for 'higher education and delayed marriage, the right to have equal inheritance of property like men, and the bi-lateral right to divorce which Bangladeshi women in general do not enjoy in a patriarchal and patrilocal society' (Afsar 1995: 269). However, it is difficult to establish that any change in attitude is an outcome of migration given the emancipative potential of education and employment among other factors.

Marriage

Marriage is a universal phenomenon in Bangladesh. In 2011, almost three out of every four men and more than nine in 10 women were married before they reached their 30th birthday. This trend is persistent since the 1990s (BBS 2012b). Although the legal age of marriage is 18 years for girls in Bangladesh, according to BDHS almost half of all girls aged between 15 and 19 years were married, divorced, or widowed (NIPORT et al. 2013). Our data shows that of the household heads, 93.5 per cent were currently married, 6 per cent were widowed, divorced, or separated, and only a fraction (0.5 per cent) were unmarried. However, given that marriage is largely arranged by families with parents playing a major role in deciding the age of marriage or selection of partners for their children, we have analysed the current marital status of the children of respondents by age group and average age to examine trends over time.

More importantly, age at marriage is often considered as an indicator of social values and norms of a population as it helps to generate understanding of the social and economic factors underlying social change (Malhotra and Tsui 1996). Based on the existing literature, we can hypothesize that age at marriage declines over time with an increase in the level of education, particularly for women, along with economic growth, women's employment outside home, and urbanization (Harwood-Lejeune 2000; Garenne 2004; Mensch et al. 2005). In the previous chapter, we found that the enrolment rates increased remarkably, and gender parity has been achieved at the primary and secondary levels. However, at the same time, the participation rate at the tertiary level has declined, and a notable gender gap has persisted over time, with young women lagging behind their male cohorts. Women's employment has also remained steady and even declined for eligible women from non-slum and long-term migrant households since the 1990s. It should be noted that Bangladesh is among those few countries in Sub-Saharan Africa and South Asia where the practice of child marriage persists (UNICEF 2014).

Differential Trends but Increased Age at Marriage for Sons and Daughters

Our data shows that in 2010 none of the respondents married off their sons before attaining the age of 21, which is the legal age of marriage for men in Bangladesh.[4] This holds for all categories of respondents, irrespective of their migration status and slum or non-slum residence. However, while nine out of every 10 boys from slum households aged 30 years or more were currently married, the proportion declined to 65 per cent for those from non-slum (Table 8.1). The remaining one-

Table 8.1 Distribution of Sons and Daughters of Respondents by Their Current Marital Status and Age Group, Slum and Non-slum Residence, Mothers' Level of Education, and Income Quintile, 2010 and 1991

	2010						1991					
	Unmarried		Married		Divorced/ Widowed		Unmarried		Married		Divorced/ Widowed	
	S	D	S	D	S	D	S	D	S	D	S	D
Slum (#)	204	154	21	4	1	0	251	188	9	10	2	0
<18 Yrs.	100	100	0	0	0	0	100	98.9	0	1.1	0	0
18–21 Yrs	100	100	0	0	0	0	88.9	55.6	7.4	44.4	3.7	0
22–9 Yrs	68.5	66.7	29.5	33.3	2.3	0	66.7	0	33.3	100	0	0
30+ Yrs.	11.1	0	88.9	100	0	0	33.3	0	66.7	100	0	0
Non-slum (#)	437	283	115	22	1	4	606	472	46	17	0	2
<18 Yrs.	100	99.5	0	0.5	0	0	99.8	99.5	0.2	0.3	0	0.3
18–21 Yrs	100	88.6	0	11.4	0	0	94.4	91.7	5.6	8.3	0	0
22–9 Yrs	74.2	76.6	25.8	19.1	0.7	0	75.7	74.2	23.4	25.8	0.9	0
30+ Yrs.	35.3	10.0	63.7	70.0	0	20.0	41.2	0	44.1	75.0	14.7	25.0
Recent Migrant (#)	60	44	7	2	0	0	85	63	1	4	1	0
<18 Yrs	100	100	0	0	0	0	98.3	100	1.7	0	1.4	0
18–21 Yrs	100	100	0	0	0	0	100	50.0	0	50.0	0	0

(Cont'd)

Table 8.1 (*Cont'd*)

	2010						1991					
	Unmarried		Married		Divorced/ Widowed		Unmarried		Married		Divorced/ Widowed	
	S	D	S	D	S	D	S	D	S	D	S	D
22–9 Yrs	33.3	100	66.7	0	0	0	100	75.0	0	25.0	0	0
30+ Yrs	28.6	0	71.4	100	0	0	88.9	0	11.1	100.0	0	0
LT Migrant (#)	420	284	95	15	1	3	610	470	43	18	6	2
<18 Yrs	100	99.5	0	0.5	0	0	99.8	99.3	0.2	0.5	0	0.2
18–21 Yrs	100	90.0	0	10.0	0	0	91.4	90.6	7.5	9.4	1.1	0
22–9 Yrs	73.4	77.8	25.9	19.4	0.7	2.8	88.9	66.7	11.1	33.3	0	0
30+ Yrs	33.0	16.7	67.0	50.0	0	33.3	0	0	0	66.7	100	33.0
Non-migrant (#)	161	109	34	9	1	1	162	127	11	5	1	0
<18 Yrs	100	100	0	0	0	0	100	100	0	0	0	0
18–21 Yrs	100	90.9	0	9.1	0	0	100	83.3	0	16.7	0	0
22–9 Yrs	72.0	66.7	26.0	26.7	2.0	6.7	70.6	50.0	29.4	50.0	0	0
30+ Yrs	36.4	0	63.6	100	0	0	12.5	0	75.0	100	12.5	0

Note: S = son; D = daughter; LT Migrant = long-term migrant

Source: Authors' estimate from the repeat surveys.

third were never married, which tends to indicate an increase in the age at marriage in conformity with the existing trends (BBS 2015).[5] In contrast, almost one-tenth and nearly half of the respondents married their sons and daughters off when they reached the age of 18 and 21, respectively, in 1991, and none of those aged 30 years or more were unmarried at the time of the survey (Table 8.1).

Trends in marriage for girls are also similar, with some noted exceptions. In 2010, except a solitary respondent, none had married their daughters off before attaining the legal age (18 years) and a few (less than one-tenth) at 21 years. The rate of marriage doubled for those aged between 22 years and 29 years and peaked to more than 90 per cent for 30 years and older daughters. More importantly, none of the daughters from slum and recent-migrants' families were married at 18 or 21 years, which supports the most rapid increase in female enrolment at the secondary levels for these two groups (compared to other cross sections) being the underlying cause for delayed marriage, as discussed in Chapter 7.

Age-specific marriage rate also explains higher rate of employment for the younger and older women from slum and recent-migrant families that we found in Chapter 2 (Table 2.10).[6] Accordingly, of the working women, the proportion of currently married women was lower for slum (67.2 per cent) compared with non-slum households (82.7 per cent). One-fifth (20.5 per cent) and over one-tenth (11.7 per cent) of working women were never married and divorced or widowed in slum. As they entered the labour market early and continued till they grew old due to economic and family necessity, this trend of economic participation by both the ever-married and never-married women from slum is not very difficult to comprehend.

Accordingly, mean age of the currently married sons and daughters increased from 28.9 years and 22.5 years, respectively, in 1991 to 31.5 years and 27.0 years, respectively, in 2010 (Table 8.2). The increase is particularly more rapid for slum dwellers compared to other groups. It is estimated at around seven years for daughters (from 20.2 years to 27 years) and four years (from 25.4 years to 29 years) for sons. We have already discussed that the growth of RMG factory and expansion of private services sector provided incentives for girls' education and delayed marriage. Research also shows that slum and non-sum residence and the level of education of the spouse influence the age at marriage (BBS 2015), which is consistent with our data.

Table 8.2 Mean Age of Marriage of Currently Married Sons and Daughters of the Respondents by Slum and Non-slum Residence, Mothers' Level of Education, and Income Quintile for 2010 and 1991

	2010		1991	
Respondents by Categories	**Son**	**Daughter**	**Son**	**Daughter**
Slum	29.0	27.0	25.4	20.2
Non-slum	31.9	27.0	30.0	24.2
All	31.5	27.0	28.9	22.5
Short-term Migrant	31.4	37.0	35.0	20.3
Long-term Migrant	30.8	24.2	28.5	22.9
Non-migrant	33.3	29.3	29.5	23.7
Mothers' Level of Education				
No Schooling	30.8	24.7	26.3	22.3
Primary/Secondary	32.2	25.2	27.4	24.2
SSC/HSC and Above	33.1	30.0	28	21.8
Households' Income on Per Capita Scale				
Top Quintile	31.6	38.5	31.2	23.5
4th Quintile	31.0	25.8	27.3	20.0
3rd Quintile	32.3	23.0	27.0	22.7
2nd Quintile	33.8	29.0	24.9	25.8
Bottom Quintile	30.1	24.9	20.5	14.0

Source: Authors' estimate from the repeat surveys.

However, it is argued that:

> Marital status does not say much about patriarchal organization of marriage. In order to grasp social control of women by men one has to look into the internalization of norms governing marriage patterns and resolution, along with the laws governing succession and inheritance of property. (Afsar 1995: 272)

Accordingly, we have analysed the attitudes of heads and spouses regarding the mode of marriage such as love or arranged, whether they support a husband marrying more than one wife at a time, and, similarly, polyandry for a wife.

Most Parents Preferred Arranged Marriages for their Children

An overwhelming majority of the heads of households and their wives, ranging between 74.2 per cent and more than 92.9 per cent, considered that marriage should be arranged by the family (Table 8.3). Although

Table 8.3 Heads' and Spouses' Attitudes towards Mode of Marriage and Men's and Women's Rights for Plural Marriages by Categories

	Marriage		Polygamy for Men	No Polygamy	Polyandry for Women	Total Number
	Arranged	Love				
			Heads' Attitudes			
Slum	82.5	10.0	51.0	43.5	18.5	200
Non-slum	82.5	11.0	48.5	44.0	21.0	400
All	82.5	10.7	49.3	43.8	20.2	600
Recent Migrant	87.8	8.1	56.8	37.8	16.2	74
LT Migrant	81.7	10.9	48.9	44.3	18.0	366
Non-Migrant	81.9	11.3	46.9	45.6	26.9	160
No Schooling	85.7	4.8	46.7	44.8	22.9	105
Secondary	78.0	12.8	46.3	46.3	22.0	227
SSC/HSC	83.2	11.2	54.4	37.6	17.6	125
Tertiary	86.7	11.2	51.7	44.8	17.5	143
Top Quintile	74.2	16.7	41.7	49.2	17.5	120
2nd Quintile	86.7	5.8	50.0	41.7	13.3	120
3rd Quintile	86.7	10.8	56.7	39.2	23.3	120
4th Quintile	85.8	8.3	55.0	39.2	29.2	120
Bottom Quintile	79.2	11.7	41.7	50	17.5	120

(Cont'd)

Table 8.3 (*Cont'd*)

	Marriage		Polygamy for Men	No Polygamy	Polyandry for Women	Total Number
	Arranged	Love				
			Spouses' Attitudes			
Slum	88.8	10.1	21.8	76.0	30.7	179
Non-slum	89.9	10.6	27.7	69.8	31.0	368
All	89.6	10.4	25.8	71.8	30.9	547
Recent Migrant	89.6	10.4	28.4	65.7	28.4	67
LT Migrant	89.5	9.9	23.4	73.7	29.6	334
Non-Migrant	89.7	11.6	30.1	70.5	34.9	146
No Schooling	92.9	6.1	29.3	71.7	30.3	99
SSC	89.7	9.9	26.2	71.4	32.5	252
SSC/HSC	87.1	14.5	25.0	71.0	26.6	124
Tertiary	88.9	11.1	20.8	75.0	33.3	72
Top Quintile	89.1	9.9	20.8	77.2	31.7	101
2nd Quintile	90.8	11.0	21.1	76.1	22.9	109
3rd Quintile	89.7	9.5	36.2	59.5	31.9	116
4th Quintile	90.2	8.9	25.9	70.5	37.5	112
Bottom Quintile	88.1	12.8	23.9	77.1	30.3	109

Note: Each column represents percentage of the total. LT = long-term migrant; SSC = Secindary School Certificate; HSC = High School Certificate
Source: Authors' estimate from the repeat surveys.

we could not see any variation in the response patterns between slum and non-slum residents, there are a few noted gender, education, and income-based differentials that draw our attention. For example, on an average a larger proportion of spouses (89.6 per cent) compared with heads (82.5 per cent) preferred retaining parents' ascendency in arranging marriage for their children. Further, heads who belonged to the highest and lowest income quintile, completed primary or secondary level education, and were born or had been living in Dhaka for more than 20 years showed a relatively progressive attitude, compared to those of other categories or their wives. However, the response patterns of their wives show no such differential.

As a corollary, only a smaller proportion of respondents—one-tenth—on average preferred marriage by self-choice or love marriage. This is similar to the 2007 Pew Global Attitudes Survey (Pew Research Centre 2007) that showed that only 12 per cent of respondents considered that it was better for a woman to choose her own husband.[7] Generally, we do not observe much variations in the response patterns. However, a small difference can be noted among those supporting love marriages, which declined to half in the case of illiterate respondents in 2010, compared with 1991. Similarly, 16.7 per cent of the heads from the highest income quintile group and 14.5 per cent of spouses who completed secondary school or higher secondary level education were in favour of self-choice marriage.

Research shows that in Bangladesh, India, and Pakistan 95 per cent or more marriages are arranged by families and there is a small increase in love marriages over time (Rubio 2014). This is despite the increase in education, employment, and urbanization and decline in agriculture, factors that are identified to be correlated with love marriage (Rubio 2014). Unlike mode of marriage, gender-based differential can be observed regarding men's and women's rights to plural marriage. Half of the heads and one-quarter of the spouses were favourably disposed to the idea of polygamy for men (Table 8.3). Further, the numbers and proportions of spouses who supported plural marriage for both men and women did not differ much. In contrast, heads who favoured women's right to plural marriage were less than half compared to those who supported polygamy. Spouses who supported monogamy were significantly larger (almost three-quarters) compared with heads (a little over two-fifths).

Stark Contrast between the Attitude of Heads and Spouses towards Polygamy

There are notable variations for different categories with respect to polygamy. For example, heads who migrated to Dhaka less than 10 years ago, belonged to lower middle class, or completed secondary or high school education were more supportive of polygamy compared to other categories. In contrast, those from the highest and lowest income quintile groups were relatively more progressive in their outlook.

Unlike heads, support for polygamy declined but monogamy increased consistently among spouses with a higher level of education. Also, slum women showed more progressive attitudes compared to non-slum women in this regard. However, a larger proportion of spouses from the lower middle class supported the idea of women's plural marriage like their male counterparts compared with other income quintile groups.

Migration and Education Influence Women's Supportive Attitude for Monogamous Marriages

Our data suggests that while migration and higher education do not appear to influence the attitude of men and women towards the mode of marriage in Bangladesh to a large extent, they matter more particularly for women who are in favour of establishing a monogamous marriage pattern in the society.[8] Using sophisticated statistical models and large-scale opinion surveys, A.C. Alexander and C. Welzel (2011) concluded that Muslim support for patriarchal values is robust against various controls. Simultaneously, however, they also found that rising levels of education, labour market participation, and an emancipative trend diminish Muslim support for patriarchy, especially among women, which is consistent with our data.

In accounting for arranged marriage, anthropologists and sociologists have emphasized its functional role such as 'to increase or secure political power, keep social status, increase wealth, and/or smooth economic transactions' by forming alliances with other kinship groups or extended families (Rubio 2014). Whether the strongly favourable disposition of our respondents towards arranged marriages by families is influenced by its functional role or due to prevalence of dowry and/or fear of marital instability needs to be studied further.

Divorce

Like polygamy, almost twice as many heads (29.8 per cent) as spouses (17.7 per cent) were in favour of men having unilateral right to divorce. In contrast, nearly two-thirds of heads (63 per cent) and most spouses

(81.9 per cent) were in view of the bilateral right to divorce for both husband and wife (Table 8.4). However, there are clear variations not only by gender but also by slum or non-slum residence, income quintile, and level of education of the respondents. Heads from non-slum households, belonging to the highest income quintile and who have completed secondary or high school and/or tertiary level were relatively more progressive in their views compared to those from slum households, belonging to the lowest income quintile and having no education at all. A similar trend is also observed in the case of spouses.

Table 8.4 Attitudes of Husbands and Wives towards Their Respective Rights to Divorce by Slum, Non-slum, Migratory Status, and Level of Education, 1991 and 2010

Husbands' Views on Right to Divorce	Only Husband Can Divorce		Both Can Divorce		Total (Number)	
	2010	1991	2010	1991	2010	1991
Slum	41.0	51.0	50.5	28.0	200	200
Non-slum	24.3	45.0	69.3	42.0	400	400
All	29.8	47.0	63.0	37.3	600	600
Migrant	31.1	45.2	62.3	39.5	440	484
Non-migrant	26.3	53.0	65.0	28.0	160	116
Illiterate	37.1	49.0	51.4	27.0	105	123
Primary/Secondary	30.0	58.8	60.4	24.7	227	194
SSC/HSC	29.6	46.0	63.2	42.2	125	124
Tertiary	24.5	31.8	75.5	56.7	143	197
Wives' Views on Right to Divorce						
Slum	26.3	39.5	72.1	29.8	179	178
Non-slum	13.6	40.8	86.7	42.4	368	356
All	17.7	40.3	81.9	38.2	547	534
Migrant	19.2	47.0	80.3	40.2	401	430
Non-migrant	13.7	39.4	86.3	29.8	146	104
Illiterate	17.2	37.8	80.8	23.8	99	214
Primary/Secondary	20.6	49.7	79.0	40.0	252	165
SSC/HSC	14.5	32.2	87.1	58.2	124	115
Tertiary	13.9	40.0	84.7	75.0	72	40

Source: Authors' estimate from the repeat surveys.

Most Spouses and Highly Educated Heads Preferred the Bilateral Right to Divorce for Husband and Wife

Over time, the heads and spouses differed greatly over their respective rights regarding the dissolution of marriage. In 1991, larger proportions of heads (47 per cent) and spouses (40.3 per cent) favoured the husband's unilateral right to divorce. Also, unlike 2010, those who considered that both husband and wife should have the right to divorce were smaller in numbers and proportions and did not differ much by gender (37.3 per cent and 38.2 per cent, respectively, for heads and spouses). However, like 2010, a positive correlation between the level of education and progressive attitudes can be observed. Also, larger numbers and proportions of migrant heads and spouses expressed more liberal views than their non-migrant counterparts, particularly in 1991.

Given that under the existing law (the Muslim Family Law Ordinance, 1961) a wife can divorce her husband if such power is delegated to her in her marriage contract, known as Kabin Nama, it is not surprising to find that more spouses and more educated respondents were favourably disposed to the bilateral rights to divorce, compared to other categories.[9] Regarding the shift towards greater gender equality over time, which we observed from this study, we can say that as migration matures migrants in general are expected to be more liberal in their attitudes. Also, as outcomes of gender parity at the primary and secondary level of education, micro-credit and social movement on women's empowerment by NGOs and mass media women are becoming more conscious about their right to divorce. According to the World Bank (2015), special initiatives taken to address gender inequality and promote women's empowerment through a schooling system that expanded girls' education, along with the role of NGOs in women's mobilization, and their 'proactive recruitment' by the RMG industry are some of the key factors behind the notable progress made by Bangladesh, particularly in the post 2000 period.[10]

Gender-Based Differential in Women's Entitlement to Inheritance

Many heads (60.8 per cent) believed that men are entitled to inherit double of the women's share as endorsed in the Shariat law, irrespective of their class and level of education (Table 8.5). In contrast, a similar

Table 8.5 Attitudes of Heads and Spouses to Gender-Based Rights to Property by Slum or Non-slum, Migratory Status, Educational Qualification, and Income Quintiles in 2010 and 1991

Respondents by Categories	Men Will Get Double than Women's Share		Men and Women Will Have Equal Share		Women Cannot Inherit/Not Applicable		Total (Number)	
	Head	Spouse	Head	Spouse	Head	Spouse	Head	Spouse
2010								
Slum	59.0	37.4	32.5	59.8	0.5	1.1	200	179
Non-slum	61.8	40.5	30.5	59.2	1.3	1.1	400	368
All	60.8	39.5	31.2	59.4	1.0	1.1	600	547
Recent Migrant	63.5	37.3	31.1	61.2	1.4	1.5	74	67
Long-term Migrant	61.5	39.5	30.3	59.3	1.1	1.2	366	334
Non-migrant	58.1	40.4	33.1	58.9	0.6	0.7	160	146
Illiterate	62.9	40.4	25.7	56.6	1.0	0.0	105	99
Primary/Secondary	58.6	44.0	31.3	54.8	0.9	1.6	227	252
SSC/HSC	60.0	33.9	33.6	66.1	0.0	0.8	125	124
Degree	63.6	31.9	32.9	68.1	2.1	1.4	143	72
Highest Quintile	56.7	33.7	33.3	66.3	1.7	1.0	120	101
2nd Quintile	61.7	42.2	29.2	57.8	1.7	1.8	120	109
3rd Quintile	70.0	41.4	25.8	56.0	0.8	0.9	120	116

(*Cont'd*)

Table 8.5 (*Cont'd*)

Respondents by Categories	Men Will Get Double than Women's Share		Men and Women Will Have Equal Share		Women Cannot Inherit/Not Applicable		Total (Number)	
	Head	Spouse	Head	Spouse	Head	Spouse	Head	Spouse
4th Quintile	62.5	44.6	30.8	52.7	0.8	1.8	120	112
Lowest Quintile	53.3	34.9	36.7	65.1	0.0	0.0	120	109
1991								
Slum	74.5	52.0	21.0	34.5	4.5	13.5	200	178
Non-slum	70.2	54.0	24.5	36.8	5.3	9.3	400	356
Permanent Migrant	71.7	53.1	23.1	36.2	5.2	10.7	484	430
Temporary Migrant	81.2	0	18.8	0	0	0	110	0
Non-migrant	71.6	54.3	24.1	35.3	4.3	10.4	116	104
Illiterate	74.8	44.4	17.1	30.3	8.1	25.3	123	214
Primary/Secondary	70.3	64.2	24.5	35.0	4.2	0.5	167	165
High School	75.0	56.5	21.2	40.0	3.3	3.5	153	115
Degree	67.4	47.5	37.8	75.0	1.9	0	157	40

Source: Authors' estimate from the repeat surveys.

proportion (59.4 per cent) of spouses were of the opinion that men and women should have an equal share in the family property, and the proportion increased for those who had a higher level of education and belonged to the highest income quintile. Despite that, wives who were favourably disposed to men's greater share in the family property were relatively larger in proportion (39.5 per cent) compared to husbands who supported equal rights of both men and women (31.2 per cent). Whether it is due to the religious influence—as per the Islamic rules of inheritance sons are entitled to inherit double the daughters' share and one-eighth share of the deceased husband's property is allocated to his wife—needs to be studied further.[11] Although Bangladesh has a National Women Development Policy since 1997 that aims to provide equal inheritance rights for women, it is not clear how this policy will be implemented without contradicting the existing laws.[12]

However, notwithstanding such gender-based differential, we can observe some important changes over time in the outlook of both heads and spouses regarding inheritance. For example, in 1991, larger proportions of heads (71.7 per cent) and spouses (53.3 per cent) favoured men's greater entitlement. Similarly, those who supported equal rights for men and women in family property were smaller, estimated at around one-quarter and one-third, respectively. Clearly, it indicates that Dhaka city dwellers are becoming more progressive in their attitudes, which is particularly the case for spouses and is consistent with the development indicators such as massive improvements in girls' education, better employment opportunities, and more income in 2010 than in the 1990s. It also indicates that migration status per se may not be sufficient to explain attitudinal changes without the concomitant changes in the level of education and income, which we have argued earlier (see Afsar 2000).

Persistence of Traditional Gender-Based Division of Labour

Roles and responsibilities of the respondents and their spouses for maintaining life and livelihoods in Dhaka remained largely traditional with a rigid gender-based division of labour (Table 8.6). Cooking, childcare, cleaning, and washing were predominantly performed by wives, while husbands were mainly engaged in regular shopping. Accordingly, many respondents considered that husbands were mainly responsible for decisions regarding family income and expenditure, while responsibilities related to domestic chores were regarded as the wives' domain. Areas

Table 8.6 Distribution of Respondents According to Who Performs Some of the Basic Daily Maintenance Activities by Slum or Non-slum Residence, Migratory Status, Level of Education, and Income Quintile, 2010

2010	Daily Cooking				Washing/Cleaning				Childcare			
Respondents	**H**	**W**	**B**	**O**	**H**	**W**	**B**	**O**	**H**	**W**	**B**	**O**
Slum	2.0	90.5	0.5	7.0	2.5	86.7	1.7	8.0	1.0	72.0	16.0	11.0
Non-slum	1.8	86.5	0.5	11.3	1.4	66.5	2.8	29.2	3.5	65.0	22.3	9.3
All	1.8	87.8	0.5	9.9	1.8	73.2	2.5	22.5	2.7	67.3	20.2	9.8
Recent Migrant	4.1	89.2	2.7	4.1	4.1	76.3	3.4	15.5	1.4	56.8	24.3	17.6
LT Migrant	1.9	86.6	0.3	11.2	1.8	71.5	2.6	24.4	3.8	66.7	21.6	7.9
Non-migrant	0.6	90.0	0	9.4	0.6	75.9	2.3	21.2	0.6	73.8	15.0	10.7
Illiterate	0	91.3	0	8.7	0.9	84.9	0.5	13.6	0	81.6	12.6	5.8
Primary/Secondary	2.9	87.3	0.4	9.4	2.5	77.5	1.8	18.2	3.7	68.6	15.9	11.9
SSC/HSC/Degree	1.6	86.9	0.5	10.7	1.4	64.3	3.9	30.3	2.8	60.3	27.4	9.5
Highest Quintile	3.3	78.3	0.8	17.5	2.5	54.6	2.1	40.8	4.2	61.7	20.0	14.1
2nd Quintile	2.5	88.3	0	9.1	0.4	71.2	2.1	26.2	2.5	88.3	0	9.1
3rd Quintile	1.7	92.5	0	5.8	3.3	75.0	3.3	18.3	1.7	65.8	20.0	12.5
4th Quintile	1.7	90.0	1.7	6.7	2.1	80.0	4.2	13.7	0.8	70.0	22.5	6.7
Lowest Quintile	0	90.0	0	10.0	0.4	85.4	0.8	13.3	0.8	77.5	12.5	9.2

Note: LT = long-term migrant; SSC = senior secondary certificate; HSC = higher secondary certificate; H = husband, W = wife, B = both, O = others including relatives, domestic help, none and not applicable, particularly if the respondents did not have any children.

Source: Authors' estimate from the repeat surveys.

in which both shared joint responsibilities for decision making included mainly children's education and marriage. However, there are some variations.

Greater Sharing of Childcare Role in Recent Migrant Families

For example, one-quarter of the respondents from non-slum households reported that they relied on domestic help or laundry service for daily washing and cleaning, compared to less than one-tenth in the case of slum dwellers. Clearly, it is a question of affordability, which has been reinforced from the variations in roles influenced largely the level of education of the respondents and their income quintiles as revealed from the analysis of the third-round survey data. More than one-third and one-quarter of the respondents belonging to the highest income quintile and having high school or tertiary qualification had such affordability. Migration per se does not appear to influence gender division of labour.

However, we observed that one-quarter of husbands and wives shared the child-caring role in recent migrant families, larger compared to non-migrants (15 per cent) and long-term migrants (21.6 per cent). This trend can be related to the higher rate of labour force participation found among the female members of recent migrant families and their lower income, compared to the other two groups (as discussed in Chapter 4 of this volume) which compelled husbands to share the child-caring role in the absence of other types of support including childcare facilities.

Between 1991 and 2010, there was little change in the gender division of labour, particularly in relation to cooking or daily shopping. However, larger proportions of respondents from non-slum (more than 40 per cent) and migrant or non-migrant households (more than one-quarter) depended on servants or non-relatives for washing and cleaning activities. This differential can be explained as an outcome of greater technological innovations and more accessibility to washing machines or other electronic devices over time that made washing and other jobs simple and less time-consuming.

However, little changes that we observed in gender roles with women continuing to bear a disproportionately larger share of unpaid work such as cooking, cleaning, and providing care for children, the elderly, and other dependents compared to men are consistent with the global trend. According to the ILO (2016), as women perform the bulk of unpaid household and care work across the world, women's working days become longer than that of men. It is estimated that women spent 7 hours and 9 minutes on paid work and unpaid household and care work per day, compared with 6 hours and 16 minutes for men in developing countries (United Nations 2015b). The difference is mostly accounted for by the fact that on average women perform at least two and a half times more unpaid household and care work than men.

'Time Use Pilot Survey' (BBS 2013c) shows that an average Bangladeshi working woman spent 3.6 hours on household work and 5.2 hours on paid work on a typical day in 2012, compared to the 1.4 hours and 6.9 hours spent, respectively, by an average working man. Unemployed women spent almost double—6.2 hours—on household work and 1.3 hours on leisure. By contrast, unemployed men spent lesser time—only 1.2 hours—on household work, comparatively less than even those who were employed, but more on leisure—2.2 hours. Clearly, these gendered work patterns draw attention to the double burden faced by women in the productive and reproductive economy.[13]

The reasons for these gender gaps can be related to the lack of services and infrastructure to reduce unpaid household and care work, but it has more to do with gender-based social norms and attitudes under which women are considered to be the primary care providers, as demonstrated in our survey (ADB 2015).[14] Following G. Kelkar (2013), we also underscore the need to 'change gendered social norms that discriminate against girls and women and redistribute women's unpaid household work and domestic care responsibilities through policy measures and media campaigns that focus on changing attitudes and values that will put the sharing of responsibilities on men'.

ATTITUDES TOWARDS WOMEN'S EDUCATION AND EMPLOYMENT

Given that women's education has emancipative potentials, as we have observed and discussed earlier, particularly regarding monogamy and women's equal rights to divorce and inheritance, it is important to examine respondents' attitudes on women's education and understand what might have influenced their attitudes. We have also included women's paid work in this discourse as it is now well recognized that the nature of women's work is critical to improve women's status (Boserup 1970; Kuhn and Wolpe 1979; ILO 2016; Kelkar 2013). According to the United Nations Family Planning Agency (UNFPA) (2014):

> Gender equality exists when both sexes are able to share equally in the distribution of power and influence, have equal opportunities for financial independence through work or through setting up businesses, enjoy equal access to educational and the opportunity to develop personal ambitions.

Most Respondents Supported Women's Higher Education

In general, most of the respondents (91.8 per cent), irrespective of their economic standing or educational background and migratory status, were disposed to women's higher education. While this is encouraging, in order to understand their attitudes towards women's higher education fully it is important to analyse the reasons for which they supported it. In their multiple responses, they mainly focused on education as a conduit to women's earning potential (53.7 per cent), their self-dependence (50.5 per cent), and good motherhood (44.3 per cent). Less than one-fifth (16.3 per cent) also emphasized that it could enhance women's marriage prospect (Table 8.7). Also, we can say that almost one-tenth of the respondents expressed a conservative attitude by disapproving, as they felt it was not necessary (2.5 per cent) or made it conditional depending on permission from a male guardian (5.7 per cent).

Reasons for Supporting Women's Education Vary by Slum and Non-slum Residence

However, importance attached to women's productive or reproductive roles or freedom as outcomes of education differed mainly depending on slum or non-slum residence, level of education, and income of the respondents. Slum dwellers and those belonging to the bottom two income quintiles emphasized increased earning potential through education over self-dependence or becoming better mothers. However, twice as many of them preferred it on the ground of good marriage prospect in comparison to those from non-slum households or other income quintiles. In the context of insufficient income and negative impact of

Table 8.7 Respondents' Attitudes towards Women's Education by Slum or Non-slum Residence, Migratory Status, Level of Education, and Income Quintile, 2010

	No Need	With Male Guardian's Permission	For Good Marriage	To Be a Good Mother	Better Income Potential	Self-reliance	Intrinsic Value	Total (#)
Slum	5.0	5.0	24.0	28.0	62.5	38.0	0	200
Non-slum	1.3	6.0	12.5	52.5	49.3	56.8	1.0	400
All	2.5	5.7	16.3	44.3	53.7	50.5	0.7	600
Recent Migrant	1.4	2.7	14.9	37.8	67.6	51.4	1.4	74
Long-term Migrant	2.5	6.0	16.4	45.6	51.4	50.8	0.3	366
Non-migrant	2.1	6.3	16.9	44.4	52.5	49.4	1.3	160
Illiterate	5.8	5.8	22.3	28.2	59.2	35.0	0	103
Primary/Secondary	2.9	7.8	18.8	33.9	60.0	42.4	0.4	245
SSC/HSC/Degree	0.8	3.6	11.5	61.1	45.2	64.7	1.2	252
Highest Quintile	1.7	5.8	7.5	68.3	44.2	61.7	2.5	120
2nd Quintile	1.7	6.7	10.8	51.7	48.3	60.8	0	120
3rd Quintile	0	4.2	17.5	45.8	55.8	49.2	0.8	120
4th Quintile	2.5	6.7	25.0	31.7	53.3	48.3	0	120
Bottom Quintile	2.5	5.0	20.8	24.2	66.7	32.5	0	120

Note: The table is compiled from multiple responses and, hence, the total does not tally with 100 per cent.
Source: Authors' estimate from the BRAC third-round urban poverty survey, 2010.

dowry on poorer and lower middle-class girls in the country, it is not difficult to comprehend their views.[15]

On the contrary, respondents from non-slum households attached high importance to self-dependence (56.8 per cent) and good motherhood (52.5 per cent), followed by increased earning potentials (49.3 per cent). Virtues of women's education in terms of self-dependence and good motherhood were also accorded higher importance compared to earning potential by those belonging to the highest income quintiles and with high school or tertiary qualification. While both long-term and non-migrants accorded almost equal importance to women's productive and reproductive roles and self-dependence, recent migrants prioritized earning potential the most, followed by self-reliance and good motherhood.

Right from Napoleon's demand for a good mother to build a good nation through to the volumes of researches by World Bank and other United Nations bodies, we have come across ample evidence that the social dividend from women's education is high. It is associated with lower infant mortality, better family nutrition and children's education, greater improvement in the poverty status and economic growth, and reduced fertility and population growth (UNDP 1990). Clearly, many of these reasons prompted more educated and higher-income groups to underscore this aspect of education. Side by side, they have also considered its virtues in making women self-reliant and independent, arguably key to women's empowerment.

Aspired Level of Education Varies by Slum And Non-slum Residence

We have observed consistency between respondents' attitudes towards women's education and their aspired level of education for sons and daughters (Table 8.8). Twice as many respondents aspired for tertiary (67.2 per cent) level of education for their daughters as those who aspired for high school-level education. However, the response pattern reversed in the case of slum dwellers, those with no formal schooling and belonging to the lowest income quintile—with the majority opting for SSC and/or HSC-level education. The logic behind their response can be explained in the light that they underscored the importance of women's education predominantly for income earning capacity, and that girls with secondary and high school education can easily get jobs in the RMG sector.

Table 8.8 Aspired Mean Level of Education for Sons and Daughters by Slum and Non-slum Residence, Migratory Status, and Level of Education of Respondents, 1991 and 2010

	Son		Daughter	
	2010	**1991**	**2010**	**1991**
Slum	12.1	10.0	11.6	7.0
Non-slum	15.0	14.0	14.6	11.0
Recent Migrant	13.1	10.5	13.7	9.5
Long-term Migrant	14.0	12.0	13.7	12.0
Non-migrant	14.2	13.0	14.0	11.0
Illiterate	12.2	9.0	11.7	7.0
Primary/Seconday	13.6	13.0	13.3	11.0
SSC/HSC	15.6	15.0	15.1	14.5
Degree	15.9	15.4	15.7	15.2

Source: Authors' estimate from the repeat surveys.

Accordingly, we found that although, over time, the enrolment rate for girls from slum households at the primary and secondary level has increased remarkably, there was little improvement at the tertiary level (Table 7.12). It should be noted that aspired mean level of education for girls across all categories was slightly lower than those for boys (Table 8.8). However, compared with 1991, there was notable reduction in the gender gap mainly because the aspired level of education for girls had increased quite significantly.[16]

What is intriguing, however, is that there is a persistent gap in the enrolment rates for young people at the tertiary level for all households, even though most from the highest income quintiles and with high school and tertiary qualification had aspired tertiary-level education for their daughters just like their sons. What is even worse is the fact that the enrolment rates at this level has declined over time, which we have discussed in Chapter 7.[17] However, when we cross-examined the enrolment rates for sons and daughters aged between 18 and 21 years, we found that a larger proportion of daughters (68.5 per cent) than sons were currently enrolled at the tertiary level. The fact that two-fifths (42 per cent) of sons were currently employed and 5.6 per cent were unemployed indicates their easy access to the labour market, which in turn explains why they were not pursuing tertiary-level education. By contrast, the rate of unemployment doubled (11 per cent) for girls and employment reduced by almost five times (9.3 per cent), which tends to justify their higher enrolment and rate of marriage (9 per cent) compared with sons (0 per cent).

Women's Paid Work

Respondents' attitudes towards women's employment can mainly be divided into three broad categories—negative, conditional, and positive. Those with a negative or conservative attitude predominantly believed that women's major role was to look after the family and children and, hence, women's paid work would bring dishonour or unrest to the family and society. Family's need, guardian's or husband's permission, and women's education were the major considerations for those who attached conditions to women's employment. Respondents who expressed favourable or progressive attitudes towards women's employment believed that it would help develop women's skills and self-dependence, improve the family's economic condition and thereby contributing to the country's prosperity, and that it is a matter of women's rights and independence.

From the multiple responses, we found that most (83.3 per cent) favoured women's employment unconditionally (Table 8.9). As expected, they belonged to the richest and middle-income brackets (92.5 per cent and 86.7 per cent, respectively), were high school or university graduates (90.5 per cent), and were from non-slum (86.8 per cent) and long-term migrant households (86.1 per cent). Those who made women's employment conditional under patriarchal norms and values constituted the second largest group with 56 per cent of the responses. We did not find much differentials in the responses by slum or non-slum residency and migratory status of the respondents in this regard. However, for income quintiles, a larger proportion of respondents belonging to the second highest income quintile (68.3 per cent) expressed cautious attitudes (or made it conditional), compared with others, while lowest income quintiles showed the opposite trend (42.5 per cent). A smaller proportion—one-tenth—of the respondents who expressed negative attitudes towards women's employment had

Table 8.9 Attitudes towards Women's Paid Work by Slum and Non-slum Residence, Migratory Status, Level of Education, and Income Quintile, 2010

	Positive	Conditional	Negative	Total (#)
Slum	76.5	52.5	13.5	200
Non-slum	86.7	57.7	9.5	400
All	83.3	56.0	10.8	600
Recent Migrant	78.4	52.7	8.8	74
Long-term Migrant	86.1	58.5	9.6	366
Non-migrant	79.4	51.8	13.7	160
Illiterate	71.8	50.5	14.5	103
Primary/Secondary	80.8	52.6	15.1	245
SSC/HSC/Degree	90.5	61.5	5.1	252
Highest Quintile	92.5	60.0	8.3	120
2nd Quintile	81.7	68.3	10.8	120
3rd Quintile	86.7	57.5	5.8	120
4th Quintile	77.5	51.7	14.2	120
Bottom Quintile	78.3	42.5	15.0	120

Note: The table is compiled from multiple responses and, hence, the total does not tally with 100 per cent.

Source: Authors' estimate from BRAC third-round urban poverty survey, 2010.

slightly greater representation from the lowest income quintiles, slum, and non-migrant households.

It should be noted that the coexistence of highly progressive and yet cautious attitudes of respondents from higher-income brackets cannot be explained by educational endowment because a majority of the respondents (between 47 per cent and 60 per cent) had tertiary-level qualification. Moreover, those with higher level of education also had similar attitudes towards women's paid work. Rather, it can be argued that class status and/or higher education does not necessarily make everybody equally progressive. In fact, it is quite natural to find stronger ideological beliefs and commitments among the most educated or upper/middle class people compared with people having lower level of education and/or class status. This proposition can be clearly supported by the narratives that emerged when we asked respondents to tell us why female members of their families were participating in the labour market or reasons for their non-participation.

Contradictory Trends in Ideological Values Regarding Women's Paid Work

Financial solvency predominated in the justification for women's paid work by many respondents from slum households (88.7 per cent) with no or low (93.5 per cent or 78.4 per cent) educational backgrounds and belonging to the lowest (96.8 per cent) or third income quintile (88.9 per cent). This is understandable in the context of the economic necessity of these households. In contrast, we have observed a coexistence of both liberal and survival-based justification in the narratives of respondents from highest income bracket and with high school and/or tertiary qualification (Table 8.10A). Clearly, it supports our argument on ideological values which can be both liberal and/or conservative. In this case, we observed a greater tilt towards liberal than conservative values. For example, the majority were of the opinion that educated women should be employed to realize their full potentials (65.6 per cent and 54.5 per cent, respectively), followed by those who supported it on grounds of financial solvency (37.5 per cent and 49.1 per cent, respectively).

However, a contradictory trend was also observed when they tried to justify non-participation of female members of their families in the labour market. In this case, larger proportions of these two groups (36.4 per cent and 30.5 per cent) prioritized women's reproductive role largely over other reasons and compared with other groups (Table 8.10B). However, like other respondents, they did not hesitate to put forward patriarchal values such as 'father-in-law did not permit' or 'women should not work outside' as reasons.

Clearly, the above analysis on gender division of labour and respondents' attitudes towards women's employment and higher education demonstrates internalization of strong patriarchal norms and values across the board. Subsequently, like Kelkar (2013), we can argue that 'the cultural ceiling that effectively prohibits women from being recognized as economic contributors needs to be overcome in order to increase the potential of human society, including women's agency and empowerment'.

Table 8.10A Reasons for Women's Employment Offered by Respondents from Households in which Women Were Employed

Respondents	Financial Solvency	Economic Independence	Productive Engagement for Educated Women	Others	Total
Slum	88.7	16.1	0	0	62
Non-slum	54.7	9.3	48.0	1.3	75
All	70.1	12.4	26.3	0.7	137
Recent migrant	83.3	12.5	16.7	0	24
LT Migrant	66.3	14.5	28.9	1.2	83
Non-migrant	70.0	6.7	26.7	0	30
Illiterate	93.5	12.9	0	0	31
Primary/ Secondary	78.4	15.7	11.8	0	51
SSC/HSC/ Degree	49.1	9.1	54.5	1.8	137
Top Quintile	37.5	12.5	65.6	0	32
2nd Quintile	50.0	21.4	35.7	3.6	28
3rd Quintile	88.9	5.6	16.7	0	18
4th Quintile	85.7	14.3	7.1	0	28
Bottom Quintile	96.8	6.5	0	0	31

Note: LT Migrant = long-term migrant; SSC = senior school certificate; HSC = high school certificate

Source: Authors' estimate from BRAC third-round urban poverty survey, 2010.

NOTES

1. Side by side, sociological literature also focuses at length on the negative aspects of urbanization such as crises of identity, anomie, drug and alcohol abuse, increasing crime, and social conflicts.

Table 8.10B Reasons for Women Not Working Offered by Respondents from Households in which Women Were not Employed

Respondents	Not Qualified	Unwilling	Not Allowed	Household Work/ Childcare	Others	Total
Slum	47.8	19.6	21.7	9.4	1.4	138
Non-slum	13.5	28.0	29.2	26.5	2.7	325
All	23.8	25.5	27.0	21.4	2.4	463
Recent Migrant	22.0	32.0	22.0	18.0	6.0	50
LT Migrant	27.9	22.6	25.4	22.3	1.8	283
Non-migrant	15.4	29.2	32.3	20.8	2.3	130
Illiterate	44.4	16.7	20.8	16.7	1.4	72
Primary/ Secondary	34.0	18.6	31.4	13.9	2.0	194
SSC/HSC/ Degree	6.1	35.5	24.9	30.5	3.0	197
Top Quintile	10.2	21.6	26.1	36.4	5.7	88
2nd Quintile	17.4	25.0	29.3	25.0	3.3	92
3rd Quintile	19.6	35.3	26.5	17.6	1.0	102
4th Quintile	35.9	21.7	23.9	17.4	1.1	92
Bottom Quintile	36.0	22.5	29.2	11.2	1.1	89

Note: LT Migrant = long-term migrant; SSC = senior secondary certificate; HSC = higher secondary certificate
Source: Authors' estimate from BRAC third-round urban poverty survey, 2010.

2. Emancipative values emphasize freedom of choice and equality of opportunities, which involves priorities of lifestyle liberty, gender equality, personal autonomy, and the voice of the people. For details, refer to World Value Survey, available at: https://en.wikipedia.org/wiki/World_Values_Survey#cite_note-FOOTNOTEWelzelInglehart201043.E2.80.9363-9 (accessed on 22 October 2016).

3. See, for example, Hayes-Pittelkow (1993), Gleason (1980), and Bisin and Verdier (2000). Research by Fernandez, Fogli, and Ottaviani (2004) shows

clearly the importance of the mothers' role in transmitting their sons' attitudes towards favouring women's participation in the labour force and acquiring higher education.

4. This is different from what we have presented in Table 7.13 in the previous chapter because here we have highlighted only the current marital status of sons and daughters of the respondents.

5. Note that in the absence of age at the time of marriage, we have used the age of the currently married offspring as a proxy indicator of changing trend. However, it should be interpreted with caution as it may not necessarily be the age at first marriage.

6. The opposite holds for women from non-slum, long-term, and non-migrant families as the rates were lower for both younger and older groups but increased for those aged between 35 and 54 years.

7. Those who believed in the family's role in the selection of a partner were three times as large, while a majority were of the opinion that the woman and her family should decide together.

8. Note that polygamy is legal in Bangladesh. A Muslim man can marry up to four women, subject to permission of prior wives. However, in reality the practice has declined over time, particularly in urban areas. The 2011 BDHS survey found that less than 1 per cent of men were in polygamous unions, much lower compared with the average rate in countries that permit polygamy. Certain cities have also placed hefty taxes on the practice of polygamy, with the tax increasing with each new wife the man takes (available at: https://en.wikipedia.org/wiki/Polygamy_in_Bangladesh [accessed on 19 December 2016]).

9. In Bangladesh, the civil divorce law applies only to Christians and the few couples that marry under the civil marriage statute (Human Rights Watch 2011). The Human Rights Watch report also noted the difficulties that women from different religious backgrounds faced in initiating divorce. In a nutshell, these difficulties include obtaining a divorce without consent and putting into effect Muslim women's entitlement to alimony, the fact that Hindu women are prohibited to obtain a divorce under the Hindu scriptures, and that exercising their legal rights to divorce and alimony after divorce can subjugate Christian women to the 'chastity question'.

10. It should be noted that Amartya Sen has particularly emphasized that Bangladesh's success in the post-independence period is largely an outcome of its 'determination to target the elimination of female disadvantages' (Sen 2013).

11. This is under the Shariat Law that governs inheritance and succession rights among Muslims. Although the *Muslim Family Law Ordinance*, 1961, did not overrule this unequal provision directly, it has allowed parents to give their daughters' equal share or even more by means of wills.

12. Please see 'Rights Are Equal: Govt Okays National Women Development Policy ahead of Int'l Women's Day Today' *Daily Star*, 26 August 2019, Available at: https://www.thedailystar.net/news-detail-176864 (accessed on 26 August 2019).

13. See Huq (2013) for a review of literature on unpaid care work in Bangladesh; Kabeer (2011); Kabeer, Mahmud, and Tasneem (2011); and Cornwall (2016).

14. Our findings are corroborated by Naved et al. (2011) in their survey 'Men's Attitudes and Practices Regarding Gender and Violence against Women in Bangladesh: Preliminary Findings', which showed that more than three-quarters of urban men (77.9 per cent) and nine out of every 10 (91.7 per cent) rural men believed that a woman's most important role is to take care of her home and cook for her family.

15. For example, case studies of Shefali and Rupa presented in Chapter 3 illustrated that often rural women are migrating to Dhaka and taking up jobs in the RMG sector to 'live with dignity and self-respect' in the context of humiliation faced due to diminishing marriage prospects arising out of high demands for dowry.

16. Factors that might have contributed to this change can be related to what they have considered important for women's education and/or paid work.

17. In Chapter 7, we have argued that the rate of marriage for female cohort aged between 18 and 21 years (Table 7.14) was high at 44 per cent, much higher than their male counterparts--2.6 per cent—which can explain the noted gender discrepancy at this level. Daughters-in-law who constituted more than one-quarter (27.6 per cent) of this age cohort and were predominantly housewives shed further light on the higher rate of marriage for this group.

9 Better Lives and Better Incomes, but Slim Prospects for Shared Prosperity

We started this book with the promise to capture the momentum of economic growth, rapid decline in poverty, and downward trend in urban inequality since the late 1990s, which we believed are conducive for developing a sustainable urban policy for Bangladesh. At the other end of the spectrum are the environmental challenges in the context of high density and the worst liveability ranking for Dhaka city, the epicentre of rapid urbanization in Bangladesh. The purpose was to answer the three compelling questions raised in the Introduction as a result of the doubts generated by these contradictory signals of rapid urbanization: is the poorer segment of the urban population that migrates with dreams for better lives and livelihoods benefitting from positive economic trends? Are these benefits sustainable in the long run? Have these benefits brought qualitative changes creating scope for this group to have a stake in the city's growing prosperity like their non-poor counterparts? Addressing these compelling questions is necessary to create a vision to make the city prosperous, inclusive, and sustainable, prerequisites for the New Urban Agenda and SDGs. To achieve the SDGs, particularly Goal 11 that calls for sustainable cities and communities (Goal 11), this understanding of the inter-relationship between migration and key development issues such as health, education, labour and livelihoods, and gender and empowerment is critical. Drawing on longitudinal data generated from three rounds of repeat surveys conducted in 1991, 1998, and 2010 of the same cross-section of 600 slum and non-slum households randomly selected from four wards of Dhaka city, the book generated the data to foster understanding and answer these questions.

THE REPORT CARD

In this chapter, we presented a 20-year report card, which analyses highlights of the major findings of the seven chapters to answer the three questions raised in the book with the help of six themes of rapid urbanization discussed in the beginning of this book. These aspects are urban poverty, income growth, and inequality; migration, the rural–urban linkage, and transformative potential; migration, better livelihoods, and inclusive development; quality of life and sustainability matters; urbanization and the demographic dividend and migration and modernization. We have observed that in this long 20-year journey, migrants and non-migrants, slum and non-slum dwellers, men and women, and young and old residents have experienced many changes that have positive, negative, and/or mixed impacts on their lives, livelihoods, well-being, and future prosperity. We captured these changes and their concomitant implications along with emerging issues from a policy development perspective with the help of a matrix table (Table 9.1). The following paragraphs provide highlights of the major achievements and challenges and the gaps that we identified from our analysis of the longitudinal data. Subsequently, the final part of this chapter presents challenges and opportunities through policy lenses which helped us to recommend measures and/or strategies to make Dhaka into a more prosperous, smart, sustainable, inclusive, and liveable city. Finally, we sum up our responses to the compelling questions we posed originally in the concluding remarks.

Table 9.1 Major Demographic, Economic, and Social Changes in the Lives of Dhaka's Residents between 1991 and 2010, Their Implications, and Emerging Issues for Policy Consideration

Areas	Changes	Impact	Issues/ Implications That Need Attention
Population changes	• Declining fertility • Smaller family size • Larger share of adult members • Smaller dependency ratio	• + • + • + • +	The demographic dividends: need appropriate policies to turn this gift to economic benefit and sustainable development
Causes and context of migration to Dhaka	• Weakening of push/ distressed migration • Migrants' birthplaces are marked with low and high decline in poverty, and not too strong or weak road connectivity for slum dwellers • Most migrants' birthplaces were well connected to primary/ secondary schools, local markets and paved roads	• + • +– • +	• Structural changes in the employment patterns of rural migrants • Roads infrastructure demands attention • Poverty reduction policies need uplift from sectoral outlook to more inclusive pathways that take advantages of rural-urban synergies to end poverty and enhance prosperity.
Occupational mobility and stagnation	• Construction and transport sectors remained the largest employers of poor migrants, scope for mobility to skilled occupations increased	• +	• Job opportunity does not necessarily mean job satisfaction

Areas	Changes	Impact	Issues/ Implications That Need Attention
	• Increased employment opportunity in manufacturing and link industries for more skilled and enterprising poor migrants • Job opportunities for poorer migrants increased in services sector but declined in business sector • Poorer migrants are creating opportunities for self-entrepreneurship by acquiring skills	• + • +– • +	• Job satisfaction depends mainly on level of skills and education and employment conditions • Lack of opportunities for finance or capital to cushion loss in business or other exigencies hinder upward mobility of poor workers • Need for affordable or subsidized short-term and hands-on training opportunity for poorer migrants to turn them from 'necessity' to 'opportunity entrepreneurs'.
Labour force, income, and poverty	• Overall improvement in the incidence of child labour but not for boys from slum	• +–	• Need greater incentives to keep poor adolescent boys and girls in school
	• Overall decline in employment, particularly for women and more for older women • Occupational shift from public to private services and	• – • +	• Lower return from female education than males'. • More job diversification and greater mobility.

Areas	Changes	Impact	Issues/ Implications That Need Attention
	formal to informal business in general, and from manual to industrial workers for slum dwellers		
	• Professional jobs, public and private service, and informal business had higher income and growth potential.	• –	• Workers' education is higher in services than other sectors. and income from services sector is more equitably distributed.
	• Increased gender disparity in incomc although rate of growth was higher for female workers between 1998 and 2010	• –+–	• Ownership of capital is becoming more skewed, major contributor to income inequality.
	• Income disparity between slum and non-slum remained high although both household and per capita income of the former doubled over time	• ––	• Higher-income groups invested more in assets, which was negligible for bottom 40 per cent.
	• Share of income increased mainly for middle 40 per cent and for top 15 per cent	• –	• Human capital is less unequally distributed compared with physical capital
	• Distribution of income from assets is most skewed.	• +	• A large proportion of households considered themselves as non-poor but at the brink of poverty.

Areas	Changes	Impact	Issues/ Implications That Need Attention
	• Income inequality declines with schooling of earners • Both moderate and extreme poverty declined significantly		
Basic services	• Housing condition and per capita space improved for poor	• +	• Distribution of land and housing in Dhaka becoming more skewed over time.
	• Average area of dwelling unit for Dhaka residents declined but increased on a per capita basis	• −+	• Housing-related expenditure more than doubled hitting harder poor than non-poor households.
	• Changing tenancy arrangements with more people living in rental accommodation and less in owner-occupied houses.	• −	• Prevalence of sub-letting to multiple tenants in the same address in many areas raises the question of legality of the practice.
	• Most slum dweller have access to electricity connection and piped gas mainly through formal channel	• +	• However, digital divide between rich and poor remained in terms of computer use.
	• The bulk of slum dwellers use cell phone as the sole mode of communication.	• +−	• Shared modes of water and sanitation cause adverse health consequences and impinge on women's time use patterns.

Areas	Changes	Impact	Issues/ Implications That Need Attention
	• Improved access to water and sanitation for slum dwellers over time although most share these facilities with multiple families.	• +	
Health and education	• Morbidity rate was lower in general than 1998 but the slum-non-slum differential remained for all age-groups, especially for children. It is higher for female across board than male members.	• +–	• Users of non-sanitary and shared latrine, long-term migrants and households with illiterate/ primary drop out spouses are more likely to be sick than others.
	• Increasing incidence of fever across board but higher among children and young people since the 1998. Incidence and types of chronic diseases differed for slum and non-slum, men and women and adult and older people.	• +/–	• Need to examine implications of the 'diseases of affluence' paradigm.
	• Slum dwellers mainly depended on pharmacy and non-slum residents relied more on specialist doctors and hospital.	• +/–	• Need to include balanced and nutritious food and physical exercises, and health education as integral part of urban health strategy.

Areas	Changes	Impact	Issues/ Implications That Need Attention
	• Adult literacy and educational attainment for adults increased since 1991, particularly for mothers and young adults. Rates of adult literacy doubled in slum.	• +	• Types of sickness and affordability influence treatment seeking behaviour.
	• Remarkable increase in enrolment for slum children and adolescents narrowing the poor and non-poor and gender gap at the primary and secondary level enrolment.	• +	• Clearly impacted on gender and generational education participation.
	• Drop out rate remains high. Rates are higher for girls and boys from recent migrant and slum households.	• +	• Women's empowerment movement and the pull of RMG and private sector in jobs for secondary school completers contributed to these changes.
	• At the tertiary level, enrolment rate declined more notably for non-slum, non-migrant cohorts and gender parity turns to gender deficit.	• –	• Poverty, lack of interest to continue study and taking up job were the other major reasons for dropping out.

Areas	Changes	Impact	Issues/ Implications That Need Attention
		• –	• It calls for effective policy measures for human capital development and turning brain drain to brain gain and brain exchange.
Attitudes, behaviours, and practices	• Age at marriage increased over time. None married their sons off before attaining 21 years and the same applies for 18 years old daughters with one exception.	• +	• Delayed marriage is a plus for fertility control, girls' education, health and women's empowerment.
	• More women preferred monogamous marriage, bi-lateral rights to divorce and women's equal rights to inheritance than men and compared with 1991.	• +	• Migration *per se* may not be sufficient to explain attitudinal changes without concomitant changes in the level of education and income.
	• Women with higher level of education were more progressive than those with lower educational level and men.	• +–	• Respondents mainly considered women's education as a conduit to women's earning potential, self-dependence, good motherhood and good marriage.
	• Arranged marriage remained as the most preferred mode and did not change.	• –	• Gender-based social norms and attitudes which promote women's

Areas	Changes	Impact	Issues/ Implications That Need Attention
	• Gendered work pattern persisted with women bearing disproportionately larger share of unpaid work such as cooking, cleaning and washing and childcare	• –	reproductive roles need to be changed.

Source: Matrix table prepared using the major findings of this study based on the first-, second-, and third-round survey data.

MAJOR ACHIEVEMENTS

A Shift from Demographic Dependence to Demographic Dividends

Over time, both family size and the dependency ratio become smaller due to fertility decline which resulted in a demographic transition transcending slum–non-slum boundary. Given that the use of modern contraception is high among eligible couples and highest for those from the lowest income quintile, arguably this transition is expected to be sustainable. There is also more gender balance in the population structure, particularly for the young adults.

Weakening of Push or Distressed Migration and Improved Connectivity between Rural and Urban Areas

We observed a weakening of push/distressed migration over time. This is partly an outcome of structural changes of the economy enhanced largely by remittances of migrant workers due to which more non-farm employment is available in rural areas. Occupational patterns of migrants prior to migration showed a waning of agricultural workers, while those employed in the services, construction, and transport sectors and those who were students increased over time. Also, we found a decline in the incidence of poverty at a varying rate in migrants' birthplaces by estimating district level poverty from the HIES data. Most of these birthplaces are well connected to primary and secondary schools, local markets, and paved roads. These trends clearly highlight that migration to Dhaka city does not necessarily occur from the most lagging region and/or that lagging regions have made some progress except for a few districts such as Jamalpur and Madaripur.

Migration Is a Journey to Realize Dreams and Aspirations for Better Lives and Livelihoods

Employment-related motivation persisted in the narratives of migrants underscoring the pull of greater economic opportunity in Dhaka as a major driver for migration. However, by focusing our attention beyond the push–pull debate, we discovered that rural poor also have dreams, aspirations, and self-confidence 'to recover the losses' and/or 'to re-establish' themselves and their families by migrating to Dhaka in the context of negative externalities of environmental vagaries and health- and wealth-related losses. By encompassing migrants' hope, aspiration, and resilience in our theoretical approach to portray migration motivation, we identified women garment factory workers' narrative of migration 'to live with dignity and self-respect' as a new gendered dimension in the context of marital breakdown and dowry-related push. Therefore, we can argue that a theoretical framework that encompasses hope, aspiration, self-confidence, and self-respect can provide a more holistic perspective to migration narratives.

Family and Social Networks—The Enablers and Providers in the Migration and Settlement Process

From migrants' narratives, we reconfirm the importance of family and social networks in the process of migration and settlement. These reflect in migrants' expressed motivations 'to enhance family income' and 'contribute to family's betterment', family's role in migration decision-making and monetary and non-monetary support to implement the decision. Also, migrants cited the role of social networks of friends and neighbours in the settlement process such as in job procurement, providing informal on-the-job training, and lending money to cushion exigencies arising out of work-related injury or lack of work.

Migrants Realized Their Dreams of Better Livelihoods and Better Incomes

Over time, there is a significant reduction in the unemployment rate and the number of unskilled workers, together with greater and more diversified job opportunities for poorer migrants after migration. We have identified some promising trends with regard to migrants' employment which is not only limited to recruitment at entry level, but also to greater scope for upward mobility to skilled occupations in the transport and construction sectors and manufacturing and linked industries. Opportunities for entrepreneurship also increased for those migrants who managed to acquire skills with the help of informal sources such as family members, friends, and neighbours. More job opportunities are created in private services and informal business compared with public services and formal business. Workers in these sectors experienced high income growth. Compared to the 1990s, Dhaka offered greater job opportunities and scope for upward occupational mobility in the job market to progress in life.

Notable Decline in the Incidence of Moderate and Extreme Poverty

Both moderate and extreme poverty declined significantly for all residents in Dhaka city and was almost wiped out for those from non-slum households. In 2010, one-third of slum dwellers (35 per cent) lived below the poverty line income threshold, compared with half (51 per cent) and nine out of every 10 (87 per cent) in 1998 and 1991, respectively. The rate of deceleration was even more rapid—fourfold—compared with 1998 (from 29.4 per cent to 7.5 per cent) and almost 10 times (from 68.8 per cent in 1991) for those living in extreme poverty in slum households. Increased earnings from both wage and self-employment, along with improvement in the educational attainment of young adults, are the primary drivers for poverty reduction in Dhaka.

Faster Income Growth from Manual Labour–Based Occupations Improved Severity of Poverty

During 1998–2010, the income of slum households grew faster (5.6 per cent) compared with those for non-slum (3.8 per cent) reducing slum–non-slum income inequality (the value of Pseudo-Gini concentration coefficient reduced from 0.51 to 0.48). Similarly, the earnings from lower-paid jobs requiring manual labour also increased at a faster rate compared to other occupations. As a result, the severity of poverty fell considerably with households at the lower end of the income scale benefitting significantly from the growing economic prosperity in recent years.

Narrowing of Poor and Non-poor and Gender Gaps in Enrolment Rates at Primary and Secondary Levels

Over the 20-year period, achievement in education has been impressive. Enrolment rates increased remarkably at the primary and secondary levels, particularly for age cohorts from slum and recent migrant households, which narrowed the gaps in the educational outcomes for children and adolescents between slum and non-slum and recent migrant and long-term migrant families. For girls, the enrolment rate was higher than for boys at both levels. Improved enrolment rates contributed to delayed marriage having implications for a virtuous cycle in terms of lowering fertility, infant and child mortality, and morbidity rates, which directly or indirectly contributed to a demographic dividend.

Improved Access and Quality of Basic Services for Slum Dwellers on a Shared Basis

There is a huge transformation in the quality of housing for slum dwellers from kutcha (non-permanent bamboo structured) to pucca (permanent structure made with CI sheet roof and concrete wall and floor and/or concrete buildings). Subsequently, slum households that were easily identifiable due to their thatched and/or CI sheet roof and wood or CI sheet walls in the 1990s were no longer so easily visible in most cases in 2010. As a result, shared mode of basic services emerged as the dominant slum identifier.

Slum dwellers' access to electricity and piped gas connection improved remarkably. More importantly, they have procured these services, which they share with multiple tenants under one roof, through formal or legal channel. Most slum dwellers now own their own cell phones, which has revolutionized the telecommunication sector. Their access to running tap water within the premises increased substantially, and moving away from unhygienic arrangements, most of them have access to shared modes of sanitary toilets.

Decline in Overall Morbidity Rate and Reliance on Modern Allopathy as the Dominant Treatment Mode

The overall morbidity rate defined as the proportion of sick members, including members who were chronically sick during a fortnight preceding the survey, to the total household members was estimated at 26.3 per cent, lower compared to our second-round survey (34 per cent) in 1998. Most sought modern allopathic treatment and perceived considerable improvements in the treatment facilities accessed in the last decade, irrespective of their backgrounds.

Wives' Attitudes Become More Progressive Favouring Gender-Based Equality to Divorce and Inheritance Rights

Most wives preferred monogamy (72 per cent) and supported women's equal right to divorce (82 per cent) and inheritance (60 per cent); the percentage was almost double compared to 1991. None of the offspring—sons and daughters—were married before attaining their legal age (21 years and 18 years for boys and girls, respectively). However, we observed that migration per se is not enough to explain attitudinal changes; one also needed to look at concomitant changes in the level of education and income.

CHALLENGES AND/OR GAPS

High Drop Out Rates for Adolescents and Declining Enrolment Rate at the Tertiary Level

We have identified a few black holes in narrating the story of the last 20 years. These include high drop out rates for the adolescent group from slum households and higher incidence of child labour for boys, while enrolment rate at tertiary level declined for the non-slum age cohort. Also, there were persistent gender and slum–non-slum gaps in the enrolment rate at the tertiary level.

Return from Education Much Lower for Female than Male Workers

There is an overall decline in the employment rate that is more pronounced for women, particularly for older women. Gender and rich–poor income disparity remained high. Return from education was staggeringly lower for female compared with male workers, which acts as a disincentive for women to join the labour market. Also, underlying this trend is the traditional gender division of labour, as a result of which women continued to bear disproportionately larger burdens of domestic work including cooking, cleaning, washing, as well as childcare compared to men, often impeding the women's scope for paid work.

Greater or Diversified Job Opportunities Do Not Necessarily Ensure Job Satisfaction

Unskilled and semi-skilled workers were the most dissatisfied with their current occupation at the time of the survey, followed by self-employed entrepreneurs. In contrast, those running their own business and employed in the services sector were more satisfied in their current occupation compared with other occupational groups. Therefore, we observed that greater and more diversified job opportunities alone cannot ensure job satisfaction. Rather, freedom, flexibility, a conducive work environment, and income matter in influencing job satisfaction.

Slum–Non-slum Income Disparity

Increasing control of physical capital by the top 10 per cent (from 39.5 per cent to 47.3 per cent) and top 5 per cent of the income quintile (from 30.7 per cent to 38.5 per cent), and declining value of fixed assets for the lowest 40 per cent (from 6.9 per cent to 6.1 per cent) during 1998–2010 contributed to the slum–non-slum income disparity. The value of Gini concentration ratio for ownership of capital was estimated at 0.57 and 0.61 in 1998 and 2010, respectively. With the help of multiple regression, we underscored the importance of accumulation of human capital because it helps to achieve more equitable distribution of income. In contrast, financial capital, which is another important source of income, contributes to its worsening.

Distribution of Land and Housing in Dhaka Becoming More Skewed

However, the distribution of land and housing in Dhaka has become more skewed over time. More people now live in rental accommodations than in the 1990s. Housing-related expenditure has more than doubled, hitting poor households harder than the non-poor. Lack of affordable housing, the high cost of living, and heavy road congestion made Dhaka the world's second-worst city to live in (Economist Intelligence Unit 2015).

POLICY IMPERATIVES

We have analysed the implications of the major findings critically from a policy perspective together with better practice analysis. Drawing lessons from across the globe, we have recommended five strategic goals encapsulating each of the themes covered in this book to address the three compelling questions raised in the Introduction. These are: (*a*) turning the demographic dividends to economic gains and shared prosperity, which covers human development aspect of quality of life; (*b*) turning poor migrants from 'necessity' to 'opportunity' entrepreneurs, which aims to provide better livelihoods; (*c*) aligning poverty reduction strategies with shared prosperity targets, which covers the question of equality and the prospects for better future for the poor and disadvantaged; (*d*) shared mode of basic services: the need for effective management and land-use planning that covers quality of life and sustainability issues; and (*e*) benefit from rural–urban synergies, and enhance competencies and capacities through partnership, which the covers poverty, space, and development nexus as well as governance issues. For effective implementation of each of these goals, we have also recommended policy measures and/or strategic actions largely based on better practice analysis.

In the context of growing recognition of the importance of urbanization in promoting economic development and urban policy to optimize the gains from urbanization and weakening of the traditional hostility of policy makers, the book has provided policy options on how cities can be transformed to better drive economic growth and poverty reduction, as well as to become better places in which to live.

In this way, the book is poised to provide coherent national direction for informed urban policy that could distribute the gains of rapid urbanization equitably, while at the same time effectively transforming Dhaka and many other similarly placed cities of the developing world into more productive, competitive, prosperous, and liveable cities. The following paragraphs present each of these goals and recommended actions.

Turning the Demographic Dividends to Economic Gains and Shared Prosperity

Dhaka is now poised to reap the benefits of the demographic dividends as an outcome of a shift in its population structure from a large base of children and adolescents to an increasing share of working age population and smaller proportion of older people, declining fertility, and smaller family size. This demographic 'gift' can be turned to economic benefit and sustained growth provided the younger population has access to quality education, adequate nutrition and health, and rewarding employment opportunities. There is no substitute for investing in quality education and creating a skilled labour force.

With the concentration ratio estimated at 0.23 for schooling of earners in 1998, which had declined further to 0.19 in 2010, we can say that investment in education has the greatest potential to reduce income inequality. However, current investment in the education of children showed the reverse trend with the increasing value of the concentration ratio from 0.36 to 0.39 during the same period, indicating that the prospect for reaping such benefit from education has not been fully realized. Unless positive action is taken to raise awareness about the importance of investment in education and equip the low-income groups by providing better access to capital and education, income equality is likely to worsen further. According to UN-Habitat 2013, continued private wealth accumulation contributed to a slowdown in the global economic growth. This is because inequality prevents low earners from realizing their human capital potential, negatively affecting the economy as a whole (OECD 2015). Some of the better practices that are proven to be effective in realizing human capital potential can be adopted in Bangladesh. These are:

Conditional Cash Transfer

Conditional cash transfer in lieu of school attendance following the home-grown success story of the female stipend scheme or Brazil's Bolsa Familia scheme can be introduced. This would help ensure continuity of education in schools and/or encourage the pursuit of vocational education by creating opportunities for apprenticeship for urban poor children and adolescent boys and girls inclusive of those from metropolitan areas.[1] The Seventh Five-Year Plan (2016–20) that aims to strive for 'just, equitable and inclusive economic growth' is consistent with the Goal 10 which calls for reduced inequality and takes into account some important issues such as equity and access related to education, the quality and content issues in the Technical and Vocational Educational Training (TVET), as well as shortage of skilled labour among others (GOB 2015c).

However, to be effective, it is important to target the right groups such as secondary school completers and those living in slum areas to enable them to access small or medium-sized loan on easy terms needed to take up informal business along with vocational training. Technical education and vocational training should be mainstreamed with the secondary and tertiary education system with a view to raise the quality of training and provide a viable alternative for those who are not interested in pursuing purely an academic career. This will enable individuals to realize their full potential, based on their own preference and talent.

Capacity Building and Greater Investment in Research and Development

There is no substitute for capacity building through education, science, and technological diffusion and greater investment in research and development (R&D). Investment in R&D is vital for innovations necessary to boost productivity of farms and industries. However, in Bangladesh, as in many developing countries, investment in R&D remained low at 1 per cent of the GDP even under the Seventh Five-Year Plan (GOB 2015c). On the contrary, research shows that strong financial support helps R&D performers in high-technology industries to achieve higher efficiency in urbanization economies (Dai, Li, and Lu 2017). It should be noted that in 2016 China's R&D investment was 2.1 per cent of the GDP, more than double compared with Bangladesh. As Bangladesh satisfies the criteria of graduation from least developed country (LDC) and can attain the lower-middle-income country status, innovation outputs are key to accelerate the growth and prosperity pathway, as witnessed from the successful examples of many East Asian countries.[2]

Improve Standards and Quality of Higher Education and Training and Establish Close Links with Domestic and International Labour Market

It should be noted that Dhaka's competitive edge and transition to the knowledge economy is dependent on the abilities of its residents to create, share, and use knowledge more effectively. Therefore, educational policies need to focus on higher education and training along with information and communication technology (ICT) infrastructure with the help of a flexible education and training system that will provide the foundation for learning and develop required competencies as a means of achieving lifelong learning. Accordingly, the importance of quality education and creating skills sets that include professional, managerial, operational, behavioural, and inter-personal and inter-functional skills becomes paramount by regulating the standards of training providers and quality of training, and analysing domestic and international labour market demands.

A better example is Ho Chi Minh City, Vietnam, where the government-led promotion of the technology and services sectors provides new opportunities for communities to switch away from conventional manual labour (Dzung 2011). Similarly, a Micro and Small Enterprise Development Strategy can be developed for the unemployed young people in urban and metropolitan areas to sustain their interest in tertiary-level education (Barlet and Aiglepierre 2017; Barkema 2018).

Turning Poor Migrants from 'Necessity' to 'Opportunity' Entrepreneurs

In the context of securing a rewarding and satisfactory job opportunity, we identified that the lack of opportunity for loans on the easy terms or capital that are needed to cushion business loss or other exigencies and develop a business hinder poorer migrants' upward mobility in the job market. Subsequently, along with the provision for credit and capital, we underscore the need for affordable or subsidized short-term hands-on training for the poorer migrants to turn them from 'necessity' to 'opportunity' entrepreneurs to drive improvements in productivity and move up the value chain. Areas in which skills training can support self-employment include carpentry, tailoring, computers, electrical, and electronic goods repair and recycling, handicrafts, motor mechanics, hairdressing, and food processing.

According to A.E. Singer (2006), the best cure for poverty is to encourage more business activity and start new ventures through entrepreneurship development. Therefore, we consider that the role of entrepreneurs who are the architects for 'capacity creation' is crucial to accelerate Dhaka's development and growth. 'Capacity creation' in turn requires a shift from low to high productivity, creation and adoption of new goods and services, new skills, and new knowledge. By targeting urban poor, particularly the bottom 40 per cent of urban households, the government can help improve their income and the overall quality of life through capacity development programmes. While micro-finance institutions (MFIs) eased entry-level access to capital, there is no such opportunity for middle-income groups to transition from micro to small and medium enterprises. Important measures for 'capacity creation' are outlined below.

Innovative Policies on Diaspora Engagement

Our analysis of occupational mobility of migrants highlights a serious dearth of short-term hands-on training facilities and apprenticeship in Dhaka for the poorer migrants that would enhance their upward mobility and increase their employability and scope to secure decent work (Goal 8). Also, it would benefit enterprises by increasing their productivity, which will ultimately help in accelerating economic growth. Apprenticeship and short-term vocational training programmes that are proven to be successful can be suitably adopted in the Bangladeshi context. Examples of such programmes can be taken from Chongqing, the largest industrial and commercial city of Western China, which supported the transition of rural migrants from unskilled manual-based to skill-based types of work, benefitting one-third of migrants (Liu and Wang 2011).

Close to 10 million people of the Bangladeshi diaspora (Monem 2018) are residing in various parts of the world as professionals, skilled migrants, entrepreneurs, and students. Innovative policies need to tap the diaspora community as a conduit for investment, marketing, and networking between the home and host countries that are paramount for economic growth and development. Elsewhere, R. Afsar (2016b: 151) recommended that diaspora could be engaged with migrant groups and entrepreneurs in the home country to provide training- and marketing-related consultancy services funded by International Financial Institutions (IFIs) and/or intermediaries such as Bangladesh Chamber of Commerce and Industry (BCCI). An effective way of engaging them is through

> a complete service package like one-stop shop, in which they will provide financial literacy, mentoring, information and training on marketing, packaging and business development, identification of projects and the scope to improve quality, productivity and innovation to small and medium entrepreneurs. Following the Indian success story of diaspora engagement, 'one-stop shop' for diaspora investment can be adapted to redress bureaucratic red tape and facilitate business-friendly legal, political and regulatory environment. (Afsar 2016b: 151)

Encourage Women's Tertiary Education and Expand Their Employment Opportunity in the Modern Services Sector

To encourage entrepreneurial activities among women and reduce the gender-based income disparity, we consider that the policies and programmes that focus on improving 'young women's access to training, education, and technology can increase economic opportunities' (Afsar 2016a: 35). Women with secondary education should be given access to credit facilities by the government and NGO sectors for entrepreneurial training and activities, irrespective of their geographic location. There is also the need to encourage women's tertiary education and expand their employment opportunity in the modern services sector. This in turn depends among others on reducing gender gap in wages, low-cost and safe housing/hostel, and public transport facilities.

Aligning Poverty Reduction Strategies with Shared Prosperity Targets

Since the late 1990s, there has been a notable reduction in poverty, but rich–poor income disparity remained high. We have identified that incomes from property and business are the major contributors to inequality with the value of the Gini concentration coefficient exceeding 0.60. Without adequate support to access capital on easy terms, poor people can never win the race of acquiring assets which is highly skewed in favour of the higher-income groups who guard it zealously by their renewed high investment in property. Similarly, despite its equalizing potential, as discussed earlier in the matrix table, investment in education is declining for the bottom 40 per cent but increasing for the middle 40 per cent and ninth decile groups, indicating that these groups are likely to reap its benefits much more than poorer residents.

Notwithstanding its rapid economic and population growth, Dhaka's per capita GDP is the lowest of all megacities indicating that agglomeration diseconomies might have wiped off a large proportion of the potential benefits associated with strong population growth (UN-Habitat 2013). It is important that government through deliberate and conscious policy measures pays serious attention to address inequality as a critical factor affecting Dhaka's prosperity. We underscore the need to 'change the prevailing urban paradigm and develop the transformative vision that will not just boost productivity of a city, or region or even country, but also broadly distribute the associated benefits for the sake of shared prosperity' (UN-Habitat 2013). Some of the important policy measures that could be adopted to address inequality and ensure shared prosperity for inclusive development are suggested below:

Realign Poverty Reduction Strategy with Progressive Taxation for the Income-Rich and Social Protection for the Urban Poor

To address inequality as a critical factor affecting Dhaka's prosperity, we recommend that the government focuses on income redistribution by aligning poverty reduction strategy with a progressive taxation system for the income-rich residents along with the provisions for social protection and a safety net for the urban poor. It should be noted that Bangladesh's average tax to GDP ratio was the lowest in South Asia. For example, between 2008 and 2018, the ratio was 10.3 per cent, which is half of either India (19.6 per cent) or Nepal (19.6 per cent). In developed countries, the average tax to GDP ratio is 35.8 per cent.[3] The government so far has made inroads to increase revenue base through an effective system of direct taxation for public sector employees and in the tax administration system.

However, simply raising marginal personal income tax rates on high earners will not necessarily bring in much additional revenue because of the danger of tax avoidance and other behavioural responses. Given that tax increases are necessary, it is important to adopt a 'growth-friendly' approach such as reducing tax-induced distortions that harm growth, including closing loopholes, raising more revenue from recurrent taxes on land and property as well as capital gains from these, and setting taxes to reduce environmental damage and correct other externalities. Arguably, the absence of regulation of land sales and appropriate rates of land, property, and capital gains tax from property transactions and stocks incentivizes investors in favour of land holdings and stock market speculation over investments in real economic activities. These also contribute to escalated land price and land speculation, particularly in the capital city of Dhaka, constraining the growth of commercial and industrial activities. Such speculative investment together with the growing population pressure and income contributed to a rapid escalation of land prices, especially in major metropolitan cities such as Dhaka and Chittagong.

Also, the soaring land prices, especially in the capital city of Dhaka, has made land a binding constraint to the growth of commercial and industrial activities, as well as adding to the woes of housing shortage and affordability issues. Although local governments have the right to value and extract tax from property owners, they often refrain from doing so, possibly due to the fear of losing popularity and votes and/or due to lack of appropriate skills and capacity that lead to loss of revenues. Following the example of India, China, and the Philippines, taxing idle land and fixed assets or assessing these as collateral for loan can be considered as a strategy to bring urban land into residential and other use (UN-Habitat 2016; UN-ESCAP 2017).

Also, the need for reviewing the effectiveness of taxation policy and tax breaks, particularly the question of whether these favour higher-income groups disproportionately, is clearly compelling. It is high time to consider an innovative taxation system that addresses income inequality without undermining the economic growth to bring high income earners such as businessmen/women and property owners into the government's tax net. To ensure social equity, it is important to allocate public expenditure for health and education that tends to favour low-income households, as well as for growth-enabling infrastructure that can also increase prospects for shared prosperity. A case in point is Venezuela where increase in investment in health and education helped improving the living standards of the urban poor (UN-Habitat 2010).

Introduce Ex-ante Measures to Stimulate and Protect Self-insurance by Reducing Risk Through Savings, Fostering Credit for the Poor

We highlighted the risks borne by low-income groups in Dhaka such as sickness of workers and or family members, work-related injury/accident, theft, and loss in business that arise largely from lack of adequate policies protecting workers from occupational hazards, which impacted mainly their health and well-being, affecting their stake in the shared prosperity. Research shows that ex-ante measures can potentially stimulate and protect self-insurance by reducing risk through savings, fostering credit for the poor as a form of social protection insurance and allow a stronger asset base to grow out of the persistent vulnerability to risk (Dercon, Bold, and Calvo 2004). In the context of Bangladesh, we underscore the need for employers to comply with the labour code and safety standards in the RMG, construction, and transport sectors through appropriate legislation and social campaign.[4] This will enable enhancing good health and well-being of migrant workers and fulfil the necessary requirements of decent work articulated in Goal 3 and Goal 8.

Also, there should be a combined social safety net of protective (such as health insurance and food aids), preventive (such as provision of basic services and adequate housing), and promotive measures (such as easy term credits and productive assets) to enhance the resilience of the most vulnerable and extremely poor households in urban areas. Such measures will also help save both human and financial assets of poor and marginalized groups of urban society from sudden erosion and increase their productivity and well-being. Effective delivery of such types of schemes requires partnership with multiple agents such as NGOs, community organizations, or the private sectors with the government playing the key role in developing and supporting an appropriate regulatory and institutional framework and sustainable and transparent institutions to monitor these activities. As a first step, it would require the formulation of a sustainable urban development policy for which we believed this book has provided a road map, particularly in the conducive environment of the Seventh Five-Year Plan, which includes urban development as a core target.

Shared Modes of Basic Services: The Need for Effective Management and Compact Urban Development

Despite the improvement in housing quality and access to basic services, the lack of affordable housing, the high cost of living, and heavy road congestion made Dhaka the world's second-worst city to live in (Economist Intelligence Unit 2015). Similarly, Dhaka secured an overall moderate (0.633) ranking in the CPI. However, it is among the cities with low prosperity factors in terms of quality of life index (0.539), which indicates inequality of opportunities, inadequate capital investment in public goods, and lack of pro-poor social programmes (UN-Habitat 2013). This is a clear evidence of policy failure because there is still no approved urban policy in Bangladesh (GOB 2015c) and 'market logic alone is congenitally incapable of regulating the urban commons in the interests of economic efficiency and social well-being' (Scott and Storper 2015: 8).

For harnessing urbanization's potential, an important precondition is improving the urban-land infrastructure nexus. Uncontrolled sprawl generates inefficiencies, injustices, and degradations that undermine economic and human development. Without adequate policy intervention such forces will severely constrain the city's ability to deliver improvements in prosperity and liveability. Key areas that require policy attention are systems of land allocation, land assembly, infrastructure investment and coordination of public (meaning both central and local government), and business and household investment decisions. This is a crucial agenda for the government that cannot be left to the market (meaning private investors, businesses, and lobby groups).

Quality infrastructure is critical to reduce business costs, increase productivity, ensure environmental sustainability by reducing transport-related carbon emissions, and enhance resilience to climate threats. Also, it is necessary to make Dhaka more liveable and inclusive by widening access to health, education, employment, and cultural opportunities. It is also required to enhance the city's innovation potential, improve environmental quality, and increase access to affordable housing and local amenities. These measures would help to attract and retain individuals with high levels of human capital and capture the positive spill-over effects for greater regional equity. Policy measures that could be adopted for effective management and land-use planning to make Dhaka more liveable and inclusive are outlined below:

Streamline Land-Use Planning to Facilitate Compact Urban Development

It is the task of the government to ensure effective urban planning, management, and an integrated approach to sustainable and inclusive urban development. However, there are serious structural, functional, financial, and social governance issues. Instead of a simple and clear-cut institutional arrangement with adequate power and resources, the current system of urban government is complex, chaotic, hierarchical, and highly inefficient. Planning, infrastructure, and basic services are delivered by a mix of central and local government and national and special purpose agencies that have limited resources, weak administrative capacity, and little coordination.

There are at least 18 main ministries responsible for urban development activities, which they deliver through their regional and local level agencies. In addition, there are 42 national level agencies such as Urban Development Directorate (UDD), National Housing Authority (NHA), and Rajdhani Unnayan Kartripakkha (RAJUK), or capital development authorities that mainly provide planning and infrastructure services to different urban jurisdictions such as city corporations, *paurashava*s (municipalities), and other urban centres. Also, special purpose agencies such as DWASA, Dhaka Electricity Supply Authority (DESA), and Road Transport Authority (RTA) deliver basic services to city dwellers. Such a haphazard system of service delivery is clearly deficient in delivering the integrated planning, implementation, and enforcement of regulations necessary for sustainable urban development as it suffers from lack of adequate resources, accountability, authority, capacity, and coordination. Therefore, it is not surprising that the bulk of the proposals, policies, and strategies stemming from a series of plans such as Dhaka Metropolitan Development Plan (DMDP) 1995–2015 have never been implemented but rather ignored (GOB 2015c).

However, it is important to acknowledge that there is a lack of a comprehensive physical plan or land-use plan equipped with population projection and an integrated view of transport and communication, trade and livelihoods, and physical and social inclusion. It should be noted that the Seventh Five-Year Plan emphasizes a coordinated 'land use and transport planning in order to encourage spatial development patterns' enabling access to multiple basic amenities such as work, school, market, and so on (GOB 2015c: 86). Also, it aims to facilitate access to land

and housing for urban poor as a strategic goal and proposes special zones for low-income settlements. Despite its good intensions, the proposed strategies for the urban poor has the potential risk of becoming exclusionary in nature if these settlements are not well connected with infrastructure and support systems such as work, networks of family and friends, schools, and other services and goods. This is because research shows that the utility of housing to households depends upon complementary investments by firms in nearby premises and by government in infrastructure (Collier and Venables 2015). 'Similarly, the productivity of premises to firms depends upon corresponding investments in infrastructure and adequately-housed workers and consumers nearby' (Turok 2018: 10).

In the context of skewed distribution of land and housing in Dhaka, we underscore the need to put housing, particularly low-cost housing, at the centre of urban policies and at the centre of cities drawing on UN-Habitat, which says:

> An incremental approach to slum upgrading can achieve this, providing adequate housing for low-income urban residents in areas that, in most cases, are already located close to city centre. This strategy will address the social and spatial implications of 'housing at the centre' while linking with broader urban renewal strategies for planned city-infill and local economic development, and meeting the density, diversity and mixed-use requirements. (UN-Habitat 2016: 58)

Side by side, there should be collective action to coordinate reciprocal investments in housing and business premises which is achieved through a long-term spatial plan or framework that provides a 'shared vision of the future form and direction of the city's growth' (Turok 2018). Land-use planning needs to be streamlined and redirected to provide safe and affordable housing together with ensuring linkages with functional transport corridors and easy connections between jobs, business premises, and housing instead of focusing on housing supply and obsolete building rules. Thus, by integrating different land uses, urban planners can facilitate more compact urban development, which is considered efficient, inclusive, and sustainable as it helps reduce the costs of doing business and infrastructure, 'improve access to services and facilities, enhance the livelihoods of urban poor and reduce social segregation' (UN-Habitat 2013).

Improve Standards for 'Safely Managed Water and Sanitation'

We found that the residents of Dhaka city who do not have access to sanitary toilets for private use, proper drainage, and waste disposal facilities have greater risk of illness compared with those having access to improved basic amenities. It is encouraging that over time Bangladesh has achieved almost universal access to safe drinking water. However, it lacks the development and implementation of proper standards such as with respect to water quality, particularly arising from E. coli and microbial contamination, and technical and service provision standards for water and sanitation systems.

However, Goal 6 calls for equitable access for all by the year 2030 to safe and affordable drinking water and environmentally responsible sanitation. To reach the new SDG water target, Bangladesh will need to measure access to 'safely managed water', based on households' access to an improved water source which is (*a*) free from faecal and chemical contamination; (*b*) continuously available when needed; and (*c*) located on the household's premises. Similarly, universal access to 'safely managed sanitation' will be measured by households' access to an unshared sanitation facility where excreta are safely disposed and treated (World Bank 2018). One major problem related to achieving sanitation target arises from the limited coverage of sewage system even in Dhaka city in which only 20 per cent of the population is connected. More than that, existing estimates suggest that only 2 per cent of the human excreta in the city is safely managed; the rest is discharged into open water, and nearly 80 per cent of the faecal sludge from on-site facilities is not being properly managed exacerbating the risk of environmental contamination (Blackett, Hawkins, and Heymans 2014).

Therefore, the DWASA's plan to ensure sanitation facilities to city dwellers from 40 per cent to 60 per cent during the Seventh Five-Year Plan period needs to take into account the pressing needs for the faecal sludge management. There should be a system of regular monitoring of performance to ensure effective service delivery with better measurable indicators of SDG. Given that the majority of the low-income settlements have shared sanitation facilities, DWASA should focus on safe containment, collection, disposal, and treatment as necessary steps to reduce faecal contamination. Following the World Bank (2018) report, we also underscore the need to explore both centralized and decentralized wastewater treatment options based on the population pressures and city plans. Local government in partnership with the relevant public and private sector can implement measures for collection, disposal, and treatment of faecal sludge. Side by side, it is necessary to ensure effective management, restoration, and operation of the natural drainage system to improve the water logging situation. Clearly, it requires adequate resources and commitment by all stakeholders along with an effective compliance and monitoring mechanism to meet SDG in pursuit of quality of life and creating scope for shared prosperity for all.

An Integrated Approach to Build a Mass Transit System for Dhaka

The shifting disease patterns over time mainly from water-borne diseases towards more communicable and chronic diseases for the residents of Dhaka city as revealed from our survey data draws attention to urban congestion, air quality, environmental issues, and the health policy. Research shows that lead and PM concentration in the air is dangerously high in Dhaka city (Mahadi 2010; Begum, Biswas, and Nasiruddin 2010) having serious implications for mortality and morbidity. The transport sector is estimated to contribute 70 per cent of carbon emissions at the national level, of which Dhaka's share ranged between 20 and 30 per cent (Alam and Rabbani 2007).

To address air pollution and sustainable environmental issues, it would be appropriate to consider an integrated approach that focuses on building an efficient mass transit system such as bus rapid transit (BRT) developed by Lagos and Bogota, Colombia, or commuter trains or the metro rail operating in many Indian cities. The government gives priority to rapid bus transit using 'high capacity dedicated bus lane' and building a rail-based mass transit system as a part of the long-term integrated transport strategy for Dhaka Metropolitan Area in the Seventh Five-Year Plan (GOB 2015c). However, implementing these goals would require an action plan with deadlines and dedicated resources, which would need to be monitored. We also recommend taxing industries and owners that use polluting technologies for vehicles and fuels; while, at the same time, providing incentives to upscale clean and energy-efficient industrial production and build credible monitoring and enforcement capacity of the local government and relevant stakeholders.

Highlight a Balanced and Healthy Diet, Physical Activities, and Health Education in the Urban Health Strategy

In the light of the paradigm shift in the disease patterns, particularly regarding chronic diseases, we underscore the need to include a balanced and healthy diet, physical activities, and health education as an integral part of the urban health strategy to reduce negative health consequences in the long term. Following WHO (2008), we also emphasize that the national health policy needs to strengthen health systems, enabling them to respond more effectively and equitably to the health care needs of the different cross-sections. There should be safer and pollution-free public spaces for health promotion activities such as physical exercise and jogging that could help prevent chronic diseases.

Effective Industrial Policies and Transformative Redevelopment

Research shows that despite Dhaka's dominance in Bangladesh's economy, its major industry—garment—which is also the country's most important industry has been shifting out of the city's core and into its peri-urban areas (Ellis and Roberts 2015). Accordingly, from more than half, DCC's share of all formal jobs declined to less than one-third between 2001 and 2009. By contrast, the share located in Dhaka's peri-urban areas almost doubled from 20 per cent to 38 per cent during the same period. These areas not only consist of garment manufacturing clusters approximately 15 kilometres from Dhaka's centre but so do municipalities of Sreepur and, to a lesser extent, Kaliakair, located outside the boundaries of metropolitan Dhaka (Ellis and Roberts 2015).

Clearly, this reflects a policy failure, particularly in relation to congestion and high land and housing prices, which failed to retain garment manufacturers within the city and drove them to relocate to suburban areas outside Dhaka. This also has had implications for workers, particularly unskilled labour, who now required to commute to peri-urban instead of more central areas, which calls on planners to provide affordable transport and infrastructure (Chandrasekhar and Sharma 2014). Moreover, the vacated buildings have not been repurposed largely because the transportation infrastructure has not been upgraded. Therefore, the movement of manufacturing out of DCC has not yet resulted in developing activities with higher economic productivity (Muzzini and Aparicio 2013). The ITC sector that emerged is not quite developed to fill the vacuum created by the garment industry.

Examples from successful and well-planned cities highlight that the areas vacated by industries are usually revitalized by high-value services. For example, Puerto Madero in Buenos Aires, Argentina, was turned to a vibrant entertainment area once it ceased to function as a maritime-oriented warehouse district. Therefore, Dhaka needs to actively 'respond to this de-concentration trend by planning and implementing policies to increase dynamism in city cores' (Ellis and Roberts 2015: 136). This would also help create more job opportunities for the under/unemployed, particularly women, whose employment rate declined over time mainly due to lack of adequate employment opportunities for the high school graduates or secondary school completers. 'New spatial planning' can be adopted for affordable transport and appropriate infrastructure because it integrates the needs of the highly skilled entrepreneurs as well as the unskilled workers of RMG sector and even the informal vendors into formal planning (UN-Habitat 2016: 82).

Benefit from the Rural–Urban Synergies to End Poverty and Ensure Shared Prosperity

Our research shows that urbanization and migration are clearly linked with building physical and social infrastructure and poverty alleviation measures such as safety nets and proliferation of micro-finance institutions. Therefore, it is important to uplift poverty discourses regarding the ways to improve livelihoods of the rural poor from an 'isolated sectoral perspective' to the inclusive pathways that take advantage of the rural–urban interactions to reduce both urban and rural poverty. At the national level, the integration of the rural and urban sectors is critical to end poverty and achieve shared prosperity. For example, the policy of Curitiba, Brazil, of developing linkages with wider access to public services, industrial development, and diversified employment opportunities available at the urban centres helped leveraging rural sector capacities to exchange resources and information and engage in social interaction with urban areas (UN 2015c). According to Ellis and Roberts (2015: 1):

> In the long run, successful urbanization is accompanied by the convergence of living standards between urban and rural areas as economic and social benefits spill beyond urban boundaries.

The following measures are recommended to leverage from rural–urban and regional connectivity to make Dhaka a more productive, competitive, and equitable city:

Plan for Integrated Investments in Transport and Urban Development

We underscore the need for an effective urban policy for Bangladesh with a shift from an overemphasis on 'balanced growth' approach to making Dhaka a globally competitive, equitable, and liveable city. This would require strategic planning, clear and accountable administrative structure, adequate investment, and appropriate action on land, infrastructure, public transport, necessary services, and sustainable environment management.

If properly designed and implemented, public transport solutions can improve the functioning of labour markets and reduce commuting time and costs for workers and thereby enhance productivity and well-being. Such measures can ensure environmental and social sustainability by reducing greenhouse gas emissions and increasing access to jobs, education, health care, and recreation, all of which would help increase Dhaka's liveability prospect. To reap these benefits, it requires planning for integrated investments in transport and urban development that operates at a regional scale and coordinating the various jurisdictions and agencies with '21st century governance mechanisms'.[5] Fear of Dhaka's primacy, that dominated the urban development discourse for long, is not only unfounded but can also jeopardize the national economic growth, given that Dhaka and Chittagong contribute nearly half of the country's GDP and comprise a little over one-tenth (13 per cent) of the total population (World Bank 2013).

Develop a Broad Regional Framework with Adequate Governance Structure and Approach

We underscore the need for a broad regional development framework to address inadequate infrastructure and poor and weak capacity of local governments to deal with the growing need for appropriate services and conducive business environment that could keep pace with the rapid urban growth and optimize urbanization for greater prosperity and better liveability. This requires a clear and accountable administrative set-up; decentralization of power, adequate resource allocation, and revenue generation system; integrated planning process and creating platform for community participation with focus on the urban poor groups and communities to reap benefits from agglomeration economies. It is also vital to enhance capabilities of the elected local representatives and officials through high-quality training facilities for efficient performance, adequate finance and budget by restructuring fiscal transfer, and facilitating local government borrowing and fostering better service and revenue performance. To achieve better service and revenue performance, the government needs to standardize methodologies for collection and analysis of data and monitoring across cities and local government. To be globally competitive, the government can consider adopting International Organization for Standardization (ISO) standard 37120: 'Sustainable development of communities: Indicators for city services and quality of life', which has been developed to provide cities with the 'comparable and relevant indicators to be used in measuring and comparing performance as well as to learn from other cities'.[6]

The importance of rural–urban interaction is widely acknowledged with cities emerging as drivers of change in rural areas. Rural areas benefit from urbanization through increased demand for rural goods, which can have a significant impact on rural poverty. Other benefits from the urban–rural linkages include increased urban–rural remittances, increased rural land/labour ratio, and increased rural non-farm employment (Cali and Menon 2013; Cuong 2014). We have presented convincing evidence of increased rural non-farm employment with expansion of construction and transportation activities in rural areas through pre-migration occupational structure of migrants. Therefore, the need to move away from the political, social, and geographical dichotomy between urban and rural areas; and the recognition and understanding of the continuum of urban and rural development is paramount to achieving sustainable development.

Creating rural–urban partnerships is critical for efficient management of rural–urban interactions. They can boost economic development by improving the production of public goods, achieving economies of scale in public service provision, coordinating decisions having cross-boundary effects, and increasing the capacity of the partners. We recommend multi-level governance instruments to implement sustainable and inclusive development policies effectively based on complementarity between different types of investments such as infrastructure, innovation, and human capital. An approach to public investment needs to take full account of regional specificities or information emanating from regional actors to be successful. It also requires an effective inter-agency and inter-sectoral coordination to learn how to engage a range of private sector and non-state actors such as the NGOs, civil society, citizens, and interest groups around complex agendas for change and development.

Uplift Urban Development and Connectivity into a National Urban Development Policy and Strategy Framework

It is encouraging that urban policy discourse in Bangladesh, as in many other developing countries, has transitioned from the conventional reservation about benefits of urbanization to greater emphasis on how to optimize such benefits for growth and prosperity. The country's Seventh Five-Year Plan, for example, includes an urbanization strategy to achieve 'compact, networked, resilient, inclusive and smart urban development' (GOB 2015c: 480). Despite incorporating many positive strategies for urban development, the plan could not overcome the geographical dichotomy between rural and urban sectoral approaches to development. Increasingly, however, the need to adopt a regional perspective and make the planning process 'inclusive and flexible' is considered as the hallmark of the most effective cities (McKinsey 2013). Also, 'the move from sectoral interventions to strategic urban planning and more comprehensive urban policy platforms' is considered crucial to transforming the city. In order to reap benefits from urbanization, it is important to have strategies for adequate and efficient management of urban growth and the extent to which the benefits accruing from urbanization are equitably distributed.

Also, well connected cities are those that deploy innovative ICT to support innovation and poverty eradication through 'promoting efficiencies in urban infrastructure leading to lower cost city services' (UN-Habitat 2016: 44). High-quality city data is essential to assess the needs for and quality of services, compliance mechanisms, and monitoring environment for an evidence-based policy, effective leadership, and decision making. The ICT has played a significant role in increasing the data availability and smart cities are adopting ICT solutions for 'better decision-making with respect to prosperity, sustainability, resilience, emergency management, or effective and equitable service delivery' (UN-Habitat 2016: 45). For example, in 2014, India announced plans to build 100 smart cities in response to its growing population and pressure on urban infrastructure (Government of India 2015). However, to realize the potential of ICT towards sustainable development (UN-Habitat and Ericsson 2014: 45), we underscore the need to create an enabling environment 'with participatory governance models, the right infrastructure and technical platforms, including capacity building, ensuring inclusion and bridging the digital divide'.

According to UN-Habitat (2016: 181):

> National Urban Policies (NUPs) are considered as fundamental 'development enablers' that ... can establish synergetic connections between the dynamics of urbanization and the overall process of national development ... contribute to building linkages between human settlements of various sizes and defining the broad parameters within which the transformative power of urbanization is activated and steered.

We recommend that the strategies for national urban development should ensure that cities 'are environmentally sustainable, resilient, socially inclusive, safe and violence-free and economically productive', connected across space and contributing to national development and shared prosperity and sustainability (UN-Habitat 2016: 1). This is in line with Goal 11 that calls to make cities and human settlements inclusive, safe, resilient, and sustainable. To achieve sustainable, resilient, and inclusive cities, we emphasize the importance of good governance that encompasses effective leadership; land-use planning; jurisdictional coordination; inclusive citizen participation; and efficient financing.

Metropolitan Government to Ensure an Effective, Accountable, Fair, and Democratic System and a Pro-poor Urban Development Agenda

Given that urban sector mandates are fragmented across various ministries in Bangladesh and there is no clear and/or unambiguous and committed political leadership, the importance of metropolitan government becomes clear for Dhaka city to ensure democratic participation, effective financing system, accountability, rule of law, along with pro-poor urban development and enabling business environment to ensure shared prosperity for all.

With strong and adequate financial autonomy, full range of capabilities, and power to ensure service delivery and optimization of the built environment, metropolitan government can enhance the scope for the national government to play a more proactive role in supporting smaller authorities governing complex rural–urban areas such as urban fringes and other urban areas which lack a clear administrative authority (UN-Habitat 2016: 113).

For metropolitan government to drive transformative agenda for sustainable development, prosperity, and social justice, it would require appropriate legal powers, adequate financial allocations, and human capacity and good governance structures. Such structures need to be participatory, accountable, and transparent creating room for participation by all including the poor, vulnerable, and marginalized groups in the service delivery planning, implementation, and budgeting process; building vertical and horizontal coordination with other sectors and jurisdictions, and with different partners and stakeholders; having a clear and effective management and monitoring mechanism and process. It is proposed that 'monitoring and managing urbanization requires new definitions based on economic function rather than administrative boundaries. Analysis of competitiveness of large metropolitan areas to guide regional development policy would benefit from a clear measure of the functional economy of these areas' (IDB and OECD 2018: 12). It also means adoption of responsibilities and activities such as education, health, and housing going beyond the traditional local government mandates (UN-Habitat 2016).

***

Dhaka has made remarkable progress to reduce poverty, enhance economic growth and quality of life through employment creation and diversification, creating the scope for upward occupational mobility, improvements in education, health, and access to basic services for the urban poor over time. In the 1990s, our major concern was whether the income gains made by the poorer migrants can be sustained in the long-run as they trailed behind not only their urban rich but also rural-poor counterparts in terms of human capital development and quality of life. In 2010, these gaps were bridged with enrolment rates accelerating for the primary and secondary school age cohorts from slum households. This resulted in their greater investment in education and health, access to improved quality of housing and basic services, compared with the 1990s. Therefore, the answers to the first and second compelling questions that we raised in the Introduction are positive meaning that *the poorer segment of urban population that migrates with dreams for better lives and livelihoods is benefitting from positive economic trends* and *these benefits can be sustained in the long run to a great extent.* However, this book comes up with a negative answer to the third question: Have these benefits brought qualitative changes creating scope for this group to have a stake in the city's growing prosperity like their non-poor counterparts?

The prospect for shared prosperity is slim as little progress has been made to reduce income disparity between the rich and poor and men and women over time, which can potentially worsen due to highly-skewed investment patterns of the rich and the poor in the sources that generate income such as property and business. Dhaka's second worst ranking in the liveability indices, and the lack of business competitiveness, adequate investment in affordable housing and infrastructure, good governance, integrated planning, and appropriate policy framework are among other factors that impede its prospects to gain from rapid urbanization and agglomeration economies. The poorer segment of the urban population had realized their dream for better livelihoods as well as better life to a great extent but their scope for having a stake in Dhaka's growing prosperity like their non-poor counterparts has not been realized yet. So long as the urban poor do not have a protective roof over their heads which they own; do not have access to the basic services for private use; are not protected from health and environmental hazards; do not have their voices heard; and are not ensured representation in the political structure and the decision-making bodies, their scope to prosper and secure their rightful claim in the city's prosperity will remain incomplete.

Dhaka's demographic and socio-economic transition as we have narrated in this book clearly highlights that the 'path to prosperity lies with cities'. Preconditions to reap the transformative potential of urbanization lie in the right vision, adequate planning, policy, human and financial resources, appropriate investment, efficient management, good governance, and a strong, clear, participatory, transparent, and an accountable institutional framework. To have the right vision, it is important for the national government to go beyond the narrow sectoral and geographic divide to encompass the New Urban Agenda adopted in 2016 Habitat III to steer the 'emerging futures' of Dhaka 'on to a sustainable, prosperous path'. For national governments, the imperative is to share urban prosperity through peri-urban and 'well organized rural–urban linkage ... guaranteeing that the benefits and services cities can offer are shared by all, regardless of income, lifestyle, place of residence and type and size of settlement' (IDB and OECD 2018: 23). 'This is why the frame for effective action on urbanization is not just the city, but the nation as a whole' (UN-Habitat 2016: 195). By defining the way in which cities should be planned and managed to best promote sustainable and equitable urbanization and integrating it with the national development agenda in this book, we have provided a road map that would create the scope for shared prosperity for all citizens.

NOTES

1. Basically, the programme makes cash transfers to low-income families on the condition that they, for example, send their children to school and ensure that they are properly vaccinated. Brazil's experience shows that four-fifths of the benefits from the scheme went to families living below the poverty line and accounted for decline in inequality by almost one-quarter (21 per cent) between 1995 and 2004 (Ni 2011; Ndegwa 2002). For Bangladesh, the achievements of female stipend scheme are well documented (see, for example, Khandker et al. 2003; World Bank 2002; Asadullah and Chaudhury 2008).
2. A country must exceed thresholds on two of the three criteria—per capita income, a human assets index, and an economic vulnerability index at two consecutive triennial reviews to be considered for graduation.
3. See https://www.dhakatribune.com/business/2018/08/02/bangladesh-s-tax-revenue-to-gdp-ratio-is-the-lowest-in-south-asia (accessed on 8 January 2018).
4. Amendments to the Bangladesh Labour Act 2006 were adopted on 15 July 2013 and to improve occupational safety and health of the workers in the workplaces and provisions for compensation for work-related deaths. However, there are some concerns about the rights of the workers by the ILO (available at: https://www.ilo.org/global/about-the-ilo/newsroom/statements-and-speeches/WCMS_218067/lang--en/index.htm [accessed on 9 January 2019]).

5. Some of the important characteristics are legitimacy, responsiveness, effectiveness and efficiency, transparency and accountability, fairness and equity, and being coordinated, and having a strategic vision.

6. See www.iso.org/iso/catalogue_detail?csnumber=62436 (accessed on 16 January 2019).

Appendices

APPENDIX 1

Table A1.1 Samples, Sampling Methods, and Selection Stages

Year/Area	First Stage Unit	Sampling Method	Second Stage Units	Sampling Method
2010 DCC	Wards # 7, 31–3, 36, 60, 62, and 90*	1. Random 2. Focus group discussion	400 Non-slum and 200 slum households Four – one each with hawkers and small shop owners, garment, transport and construction workers. 32 participants – 8 from each group	Stratified random sampling proportionate to population based on occupation of the electorate drawn from 2008 Electoral Rolls Purposive and snowballing

Year/Area	First Stage Unit	Sampling Method	Second Stage Units	Sampling Method
		3. In-depth interviews	Eight workers – two hawkers, two garment workers, two construction labours, one rickshaw puller and one auto driver	Purposive and snowballing
1998 and 1991 DCC	Wards # 7, 25, 48, and 64	1. Random 2. Random	400 Non-slum and 200 slum households 110 Temporary migrants	Same SRS as above drawn from 1990–91 and 1996 Electoral Rolls. Supplementary censuses held to cover all slums in four wards in 1996. Slum households drawn using SRS. SRS in 1991
1991 Villages	Migrants' birthplaces	3. Purposive sampling and tracing	30 Non-migrant households and 20 temporary migrant households	Quota sample selected by age and occupation

Note: * For Ward names and boundaries, see Table 1.2 and the discussion in Chapter 1 under the section titled 'Methodology'.
Source: Author.

APPENDIX 2

Types of information collected for the study

I. Quantitative: Survey Questionnaire
   A. Demographic and Socio-Economic Information (For All Members)
      A.1. Name, relationship with household head, gender, age, marital status, grades/degree completed, current students, drop outs and reasons, occupation/s, health status, disability, immunization status (under-5 children)
      A.2. Information about sickness (last 15 days) and sick members including treatment seeking behaviour and cost
      A.3. Information about mortality last 10 years (2001–10)
      A.4. Information about the out-migrant members (2001–10) and remittances
      A.5. Information about the incoming members (if stayed out of house for more than 6 months) (2001–10)
   B. Quality of Life (For All Members)
      B.1. Housing quality, ownership, per capita space availability
      B2. Source of drinking water, types of toilet, distance between water source from house, bathing arrangement, waste disposal, water logging, electricity connection and sources, cooking arrangement and piped gas connection, type of telephone used and period
   C. Migration and Rural–Urban Linkage (For Household Heads)
      C.1. Birthplace, transportation used for going to birthplace, infrastructure/facilities in the birthplace such as paved road, market, primary school, secondary school, college, bank, health centre/hospital, NGO office, and distance from village for each.
      C2. Migration history prior coming to Dhaka, length of stay in Dhaka, reason/s for migration, migration decision-making, and problems encountered during the implementation process, and sources who accompanied at the time of migration
      C3. Settlement and accommodation immediately after coming to Dhaka, money brought at the time of migration—amount,

source, reason, mobility/change of accommodation and reasons

C4. Pre-migration occupation; first job after coming to Dhaka, waiting period for first job, sources who helped in job search and procurement, duration in the first job, and reasons for job change; any other job between first and current job; current job at the time of survey, duration, job satisfaction, and plan for job change

C.4. Problems faced after coming to Dhaka such as financial problems, health-related problems, death/mortality, and environmental hazards, how these challenges were addressed, and sources who helped, migration-related information for spouse

C.5. Birthplace, length of stay in Dhaka, reason/s for migration, sources who accompanied at the time of migration, and whether and how connection is maintained with natal family

D. Migration and Modernization (For Household Heads and Spouse)

D.1. Who makes the decision regarding family's income and expenditure, domestic chores, caring for family members, children's education and marriage, looking after elderly parents/in-laws

D.2. Who cooks, looks after children, cleans house, undertakes repairing activities, goes for shopping, supervises children's studies, caring for elderly parents/in-laws

D.3. Whether spouse, daughter, daughter-in-law, mother/in-law continued studies after marriage

D.4. Whether female members in the family are employed, reasons for those who are employed and those who are not, perception regarding women's employment and justification

D.5. Aspired level of education for sons and daughters, aspired age of marriage for sons and daughters, attitude towards dowry and dower's money

D.6. Attitudes towards women's higher education

D.7. Attitudes towards marriage, divorce, and inheritance

D.8. Perception about who will bear aged care responsibility when self/spouse will get old

D.9. For eligible couples only—desired number of children, attitude towards family planning, contraceptive use, sources from which contraceptives are procured

D.10. Details about NGO membership, if any, and types of benefits, if received any social welfare assistance or relief in the last year

E. Household Expenditure Related Information (For Head or Spouse)

E.1. All types of expenditure on food, fuel, transport, and miscellaneous (one week recall period)

E.2. House rent, bills and service charges, education, toiletries, entertainment, and miscellaneous expenditure (one month recall period)

E.3. Shoes and clothing, utensils, furniture, bedding and upholstery, electrical and electronic goods, tax, ceremonial, travel and holidays, medical, buying modes of transportation, charity/donation, religious ceremony and festivals and miscellaneous expenditure (one-year recall period)

F. Information Regarding Loans and Savings

G. Income and Asset Related Information

G.1. Income sources and income—house ownership, shops and establishment, industries/factories, occupation, other sources including land, remittances, share and investment

G.2. Information about assets including all electrical devices, furniture, means of transportation, gold jewellery, land, ponds, and other assets

H. Perception Regarding Changes in Households' Economic Condition in Last 10 Years (2001–10)

H.1. Family related—safety and security, income, relationship with family members/friends and neighbours, treatment facilities, children's education, threat by *mastaans* (goons)

H.2. Type of family prior to migration

H.3. Whether household's economic condition changed in the last 10 years and reasons for that

II. Qualitative Information

A. Guidelines for FGD

Focus group discussion was conducted primarily with four groups of informal and formal sector workers in the same wards as the survey. These are:

1. Female workers of RMG factory (formal), Jurain
2. Male workers of construction sector (informal), Mirpur/Purana Paltan
3. Male hawkers/vendors (informal) Motijheel
4. Male transport operators (informal) Mirpur/Lalbagh
   - Introducing/Ice breaking
     – Introducing the FGD conductors and workers
     Explain the purpose of the discussion. Make sure that every participant understands the purpose of the discussion and confirm that they are willing to participate voluntarily in the discussion. Make it clear that their identity will not be disclosed and that the information they provide may not help them directly. But insights generated from the discussion will help generate better understanding of the factors and process underlying occupational changes; identify major constraints in the process of occupational mobility and outcomes, and specific needs of each group. Understanding thus generated will help us to recommend appropriate policy masseurs and design programmatic interventions to address these issues and needs.
   - Current occupation
     – General information
     (Duration, type, who helped in getting job, sources of information)
     – Skills-related information
     (Whether they had requisite skills for the job? Where did they learn? How long it took? Who helped them in learning skills? Whether their wages increased? Do they need more skills? What? Why? Whether skills acquisition helped them to change job? Which jobs? Why? Do they need more skills? What types of skills and why?
     – Capital investment-related information
     (How much capital they invested so far and last year? Whether investment is increasing along with the rate of

return? Sources from where they manage the capital; who helped them and who did not in the process of capital accumulation? What would they recommend for meeting their capital needs?)

– Information related to occupational mobility

(Number and frequency of job changes after migration? How and why? Job satisfaction, job security, occupational hazards, and major issues from current compared with previous jobs; sources who constitute major help and major threats? How do they address occupational problems, current working condition, and environment, security threats; examples of collective bargaining)

– Fallback and solidarity

(Examples of when and where they helped migration of other family members/friends/neighbours for job-related reasons? Do they have district based migrant networks as a source of fall back and collective bargaining?)

– Future plans for occupational changes, migration, and settlement

B. Guidelines for the in-depth Interviews

In-depth interviews were conducted with the following categories of workers:

1. One male and one female RMG sector workers
2. One male and one female construction sector workers
3. One male transport operator
4. One male and one female hawkers/vendors

- Introduction/Ice breaking

  Introducing the interviewers and informal greetings with respondent

  Explain the purpose of the in-depth interviews. Make sure that every participant understands the purpose of the discussion and confirm that they are willing to participate voluntarily in the discussion. Make it clear that their identity will not be disclosed and that the information they provide may not help them directly. But insights generated from the interviews will help us understand settlement-related opportunities and constraints; identify specific needs, challenges and opportunities in their work, family, and plans for the future. Understanding thus generated will help us to recommend appropriate policy measures and design programmatic interventions to address these issues and needs.

- General information
  (Current housing characteristics; duration in this place; length of and reason for migration; family composition including age–sex distribution of the family members, occupation, education and a rough idea about incomes and assets)
- Major differences between rural and urban living that they have experienced (need to explore from their own experiences)
- Exploring temporal dimensions of the rural–urban differences
  - Are the forms of social and political violence that they have experienced changing over time?
  - Why and how?
  - Generate insights from personal experiences.
- Way-out and risk minimization strategies
  - Major attractions and threats
  - Social connections and social security
  - Major channels and processes through which such problems were redressed
  - Types and modes of collective action

Glossary

auto-rickshaw	a motorized three-wheel vehicle, a common form of urban transport, mostly for hire, in many developing countries around the world
bostee	slum
chingri gher	prawn farm
chashar chele	son of a peasant
jogal/jogan	helper in a construction and building industry
hata daridra	extreme poor
haat	weekly/biweekly market
Kabin Nama	Muslim marriage contract
kutcha	non-permanent
jowan pola	young and strong son
mahalla	the smallest unit in the urban administrative structure, locality
mastaan	goons or gangsters, brokering power, running extortion networks, and providing political muscle
paurashava	municipalities
pucca	permanent
rickshaw puller	a person who pulls or pedals a rickshaw, which is mainly a cycle with a covered seating arrangement for two people
thana	police district

ward	a unit that occupy an intermediate position between thana and the smallest unit mahalla in the urban administrative heirarchy
upazila	sub-district

References

Abegunde, D.O., C.D. Mathers, T. Adam, M. Ortegon, and K. Strong. 2007. 'The Burden and Costs of Chronic Diseases in Low-Income and Middle-Income Countries'. *The Lancet* 370(9603): 1929–38.

Afsar, Rita. 2016a. 'Reconstructing Labour Migration Theory from the Bangladesh Experience'. Paper presented at Panel 34, 24th European Conference for South Asian Studies (EASAS), University of Poland, Warsaw, Poland.

———. 2016b. 'Remittances and SME Development: Reflections from South Asia'. In *Migrant Remittances in South Asia: Social, Economic and Political Implications*. Edited by M.M. Rahman, T.T. Yong, and A.K.M.A. Ullah (Hampshire: Palgrave Macmillan), 135–57.

———. 2016c. 'Urban Development and Urban Poverty Reduction Approaches: Gender Implications and Development Outcomes'. In *State of the Urban Poor Report 2015: Gender and Urban Poverty 2015*. Edited by O.P. Mathur and Ministry of Housing and Urban Poverty Alleviation, Government of India (New Delhi: Oxford University Press), 29–43.

———. 2011. 'Contextualizing Gender and Migration in South Asia'. *Gender, Technology and Development* (Special Issue: Gender and Space: Themes from Asia) 15(3): 389–410.

———. 2005. 'Internal Migration and Development Nexus: The Case of Bangladesh'. In *Migration and Development: Pro-poor Policy Choices*. Edited by T. Siddiqui (Dhaka: University Press Limited), 39–70.

———. 2004. 'Dynamics of Poverty, Development and Population Mobility: The Bangladesh Case'. *Asia-Pacific Population Journal* 19(2): 69–91.

———. 2003. 'Rural–Urban Dichotomy and Convergence: Emerging Realities in Bangladesh'. *Environment and Urbanization* 11(1): 235–46.

———. 2000. *Rural–Urban Migration in Bangladesh: Causes, Consequences and Challenges* (Dhaka: University Press Limited).

———. 1999. 'Is Migration Transferring Rural Poverty to Urban Areas? An Analysis of Longitudinal Survey Data of Dhaka City'. Paper presented at the Workshop on Changes and Determinants of Urban Poverty, Grameen Trust, Grameen Bank, Dhaka.

———. 1995. 'Causes, Consequences and Challenges of Rural–Urban Migration in Bangladesh'. PhD thesis submitted at University of Adelaide, South Australia.

Ahmed, R., and M. Hossain. 1990. 'Development Impact of Rural Infrastructure in Bangladesh'. International Food Policy Research Institute Research (IFPRI) Report 83. (Washington, DC: IFPRI).

Ahmed, S. 1986. *Dacca: A Study in Urban History and Development* (London: Curzon Press/Riverdale Company).

Ahmed, S.M., M.A. Hossain, and M.R. Chowdhury. 2009. 'Informal Sector Providers in Bangladesh: How Equipped Are They to Provide National Health Care?' *Health Policy and Plan* 24(6): 467–78.

Alam, M., and G. Rabbani. 2007. 'Vulnerabilities and Responses to Climate Change for Dhaka'. *Environment and Urbanization* 19(1): 81–97.

Alexander, A.C., and C. Welzel. 2011. 'Islam and Patriarchy: How Robust Is Muslim Support for Patriarchal Values?' *International Review of Sociology* 21(2): 249–76.

Ali, Z., S. Begum, Q. Shahabuddin, and M. Khan. 2006. 'Rural Poverty Dynamics 2005/2006: Evidence from 64 Village Census Plus'. Programme for Research on Chronic Poverty in Bangladesh, Bangladesh Institute of Development Studies, Dhaka.

Anand, S., and M. Ravallion. 1993. 'Human Development in Poor Countries: On the Role of Private Incomes and Public Services'. *Journal of Economic Perspectives* 7(Winter): 133–50.

Annez, P., and R. Buckley. 2009. 'Urbanisation and Growth: Setting the Context'. In *Urbanisation and Growth*. Edited by M. Spence, P. Annez, and R. Buckley (Washington, DC: World Bank), pp. 1–46.

Appadurai, A. 2004. 'The Capacity to Aspire: Culture and Terms of Recognition'. In *Culture and Public Action*. Edited by V. Rao and M. Walton (Stanford: Stanford University Press), 59–84.

Asadullah, N., and N. Chaudhury. 2009. 'Reverse Gender Gap in Schooling in Bangladesh: Insights from Urban and Rural Households'. *Journal of Development Studies* 45(8): 1360–80.

Arias-Granada, Y., S.S. Haque, G. Joseph, and M. Yanez-Pagans. 2018. 'Informal Markets for Water and Sanitation Services within Dhaka Slums'. Policy Research Working Paper, World Bank, Washington, DC.

Arthur, W.B., and G. McNicoll. 1978. 'An Analytical Survey of Population and Development in Bangladesh'. *Population and Development Review* 4(1): 23–80.

Asadullah, N., and N. Chaudhury. 2008. 'Reverse Gender Gap in Schooling in Bangladesh: Insights from Urban and Rural Households'. *Journal of Development Studies* 45(8): 1360–80.

Asian Development Bank. 2015. *Balancing the Burden? Desk Review of Women's Time Poverty and Infrastructure in Asia and the Pacific* (Manila: Asian Development Bank).

Atkinson, S.J., and J. Chyne. 1994. 'Immunization in Urban areas: Issues and Strategies'. *Bulletin of the World Health Organization* 72(2): 183–94.

Awumbila, M., G. Owusu, and J.K. Teye. 2014. 'Can Rural–Urban Migration into Slums Reduce Poverty? Evidence from Ghana'. Working Paper 13, Migrating out of Poverty Research Consortium, University of Sussex, Falmer, UK.

Baldacci, E., E. Clements, S. Gupta, and Q. Cui. 2004. 'Social Spending, Human Capital, and Growth in Developing Countries: Implications for Achieving the MDGs'. Working Paper WP/04/217, International Monetary Fund (IMF), Washington, DC.

Bangladesh Bureau of Statistics. 2015. 'Census of Slum Areas and Floating Population 2014'. Bangladesh Bureau of Statistics, Dhaka.

———. 2013a. 'Health and Morbidity Status Survey 2012'. Bangladesh Bureau of Statistics, Dhaka.

———. 2013b. 'Statistical Yearbook of Bangladesh—2012'. Bangladesh Bureau of Statistics, Dhaka.

———. 2013c. 'Time Use Pilot Survey 2012'. General Economic Division, Planning Commission, Government of Bangladesh, Dhaka.

———. 2012a. 'Population and Housing Census 2011: Preliminary Results'. Bangladesh Bureau of Statistics, Dhaka. Available at: http://www.bbs.gov.bd/WebTestApplication/Userfiles/Image/Census2011/Dhaka/Dhaka/Dhaka_CO1.pdf (accessed on 14 February 2013).

———. 2012b. 'Statistical Yearbook of Bangladesh-2011'. Bangladesh Bureau of Statistics, Dhaka.

———. 2011a. 'Report on the Household Income and Expenditure Survey 2010'. Bangladesh Bureau of Statistics, Dhaka.

———. 2011b. 'Report on Labour Force Survey 2010'. Bangladesh Bureau of Statistics, Dhaka.

———. 2007a. 'Report on the Household Income and Expenditure Survey 2005'. Bangladesh Bureau of Statistics, Dhaka.

———. 2007b. 'Statistical Pocketbook of Bangladesh 2007'. Bangladesh Bureau of Statistics, Dhaka.

———. 1996. 'Report on Labour Force Survey 1995–1996'. Bangladesh Bureau of Statistics, Dhaka.

———. 1992. 'Supplement No. 1 to the Preliminary Population Census 1991'. Bangladesh Bureau of Statistics, Dhaka.

Barlet, S., and R. D'Aiglepierre. 2017. 'Supporting Youth Insertion into the African Labor Market'. Available at: https://issuu.com/objectif-developpement/docs/youth_insertion_web (accessed on 13 September 2019).

Barkema, H. 2018. 'Final Findings: Multipliers for Employment Creation: The IT-Industry in Kenya'. *Include*, 24 October. Available at: http://include-platform.net/downloads/final-findings-multipliers-employment-creation-industry-kenya/ (accessed on 13 September 2019).

Bates, R.H. 1981. *Markets and States in Tropical Africa* (Berkeley: University of California Press).

Begum, B.A., S.K. Biswas, and M. Nasiruddin. 2010. 'Trend and Spatial Distribution of Air Particulate Matter Pollution in Dhaka City'. *Journal of Bangladesh Academy of Sciences* 34(1): 33–48.

Bhuyan, A.R., A. Khan, and S.U. Ahmed. 2001. 'Rural–Urban Migration and Poverty: The Case for Reverse Migration in Bangladesh'. MAP Focus Study Series 10, Centre for Integrated Development for Asia and the Pacific, Dhaka.

Bisin, A., and T. Verdier. 2000. 'Beyond the Melting Pot: Cultural Transmission, Marriage, and the Evolution of Ethnic and Religious Traits'. *Quarterly Journal of Economics* 115(3): 955–88.

Biswas, S.K., S.B. Mahtab, and M.M. Rahman. 2010. 'Integrated Water Resources Management Options for Dhaka City'. Proceedings of International Conference on Environmental Aspects of Bangladesh (ICEAB10), Japan.

Boserup, E. 1970. *Women's Role in Economic Development* (London: George, Allen and Unwin).

Boulding, K.E. 1963. 'The Death of the City: A Frightened Look at Postcivilization'. In *The Historian and the City*. Edited by Oscar Handlin and J. Burchard (Cambridge, Massachusetts: The M.I.T. Press), 133–46.

Bangladesh Rehabilitation Assistance Committee (BRAC). 2004. 'Towards a Profile of the Ultra Poor in Bangladesh: Findings from CFPR/TUP Baseline Survey'. Research and Evaluation Division, Bangladesh Rehabilitation Assistance Committee and Aga Khan Foundation, Dhaka and Ottawa.

Blackett, I.C., P. Hawkins, and C. Heymans. 2104. 'The Missing Link in Sanitation Service Delivery: A Review of Faecal Sludge Management in 12 Cities'. *Water and Sanitation Program Research Brief*. World Bank Group, Washington DC. Available at: http://documents.worldbank.org/curated/en/395181468323975012/The-missing-link-in-sanitation-service-delivery-a-review-of-fecal-sludge-management-in-12-cities (accessed on 9 January 2019).

Bridges, S., D. Lawson, and S. Begum. 2011. 'Labour Market Outcomes in Bangladesh: The Role of Poverty and Gender Norms'. *European Journal of Development Research* 23(3): 458–87.

Bryan, G., S. Chowdhury, and A. Mobarak. 2013. 'Seasonal Migration and Risk Aversion'. Allied Social Sciences Association Annual Meeting. American Economic Association, San Diego, California, USA.

Calderon, C., and L. Serven. 2004. 'The Effects of Infrastructure Development on Growth and Income Distribution'. Working Paper Series 3,400, World Bank, Washington, DC. Available at: http://www1.worldbank.org/publicsector/pe/PEAMMarch2005/WPS3400.pdf (accessed on 8 May 2019).

Calì, M. 2013. 'Urbanization Is Good for Rural Poverty (At Least in India): Let's Talk Development'. Cited in UN-Habitat (2016), 'Urbanization and Development: Emerging Futures. World Cities Report 2016'. United Nations Human Settlements Programme (UN-Habitat), Nairobi, Kenya.

Cali, M., and C. Menon. 2013. 'Does Urbanization Affect Rural Poverty? Evidence from Indian Districts'. *World Bank Economic Review* 27(2): 171–201.

Canning, D., and E. Bennathan. 2007. 'The Rate of Return to Transportation Infrastructure'. World Bank Working Paper 3293. World Bank, Washington, DC.

———. 2000. 'The Social Rate of Return on Infrastructure Investments'. World Bank Policy Research Working Paper 2390. World Bank, Washington, DC.

Castles, S. 2008. 'Understanding Global Migration: A Social Transformation Perspective'. Conference on Theories of Migration and Social Change, St Anne's College, Oxford, UK.

Centre for Urban Studies (CUS). 1996. 'Survey of Slums and Squatter Settlements in Dhaka City'. CUS, Dhaka.

———. 1990. 'The Urban Poor in Bangladesh: Comprehensive Summary Report'. CUS, Dhaka.

Chandrasekhar, S., and A. Sharma. 2014. 'On the Spatial Concentration of Employment in India'. *Economic and Political Weekly* 49(21): 16–18.

Chant, S. 2014. 'Exploring the "Feminization of Poverty" in Relation to Women's Work and Home-based Enterprise in Slums of the Global South'. *International Journal of Gender and Entrepreneurship* 6(3): 296–316.

———. 2013. 'Cities through a "Gender Lens": A Golden "Urban Age" for Women in the Global South?' *Environment and Urbanization* 25(1): 9–19.

Chaudhury, R.H. 1980. 'Urbanisation in Bangladesh'. CUS, Dhaka.

Chowdhury, I.A. 2014. 'Impacts of Remittance on the Socioeconomic Condition of Bangladesh: an Analysis'. Dalhousie University, Halifax, Canada.

City Mayors. 2007. 'The Largest Cities in the World by Land Area, Population and Density'. Available at: http://www.citymayors.com/statistics/largest-cities-density-125.html (accessed on 25 January 2016).

Cleland, J., J.F. Phillips, S. Amin, and G.M. Kamal. 1994. 'The Determinants of Reproductive Change in Bangladesh: Success in a Changing

Environment'. World Bank Regional and Sectoral Studies, World Bank, Washington, DC. Available at: http://documents. worldbank.org/curated/en/991321468768584526/The-determinants-of-reproductive-change-in-Bangladesh-success-in-a-challenging-environment (accessed on 8 May 2019).

Collier, P., and A.J. Venables. 2015. 'Housing and Urbanisation in Africa: Unleashing a Formal Market Process'. In *The Urban Imperative: Towards Competitive Cities*. Edited by E. Glaeser and A. Joshi-Ghani (Oxford: Oxford University Press), pp. 413–36.

Collinson, S. 2009. 'The Political Economy of Migration Processes: An Agenda for Migration Research and Analysis'. International Migration Institute Working Paper 12, University of Oxford, Oxford.

Cox, W. 2012. 'Evolving Urban Form: Dhaka'. *Newgeography*. Available at: http://www.newgeography.com/content/003004-evolving-urban-form-dhaka (accessed on 8 May 2019).

Cuong, N.V. 2014. 'Does Urbanization Help Poverty Reduction in Rural Areas? Evidence from a Developing Country'. IPAG Working Paper Series. Available at: https://www. ipag.fr/wp-content/uploads/recherche/WP/IPAG_WP_2014_178.pdf (accessed on 28 March 2016)

Curran, S.R., and A.C. Saguy. 2001. 'Migration and Cultural Change: A Role for Gender and Social Networks?' *Journal of International Women's Studies* 2(3): 54–77.

Dai, M., X. Li, and Y. Lu. 2017. 'How Urbanization Economies Impact TFP and R&D Performers: Evidence from China'. *Sustainability* 9(10): 1–17.

Dani, A.H. 1956. *Dacca: A Record of Its Changing Fortunes* (Dhaka: Safia Dani).

Demographia. 2018. 'Demographia World Urban Areas: Built Up Urban Areas or Agglomerations', 14th Edition, April. Available at: http://demographia.com/db-worldua.pdf (accessed on 8 May 2019).

Dercon, S., T. Bold, and C. Calvo. 2004. 'Insurance for the Poor?' Working Paper Number 125. Queen Elizabeth House (QEH) Working Paper Series—QEHWPS125, London, UK.

Dev, U., Z. Hoque, N. Khaled, and S.K. Bairagi. 2008. 'Growth, Income Inequality and Poverty in Bangladesh: Implications for Development Strategy'. Paper presented at the Dialogue on Addressing Regional Inequalities, Policy Options and Strategies, Centre for Policy Dialogue, Dhaka.

Dhaka Water Supply and Sewerage Authority (DWASA). 2011. 'Monthly Information Report (MIR)'. Cited in *Water Supply of Dhaka City: Murky Future. The Issue of Access and Inequality*. Edited by A.F.M.A. Uddin and A. Baten (Dhaka: Unnayan Onneshan-The Innovators).

Dower, M. 2013. 'Rural Development in the New Paradigm'. In *New Paradigm in Action Successful Partnerships*. Edited by M. Kolczyński (Warsaw: Polish Ministry of Regional Development), pp. 30–50.

Duranton, G. 2014. 'The Urbanisation and Development Puzzle'. In *The Buzz in Cities: New Economic Thinking*. Edited by S. Yusuf (Washington DC: The Growth Dialogue), pp. 1–17.

Durkheim, E. 1982. *The Rules of Sociological Method* (New York: The Free Press).

———. 1933. *The Division of Labour in Society* (New York: Macmillan).

Dwyer, D.J., ed. 1972. *The City as a Centre of Change in Asia* (Hong Kong: University of Hong Kong Press).

Dzung, D.D. 2011. 'City Report on Ho Chi Minh City'. Unpublished UN-Habitat background study for State of the World's Cities Report 2012/2013. Nairobi, Kenya.

Economist Intelligence Unit (EIU). 2015. 'Livability Ranking and Overview'. Available at: https://media.heraldsun.com.au/files/liveability.pdf (accessed on 13 September 2019.

Ellis, P., and M. Roberts. 2016. 'Leveraging Urbanization in South Asia: Managing Spatial Transformation for Prosperity and Livability'. World Bank Groups, International Bank for Reconstruction and Development/The World Bank, Washington, DC.

Eisenstadt, S.N. 1966. *Modernisation, Protest and Change* (Englewood Cliffs, New Jersey: Prentice-Hall).

———. 1964. 'Institutionalization and Social Change'. *American Sociological Review* 29(2): 235–47.

Ellis, P., and M. Roberts. 2015. 'Leveraging Urbanization in South Asia: Managing Spatial Transformation for Prosperity and Livability'. World Bank Groups, International Bank for Reconstruction and Development/World Bank, Washington, DC.

Epstein, A.L., E.M. Bruner, P.C.W. Gutkind, M.M. Horowitz, K.L. Little, D.F. McCall, P. Mayer, et al. 1967. 'Urbanisation and Social Change in Africa'. *Current Anthropology* 8(4): 275–95.

Esser, H. 1993. 'Social Modernization and the Increase in the Divorce Rate'. *Journal of Institutional and Theoretical Economics* 149(1): 252–77.

Ezzati, M., S.V. Hoorn, C.M.M. Lawes, R. Leach, W.P.T. James, A.D. Lopez, A. Rodgers, and C.J.L. Murray. 2005. 'Rethinking the "Diseases of Affluence" Paradigm: Global Patterns of Nutritional Risks in Relation to Economic Development'. *PLoS Med* 2(5): e133.

Fan, S., C. Chang-Kan, and A. Mukherjee. 2005. 'Rural–Urban Dynamics and Poverty: Evidence from China and India'. Food Consumption and Nutrition Division (FCND) Discussion Paper 196, International Food Policy Research Institute, Washington, DC.

Fan, Shenggen, P.B.R. Hazell, and T. Haque. 1998. 'Role of Infrastructure in Production Growth and Poverty Reduction in Indian Rainfed Agriculture'.

Project Report to the Indian Council for Agricultural Research (ICAR) and the World Bank, International Food Policy Research Institute, Washington, DC.

Favell, A. 2008. 'Rebooting Migration Theory. Inter-disciplinarity, Globality and Post-Disciplinarity in Migration Studies'. In *Migration Theory: Talking Across Disciplines*. Edited by C.B. Brettell and J.F. Hollifield (New York, London: Routledge), pp. 259–78.

Fernández, R., A. Fogli, and C. Olivetti. 2004. 'Mothers and Sons: Preference Formation and Female Labor Force Dynamics'. *Quarterly Journal of Economics* 119(4): 1249–99.

Field, E., and A. Ambrus. 2008. 'Early Marriage, Age of Menarche, and Female Schooling Attainment in Bangladesh'. *Journal of Political Economy* 116(5): 881–930.

Findley, S.E. 1987. *Rural Development and Migration: A Study of Family Choices in the Philippines*. Brown University Studies in Population and Development (Boulder: Westview Press).

Foster, J.G., and E. Thorbek. 1984. 'A Class of Decomposable Poverty Measure'. *Economtrics* 52(3): 761–6.

Freeman, Gary P., and Alan E. Kessler. 2008. 'Political Economy and Migration Policy'. *Journal of Ethnic and Migration Studies* 34(4): 655–78.

Gardner, K., and F. Osella. 2003. 'Migration, Modernity and Social Transformation in Asia: An Overview'. *Contributions to Indian Sociology* 37(1–2): v–xxviii.

Garenne, M. 2004. 'Age at Marriage and Modernisation in Sub-Saharan Africa'. *Southern African Journal of Demography* 9(2): 59–79.

Garrett, J., and S. Chowdhury. 2004. 'Urban–Rural Links and Transformation in Bangladesh: A Review of the Issues'. Care Discussion Paper, Dhaka, Bangladesh.

Ghana Statistical Services (GSS). 2008. 'Ghana Living Standards Survey: Report of the Fifth Round'. Accra, Ghana. Available at: https://www.cleancookingalliance.org/binary-data/RESOURCE/file/000/000/87-1.pdf (accessed on 13 September 2019).

Glaeser, E. 2011. *Triumph of the City: How our Greatest Invention makes us Richer, Smarter, Greener, Healthier, and Happier* (London: Macmillan).

Glaeser, E., and A. Joshi-Ghani, eds. 2015. *The Urban Imperative: Towards Competitive Cities* (Oxford: Oxford University Press).

———. 2013. 'Rethinking Cities: Towards Shared Prosperity'. 126, Economic Premise, Poverty Reduction and Economic Management Network (PREM), World Bank, Washington, DC.

Gleason, P. 1980. 'American Identity and Americanization'. In *Harvard Encyclopedia of American Ethnic Groups*. Edited by S. Thernstrom, A. Orlov, and O. Handlin (Cambridge: Harvard University Press), 31–58.

Global Monitoring Report. 2013. 'Rural–Urban Dynamics and the Millennium Development Goals'. International Monetary and Reconstruction Bank and World Bank joint publication, Washington, DC.

Goel, P., D. Ross-Degnan, P. Berman, and S. Soumerai. 1996. 'Retail Pharmacists in Developing Countries: A Behaviour and Intervention Framework'. *Social Science and Medicine* 42(8): 1155–61.

Government of the People's Republic of Bangladesh. 2015a. 'Bangladesh Economic Review 2015'. Economic Adviser's Wing, Finance Division, Ministry of Finance, Dhaka.

———. 2015b. 'Millennium Development Goals: Bangladesh Progress Report 2015'. Planning Commission in assistance from Support to Sustainable and Inclusive Planning (SSIP) Project, General Economic Division (GED) UNDP, Dhaka.

———. 2015c. 'Seventh Five Year Plan FY 2016–FY2020: Accelerating Growth, Empowering Citizens'. GED, Planning Commission of Bangladesh, Dhaka.

———. 2011. 'Sixth Five Year Plan FY 2011–FY2015: Accelerating Growth and Reducing Poverty'. Part: 1–3, General Economic Division, Planning Commission, Government of the People's Republic of Bangladesh, Dhaka.

———. 2008. 'Strategy for Poverty Reduction in the Lagging Regions of Bangladesh'. General Economics Division, Planning Commission of Bangladesh, Dhaka.

———. 2005. 'Bangladesh Unlocking the Potential: National Strategy for Accelerated Poverty Reduction'. General Economics Division, Planning Commission of Bangladesh, Dhaka.

Government of India. 2014. 'Draft Concept Note on Smart City Scheme'. Smart Cities of Tomorrow, 3 December. Available at: https://www.smartcitiesoftomorrow.com/wp-content/uploads/2014/09/CONCEPT_NOTE_-3.12.2014__REVISED_AND_LATEST_.pdf (accessed 13 September 2019).

Gugler, J., and W. Flanagan. 1978. *Urbanisation and Social Change in Western Africa* (New York: Cambridge University Press).

De Haan, A., and B. Rogaly. 2002. 'Introduction: Migrant Workers and Their Role in Rural Change'. *Journal of Development Studies* 38(5): 1–14.

De Haas, H. 2008. 'Migration and Development: A Theoretical Perspective'. International Migration Institute Working Paper 9, University of Oxford, Oxford.

Hakim, C. 1987. *Research Design: Strategies and Choices in the Design of Social Research* (Boston: Unwin Hyman).

Haq-Hossain, S. 1996. 'Female Migrants' Adaptation in Dhaka: A Case of the Process of Urban Socio-Economic Change'. *Oriental Geographer* 39(1 and 2): 86–105.

Harttgen, K., and S. Klasen. 2009. 'A Human Development Index by Internal Migrational Status'. Human Development Research Paper 2009/54, United Nations Development Programme, New York.

Harwood-Lejeune, A. 2000. 'Rising Age at Marriage and Fertility in Southern and Eastern Africa'. *European Journal of Population* 17(3): 261–80.

Hayes, G., and G. Jones. 2015. 'The Impact of Demographic Transition on Socioeconomic Development in Bangladesh: Future Prospects and Implications for Public Policy'. The United Nations Population Fund (UNFPA), Bangladesh Country Office, Dhaka.

Hayes, B.C., and Y. Pittelkow. 1993. 'Religious Belief, Transmission, and the Family: An Australian Study'. *Journal of Marriage and the Family* 55(3): 755–66.

Henderson, V. 2010. 'Cities and Development'. *Journal of Regional Science* 50(1): 515–40.

———. 2003. 'The Urbanization Process and Economic Growth: The So-What Question'. *Journal of Economic Growth* 8(1): 47–71.

Herrmann, M., and D. Svarin. 2009. 'Environmental Pressures and Rural–Urban Migration: The Case of Bangladesh'. Munich Personal RePEc Archive 12879. Available at: http://mpra.ub.uni-muenchen.de/12879/ (accessed on 8 May 2019).

Hoselitz, B. 1957. 'Urbanization and Economic Growth in Asia'. *Economic Development and Cultural Change* 6(1): 42–54.

Hossain, I.M., I.A. Khan, and J. Seeley. 2003. 'Surviving on Their Feet: Charting the Mobile Livelihoods of the Poor in Rural Bangladesh'. Paper presented at the Conference on Staying Poor: Chronic Poverty and Development Policy, 7–9 April. University of Manchester, Manchester, UK.

Hossain, M.Z. 2001. 'Rural–Urban Migration in Bangladesh: A Micro Level Study'. Paper presented at the 21st Conference Bangladesh Association for the Advancement of Science (BAAS), Dhaka.

Hossain, M., and A. Bayes. 2015. *Rural Economy and Livelihoods: Insights from Bangladesh* (Dhaka: A.H. Development Publishing House).

———. 2009. *Rural Economy and Livelihoods: Insights from Bangladesh* (Dhaka: AH Development Publishing House).

Hossain, M., and B. Sen. 1992. 'Rural Poverty in Bangladesh: Trends and Determinants'. *Asian Development Review* 10(1): 1–34.

Hossain, M., R. Afsar, and M.L. Bose. 1999. 'Growth and Distribution of Income and Incidence of Poverty in Dhaka City'. Paper presented at the Conference on Changes and Determinants of Urban Poverty, Grameen Trust, Grameen Bank, Dhaka.

Hossain, S. 2008. 'Rapid Urban Growth and Poverty in Dhaka City'. *Bangladesh e-Journal of Sociology* 5(1): 1–24.

Hugo, G.J. 1994. 'Migration and the Family'. Paper prepared for Occasional Paper Series for the International Year of the Family, United Nations Department of Policy Coordination and Sustainable Development Secretariat for the International Year of the Family, New York.

———. 1992. 'Migration and Rural–Urban Linkages in the ESCAP Region'. Paper prepared for Pre-Conference Seminar of the Fourth Population Conference on Migration and Urbanisation: Inter-Relationship with Socio-Economic Development and Evolving Policy Issues, Seoul, Republic of Korea.

———. 1991. 'Rural–Urban Migration, Economic Development and Social Change: Some Important Issues'. Paper Presented in the Workshop on the Urbanisation and Urban Poor, Bangladesh Institute of Development Studies, Dhaka, 355–86.

———. 1981. 'Road Transportation, Population Mobility and Development in Indonesia'. In *Population Mobility and Development: South East Asia and the Pacific*. Edited by G.W. Jones and H.V. Richter, Monograph 27 (Canberra: Australian National University).

Hulme, D., and M. Green. 2005. 'From Correlates and Characteristics to Causes: Thinking about Poverty from a Chronic Poverty Perspective'. *World Development* 33(6): 867–79.

Human Rights Watch. 2011. 'Bangladesh—Social Institutions and Gender Index'. OECD Development Centre, Geneva, Switzerland. Available at: http://www.genderindex.org/wp-content/uploads/files/datasheets/BD.pdf (accessed on 8 May 2019).

Huq, L. 2013. 'Review of Literature on Unpaid Care Work Bangladesh'. Centre for Gender and Social Transformation (CGST), BRAC Development Institute and BRAC University, Dhaka.

Huq, S., and M. Alam. 2003. 'Flood Management and Vulnerability of Dhaka City'. Bangladesh Centre of Advance Studies (BCAS), Dhaka.

Inter-American Development Bank (IDB) and Organisation for Economic Cooperation and Development (OECD). 2018. 'Regional Planning for Sustainable Habitat'. Background Paper prepared on the 1st Meeting of the G20 Development Working Group (DWG) in Buenos Aires, Argentina.

International Cholera and Diarrhoeal Disease Research, Bangladesh (ICDDR, B). 2009. 'Pandemic (H1N1) 2009 in Bangladesh'. *Health and Science Bulletin* 7(3): 1–8.

International Labour Organisation (ILO). 2016. *Women at Work: Trends 2016* (Geneva: International Labour Office).

———. 2008. *Global Employment Trends for Women*. March International Labour Office (Geneva: International Labour Organisation).

Islam, M.S., M.R. Rahman, A.K.M. Shahbuddin, and R. Ahmed. 2010. 'Changes in Wetland in Dhaka City: Trends and Physio-environmental Consequences'. *Journal of Life Earth Science* 5: 37–42.

Islam, N. 2005. *Dhaka Now: Contemporary Urban Development* (Dhaka: Bangladesh Geographical Society).

———. 1996. 'Dhaka: From City to Megacity—Perspectives on People, Places, Planning and Development Issues'. Urban Studies Programme, Dhaka University, Dhaka, p. 256.

Islam, N., A. Mahbub, N.I. Nazem, G. Angeles, and P. Lance. 2006. 'Slums of Urban Bangladesh: Mapping and Census, 2005'. CUS, Measure Evaluation, NIPORT, and USAID, Dhaka.

Islam, N., N. Huda, F.B. Narayan, and P.B. Rana. 1997. *Addressing the Urban Poverty Agenda in Bangladesh*. Dhaka: University Press Limited.

Ishtiaque, A., and M.S. Mahmud. 2011. 'Migration Objectives and Their Fulfillment: A Micro Study of the Rural–Urban Migrants of the Slums of Dhaka City'. *Geografia* 7(4): 24–9.

Ishtiaque, A., and M.S. Ullah. 2013. 'The Influence of Factors of Migration on the Migration Status of Rural-Urban Migrants in Dhaka, Bangladesh'. *Human Geographies—Journal of Studies and Research in Human Geographies* 7(2): 45–52

Jackson, J.A., ed. 1969. *Migration* (Cambridge: Cambridge University Press).

Jahan, N.A., S.R. Howlader, N.A. Sultana, F. Ishaq, Md Z.H. Sikder, and T. Rahman. 2015. 'Health Care Seeking Behavior of Slum-Dwellers in Dhaka City: Results of a Household Survey'. Report prepared for Health Economics Unit (HEU) of Ministry of Health and Family Welfare (MoHFW) and World Health Organization (WHO), Institute of Health Economics, University of Dhaka, Dhaka.

Jalan, J., and M. Ravallion. 2002. 'Geographic Poverty Traps?: A Micro Model of Consumption Growth in Rural China'. *Journal of Applied Econometrics* 17(4): 329–46.

Kabeer, N. 2001. *Bangladeshi Women Workers and Labour Market Decisions: The Power to Choose* (Dhaka: The University Press Limited).

Jin, L., and Y. Liu. 2011. 'City Report on Shenzhen'. Unpublished UN-Habitat background study for State of the World's Cities Report 2012/2013, Nairobi, Kenya.

Jones, G.A., and S. Corbridge. 2010. 'The Continuing Debate about Urban Bias: The Thesis, Its Critics, Its Influence and Its Implications for Poverty-Reduction Strategies'. *Progress in Development Studies* 10(1): 1–18.

Jones, G., A.Q.M. Mahbub, and I. Haq. 2016. *Urbanization and Migration in Bangladesh* (Dhaka: UNFPA Country Office).

Kabeer, N., S. Mahmud, and S. Tasneem. 2011. 'Does Paid Work Provide a Pathway to Women's Empowerment?: Empirical Findings from Bangladesh'. Working Paper 375, Institute of Development Studies Brighton, Sussex.

Kabir, M., M. Haque, and H. Chaklader. 2005. 'Mainstreaming Ageing in Health: Will It Be Possible'. Paper presented in the International conference on mainstreaming ageing in health system and rural development, Dhaka.

Kamruzzaman, M., and N. Ogura. 2007. 'Apartment Housing in Dhaka City: Past, Present and Characteristic Outlook'. Working Paper, Building Stock Activation, Tokyo, Japan. Available at: http://tmu-arch.sakura.ne.jp/pdf/26_proc_bsa_e/Proceedings_pdf/081-088 011SS_A1-4.pdf (accessed on 8 May 2019).

Kelkar, G. 2013. 'At the Threshold of Economic Empowerment: Women, Work and Gender Regimes in Asia'. Working Paper Series 2227–4391; 2227–4405, International Labour Organization (ILO) Asia-Pacific, International Labour Organization, ILO DWT for South Asia and ILO Country Office, New Delhi.

Keraita, B., P.K.M. Jensen, F. Konradsen, M. Akple, and T. Rheinlander. 2013. 'Accelerating Uptake of Household Latrines in Rural Communities in the Volta Region of Ghana'. *Journal of Water Sanitation Hygiene and Development* 3(1): 26–34.

Khan, A.R. 1976. 'Poverty and Inequality in Rural Bangladesh'. *Poverty and Landlessness in Rural Asia*, International Labour Organisation, Geneva.

Khanam, M.A., C. Qiu, W. Lindeboom, P.K. Streatfield, Z.N. Kabir, and A. Wahlin. 2011. 'The Metabolic Syndrome: Prevalence, Associated Factors, and Impact on Survival among Older Persons in Rural Bangladesh'. *PLoS One* 6(6): e20259.

Khandker, S.R. 1988. 'Determinants of Women's Time Allocation in Rural Bangladesh'. *Economic Development and Cultural Change* 37(1): 111–26.

Khandker, S.R., M.M. Pitt, and N. Fuwa. 2003. 'Subsidy to Promote Girls' Secondary Education: The Female Stipend Program in Bangladesh'. World Bank Report No. 81464. World Bank, Washington, DC.

Kharas, H., and G. Gertz. 2010. 'The New Global Middle Class: A Crossover from West to East'. In *China's Emerging Middle Class: Beyond Economic Transformation*. Edited by Cheng Li (Washington, DC: Brookings Institution Press), 32–51.

Kibria, N. 2001. 'Becoming Garment Factory Worker: The Mobilisation of Women into the Garment Factories of Bangladesh'. In *Globalisation and Gender: Changing Patterns of Women's Employment in Bangladesh*. Edited by R. Sobhan and N. Khundker (Dhaka: Centre for Policy Dialogue and University Press Limited), 64–90.

Klugman, J., F. Rodriguez, and H.J. Choi. 2011. 'The HDI 2010: New Controversies, Old Critiques'. UNDP-HDRO Occasional Papers No. 2011/1, Human Development Report Office (HDRO), United Nations Development Program (UNDP), New York.

Kols, A., and D. Lewison. 1983. 'Migration, Population Growth and Development'. Population Reports: Series M (7), Population Information Program, John Hopkins University, Baltimore, Maryland, USA.

Kothari, U. 2002. 'Migration and Chronic Poverty'. Working paper 16, Chronic Poverty Research Centre (CPRC), Institute for Development and Policy Management, University of Manchester, UK.

Kuhn, R. 2000. 'The Logic of Letting Go'. Paper presented at BRAC, Mohakhali, Dhaka.

Kuhn, A., and A.M. Wolpe. 1979. 'Feminism and Materialism'. *Feminism and Materialism: Women and Modes of Production*. Edited by A. Kuhn A.M. and Wolpe (London: Routledge and Kegan Paul), 1–10.

Lipton, M. 1977. *Why Poor People Stay Poor: A Study of Urban Bias in World Development*. London: Temple Smith.

Liu, Y., and Y. Wang. 2011. 'City Report on Chongqing'. Unpublished UN-Habitat background study for State of the World's Cities Report 2012/2013, Nairobi, Kenya.

Lopez-Acevedo, G., and R. Robertson, eds. 2012. *Sewing Success? Employment, Wages, and Poverty following the End of the Multi-fibre Arrangement* (Washington, DC: The World Bank).

Mahadi, M. 2010. 'Air Pollution in Dhaka'. Available at: http://www.scribd.com/doc/10304145/-Air-Pollution-in-Dhaka-City (accessed on 8 May 2019).

Majumder, P.P., S. Mahmud, and R. Afsar. 1996. *The Squatters of Dhaka City: Dynamism in the Life of Agargoan Squatters* (Dhaka: University Press Limited).

Mantra, I.B. 1981. *Population Movement in Wet Rice Communities: A Case Study of Two Dukuh in Yogyakarta* (Yogyakarta: Gadjah Mada University Press).

McKay, A., and P. Deshingkar. 2014. 'Internal Remittances and Poverty: Further Evidence from Africa and Asia', Working Paper 12, Migrating out of Poverty Research Consortium, University of Sussex, Falmer, UK.

McKinsey Global Institute (MGI). 2015. *The Power of Parity: How Advancing Women's Equality Can Add $12 Trillion to Global Growth* (London, San Francisco, and Shanghai: McKinsey and Company). Available at: https://www.mckinsey.com/~/media/McKinsey/Featured%20Insights/Employment%20and%20Growth/How%20advancing%20womens%20equality%20can%20add%2012%20trillion%20to%20global%20growth/

MGI%20Power%20of%20parity_Full%20report_September%202015.ashx (accessed on 13 September 2019).
———. 2011. 'Urban World: Mapping the Economic Power of Cities'. McKinsey. Available at: https://www.mckinsey.com/~/media/mckinsey/featured%20 insights/urbanization/urban%20world/mgi_urban_world_mapping_economic_power_of_cities_full_report.ashx (accessed on 13 September 2019).
McKinsey and Company. 2013. 'How to Make a City Great: A Review of the Steps City Leaders around the World Take to Transform Their Cities into Great Places to Live and Work'. McKinsey & Company. Available at: https://www.mckinsey.com/~/media/mckinsey/featured%20insights/urbanization/how%20to%20make%20a%20city%20great/how_to_make_a_city_great.ashx (accessed on 13 September 2019).
Mahbub ul Haq Human Development Centre (MHHDC). 2014. *Human Development Report in South Asia 2014: Urbanisation-Challenges and Opportunities* (Lahore: Mahbub ul Haq Human Development Centre, Lahore University of Management Sciences).
Malhotra, A., and A. Tsui. 1996. 'Marriage Timing in Sri Lanka: The Role of Modern Norms and Ideas'. *Journal of Marriage and Family* 58(2): 476–90.
Mark, O., and A. Chusit. 2002. 'Modelling of Urban Runoff in Dhaka City'. Asian Institute of Technology (AIT), Thailand.
Massey, D.S., J. Arango, G. Hugo, A. Kouaouci, A. Pellegrino, and J.E. Taylor. 1993. 'Theories of International Migration: A Review and Appraisal'. *Population and Development Review* 19(3): 431–66.
Menard, S. 1991. *Longitudinal Research*. Quantitative Applications in Social Sciences Series (London: SAGE).
Mensch, B.S., D. Bagah, W.H. Clark, and F. Binka. 1999. 'The Changing Nature of Adolescence in the Kassena-Nankana District of Northern Ghana'. *Studies in Family Planning* 30(2): 95–111.
Mezzadra, S. 2004. 'The Right to Escape'. *Ephemera* 4(3): 267–75.
Mohan, R., and P. Thottan. 1988. 'The Regional Spread of Urbanisation, Industrialisation and Urban Poverty'. Planning Commission, Government of India.
Monem, M. 2018. *Engagement of Non-resident Bangladeshis (NRBs) in National Development: Strategies, Challenges and Way Forward* (Dhaka: Economic Relations Division, Ministry of Finance, Government of the People's Republic of Bangladesh).
Mowla, Q.A. 2005. 'Eco-Systems and Sustainable Urban Design Nexus: A Borderless Concept'. Paper presented in the International Alumni Conference on Technology without Borders, organized by the Global IIT, Bethesda, Washington, DC, USA, 20–2 May.

Mowla, Q.A., and M.S. Islam. 2013. 'Natural Drainage System and Water Logging in Dhaka: Measures to address the Problems'. *Journal of the Institute of Planners* 6: 23–33.

MRC Mode Limited. 2009. 'Impact Assessment of Health Care for Slum Dwellers'. Prepared by MRC Mode Limited, December.

Muqtada, M. 1986. 'Poverty and Inequality: Trends and Causes'. *Bangladesh: Selected Issues in Employment and Development*. Edited by R. Islam and M. Muktada (New Delhi: International Labour Organisation), 75–92.

Muzzini, E., and G. Aparicio. 2013. *Bangladesh: The Path to Middle-Income Status from an Urban Perspective. Directions in Development; Countries and Regions* (Washington, DC: World Bank). Available at: https://www.citiesalliance.org/resources/knowledge/cities-alliance-knowledge/bangladesh-path-middle-income-status-urban (accessed on 13 September 2019).

Nabi, A.K.M.N. 1992. 'Dynamics of Internal Migration in Bangladesh'. *Canadian Studies in Population* 19(1): 81–98.

National Institute of Population Research and Training (NIPORT), Measure Evaluation, UNC-Chapel Hill, USA, and International Centre for Diarrhoeal Disease Research, Bangladesh (ICDDR, B). 2014. *Bangladesh Urban Health Survey 2013: Preliminary Results* (Dhaka: NIPORT).

National Institute of Population Research and Training (NIPORT), Mitra and Associates, and ICF International. 2013. *Bangladesh Demographic and Health Survey 2011* (Dhaka, Bangladesh, Maryland, USA: NIPORT, Mitra and Associates and ICF International).

National Institute of Population Research and Training (NIPORT), MEASURE Evaluation, International Centre for Diarrhoeal Disease Research, Bangladesh (ICDDR, B), and Associates for Community and Population Research (ACPR). 2008. *2006 Bangladesh Urban Health Survey* (Dhaka, Bangladesh, and Chapel Hill, NC, USA: NIPORT, MEASURE Evaluation, ICDDR, B, and ACPR).

Naved, R.T., H. Huque, S. Farah, and M.M.R. Shuvra. 2011. 'Men's Attitudes and Practices Regarding Gender and Violence Against Women in Bangladesh: Preliminary Findings'. ICDDR, B Special Report 135. Research Supported by ICDDR, B., UNFPA, Partners for Prevention, The Change Project (Dhaka: ICDDR, B).

Ndegwa, S.N. 2002. 'Decentralization in Africa: A Stocktaking Survey'. Africa Region Working Paper Series No. 40. World Bank, Washington DC.

Nguyen, M.C., and Q. Wodon. 2012. 'Measuring Child Marriage'. *Economics Bulletin* 32(1): 398–411.

Ni, P. 2011. 'Driving Factors of Prosperity: An Empirical Analysis Global Cities'. Background paper for UN-Habitat, 'State of the World Cities 2012/2013: Prosperity of the Cities'.

Organisation for Economic Cooperation and Development (OECD). 2015. *In It Together: Why Less Inequality Benefits All* (Paris: OECD Publishing). Available at: www.oecd. org/social/in-it-together-why-lessinequality-benefits-all-9789264235120-en.htm (accessed on 8 May 2019).

Osmani, S.R. 2015. 'Linking Equity and Growth in Bangladesh'. Background paper prepared for the Seventh Five-Year Plan of the Government of Bangladesh, Planning Commission, The Government of the People's Republic of Bangladesh, Dhaka. Available at: http://www.plancomm.gov.bd/wp-content/uploads/2015/02/24_Linking-Equity-and-Growth-in-Bangladesh.pdf (accessed on 8 May 2019).

Osmani, S.R., and B. Sen. 2011. 'Inequality in Rural Bangladesh in the 2000s: Trends and Causes'. *Bangladesh Development Studies* 34(4): 1–36.

Parsons, T. 1960. 'Patten Variables Revisited'. *American Sociological Review* 25: 467–83.

Pew Research Centre. 2007. 'Pew Global Attitudes Project: Spring 2007 Survey'. Pew Research Centre, 28 May. Available at: https://www.pewresearch.org/global/2007/05/28/spring-2007-survey-data/ (accessed on 13 September 2019).

Putman, R.D. 2000. *Bowling Alone: The Collapse and Revival of American Community* (New York: Simone & Schuster).

Rahman, A.K.M.F. 2005. 'Transport Infrastructure and Poverty Reduction: Experiences of Bangladesh'. Paper presented at the Asian Development Bank Institute (ADBI) Transport Infrastructure and Poverty Reduction Workshop, Manila, 18–22 July.

Rahman, H.Z., M. Hossain, and B. Sen. 1996. 'Dynamics of Rural Poverty in Bangladesh 1987–1994'. Analysis of Poverty Trends Project, Final Report, Bangladesh Institute of Development Studies, Dhaka.

Rahman, R.I. 2006. 'Gender and Labour Market: Trends and Determinants'. Working paper for the World Bank, Dhaka.

Rahman, R.I., and R. Islam. 2013. 'Female Labour Force Participation in Bangladesh: Trends, Drivers and Barriers'. ILO Asia-Pacific Working Paper Series. International Labour Organization (ILO), Geneva.

Raihan, S. 2012. *Economic Reforms and Agriculture in Bangladesh: Assessment of Impacts Using Economy-wide Simulation Models*. ILO, ILO Country Office for Bangladesh.

Ravallion, M., and B. Sen. 1996. 'When Method Matters: Monitoring Rural Poverty in Bangladesh'. *Economic Development and Cultural Change* 44(4): 761–92.

Ravallion, M., S. Chen, and P. Sangruala. 2007. 'New Evidence on the Urbanisation of Global Poverty'. *Population and Development Review* 33(4): 667–701.

Real Estate and Housing Association of Bangladesh (REHAB). 2012. 'A Comprehensive Study of the Real Estate Sector of Bangladesh'. Available at: http://www.rehab-bd.org/mis/attachment/add_page/page_94.pdf (accessed on 8 May 2019).

Reuveny, R. 2007. 'Climate Change-induced Migration and Violent Conflict'. *Political Geography* 26(6): 656–73.

Rheinlander, T., F. Konradsen, B. Keraita, P. Apoya, and M. Gyapong. 2015. 'Redefining Shared Sanitation'. *Bulletin of the World Health Organization* 93(7): 509–10. Available at: https://www.who.int/bulletin/volumes/93/7/14-144980.pdf (accessed on 13 September 2019).

Robertson, S. 2006. 'Brain Drain, Brain Gain and Brain Circulation'. *Globalisation, Societies and Education* 4(1): 1–5.

Romano, D., and S. Travorso. 2016. 'The Impact of International Migration on Household Food Security: Evidence from Bangladesh'. Paper submitted to the Third Conference of the Italian Association of Development Economists (SITES), Florence, 29–30 September.

Rosenthal, M. 2000. 'Rural–Urban Relations and Representations: Comparative Perspectives'. *Anthropology Today* 16(5): 23–34.

Rubio, G. 2014. 'How Love Conquered Marriage: Theory and Evidence on the Disappearance of Arranged Marriages'. Job Market Paper, University of California, Merced, California. Available at: http://faculty.ucmerced.edu/grubio4/Job_market_paper.pdf (accessed on 25 November 2016).

Sarker, A.R., R.A. Mahmud, M. Sultana, S. Ahmed, W. Ahmed, and J.A.M. Khan. 2014. 'The Impact of Age and Sex on Healthcare Expenditure of Households in Bangladesh'. SpringerPlus 3(435). Available at: https://www.ncbi.nlm.nih.gov/pmc/articles/PMC4153877/ (accessed on 8 May 2019).

Satapathy, B.K. 2014. 'Safe Drinking Water in Slums: From Water Coverage to Water Quality'. *Economic and Political Weekly* 20(24): 50–5.

Satterthwaite, D. 2004. 'The Under-Estimation of Urban Poverty in Low and Middle-Income Nations'. IIED Poverty reduction in urban areas series working paper 14, International Institute for Environment and Development (IIED), London.

Schultz, T.P. 1990. 'Women's Changing Participation in the Labor Force: A World Perspective'. *Economic Development and Cultural Change* 38: 457–88.

Scott, A.J., and M. Storper. 2015. 'The Nature of Cities: The Scope and Limits of Urban Theory'. *International Journal of Urban and Regional Research* 39(1): 1–15.

Scott, M.F. 1977. 'Peasants Farmers, Masons and Maids: Migration and Family Structure in Tlaxcala, Mexico'. University Micofilm Order 77–25. 607 Santa Barbara, University of California, California.

Sen, B. 2005. 'Sub-National Growth Dynamics in Bangladesh: Insights from the Macro- GDP and Micro-Survey Data'. Mimeo (Dhaka: Bangladesh Institute of Development Studies).

Sen, A. 1999. *Development as Freedom* (Oxford: Oxford University Press).

Sen, B., and Z. Ali. 2005. 'Spatial Inequality in Social Progress in Bangladesh'. PRCB Working Paper No. 7, Bangladesh institute of Development Studies, Dhaka.

Sen, B., and D. Hulme, eds. 2006. *The State of the Poorest 2005/2006 – Chronic Poverty in Bangladesh: Tales of Ascent, Descent, Marginality and Persistence* (Dhaka: Bangladesh Institute of Development Studies and Manchester: Chronic Poverty Research Centre, Institute for Development and Policy Management, University of Manchester).

Sen, B., M. Ahmed, M. Yunus, and Z. Ali. 2014. *Regional Inequality in Bangladesh in the 2000s: Re-Visiting the East–West Divide Debate* (Dhaka: Bangladesh Institute of Development Studies).

Seraj, T.M. 2012. *Private Sector Housing*. Dhaka: Pearl Publications.

Shah, A. 2006. 'The Labour of Love: Seasonal Migration from Jharkhand to the Brick Kiln of other States in India'. *Contribution to Indian Sociology* 40(1): 91–118.

Siddiqui, T., ed. 2005. *Migration and Development: Pro-poor Policy Choices* (Dhaka: University Press Limited).

———. 2003. *Migration as a Livelihood Strategy of the Poor: The Bangladesh Case* (Dhaka: Refugee and Migratory Movements Research Unit, Dhaka University).

Siddiqui, K., S.R. Qadir, S. Alamgir, and S. Haq. 1993. *Social Formation in Dhaka City* (Dhaka: University Press Limited).

Siddiqui, K., J. Ahmed, K. Siddique, S. Huq, A. Hossain, S. Nazimud-Doula, and N. Rezawana. 2010. *Social Formation in Dhaka, 1985–2005: A Longitudinal Study of Society in Third World Megacity* (Farnham, Surrey: Ashgate).

Singer, A.E. 2006. 'Business Strategy and Poverty Alleviation'. *Journal of Business Ethics* 66 (2–3): 225–31.

Skeldon, R. 2003. 'On Migration and Migration Policy in Asia: A Synthesis of Selected Cases'. Mimeo (Brighton: University of Sussex).

———. 1997a. *Migration and Development: A Global Perspective* (London: Longman Limited).

———. 1997b. 'Rural to Urban Migration and Its Implications for Poverty Alleviation'. *Asia-Pacific Population Journal* 12(1): 3–16.

Smith, F. 2009. 'Private Local Pharmacies in Low- and Middle-Income Countries: A Review of Interventions to Enhance their Role in Public Health'. *Tropical Medicine and International Health* 14(3): 362–72.

Smith, R.C. 2006. *Mexican New York: Transnational Lives of New Immigrants* (Berkeley: University of California Press).

Stark, O. 1991. *The Migration of Labour* (Cambridge, Mass.: Harvard University Press).

Stoeckel, J., A.K.M.A. Chowdhury, and K.M.A. Aziz. 1972. 'Out-Migration from Rural Areas in Bangladesh'. *Rural Sociology* 37 (2): 236–45.

Storper, M. 2013. *Keys to the City: How Economics, Institutions, Social Interaction, and Politics Shape Development* (Princeton, N.J.: Princeton University Press).

Storper, M., and T. Venables. 2004. 'Buzz: Face-to-Face Contact and the Urban Economy'. *Journal of Economic Geography* 4(4): 351–70.

Suttie, D., and R. Vargas-Lundius. 2016. *Migration and Transformative Pathways: A Rural Perspective* (Rome: IFAD).

Tacoli, C. 2012. *Earthscan Reader in Rural–Urban Linkages* (London: Earthscan).

———. 2003. 'The Links between Rural and Urban Development'. *Environment and Urbanization* 15(1): 3–12.

———. 1998. 'Rural–Urban Interactions: A Guide to the Literature'. *Environment and Urbanization* 10(1): 147–66.

Tacoli, C., and D. Satterthwaite. 2013. 'Gender and Urban Change'. *Environment and Urbanization* 25(1): 3–8.

Tacoli, C., G. McGranahan, and D. Satterthwaite. 2015. 'Urbanisation, Rural–Urban Migration and Urban Poverty'. International Institute of Environment and Development (IIED) Working Paper, IIED, London.

Todaro, M.P. 1976. *Internal Migration in Developing Countries: A Review of Theory, Evidence, Methodology and Research Priorities* (Geneva: International Labour Organisation).

Udall, A.T. 1981. 'Transport Improvement and Rural Out-Migration in Columbia'. *Economic Development and Cultural Change* 29(3): 613–29.

Turok, I. 2018. 'Urbanisation and Development: Reinforcing the Foundation'. In *The Routledge Companion to Planning in the Global South*. Edited by G. Bhan, S. Srinivas, and V. Watson (New York: Routledge), 93–103.

———. 2016. 'Housing and the Urban Premium'. *Habitat International* 54(3): 234–40.

Uddin, A.F.M.A., and A. Baten. 2011. *Water Supply of Dhaka City: Murky Future. The Issue of Access and Inequality* (Dhaka: Unnayan Onneshan-The Innovators).

Uddin, M.J., C.P. Larson, E. Oliveras, A.I. Khan, M.A. Quiyum, and N.C. Saha. 2009. 'Child Immunization Coverage in Urban Slums of Bangladesh: Impact of an Intervention Package'. *Health Policy and Planning* 25(1): 50–60.

Ullah, A.K.M.A. 2004. 'Bright City Lights and Slums of Dhaka City: Determinants of Rural–Urban Migration in Bangladesh'. *Migration Letters* 1 (1): 26–41.

United Nations. 2018. 'World Urbanization Prospects: 2018 Revision'. Department of Economic and Social Affairs, Population Division, United Nations, New York.

———. 2015a. 'World Urbanization Prospects: 2015 Revision'. Department of Economic and Social Affairs, Population Division, United Nations, New York.

———. 2015b. *The World's Women 2015: Trends and Statistics* (New York: United Nations, Department of Economics and Social Affairs, Statistics Division).

———. 2015c. 'Transforming Our World: The 2030 Agenda for Sustainable Development'. United Nations, New York.

———. 2014. 'World Urbanization Prospects: 2014 Revision'. Department of Economic and Social Affairs, Population Division, United Nations, New York.

———. 2012. *World Urbanization Prospects: 2012 Revision* (New York: Department of Economic and Social Affairs, Population Division, United Nations.

———. 2010. *World Urbanization Prospects: 2010 Revision* (New York: Department of Economic and Social Affairs, Population Division, United Nations).

United Nations Development Program (UNDP). 2015. *Human Development Report 2015*. Available at: http://hdr.undp.org/en/composite/MPIchanges (accessed on 14 April 2016).

———. 2014. *World Urbanization Prospects Database: The 2011 Revision*. Available at: https://www.un.org/en/development/desa/population/publications/pdf/urbanization/WUP2011_Report.pdf (accessed on 13 September 2019).

———. 2013. *World Population Prospects Database: The 2011 Revision*. Available at: https://population.un.org/wpp/Publications/Files/WPP2012_HIGHLIGHTS.pdf (accessed on 13 September 2019).

———. 1990. 'Women Watch Fact Sheet'. Available at: http://www.un.org/womenwatch/feature/urban/downloads/WomenWatch_Gender_Equality_and_Sustainable_Urbanisation-fact_sheet.pdf (accessed on 21 December 2016).

United Nations Economic and Social Commission for Asia and the Pacific (UNESCAP). 2017. 'Urbanization and Sustainable Development in Asia and the Pacific: Linkages and Policy Implications'. Note by the Secretariat. Seventy-third session, Bangkok, Thailand, 15–19 May.

United Nations Education and Cultural Organisation (UNESCO). 2012. 'Education and Skills for Inclusive and Sustainable Development beyond 2015: Thematic Think Tank Piece'. UNESCO, Paris.

———. 2005. 'Youth in Transition: The Challenges of Generational Change in Asia'. Proceedings of the 15th Biennial General Conference of the Association of Asian Social Science Research Councils (AASSREC), UNESCO Office Bangkok and Regional Bureau for Education in Asia and the Pacific, Bangkok.

United Nations Family Planning Agency (UNFPA). 2014. 'Gender Equality: Empowering Women'. Available at: http://www.unfpa.org/gender/empowerment.htm (accessed on 8 May 2019).

United Nations Human Settlement Programme (UN-Habitat). 2016. 'Urbanization and Development: Emerging Futures'. World Cities Report 2016, Nairobi, Kenya.

———. 2013. *State of the World's Cities 2012/13: Prosperity of Cities* (New York: Routledge Taylor and Francis Group).

———. 2012. *Sustainable Housing for Sustainable Cities: A Policy Framework for Developing Countries* (Nairobi: United Nations Human Settlement Programme).

———. 2010. *UN-Habitat, State of the World's Cities 2010/2011: Bridging the Urban Divide* (Nairobi: UN-Habitat).

United Nations Human Settlement Programme (UN-Habitat), and Ericsson. 2014. *The Role of ICT in the Proposed Urban Sustainable Development Goal and the New Urban Agenda* (Nairobi: UN-Habitat).

United Nations International Children's Fund (UNICEF). 2014. 'Ending Child Marriage: Progress and Prospects'. Available at: https://www.unicef.org/media/files/Child_Marriage_Report_7_17_LR..pdf (accessed on 13 September 2019).

United States Agency for International Development (USAID). 2015. 'Wage Labour, Agricultural-Based Economies, and Pathways Out of Poverty: Taking Stock of the Evidence'. Leveraging Economic Opportunities Report 15, USAID, Washington, DC.

Uteng, T.P. 2011. 'Gender and Mobility in the Developing World'. Background Paper, World Development Report.

Varshney, A. 1995. *Democracy, Development and the Countryside* (Cambridge: Cambridge University Press).

Varshney, A., ed. 1993. *Beyond Urban Bias* (London: Frank Cass).

Wickramasekara, P. 2015. 'Mainstreaming Migration in Development Agendas: Assessment of South Asian countries'. Working paper 2015/02. Arndt-Corden Department of Economics Crawford School of Public Policy ANU College of Asia and the Pacific, Australian National University, Canberra, Australia.

Wickramasekara, P. 2003. 'Policy Responses to Skilled Migration: Retention, Return and Circulation'. International Labour Organization, Geneva. Available at: http://www.ilo.org/wcmsp5/groups/public/---ed_protect/---protrav/--migrant/documents/ publication/wcms_232366.pdf (accessed on 4 September 2016).

Winkel, J. 2015. 'Inequality and the 2030 Agenda for Sustainable Development'. Development Issues No. 4., Development Strategy and Policy Analysis Unit,

Development Policy and Analysis Division, Department of Economic and Social Affairs, United Nations, New York.

World Bank. 2018. 'Promising Progress: A Diagnostic of Water Supply, Sanitation, Hygiene, and Poverty in Bangladesh'. WASH Poverty Diagnostic. World Bank, Washington, DC.

———. 2015. *Bangladesh: More and Better Jobs to Accelerate Shared Growth and End Extreme Poverty. A Systematic Country Diagnostic* (Washington, DC: World Bank Group, South Asia Region).

———. 2014. *World Development Indicators* (Washington, DC: World Bank).

———. 2013. 'Building Sustainability in an Urbanizing World'. Urban Development Series 13. World Bank, Washington DC.

———. 2012. 'Bangladesh—Towards Accelerated, Inclusive and Sustainable Growth: Opportunities and Challenges', Vol. 2: Main Report, Report Number 67991 (Washington, DC: International Bank for Reconstruction and Development/the World Bank). Available at: http://documents.worldbank.org/curated/en/280061468006660483/pdf/NonAsciiFileName0.pdf (accessed on 13 September 2019).

———. 2009. *Reshaping World Geography: World Development Report 2009* (Washington, DC: The International Bank for Reconstruction and Development/The World Bank).

———. 2008. 'Bangladesh Poverty Assessment for Bangladesh: Creating Opportunities and Bridging the East–West Divide'. Report No. 44321BD, The World Bank, South Asia Region.

———. 2007. *Dhaka: Improving Living Conditions for the Urban Poor* (Dhaka: World Bank Office).

———. 2005. *World Development Report 2006: Equity and Development* (Washington, DC: International Bank for Reconstruction and Development/The World Bank).

———. 2002. 'Implementation Completion Report (IDA 24690) on a Credit to the Peoples' Republic of Bangladesh for a Female Secondary School Assistance Project'. World Bank, Washington, DC.

World Health Organization (WHO). 2008. *The World Health Report 2008: Primary Health Care Now More Than Ever* (Geneva: World Health Organization).

———. 2011. *Global Health Status on Noncommunicable Diseases 2010* (Geneva: WHO).

World Health Organisation (WHO), and UNICEF. 2014. *Progress on Drinking Water and Sanitation: 2014 Update* (Geneva: World Health Organization).

Zaman, A.K.M.H., K.M.T. Alam, and M.J. Islam. 2010. 'Urbanization in Bangladesh: Present Status and Policy Implications'. *ASA University Review* 4(2): 1–16.

Index

About the Authors

Rita Afsar is an honorary research fellow at the Faculty of Arts, School of Social Sciences, University of Western Australia (UWA), Perth, and works for the Western Australian Government. She has been a senior research fellow at the Bangladesh Institute of Development Studies (BIDS), Dhaka, Bangladesh, and an honorary research fellow at the Centre of Muslim States and Societies (CMSS), UWA. She obtained her PhD in population studies from Adelaide University, Australia, and two master's degrees, one each in sociology and social work, from University of the Philippines and University of Delhi, respectively. She has developed expertise in the areas of urbanization, migration, poverty and inequality, women's empowerment, and development issues in Bangladesh and South Asia. Her published works in these areas include articles such as 'Urban Development and Urban Poverty Reduction Approaches: Gender Implications and Development Outcomes' in *State of the Urban Poor Report 2015: Gender and Urban Poverty*, by the Ministry of Housing and Urban Poverty Alleviation, Government of India, in 2016: 'Revisiting the Saga of Bangladeshi Labour Migration to the Gulf States: Need for New Theoretical and Methodological Approaches' in *South Asian Migration to Gulf Countries: History, Policies and Development*, edited by P.C. Jain and G.Z. Oommen in 2016; and 'Remittances in SME Development: Reflections from South Asia' in *Migrant Remittances in South Asia: Social, Economic and Political Implications*, edited by M.M. Rahman, T.T. Yong, and A.K.M.A. Ullah, in 2014, as well as authored volumes, such as *Rural–Urban Migration in Bangladesh: Causes, Consequences and Challenges* in 2000.

Mahabub Hossain was advisor to the executive director, Bangladesh Rural Advancement Committee (BRAC), Dhaka, and distinguished professor and chair, Department of Economics and Social Sciences, BRAC University. He had also been the former director general at BIDS. He completed his PhD in economics at the University of Cambridge, UK, and his master's degree in economics at the University of Dhaka, Bangladesh. His extensive list of publications includes articles such as 'Rice Research, Technological Progress and Poverty: The Bangladesh Case' in *Agricultural Research, Livelihoods and Poverty: Studies of Economic and Social Impact in Six Countries,* edited by M. Adato and R.S. Meinzen-Dick in 2007 (with David Lewis, M.L. Bose, and Alamgir Chowdhury), authored volumes, such as *Rural Transformation: Insights from Bangladesh* in 2018 (with Abdul Bayes), as well as edited volumes such as *Leading Issues in Rural Development: Bangladesh Perspective* in 2015 (with Abdul Bayes) and *Adoption and Diffusion of Modern Rice Varieties in Bangladesh and Eastern India* in 2012 (with W.M.H. Jaim and T. Paris).